Bloom's Modern Critical Views

Bloom's Modern Critical Views

Bloom's Modern Critical Views

Julio Cortázar

Edited and with an introduction by
Harold Bloom
Sterling Professor of the Humanities
Yale University

CHELSEA HOUSE
PUBLISHERS
A Haights Cross Communications ✦ Company ®
Philadelphia

A Haights Cross Communications ◀✦ Company ®

http://www.chelseahouse.com

Introduction © 2005 by Harold Bloom.

Printed and bound in the United States of America.
10 9 8 7 6 5 4 3 2 1

Library of Congress Cataloging-in-Publication Data

Bloom, Harold.
  Julio Cortázar / Harold Bloom.
      p. cm. — (Bloom's modern critical views)
  Includes bibliographical references
  ISBN 0-7910-8134-6 (alk. paper)
  1. Cortázar, Julio—Criticism and interpretation. I. Title. II. Series.
  PQ7797.C7145Z5947 2004
  863'.64—dc22
                                        2004026652

Contributing Editor: Elizabeth Beaudin

Cover designed by Keith Trego

Cover photo: © Bettman/CORBIS

Layout by EJB Publishing Services

Contents

Editor's Note

My Introduction centers upon Cortázar as a short story writer, since I prefer his Borgesian tales to his novels and purely experimental works.

Jaime Alazraki, in a fully informed overview of Cortázar, emphasizes this fabulist's art of hindering the reader's presuppositions, while Roberto González Echevarría illuminates a Nietzschean element in Cortázar's "mythology of writing."

A Manual for Manuel, a political novel, is judged by Steven Boldy to be a richly confused work, after which Ana Hernández del Castillo traces the effect of John Keats upon Cortázar's work (a radically misread Keats), particularly in regard to visions of the Circe-like goddess la Maga in *Rayuela* (translated as *Hopscotch*).

Rayuela, a novelistic labyrinth, returns in Gordana Yovanovich's interpretation, which concludes that the reader must tease out the meanings strictly for herself, while Doris Sommer discovers in the jazz novella *The Pursuer* Cortázar's profound critique of his own narrator, a jazz critic.

Isabel Alvarez Borland extends this critique by suggesting that for Cortázar the critic must become the artist's double, after which Ilan Stavans defends Cortázar against those who might see him as a writer of period pieces. For Stavans, Cortázar was the true heir of Surrealism, and as an endless experimenter was central to the era of the 1960s and 1970s, the so-called "Counterculture."

The major writer Mario Vargas Llosa memorializes Cortázar as a great fantasist, while Lucille Kerr gives us an appreciation of the indescribable text *62: A Model Kit*.

In this volume's final essay, Aníbal González analyzes the story "Press Clippings" as an instance of Cortázar's curious variety of "the ethics of reading."

HAROLD BLOOM

Introduction

Despite the indisputable influence upon him of his fellow Argentine, Jorge Luis Borges, Julio Cortázar preferred to see himself as a writer more in the mode of their common ancestor, Edgar Poe. The American Romantic was safely distant, in time and place, and more deliciously unhealthy than the personally staid Borges. Cortázar, like Borges, evaded Freud, as did Nabokov, another elegant fantasist. The evasions seem curious in Cortázar, who must have known that Surrealism, his preferred aesthetic, had Freudian sources and affiliations.

Hopscotch remains the most famous of Cortázar's longer fictions, but I fear that it eventually will seem a period piece, as will *One Hundred Years of Solitude*, the equally illustrious narrative of Gabriel García Márquez. Both novels wear out further for me with each rereading. García Márquez did better with the later *Love in the Time of Cholera*, and Cortázar seems most effective to me in his tales, which are at once varied and off-the-beat, like the Bop jazz he admired.

The novella called, in English, *The Pursuer* is Cortázar at his impressive best. It is a kind of elegy for Charlie Parker, founder of Bop with Dizzy Gillespie, Charles Mingus, Bud Powell, and Max Roach among others. They had a long foreground in jazz masters from Louis Armstrong through Duke Ellington, Coleman Hawkins, Art Tatum and other strong precursors, yet they were as much a breakthrough as Walt Whitman and Charles Baudelaire had been. Parker appears in *The Pursuer* as Johnny Carter, down and out in a wretched Parisian hotel room, his alto saxophone lost in the Metro. Bruno, an admiring but self-serving critic, narrates this extraordinary and celebratory lament for the greatest jazz artist after Louis Armstrong but, unlike the wise Armstrong, addicted to alcohol and heroin.

1

There are apocalyptic overtones in *The Pursuer*, and yet the story is a naturalistic triumph, far removed from Surrealism. The pathos of Charlie Parker, a genius trapped by his self-destructive temperament, is conveyed with superb clarity. But so is the human inadequacy of the critic Bruno, who apprehends greatness, but stands aside from the apocalyptic abyss of Parker's fate.

Michael Wood wisely said of Cortázar that the art of his stories "is the avoidance of allegory where it seems virtually unavoidable." Allegory is a kind of extended irony, in which you say one thing yet mean another. What you mean wanders off anyway in irony, and Cortázar, unlike Borges, is not essentially an ironic storyteller. Borges truly resembles Kafka, who made himself uninterpretable. Cortázar, closer to Poe, longs both for fact and fantasy, and so far as I know was the first translator of Poe into Spanish.

The mingling of bisexual fact and sublime fantasy is absolute in the wonderful "Bestiary," which condenses a novella into just twenty pages. Isabel, an adolescent, goes off to spend a summer with her aunt-by-marriage, Rema, at a country house inexplicably containing, at intervals, a tiger. In love with Rema, Isabel contrives the devouring of Rema's brother-in-law, a sadistic fellow called "the Kid," by the convenient tiger. Cortázar subtly implies a lesbian passion between Isabel and Rema, which is expedited by the demise of the Kid.

Cortázar himself was bisexual, and is believed to have died of AIDS. The tiger in "Bestiary" is not an allegory; sometimes a tiger *is* only a tiger. "Bestiary" may be an unusual love story, but it is an endearing and persuasive one. Like Joyce and D.H. Lawrence, Hemingway and Isaac Babel, Borges and Calvino, Cortázar was one of the canonical story-writers of the twentieth century.

JAIME ALAZRAKI

Toward the Last Square of the Hopscotch

Julio Cortázar, the most Argentine among Argentine writers, is also, together with Borges and Octavio Paz, the most universal in a generation of Spanish American writers which has so definitely changed the status of its literature and its place in the letters of our time. *Hopscotch* was the turning point. Published in Spanish in 1963, it was successively translated into French, English, Italian, Polish and Portuguese. The English translation by Gregory Rabassa received the first National Book Award given in this country for the work of a translator. It was greeted by *The New Republic*'s reviewer, C.D.B. Bryan, as "the most powerful encyclopedia of emotions and visions to emerge from the post-war generation of international writers," by the London *Times Literary Supplement* as the "first great novel of Spanish America," and by Carlos Fuentes, who reviewed the book for the prestigious magazine *Commentary*, as the novel which "in its depth of imagination and suggestion, in its maze of black mirrors, in its ironical potentiality-through-destruction of time and words, marks the true possibility of encounter between the Latin American imagination and the contemporary world."[1] Donald Keene reviewed *Rayuela*'s English version for *The New York Times Book Review* and concluded that if *The Winners*, published in English a year earlier, "earned respectful reviews, *Hopscotch*, a superb work, should establish Cortázar as an outstanding writer of our day."[2] A year later the American

From *The Final Island: The Fiction of Julio Cortázar*. © 1978 University of Oklahoma Press.

reader was to discover that the author of one of the most prominent novels of the century was also a master of the short story. A selection of his short fiction, translated by Paul Blackburn, was published under the title *End of the Game and Other Stories* (Pantheon, 1967).

*

Cortázar was born in Brussels in 1914 of Argentine parents whose descent included Basque, French and German forebears. This apparent non-Argentine background is, however, his most Argentine asset, if one remembers that 97% of the population in Argentina is of European extraction. About the circumstances of his birth, he has explained:

> My birth in Brussels was the result of tourism and diplomacy. My father was on the staff of a commercial mission stationed near the Argentine legation in Belgium, and since he had just gotten married he took my mother with him to Brussels. It was my lot to be born during the German occupation of Brussels, at the beginning of World War I. I was almost four when my family was able to return to Argentina. I spoke mainly French and from that language I retained my rolling *r* which I could never get rid of. I grew up in Bánfield, a town on the outskirts of Buenos Aires, in a house with a large garden full of cats, dogs, turtles and parrakeets: paradise. But in that paradise I was already Adam, in the sense that I don't have happy memories from my childhood—too many chores, an excessive sensitivity, a frequent sadness, asthma, broken arms, first desperate loves (my story "The Poisons" is very autobiographical).[3]

As for his beginnings as a writer, he made the following comments:

> Like all children who like to read, I soon tried to write. I finished my first novel when I was nine years old ... And so on. And poetry inspired by Poe, of course. When I was twelve, fourteen, I wrote love poems to a girl in my class ... But after that it wasn't until I was thirty or thirty-two—apart from a lot of poems that are lying about here and there, lost or burned—that I started to write stories. I knew instinctively that my first stories shouldn't be published. I'd set myself a high literary standard and was determined to reach it before publishing anything. The

stories were the best I could do at the time, but I didn't think they were good enough, though there were some good ideas in them. I never took anything to a publisher.

I'm a schoolteacher. I graduated from Mariano Acosta School in Buenos Aires, completed the studies for a teacher's degree, and then entered the Buenos Aires University School of Liberal Arts. I passed the first-year exams, but then I was offered a teaching job in a town in the province of Buenos Aires, and since there was little money at home, and I wanted to help my mother, who educated me at great cost and sacrifice—my father had left home when I was a very small child and had never done anything for the family—, I gave up my university studies at the first chance I had to work, when I was twenty years old, and moved to the country. There I spent five years as a high school teacher. And that was where I started to write stories, though I never dreamed of publishing them. A bit later I moved West, to Mendoza, to the University of Cuyo, where I was offered to teach some courses, this time at the university level. In 1945–46, since I knew I was going to lose my job because I'd been in the fight against Perón, when Perón won the presidential election, I resigned before I was backed against the wall as so many colleagues who held onto their jobs were. I found work in Buenos Aires and there I went on writing stories. But I was very doubtful about having a book published. In that sense I think I was always clear-sighted. I watched myself develop, and didn't force things. I knew that at a certain moment what I was writing was worth quite a bit more than what was being written by others of my age in Argentina. But, because of the high idea I had of literature, I thought it was a stupid habit to publish just anything as people used to do in Argentina in those days when a twenty-year-old youngster who'd written a handful of sonnets used to run around trying to have them put into print. If he couldn't find a publisher, he'd pay for a personal edition himself ... So I held my fire.[4]

Cortázar's reference to the anonymous twenty-year-old author of a book of sonnets describes his generation's hasty attitude toward publishing, but it also alludes to his own first collection of sonnets published in 1938 under the title *Presencia* and pseudonymously signed Julio Denís. This is, so far, the earliest evidence of his writings and the only book he never allowed to be reprinted. Copies of this limited first edition, not available today in most libraries or collections, circulate nonetheless among friends and devotees, sometimes in xeroxed copies of the original. Cortázar doesn't care to talk about this early volume and discards the collection altogether as a "very Mallarméan" type of poetry. The presence of Mallarmé is apparent, but in addition Baudelaire, Rosetti and Cocteau are quoted in three epigraphs, and two poems are devoted to Góngora and Neruda. His reading of Rimbaud is also evident, supported by one of his earliest prose pieces, "Rimbaud," published in 1941 in the literary magazine *Huella*. Cortázar acknowledges Rimbaud as one of the most influential poets on his generation and on surrealism because, he explains there, "Rimbaud is above all a man. His problem was not a poetic problem but one posed by an ambitious human realization, to which end the Poem should he the key. This brings him near to those of us who see poetry as the fulfillment of the self, as its absolute embodiment and its entelechy."[5] In later essays Cortázar further elaborates and refines this point concerning surrealism as a world view and poetry as "an extension of life." As a young poet he voiced some of the preoccupations of his generation: poetry as a journey to the self; life as an insoluble mystery; authenticity as the ultimate test; time, solitude and death. The tone is grave, elegiac and at times sibylline: "Because this that you call my life / Is my death feigning my life."[6] One thinks of Quevedo, but from the quotation heading the poem Cortázar makes clear that his context is not the Spanish conceptist, but a writer who is to leave a strong impression on him—Jean Cocteau. *Presencia* also reveals Cortázar's early enthusiasm for music in general and for jazz in particular, and more revealing still is one sonnet in which his fascination for the fantastic finds a first formulation in a closing triplet:

> And what once was true is no longer true,
> And night enters through the windows
> Open to the realm of the unknown.[7]

One can understand Cortázar's reluctance to permit the reedition of this early volume and his dismissal of its literary merits. As much as he displays profuse and at times cryptic language and handles the sonnet form with the skill of a virtuoso, this poetry is still the probing of a poet attitudinizing, echoing the prestige and elegance of a polished dictionary, conjuring the spell of the old masters. Cortázar has not yet found his own poetic voice, which when fully achieved in his more mature poetry of *Pameos y meopas*, published in 1971 but including poems written as early as 1951, will prove to be of such different tenor and timbre—straightforward, attuned to his circumstance, free of any affectation, masterfully plain and yet by far more complex and intense than his early attempts. His first volume of poems is reminiscent of the literary beginnings of another Argentine, Borges, who never allowed the reprinting of his first three volumes of essays because, he has explained,

> I began writing in a very factitious and baroque style. I believe that what happened to me was happening to many young writers. Out of timidity, I thought that if I used a plain language people would suspect that I didn't know how to write. I felt compelled to prove that I knew many rare words and that I knew how to combine them in a surprising way.[8]

Curiously, it was Borges who published Cortázar's first short story, "House Taken Over," in *Los anales de Buenos Aires*, a literary journal he edited and which, together with *Sur*, was among the most influential literary magazines published in Argentina at the time. The year, 1946. Talking about these early contacts with Cortázar, Borges observed:

> I don't know Cortázar's work at all well, but the little I do know, a few stories, seems to me admirable. I'm proud of the fact that I was the first to publish any work by him. When I was the editor of a magazine named *Los anales de Buenos Aires*, I remember a tall young man presenting himself in the office and handing me a manuscript. I said I would read it, and he came back after a week. The story was entitled "La casa tomada" (House Taken Over). I told him it was excellent; my sister Norah illustrated it.[9]

It couldn't have been a more auspicious beginning for Cortázar as a fiction writer. A year later the same journal published his second short story, "Bestiary," and a third, "Lejana" (The Distances), appeared the year after in *Cabalgata*, a Buenos Aires monthly magazine of arts and letters. It was not until 1951, the year he left for France not to return except for occasional visits, that he collected these three stories together with five others in a volume entitled *Bestiario*. The book was published at the insistence of a few close friends who read the stories in manuscript form. About his unhurriedness, Cortázar has explained: "I was completely sure that from about, say, 1947, all the things I'd been putting away were good, some of them even very good. I am referring, for example, to some of the stories of *Bestiario*. I knew nobody had written stories like those before in Spanish, at least in my country. There were others, the admirable tales by Borges, for instance, but what I was doing was different."[10]

And indeed it was. There are some stories whose subjects bring to mind those of Borges, sort of variations on a same theme; but even when that is the case, the common subject only underlines the differences. A good example is Borges's "Streetcorner Man" and Cortázar's "El móvil" (The Motive). Both stories deal with a similar character (the *compadre* as the city counterpart in courage and sense of honor to the gaucho in the countryside), both present a similar plot (an infamous act that must be avenged), and both surprise the reader with an unexpected turn in the sequence of events leading to their denouement. Yet Cortázar's treatment of this common theme differs considerably from the one adopted by Borges. While Borges follows a linear unfolding of the basic conflict, in Cortázar's story the plot ramifies into a double conflict, thus creating within a single narrative space two spaces that the reader must discover as a hidden double bottom. Stylistically, Borges has fused some living speech patterns of the *compadre* with a language in which the reader recognizes the traits of Borges's own playful style. This deliberate hybridization works, because in re-creating the *compadre*'s speech as the narrator of the story, Borges proceeds with the knowledge that the problem confronting a writer is not that of reproducing with the fidelity of a tape recorder the voice of his protagonists but that of producing the illusion of his voice, and this illusion is based on a literary convention. Cortázar's stylistic solution, on the other hand, is different. Since his character-narrator lives in an Argentina contemporaneous with his own writing, he rejects the use of an exclusive vernacular to adopt instead a Spanish closer to that used by a *Porteño* type he is fully familiar with and not too different from his own—in summary, a Spanish which best captures the tone of the narrative, which best fits the theme and intention of the story and which becomes its most powerful vehicle of characterization.

This stylistic answer typifies Cortázar's overall approach to the use of language in his stories. He himself has pointed out that:

> ... in a great style language ceases to be a vehicle for the expression of ideas and feelings and yields to a borderline state in which it is no longer a mere language to become actually the very presence of what has been expressed.... What is told in a story should indicate by itself who is speaking, at what distance, from what perspective and according to what type of discourse. The work is not defined so much by the elements of the *fabula* or their ordering as by the modes of the fiction, tangentially indicated by the enunciation proper of the *fabula*.[11]

In most of his stories the challenge lies precisely in the search for a voice without falsetto, a genuine voice through which his characters embody themselves. In a strange way, mimesis at its best, the author keeps quiet so that the narrative can speak for itself, from within, and find the language which suits in the most natural manner its inner needs and own intents, a paradoxical immanence by means of which the characters lend their voices to the author.

It has also been a facile operation to throw Borges and Cortázar into the same bag loosely labeled as the fantastic. The truth is that neither of them has much in common with the nineteenth-century European and American writers who, between 1820 and 1850, produced the masterpieces of the fantastic genre.[12] Sensing the imprecision of the designation, Cortázar himself has said about this, "Most of the stories I have written belong to the genre called fantastic for lack of a better name."[13] And on the same subject, he has explained to the interviewer of *La Quinzaine Littéraire*:

> Le grand fantastique, le fantastique qui fait les meilleurs contes, est rarement axé sur a joie, l'humour, les choses positives. Le fantastique est négatif, il approche toujours de l'horrible, de l'épouvante. Ça a donné le roman "gothique," avec ses chaînes et ses fantômes, etc. Puis ça a donné Edgar Allan Poe qui a vraiment inventé le conte fantastique moderne—toujours horrible aussi. Je ne suis pas arrivé á savoir pourquoi le fantastique est axé sur le côté nocturne de l'homme et non sur le côté diurne.[14]

Neither Borges nor Cortázar is interested in this nocturnal side of man, in assaulting the reader with the fears and horrors which have been defined as the attributes of the fantastic.[15] Yet it is clear that in their stories there is a fantastic dimension which runs against the grain of the realist or psychological forms of fiction, allowing for uncanny events intolerable within a realist code. Accepting this fact, and acknowledging at the same time that the definition of "fantastic" for this type of narrative is incongruous, I have suggested elsewhere to refer to them as "neofantastic" as a way of distinguishing them from their distant, nineteenth-century relatives.[16] This is not the place to expand on a proposal for a poetics of this new genre, but it seems reasonably acceptable to view certain works by Kafka, Blanchot, Borges, Cortázar and several others in Latin America as expressions of the neofantastic. Rather than "playing with the readers' fears," as the fantastic sought, the neofantastic, as Cortázar has put it in defining his own short fiction, "seeks an alternative to that false realism which assumed that everything can be neatly described as was upheld by the philosophic and scientific optimism of the eighteenth century, that is, within a world ruled more or less harmoniously by a system of laws, of principles, of causal relations, of well defined psychologies, of well mapped geographies." Cortázar concludes, "In my case, the suspicion of another order, more secret and less communicable, and the fertile discovery of Alfred Jarry, for whom the true study of reality did not rest on laws but on the exceptions to those laws, were some of the guiding principles of my personal search for a literature beyond overly naïve forms of realism."[17]

Much as Borges and Cortázar approach the fantastic in an effort not to terrify the reader but to shake his epistemological assumptions, to immerse him in a world where "the unreal" invades and contaminates the real, their stories can be described as the obverse and the reverse of that same effort. Borges has said that everything that has happened to him is illusory and that the only thing real in his life is a library. This would be a dubious statement were it not for the fact that the world, as we know it, is a creation of culture, an artificial world in which, according to Lévi-Strauss, man lives as a member of a social group.[18] Leaning on the nature of culture as a fabrication of the human mind, Borges has written, "We have dreamed the world. We have dreamed it strong, mysterious, visible, ubiquitous in space and secure in time; but we have allowed tenuous, eternal interstices of unreason in its structure so we may know that it is false."[19] Borges penetrates these illogical interstices in an attempt to unweave that tidy labyrinth of reason woven by culture to find finally that art and language (and science, for that matter) are, can only be, symbols—however, "not in the sense of mere figures which refer to some given reality by means of suggestion and allegorical renderings, but in the sense of forces each of which produces and posits a world of its own."[20]

Motivated by this inference, Borges finds the road that leads to the universe of his fiction: "Let us admit what all idealists admit the hallucinatory nature of the world. Let us do what no idealist has done: let us seek unrealities that confirm that nature."[21] He has found those unrealities not in the realm of the supernatural or the marvelous but in those symbols and systems which define our own reality in philosophies and theologies which in some way constitute the core of our culture. Hence the countless references in his stories to authors and books, to theories and doctrines; hence the aura of the bookishness and intellection that pervades his work; and hence his constant insistence on his having said nothing new, because what he wrote was already written in other literatures. It was written in the same way that the *Quixote* had been written before Pierre Menard, but Menard's merit lies in his reading the *Quixote* as it couldn't have been read in Cervantes's time.

Borges, for whom "one literature differs from another, either before or after it, not so much because of the text as for the manner in which it is read,"[22] reads that "respected system of perplexities we call philosophy" in a new context. The ingredients do not change, just as the number of colored glass bits contained in a kaleidoscope is always the same, but with each movement of the tube the symmetrical image does change. Borges deals with human culture as if he were holding a kaleidoscope, but after his master stroke the image is no longer the same. The alchemy consists in presenting our reality, what we have come to accept as our reality, transfigured in a dream, in one more phantasmagoria of the mind which has little or nothing to do with the real world it seeks to penetrate.

Cortázar's fictional world, on the other hand, rather than an acceptance, represents a challenge to culture, a challenge, as he puts it, to "thirty centuries of Judeo-Christian dialectics," to "the Greek criterion of truth and error," to the homo sapiens, to logic and the law of sufficient reason and, in general, to what he calls "the Great Habit." If Borges's fantasies are oblique allusions to the situation of man in a world he can never fully fathom, to an order he has created as a substitute labyrinth to the one created by a divine mind, Cortázar's stories strive to transcend the schemes and constructs of culture and seek precisely to touch that order Borges finds too abstruse and complex to be understood by man. The first stumbling block Cortázar encounters in this quest is language itself: "I've always found it absurd," he says, "to talk about transforming man if man doesn't simultaneously, or previously, transform his instrument of knowledge. How to transform oneself if one continues to use the same language Plato used?"[23] He found a first answer in surrealism. As early as 1949 he defined surrealism as "the greatest undertaking of contemporary man as an anticipation and attempt toward an integrated humanism."[24] Cortázar saw in surrealism not a mere literary technique or a simple esthetic stand, but a world view or, as he said in the same article, "not a school or an ism but a Weltanschauung." When surrealism settled for less than "an integrated humanism," Cortázar confronted some of its inconsistencies through the pages of *Hopscotch*. One of its characters, Étienne, says in chapter 99:

> The surrealists thought that true language and true reality were censored and relegated by the rationalist and bourgeois structure of the Western world. They were right, as any poet knows, but that was just a moment in the complicated peeling of the banana. Result, more than one of them ate it with the skin still on. The surrealists hung from words instead of brutally disengaging

themselves from them, as Morelli would like to do from the word itself. Fanatics of the *verbum* in a pure state, frantic wizards, they accepted anything as long as it didn't seem excessively grammatical. They didn't suspect enough that the creation of a whole language, even though it might end up betraying its sense, irrefutably shows human structure, whether that of a Chinese or a redskin. Language means residence in reality, living in a reality. Even if it's true that the language we use betrays us ..., wanting to free it from its taboos isn't enough. We have to relive it, not re-animate it.[25]

The second obstacle Cortázar stumbles upon in this search for authenticity is the use of our normative categories of thought and knowledge, our rational tools for apprehending reality. He believes in a kind of marvelous reality (here again the affinity with surrealism is obvious). "Marvelous," he explains, "in the sense that our daily reality masks a *second reality* which is neither mysterious nor theological, but profoundly human. Yet, due to a long series of mistakes, it has remained concealed under a reality prefabricated by many centuries of culture, a culture in which there are great achievements but also profound aberrations, profound distortions."[26]

Among those distorted notions which obstruct man's access to a more genuine world, Cortázar points a finger to our perception of death and to two of the most established concepts in the Western grasp of reality—time and space.

The notions of time and space, as they were conceived by the Greeks and after them by the whole of the West, are flatly rejected by Vedanta. In a sense, man made a mistake when he invented time. That's why it would actually be enough for us to renounce mortality, to take a jump out of time, on a level other than that of daily life, of course. I'm thinking of the phenomenon of death, which for Western thought has been a great scandal, as Kierkegaard and Unamuno realized so well; a phenomenon that is not in the least scandalous in the East where it is regarded not as an end but as a metamorphosis.[27]

As much as Cortázar sees the East as an alternative to this preoccupation with time and space, he also realizes that it cannot be an answer for Western man, who is the product of a different tradition, a tradition one cannot simply undo or replace. If there is an answer to the questions of time and space, it lies in a relentless confrontation with them in a manner similar to the struggle Unamuno memorably represented in the fight between Jacob and the Angel. "*Rayuela*, like so much of my work," Cortázar says, "suffers from hyperintellectuality. But, I'm not willing or able to renounce that intellectuality, insofar as I can breathe life into it, make it pulse in every thought and word."[28]

It is this kind of coalescence between two diametrically opposed dimensions—one natural and one supernatural, one historical and one fantastic—that constitutes the backbone of Cortázar's neofantastic short fiction. The beggar whom the protagonist of "Lejana" meets in the center of a bridge in Budapest, the noises that expel the brother and sister from their "house taken over," the rabbits that the narrator of "A Letter to a Lady in Paris" helplessly vomits, the tiger that roams freely through the rooms of a middle-class family's house in "Bestiary," the dead character who is yet more alive than the living ones in "Cartas de mamá," the dream that becomes real and converts its dreamer into a dream in "The Night Face Up," the reader who enters the fiction and ends up fictionalizing reality in "Continuity of Parks"—these are but a few examples of how the realist code yields to a code which no longer responds to our causal categories of time and space. In these stories the reverse side of the phenomenal world is sought, an order scandalously in conflict with the order construed by logical thinking; hence the incongruities we call "fantastic."

But the fantastic event in these tales does not aim, as it did in the nineteenth century, at assailing and terrifying us with "a crack," as Roger Caillois says of the fantastic genre.[29] From the outset the realist scale is juxtaposed with the fantastic one. In "Axolotl" the opening paragraph reads, "There was a time when I thought a great deal about axolotls. I went to see them in the aquarium at the Jardin des Plantes and stayed for hours watching them, observing their immobility, their faint movements. Now I am an axolotl."[30] In this text there is not, as is the case in most neofantastic fiction, a gradual process of presentation of the real which finally yields to a fissure of unreality. In contrast to the nineteenth-century fantastic fiction in which the text moves from the familiar and natural to the unfamiliar and supernatural, like a journey through a known and recognizable territory which eventually leads to an unknown and dreadful destination, the writers of the neofantastic bestow equal validity and verisimilitude on both orders. They have no difficulty in moving with the same freedom and ease in both. This unbiased approach is in itself a profession of faith. The unstated assumption declares that the fantastic level is just as real (or unreal, from a realist standpoint) as the realist level. If one of them produces in us a surreal or fantastic feeling, it is because in our daily lives we follow logical notions similar to those that govern the realist mode.

The neofantastic writer, on the other hand, ignores these distinctions and approaches both levels with the same sense of reality. The reader senses, nevertheless, that Cortázar's axolotl is a metaphor (a metaphor and not a symbol) that conveys meanings unconveyable through logical conceptualizations, a metaphor that strives to express messages inexpressible through the realist code. The metaphor (rabbits, tiger, noises, axolotl, beggar) provides Cortázar with a structure capable of producing new referents, even if their references are yet to be established or, to use I. A. Richards's terminology, the *vehicles* with which these metaphors confront us point to unformulated *tenors*. We know we are dealing with vehicles of metaphors because they suggest meanings that exceed their literal value, but it is the reader's task to perceive and define those meanings, to determine the tenor to which the vehicle points.

When personally asked about the meanings implied in those metaphors, Cortázar has answered: "I know as much as you do." This is not a subterfuge. He once explained, "The great majority of my stories were written—how should I say—in spite of my own will, above or below my reasoning consciousness, as if I were but a medium through which a strange force passed and manifested itself."[31] Some even originated as dreams or nightmares:

> Il est vrai que certain de mes contes sont nés directement de cauchemars ou de rêves. Un des premiers contes que j'ai écrits, "La maison occupée", procède d'un cauchemar. C'en est la transcription très fidèle bien que travaillée littérairement, évidemment.... Si je faisais une statistique de ceux de mes contes que je dois aux rêves, ils se situeraient en nette minorité. Quelques-uns évidemment sont faits de lambeaux de rêves, mais c'est lorsque je suis éveillé que le fantastique tombe sur moi comme une pierre.[32]

All this may sound too close to the surrealist explorations of the unconscious, to the prescriptions included by Breton in the *Manifestos* regarding automatic writing and transcription of dreams. Any page written by Cortázar will suffice, however, to dispel that impression. If he, on one hand, acknowledges the strong influence surrealism had on him at the beginning of his work, it is equally true, on the other, that it was an influence on outlook and philosophy rather than on technique and style. Cortázar's stories are built with the rigorous precision and, at the same time, subtle naturalness of a cobweb. The text flows with the same perfection one finds in those fragile fabrics beautifully spun between two wires of a fence or in the branches of a tree. But there is nothing fragile in the texture of any of his stories. Quite the contrary. The text displays such an economy of means, it streams with such ease and determination, it arrives so convincingly at its destination, one is tempted to say the story has been told by itself, that what the reader has in front of him is a structure woven by the text itself and that, like those seashells which have engraved on themselves with silent perfection traces of undefiled beauty, on that limpid surface nothing is in excess and nothing is lacking.

*

Cortázar likes to think that with his novels, and more specifically with the long story "The Pursuer," he begins to unloose the stylistic perfection with which his stories are knitted. He also believes that with this change he moves to a new stage in his development as a writer.

> When I wrote "The Pursuer," I had reached a point where I felt I had to deal with something that was looser to me. I wasn't sure of myself any more in that story. I took up an existential problem, a human problem which was later amplified in *The Winners*, and above all in *Hopscotch*. Fantasy for its own sake had stopped interesting me. By then I was fully aware of the dangerous perfection of the storyteller who reaches a certain level of achievement and stays on that same level forever, without moving on. I was a bit sick and tired of seeing how well my stories turned out. In "The Pursuer" I wanted to stop inventing and stand on my own ground, to look at myself a bit. And looking at myself meant looking at my neighbor, at man. I hadn't looked too closely at people until I wrote "The Pursuer."[33]

But, of course, the new linguistic mood he finds in this long story, and later in his subsequent novels, is not the deterioration of his previous style but a new form of expression which tackles more effectively the nature of his new concerns. Cortázar defines those new concerns as "existential and metaphysical" as opposed to his esthetic pursuits in the short story.

The truth is, though, as Cortázar well knows, that his short stories and his novels are motivated by a common search, by a quest for authenticity which is of one piece in both genres. Otherwise, how does one understand his own definition of *Hopscotch* as "the philosophy of my stories, as an examination of what determined, throughout many years, their substance or thrust"?[34] *Hopscotch* articulates the same questions around which the stories are built; but if the novel is a reflection, an effort to brood upon those questions the stories are narrative translations of those same questions. *Hopscotch* traces the mandala through which the characters of the stories are constantly journeying. Those characters do not speculate or intellectualize; they simply deliver themselves to the passions and games sweeping their lives, moved and battered by forces they don't understand. *Hopscotch* seeks to understand those forces, and as such it represents the intellectual bow from which the stories were shot. The proof that this is indeed the case lies in the fact that some of the central inquiries found in *Hopscotch* were already outlined in the early essays and reviews Cortázar wrote before and during his writing of the short stories. His tales were fantastic responses to those problems and questions which occupied his mind at the time and which eventually found a masterful formulation in *Hopscotch*. It goes without saying that *Hopscotch*'s hyperintellectual ponderings alone do,not explain the stories; Cortázar combined his intellectual spurs with his own passions and phobias, and the latter are as enigmatic to him as to the reader.

If Horacio Oliveira seeks through the pages of *Hopscotch* a second reality which has been covered by a it and culture in our present version of reality, and Johnny Carter in "The Pursuer" perceives through intuition and artistic imagination dimensions of reality which have been buried by conceptualization, the characters of the stories also find their ultimate realization on a fantastic plane that is the reverse of that stiff reality to which habit and culture have condemned them. In "Lejana," for instance, one of Cortázar's earliest short stories, the protagonist searches for a bridge at whose center she hopes to find that part of her self rejected and suffocated by family, friends and environment. She does find it, as a beggar waiting on a Budapest bridge, a beggar in whom she recognizes her true self, a sort of double whose reality bursts from her imagination, like a fantastic event, onto a historical plane. Similarly, the protagonist of "The Pursuer," a jazzman modeled after saxophonist Charlie Parker, searches for "a reality that escapes every day" and that sometimes presents itself as "holes": "In the door," he explains, "in the bed: holes. In the hand, in the newspaper, in time, in the air: everything full of holes, everything spongy, like a colander straining itself...."[35] Those holes, invisible or covered for others, are for Johnny the residence of "something else," of a second reality whose door Johnny senses and seeks to open: "It's impossible there's nothing else, it can't be we're that close to it, that much on the other side of the door ... Bruno, all my life in my music I looked for that door to open finally. Nothing, a crack...." (215–16). What is behind that door is a world that Johnny sees only on one occasion, through his music, but whose substance one glimpses throughout the narrative. A good example is the biography of Johnny written by Bruno: very well informed, very complete, very successful, but with one omission—the biographee. Or as Johnny puts it, "It's very good your book.... You're much better informed than I am, but it seems to me like something's missing.... Don't get upset, Bruno, it's not important that you forgot to put all that in. But Bruno, ... what you forgot to put in is me" (207, 212).

Cortázar has acknowledged that Johnny Carter is a first draft of Horacio Oliveira, a precursor in that search which takes the protagonist of *Hopscotch* into a revision of the very foundations of Western culture—its writers and artists, its music and language, its philosophy and ethics, its religion and science—a task Oliveira undertakes together with his friends of the Serpent Club with the casualness and poignancy that makes fiction more credible and convincing than pure intellection. Jung has said of Freud that "he has given expression to the fact that Western man is in danger of losing his shadow altogether, of identifying himself with his fictive personality and of identifying the world with the abstract picture painted by scientific rationalism."[36] This is also Oliveira's concern; but to show that man has become "the slave of his own fiction, and that a purely conceptual world progressively replaces reality," as Jung has said of the products of man's conscious activity, Cortázar proceeds to disassemble that fictitious apparatus manufactured by culture to show that it has become a substitute of reality, a mask that must be removed if man is to retain touch with the real world and with himself. In this sense, *Hopscotch* is a devastating criticism of rationalism:

> ... this technological reality that men of science and the readers of *France-Soir* accept today, this world of cortisone, gamma rays, and the elution of plutonium, has as little to do with reality as the world of the *Roman de la Rose*.... Man, after having expected everything from intelligence and the spirit, feels that he's been betrayed, is vaguely aware that his weapons have been turned against him, that culture, *civiltà*, have misled him into this blind alley where scientific barbarism is nothing but a very understandable reaction. (444–45)

As in "The Pursuer," in *Hopscotch* reality lies also somewhere behind: "Behind all that (it's always behind, convince yourself that this is the key idea of modern thought) Paradise, the other world, trampled innocence which weeping darkly seeks the land of Hurgaly?" (377). How does one get there? How does one reach that center, the "kibbutz of desire" which Oliveira seeks? In his short stories the road is a fantastic event; the conflict between a hollow reality and one which, like an epiphany, reveals to the characters a time outside time and a space that transcends geometric space, resolves itself in metaphors that by defying physical laws appear as fantastic occurrences. In "The Pursuer" Johnny Carter peeps through those "holes" of a second reality via his jazz music; the artistic phenomenon becomes what it has always been—"a bridge toward true reality," in Nietzsche's dictum—but now Johnny transports his visions to the trivial act of riding a subway and indicts the fallacy inherent in our concepts of time and space. In *Hopscotch* our logical order of reason and science is described as totally absurd: "Reason is only good to mummify reality in moments of calm or analyze its future storms, never to resolve a crisis of the moment.... And these crises that most people think of as terrible, as absurd, I personally think they serve to show us the real absurdity, the absurdity of an ordered and calm world" (163–64). Oliveira muses on this absurd world when he concludes that "only by living absurdly is possible to break out of this infinite absurdity" (101). *Hopscotch* offers an answer different from the one found in the short stories and even in "The Pursuer," where Johnny, as much as he lives a life which in Bruno's eyes can only be described as "absurd," engages in a life style of a musical genius who indulges in his allotted share of "absurdity"; it is music which in the end provides for Johnny a bridge to those "holes." The characters of *Hopscotch*, on the other hand, are unprofessional, simple, though extremely well-read and informed people who, as much as they live a bohemian life, share the pettiness and trivia of plain people.

Thus the solution *Hopscotch* resents to Cortázar's basic quest for authenticity is a kind of existential absurdity, a solution that also had a very strong appeal to surrealists since Mallarmé's *Igitur*: "Igitur is a person 'who feels in himself, thanks to the absurd the existence of the Absolute.' After him the Surrealists will enlarge and maintain the domain of the absolute through this very same type of cult of the absurd which will tend to become the basis of artistic creation and a means of liberating art from the finite or natural aspects of things and beings."[37] It is in this context that some of the most momentous chapters of *Hopscotch* should be read: the concert by Berthe Trépat, the death of Rocamadour, the encounter with the *clocharde*, the episodes of the board, the circus and the mental clinic. These seemingly preposterous situations impress us as a absurd because they run against the grain of our accepted order, which for Oliveira has become absurdity at its best. For him, reason contains a sophism as huge as the world it has created, and logic leads to a gargantuan and catastrophic nowhere. To pull out from this dead end, Oliveira embarks on feats and situations which, though they offer him on one hand a route to further exploration of that dead end, act on the other hand as a modified virus of the same disease which hopefully will immunize him. And although *Hopscotch* presents no answers, no prescriptions for guaranteed salvation it offers a possibility of reconciliation. Toward the end of his absurd odyssey Horacio meditates on the significance of his friend Traveler's last efforts to lend him a helping hand. Horacio seems to have reached the last square of his hopscotch:

> After what Traveler had just done, everything had something like a marvelous feeling of conciliation and that senseless but vivid and present harmony could not be violated, could no longer be falsified, basically Traveler was what he might well have been with a little less cursed imagination, he was the man of the territory, the incurable mistake of the species gone astray, but how much beauty in the mistake and in the five thousand years of false and precarious territory, how much beauty in those eyes that had filled with tears and in that voice that had advised him: "Throw the bolt, I don't trust them," how much love in that arm that held the waist of a woman. "Probably," Oliveira thought while he answered the friendly gestures of Dr. Ovejero and Ferraguto, ... "the only possible way to escape from that territory is to plunge into it over one's head." (347)

Cortázar's next novel, *62: A Model Kit*, derives from chapter 62 of *Hopscotch* and represents his novelistic answer to Oliveira's search for alternatives to that fabricated reality criticized in the earlier novel. In chapter 62 Morelli sketches the outline of "a book he had been planning but that never got beyond a few scattered notes." "If I were to write this book," he continues, "standard behavior ... would be inexplicable by means of current instrumental psychology.... Everything would be a kind of disquiet, a continuous uprooting, a territory where psychological causality would yield disconcertedly, and those puppets would destroy each other or love each other or recognize each other without suspecting too much that life is trying to change its key in and through and by them, that a barely conceivable attempt is born in man as one other day there were being born the reason-key, the feeling-key, the pragmatism-key" (363). *62: A Model Kit* is the implementation of this attempt.

The novel is, as Cortázar advances in the foreword, a transgression, not only at the most manifest level of language but also as an effort to understand life by cognitive means other than the ones rationally codified by science. Hence psychology is no longer the yardstick. What replaces psychology as the criterion to measure human behavior? A mixture of game, vampirism[38] and an intangible magnetic force that groups people into what Cortázar calls *figuras* or human constellations. The notions of time and space as traditionally accepted are no longer the ordinate and the abscissa which frame and regulate life. In *62* the action takes place in Paris, London and Vienna, but the characters move and act in these different cities as if they were one single space referred to as *la ciudad* (the city). This new space is no longer a confining area which imposes on the characters the limitations of its own perimeter; it is a new medium that the characters stretch, shape and dispose of like a chessboard to play their own games. It matters not if Marrast and Nicole are in London, Hélène and Celia in Paris, Juan and Tell in Vienna; they move and interact from one city to the other horizontally, vertically and diagonally, using the cities as square spaces for their traps, gambits and inevitable checks. But they ignore the rules of the game they play. Their movements are controlled by forces they dimly grasp and which ultimately escape their consciousness, like chess pieces unaware of the player's designs and strategies. Physical or conventional time also recedes to a sort of mythical time in which "the before and the after touch and are one and the same."[39] The characters' nights and days are pivoted around the ominous and invisible rule of the Countess (Erszebet Báthory), whose legendary past marks the birth of vampirism. That past becomes present, and the present in which the characters reside sends them back to that legendary past, in which context one begins to understand in part the patterns that shape their destiny.

The model kit in the title alludes, as Cortázar points out in the foreword, not so much to the structure of the novel as to the task of assembling an intimated meaning by putting together the various elements of a possible *combinatoria*. In form, the novel is built with the precision and cleverness of a clockwork. The first thirty pages that introduce the rest of the narrative contain, like the slide in Nicolas Roeg's memorable film *Don't Look Now*, the basic ingredients of which the novel is made: the name of the restaurant, the mistranslation of a customer's order, Juan's own order of a bottle of Sylvaner, the book Juan carries and opens by chance to a certain page, the date (Christmas Eve) and fragments of the story the novel is about to unfold. In this long soliloquy that streams through Juan's consciousness as he sits facing a mirror in the restaurant, Cortázar has disclosed the leading strands that tie together the meandering ramifications of the entire novel. In this sense, the overture is like a cocoon which already holds the full length of the thread the text patiently and skillfully unwinds. The mirror Juan faces in the restaurant anticipates the reflective quality of the introductory passage and also defines the mirrorlike symmetries with which the novel is constructed. Each character seems to be a reflection or double of another: Frau Marta echoes Erszebet Báthory, and the English girl she violates has a counterpart in Celia, who is violated by Hélène, who in turn seems to be under the spell of Countess Báthory; Marrast loves Nicole, who loves Juan, who loves Hélène; the seduction of an adolescent girl (Celia) is matched by the seduction of an adolescent boy (Austin); Polanco and Calac are each like the inverted image of the other; the long section about Frau Marta and the possession of the English girl parallels and crisscrosses, at the same time, the equally long section about the possession of Celia by Hélène, and the doll made by monsieur Ochs that Juan gives to Tell and Tell sends to Hélène bridges the two sections as the clue to both stories. Finally, Hélène is guilt-ridden by the death of one of her patients, who hauntingly reminds her of Juan, and toward the end of the novel she is killed by Austin, who loves Celia; Hélène is thus the vertex of two triangles, in each of which there is a deceased and in each of which a member of one sex is linked to two of the other: Hélène–Patient–Juan and Austin–Hélène–Celia.

The text itself, as discourse, shares these equidistances: first, in the relation between the introduction and the body of the novel in a proportion similar to the one between a code and its decoder; second, in the way the myth of the Countess Báthory and the "blood castle" at the very beginning of the novel exchanges signals toward the end with a second myth, the story of Diana and Acteon from Greek mythology, mentioned by Juan on page 235 and subsequently discussed by him and Hélène in the following pages; and third, the black pontoon that mysteriously appears at the end of the introduction carrying Frau Marta and reappears towards the end of the novel with Frau Marta on it, but this time bewitching Nicole, who also travels through the canal on "the same" black pontoon. In addition, the scene in the restaurant is described as the point where the various pieces of a puzzle finally fall into place, bringing the bizarre and liquid ingredients of Juan's blood story to "coagulation," to a curdling point and a frozen time where for Juan "the before and the after had fallen apart in his hands, leaving him a light, useless rain of dead moths" (24).

But if for a moment this curdled *figura*, which creates its own space and generates its own time, which seeks to perceive and define reality in terms that defy causality, makes us think of or suspect a flight from history, it is only so because we have tended for too long to associate the concern for man and his social plight with facile pamphlets mistakenly taken as "literature" of protest. Cortázar knows too well that there are no easy answers, that the fires and horrors of history cannot be put out or even placated by making literature impersonate roles and gestures which create false illusions and hollow expectations and end up adulterating and finally canceling its true capabilities. His next and latest novel so far, *Libro de Manuel*, is an effort to show that a writer can undertake to deal with the social problems of his time without turning into a puppeteer whose script has been set beforehand as an adaptation of political slogans and ideological platitudes. Cortázar is torn in this novel between his responsibilities as a writer who respects and values his craft and his responsibilities as a man who lives immersed in his time and feels part of the Latin American destiny. And again the answer is neither simple nor clear-cut. In *Hopscotch* Horacio ponders the dilemma and its double-edged nature:

> Besides, what was the true morality of action? A social action like that of the syndicalists was more than justified in the field of history. Happy were those who lived and slept in history.... There was no objection to that action as such, but he pushed it aside with doubts about his personal conduct. He would suspect a betrayal the moment he gave in to posters on the street or activities of a social nature; a betrayal disguised as satisfactory work, daily happiness, satisfied conscience, fulfilled duty. He was too well acquainted with certain communists in Buenos Aires and Paris, capable of the worst villainy but redeemable in their own minds by "the struggle," by having to leave in the middle of dinner to run to a meeting or finish a job. Social action in those people seemed too much like an alibi, the way children are usually the alibi for mothers' not having to do anything worth while in this life, the way learning with its blinders is useful in not learning that in the jail down the street they are still guillotining guys who should not be guillotined. False action is almost always the most spectacular, the kind that tears down respect, prestige, and whequestrian wheffigies. (417–18)

Andrés, the protagonist of *Libro de Manuel* and a sort of outgrowth of Horacio Oliveira, seeks a political answer without suppressing his human condition and without impinging on his individual rights and endeavors. Thus his political search becomes an act of assertion of his freedom and of his personal realization. The road leading to this ultimate goal is a tortuous and agonizing one, since in the long run any genuine social struggle implies the suppression or assimilation of personal struggles, or at least their postponement, to the cause one is engaged in. In his last conversation with Lonstein, Andrés defends his rights up to the last, sensing that the slightest form of mutilation conceals a betrayal:

> —You, sir, want a lot of things, but you don't give up any.
> —No, I don't give up anything, pal.
> —Not even a tiny bit? Say, an exquisite author? A Japanese poet known only to you?
> —No, not even that.
> —What about your Xenakis, your aleatory music, your free jazz, your Joni Mitchell, your abstract lithographs?
> —No, brother. Nothing. I take everything with me wherever I go.
> —You really have it your way. don't you?—said Lonstein—. You want to have the pie and eat it too, right?
> —Yes sir—said Andrés.[40]

But as much as this novel takes Cortázar into exploring his own social and political concerns, *Libro de Manuel* is also, like his previous works, part of his relentless effort to liberate man. This new man should be the product of a new kind of humanism Cortázar has striven to outline throughout his poetry, essays and fiction. Each of them is a stretch of a route seeking to arrive at a center, at a final island, at a world that "exists in this one" but that "one has to create like the phoenix." As there are no easy answers for Cortázar, there are no final answers either. He is a nonconformist, a rebel or, what amounts to the same thing, a poet who searches through literature "to earn the right to enter the house of man."

NOTES

1. Carlos Fuentes, "A Demanding Novel," *Commentary* (New York), October 1966, pp. 142–43.

2. Donald Keene, "Moving Snapshots," *The New York Times Book Review*, 10 April 1966, p. 1.

3. Graciela de Sola, *Julio Cortázar y el hombre nuevo*, Buenos Aires, Sudamericana, 1968, p. 9 (my translation).

4. Luis Harss, Barbara Dohmann, *Into the Mainstream*, New York, Harper & Row, 1967, pp. 214–15.

5. Julio Denís (Julio Cortázar), "Rimbaud," *Huella* (Buenos Aires), no. 2 (July 1941); Quoted by G. De Sola, p. 14.

6. Julio Denís (Julio Cortázar), "Quitadme," from his *Presencia*, Buenos Aires, El Bibliófilo, 1938, p. 40 (my translation).

7. Ibid., p. 94 (my translation). The Spanish pun *cierto/incierto* is lost in translation.

8. James E. Irby, "Encuentro con Borges," *Vida universitaria* (Monterrey, Mex.), 12 April 1964, p. 14.

9. Rita Guibert, *Seven Voices*, New York, Vintage, 1973, p. 108.

10. Harss, p. 61.

11. Julio Cortázar, *La vuelta al día en ochenta mundos*, Mexico City, Siglo XXI, 1967, p. 94. In the second part of the quotation Cortázar cites a passage by Michel Foucault, as he clearly indicates in his book.

12. See Roger Caillois, *Imágenes, imágenes* ..., Buenos Aires, Sudamericana, 1970, pp. 23, 24.

13. Julio Cortázar, "Algunos aspectos del cuento," *Casa de las Américas* (Havana), 1962, nos. 15–16, p. 3 (my translation).

14. C.G. Bjurström, "Julio Cortázar, Entretien," *La Quinzaine Littéraire* (Paris), 1 August 1970, p. 17.

15. See Caillois, op. cit.; Louis Vax, *L'art et la littérature fantastique*, Paris, 1960; and Peter Penzoldt, *The Supernatural in Literature*, New York, 1965.

16. See my article "The Fantastic as Surrealist Metaphors in Cortázar's Short Fiction," *Dada/Surrealism* (New York), 1975, no. 5, pp. 28–33.

17. "Algunos aspectos del cuento," pp. 3–4.

18. See Claude Lévi-Strauss, *Arte, lenguaje, etnología* (*Entrevistas con Georges Charbonier*), Mexico City, Siglo XXI, 1968, p. 132.

19. Jorge Luis Borges, *Other Inquisitions*, R. L. Simms, tr., New York, Washington Square, 1966, p. 120.

20. See Ernest Cassirer, *Language and Myth*, New York, Dover, 1953, p. 8.

21. Borges, p. 120.

22. Ibid., p. 173.

23. Harss, p. 235.

24. Julio Cortázar, "Irracionalismo y eficacia," *Realidad: revista de ideas* (Buenos Aires), nos. 17–18 (September–December 1949), p. 253.

25. Julio Cortázar, *Hopscotch*, Gregory Rabassa, tr., New York, Pantheon, 1966, p. 441. Subsequent quotations are taken from this edition.

26. Margarita García Flores, "Siete respuestas de Julio Cortázar," *Revista de la Universidad de México* (Mexico City), vol. 21, no. 7 (March 1967), p. 11 (my translation).

27. Harss, p. 219.

28. Ibid., pp. 244–45.

29. Caillois, p. 14.

30. Julio Cortázar, *Blow-Up and Other Stories*, Paul Blackburn, tr., New York, Collier, 1968, p. 3.

31. "Algunos aspectos del cuento," p. 7.

32. Bjurström, p. 17. In this regard Cortázar also noted in one of his lectures at the University of Oklahoma in November 1975: "And since I have mentioned dreams, it seems appropriate to say that many of my fantastic stories were born in an oneiric territory and that I had the good fortune that in some cases the censorship was not merciless and

permitted me to carry the content of the dreams into words.... One could say that the fantastic which they contain comes from archetypal regions which in one way or another we all share, and that in the act of reading these stories the reader witnesses or discovers something of himself. I have seen this phenomenon put to the test many times with an old story of mine entitled "The House Taken Over," which I dreamed with all the details which figure in the text and which I wrote upon jumping out of bed, still enveloped in the horrible nausea of its ending." From "The Present State of Fiction in Latin America," Margery A. Safir, tr., *Books Abroad* 50:3 (Summer 1976), p. 522–32, and included in this volume.

33. Harss, p. 224.

34. *La vuelta al día*, p. 25.

35. *Blow-Up and Other Stories*, pp. 190–91. Subsequent quotations are from this edition.

36. C.G. Jung, *The Undiscovered Self*, Boston, Little, Brown, 1957, p. 82.

37. Anna Balakian, *Surrealism: The Road to the Absolute*, New York, Noonday, 1959, p. 12.

38. On game, see Linda Cummings Baxt, "Game in Cortázar," unpublished Ph.D. dissertation (Yale University), 1974; and also my article "*Homo sapiens vs. homo ludens* en tres cuentos de Cortázar," *Revista Iberoamericana* (Pittsburgh University), nos. 84–85 (July–December 1973), pp. 611–24. On vampirism in *62: A Model Kit*, see chapter 8 of Baxt's dissertation; and also Ana Maria Hernández, "Vampires and Vampiresses: A Reading of *62*," *Books Abroad* 50:3 (Summer 1976), pp. 570–76, included in this volume.

39. Julio Cortázar, *62: A Model Kit*, Gregory Rabassa, tr., New York, Pantheon, 1972, p. 148. Subsequent quotations are from this edition.

40. Julio Cortázar, *Libro de Manuel*, Buenos Aires, Sudamericana, 1973, p. 343 (my translation).

ROBERTO GONZÁLEZ ECHEVARRÍA

Los reyes: *Cortázar's Mythology of Writing*

Although I refer to *Los reyes* in my title, I do not intend to carry out an independent literary analysis of what no doubt is a callow work of Cortázar's. My design, at once broad and reductive, is to deal with the somewhat dated and embarrassing problem of how to read an author, not a book.[1] Is "holistic" criticism viable? Is it possible, in other words, to read Cortázar instead of engaging in a series of isolated exegeses of his works? And if it is worth attempting such a reading, how does one avoid turning it into a thematic gloss, a formalistic reduction or a biographical narrative? How, other than as a rhetorical license, can we continue to use Cortázar's name in reference to what is already a vast and diverse body of writing, encompassing texts belonging not only to various genres but also to criticism and theory? And what can one make of a text as bizarre as *Los reyes*? In what way is it also Cortázar's?

These questions do not arise from an abstract, speculative whim, but from Cortázar's work itself. They are, as I hope to be able to argue here, the fundamental questions posed by Cortázar's texts, and not only by such obviously autobiographical books as *La vuelta al día en ochenta mundos*, *Ultimo round* and *Fantomas contra los vampiros multinacionales*. I intend to use *Los reyes* to sketch a primal scene, to delineate what might very broadly be called Cortázar's conception of writing—conception, that is, both in its etymological sense of

From *The Final Island: The Fiction of Julio Cortázar.* © 1978 University of Oklahoma Press.

insemination or generation, and in its more common meaning of notion or idea. By determining Cortázar's conception of writing in both these senses, I hope to legitimize a critical discourse that will atone for its seductiveness by providing a critical insight into the totality of a literary enterprise.

While discussing a problem similar to the one just sketched, Roland Barthes remarks in *Critique et vérité*:

> There is no doubt that the "civilized" work cannot be dealt with as myth, in the ethnological sense of the term. But the difference [between the "civilized" work and that of the "primitive"] has less to do with the signature of the message than with its substance. Our works are written; that imposes upon them certain constraints of meaning that the oral myth could not know. It is a mythology of writing that awaits us, which shall have as its object not certain *determined* works, that is to say, which are inscribed in a process of determination where a person (the author) would be the origin, but works *traversed* by the great mythic writing in which humanity tries out its significations, i.e., its desires.[2]

As often happens in discussions of myth, whether they be "civilized" or not, Barthes's own formulation has become part of the myth that it attempts to uncover. For if there is a modern mythology of writing, it centers on the question of authorship versus general determination—a question, in other words, of the origin or generation of writing. That "great mythic writing" of which Barthes speaks has as its object the disappearance of the author, or in more current critical idiom, the abolition of the subject; it is a search for meaning in a universe abandoned both by man and the gods.

While current and certainly modern, the abolition of the author is not new. In *The Dehumanization of Art*, synthesizing a whole current of modern thinking, Ortega said that "the poet begins where man ends," and added, referring to Mallarmé, that the fate of the "poor face of the man who officiates as poet" is to "disappear, to vanish and become a pure nameless voice breathing into the air the words—those true protagonists of the lyrical pursuit. This pure and nameless voice, the mere acoustic carrier of the verse, is the voice of the poet who has learned to extricate himself from the surrounding man."[3] The work of philologists and mythographers during the nineteenth century (the Grimm brothers, later Bédier and Menéndez Pidal) brought to the fore the question of authorship. As Foucault has shown, once representation as a synchronic, complete system mediating between the subject and the world is shattered, the various languages of literary expression, as well as the question of being, become historical—language and being become a matter of depth.[4] Philology seeks the origin of language, just as ontology seeks the origin of being in man's passions (Rousseau). The urgency of this question of origins—in its double thrust: language, being—determines that most salient characteristic of modern writing, self-referentiality. By alluding to itself and by probing into its own mode of being, modern wasting is always in the process of offering an implicit statement about its own generation, a conception of its conception, as it were.

It would be a naïve and predictable undertaking to show that self-referentiality occurs in Cortázar, since *Hopscotch* has already become a classic of self-referential writing. But it is precisely in self-referentiality that the mythology which I intend to isolate manifests itself. As Hyppolite has shown in his study of Hegel, self-reflexiveness is a regressive movement, a circular journey back to the source.[5] In literature self-referentiality is a return to origins in order to take away from conception its claim of originality, of constituting a single, fresh moment of beginning, an ordering principle and principium. Rather than the joyful game that it is often taken to be, self-referentiality is a deadly game in Cortázar, a violent ritual where Cortázar is at stake. *Los reyes*, the first book that he signed with his own name (as is known, an earlier work had appeared under a pseudonym), presents, under the guise of the Theseus myth; this ritual. By the reenactment of this ritual, Cortázar's writing labors to define itself, to cope with the opposition of the individual/original versus the general/collective, in short, the issue of generation. Who writes?

The most superficial consideration of *Los reyes* immediately leads to the issue of individuality and origin. The very appeal to classical mythology, to the dawn of Western literary tradition, is suggestive of a concern about the beginning of writing. The recourse to classical mythology is in itself hardly original, but rather a characteristic of the modern tradition: Nietzsche, Freud, Joyce, Pound, Unamuno; all take recourse to classical figures. In Latin America there is a strain of classicism of this sort that runs from Lugones and Borges through Reyes, Carpentier and Paz. It is not a neoclassical spirit that leads these modern writers to the classical tradition, since they do not imitate classical models, but instead (particularly in Nietzsche and Freud) a philological quest for a mythology of origins: a perfect example of this would be Carpentier's story "Like the Night," which begins and ends with an episode drawn from the *Iliad*, a double thrust away from and back to the origin of Western literary tradition. There is throughout Cortázar's work a recurrence of classical motifs and figures that answers to this general philological trend.

All myths, as we know, appear in many versions; but if one reads the most complete account of the Theseus myth, that of Plutarch, one is struck by the confusing number of contradictory accounts extant of this particular story. The charm, in fact, of Plutarch's rendition is his juggling of so many different versions in one and the same text, versions that cancel each other and blur or abolish altogether the possibility of a master version. To read Plutarch is to realize that the myth, while organized around a certain implied narrative core, is not a fixed text but a set of superimposed narratives. Thus we already have in the myth chosen by Cortázar the outlines of the question of conception: while being set at the dawn of Western tradition that classical mythology represents, the myth cannot claim originality in the sense of constituting a single source.

If the versions of the myth of Theseus offer, simultaneously, the promise of uniqueness and multiplicity, of singularity and plurality, so do the many readings of which the particular incident of the Minotaur has been the object. Theseus's slaying of the Minotaur and his escape from the labyrinth have often been interpreted as the victory of reason over ignorance, so much so that to some the myth is a parable of the Greeks' founding of Western thought after conquering superstition. According to this reading the Theseus myth would mark the birth of reason. Moralistic interpretations also abound in the form of allegories, particularly in the Middle Ages. A creature half bull and half man is the image of man driven by his lower instincts, imprisoned in the materiality of his senses, unable to exercise his spiritual and intellectual powers. Dante's inversion of the figure, making the lower half of the Minotaur the animal part, points to such a moralistic interpretation.[6] Theseus's victory would in this case be a moral one, the triumph of the higher faculties of man over his lower instincts. His victory would thus mark the birth of morals. A political reading is also possible and common. Theseus's victory over Minos is the triumph of political principle over arbitrary rule, of Athens over Crete, the defeat of the old order and the coming of the new. The very abstractness of these readings underscores again the question of singularity, of individuation: Theseus's victory is that of reason, of higher instincts, of political principle. The specificity of the text vanishes as we glide into allegorical abstraction and accept the plurality of potential readings that the myth contains.

The same problematics appear when it becomes evident that Theseus's slaying of the Minotaur displays a series of elements that relates the episode to other myths. The confrontation of Theseus and Minos is the well-known struggle between the old king and the prince; Theseus's journey into the labyrinth, the regressive voyage in search of origins, the slaying of the

Minotaur (who is after all also a young prince), the hero's struggle to assert his individuality—all of these elements link the myth to other myths of generation, such as the Oedipus myth. It might be remembered here that Theseus not only defeats Minos, but also, though inadvertently like Oedipus, kills his own father Aegeus by forgetting to change the sails. Moreover, as in the cases of Oedipus and the Minotaur, Theseus's origins are clouded by mystery: it is not clear whether he is the son of Neptune or the son of Aegeus. His journey to the center of the labyrinth, like his earlier journey to Athens, is a journey back to the source to establish (or reestablish) his own beginning. As soon as we insert the Theseus story into a general mythology, it begins to lose its specificity; its own origins begin to recede into infinity or to dissolve and multiply as if in a gallery of mirrors. The thematics of genealogy that pervade the readings of the myth—it represents the birth of reason, of morals, of political principle—perhaps reflect this dialectic that subtends its structure.

What we find in *Los reyes* is then necessarily not a version but a subversion of the myth of Theseus. To begin with, as Cortázar himself has emphasized on many occasions, his Ariadne gives Theseus the clew only in order to free the Minotaur, once the monster has killed the hero. As Alfred MacAdam perceptively notes, *Los reyes* contains a "double tragedy."[7] Instead of a triumph, Cortázar's version offers a mutual defeat: Theseus's quest leads not to heroic distinction, but to indifferentiation. The Minotaur, who would represent such indifferentiation and thus be the victor, is dead. Theseus's pursuit of individuation is thwarted from the start: he constantly recognizes himself in others, not only in the Minotaur, but also in Minos. What is emphasized in Cortázar's version is the violence that Theseus commits against himself in defeating Minos and killing the Minotaur. Instead of the erection of individual presence, Theseus's regressive voyage creates a vacuum at the center; the Minotaur is dead, Theseus has fled. The clash, the violence of conception suggested by the erotic act *contra naturam* by which the Minotaur was conceived, is repeated at the end of Theseus's journey. The blood of Pasiphae has been spilled again. Whereas previously the labyrinth was inhabited by the "lord of games" (the Minotaur),[8] it now stands as an empty gallery of winding walls. Theseus's victory has led to that other labyrinth suggested by Borges: the labyrinth of total indifferentiation, the desert, the white page. The I, the you and the we float in a space without perspectives and dimensions, as interchangeable masks of primeval chaos and apocalypse.

This confrontation of the monster and the hero constitutes the primal scene in Cortázar's mythology of writing: a hegemonic struggle for the

center that resolves itself in a mutual cancellation and in the superimposition
of beginnings and ends. The very image of man unborn, the Minotaur is the
possessor of the immediate but naîve knowledge of man before the Fall. His
speech is the incoherent, symbolic language of a savage god. Theseus, on the
other hand, is not only a dealer in death, but is the very image of death. His
linear, cogent language is temporal, discursive—it is discourse. In his
enclosure the Minotaur speaks a perishable language that is not temporal but
that is reinvented every day. The words he utters are, even if momentarily,
attached to the things they represent:

> Oh, his pained monologues, which the palace guards heard in
> wonder, without understanding them. His profound recitals of
> the recurring waves, his taste for celestial nomenclatures and the
> catalogues of herbs. He ate them pensively, and then gave them
> names with secret delight, as if the flavor of stems had revealed
> their names to him ... He raised the whole enumeration of
> celestial bodies, and seemed to forget it with the dawn of a new
> day, as if also in his memory dusk dimmed the stars. And the next
> night he took delight in inaugurating a new nomenclature,
> ordering sonorous space with ephemeral constellations.[9]

If in other versions of the myth the birth of reason, morals or politics is at
stake, what we have in *Los reyes* is the violent birth of writing. The catalogue
of herbs that the Minotaur "tastes" is a series of disconnected words, without
syntactical and therefore temporal structure, linked to their individual origin
through their "stems." By killing the Minotaur, Theseus attempts to replace
the perishable sound of individual words with the linear, durable cogency of
discourse, a cogency predicated not on the stems of words but on their
declensions, on the particles that link them in a structure whose mode of
representation would not be sonorous but spatial—writing. The irony, of
course, is that once writing is instituted, Theseus does not gain control of the
labyrinth but becomes superfluous and flees. Because writing cannot be
dimmed like the stars with each dawn, because it is not a memory whose
traces can be erased, Theseus is not needed to reinvent it, as the Minotaur
reinvented his nomenclatures every day. Writing is the empty labyrinth from
which both the Minotaur and Theseus have been banished.

This primal scene appears with remarkable consistency in Cortázar's
writing. I do not mean simply that there are monsters, labyrinths and heroes,
but rather that the scene in which a monster and a hero kill each other, cancel
each other's claim for the center of the labyrinth, occurs with great

frequency, particularly in texts where the nature of writing seems to be more obviously in question. The most superficial consideration of Cortázar's first novel, *The Winners*, will no doubt reveal the existence of the primal scene. But I would like to examine two briefer texts, "All Fires the Fire" and "The Pursuer."

The title of "All Fires the Fire" is drawn from Heraclitus and suggests the indifferentiation obtained when all things return to their primal state and ends and beginnings resolve into one.[10] The story is in fact two stories that reflect each other, being told simultaneously. One is a lover's triangle taking place presumably in contemporary Paris and told for the most part through a telephone conversation. The other also involves a lover's triangle of sorts: it is the story of a gladiator who is made to fight a gigantic black slave by a Roman consul who is jealous of his wife's interest in the gladiator. In the first story (I use first here for the sake of clarity, but there is no hierarchy of this kind in the text) Sonia calls Roland to plead with him and to announce that Irene is on her way to his apartment. Their conversation is made difficult by a bad connection. A mysterious voice in the background keeps reading a series of figures—is it a gambler? These figures, in their stark meaninglessness, are remindful of the Minotaur's "celestial nomenclatures." They oppose the flow of speech, the discursiveness that Roland wants to achieve. The dark depths from which the sounds in the telephone line seem to emerge also evoke the labyrinth and Ariadne's clew. Roland's cool and logical entreaties to Sonia, who finally commits suicide, are Theseus-like in their reasoned discursiveness. There is, furthermore, although very obliquely suggested, a potential monstrosity in Sonia, whose interest in Irene seems to be as strong as her interest in Roland. In the other strand of the story the primal scene is present in much more obvious fashion. The hero-monster confrontation is clear, and there is, moreover, an echo of one of the versions of the Theseus myth offered by Plutarch in which the Minotaur, instead of being a monstrous creature, is a powerful and hateful man named Taurus, whom Theseus defeats in combat at the Cretan games.[11] Although, naturally, some of the details are different in Cortázar's story, the basic situation is essentially the same. The young gladiator has risen from the ranks because of his heroic deeds to become known as an individual, and by competing for the affections of the consul's wife he has also become a potential usurper.

There are other, more direct echoes of the primal scene in the text of the story. When the black giant enters the arena, he does so through the gallery used by the beasts, and the description of the gate through which he passes evokes the act of birth: "They have raised the creaking gates of the dark passage where they have wild animals come out, and Marcus sees the gigantic figure of the Nubian retiarius appear, until then invisible against the background of mossy stone."[12] The labyrinth is evoked in the description of the arena, where it appears sketched on the sand as a trace, "the enormous bronze eye where hoes and palm leaves have sketched their curved paths darkened by traces of preceding fights." It is, of course, at the center of that maze that Marcus and the Nubian retiarius stage their combat.

As in *Los reyes*, there is no victory at the end of "All Fires the Fire," but rather a mutual annihilation. The fight between the Nubian retiarius and the gladiator is resolved when both fall dead upon each other in the sand. The mutual killing and the sand, which suggests the desert, prefigure the fire that kills everyone at the end, the fire that destroys the arena and which also levels the apartment building where, centuries later, Roland and Irene have fallen asleep on each other, like the dead gladiators, after making love. The stories merge at the end, not only on the level of the action but also at a conceptual level; love and war, presumably opposites, mingle to evoke the topic of the *ars amandi, ars bellandi*. Like the two gladiators and the lovers, the two stories have a common end that abolishes their difference and returns the text to the indifferentiation of origins—all texts the text.

In "The Pursuer" the various elements of this mythology are even more directly related to writing. The story tells of the last months in the life of the jazz saxophonist Johnny Carter, as reported by Bruno, a writer who had previously published a biography of the musician. It is rather easy to discern in the story the general outline of the primal scene. Bruno's visit to Johnny as the story opens is reminiscent of Theseus's journey into the labyrinth; the jazzman lives in a small, dark walk-up apartment, a sort of lair, and he is described in animal terms: "But he's making gestures, laughing and coughing at the same time, shivering away under the blanket like a chimpanzee."[13] Johnny is also described as a huge fetus or newborn monster, naked and coiled onto himself and making inarticulate sounds: "And I saw Johnny had thrown off the blanket around him in one motion, and I saw him sitting in the easy chair completely nude, his legs pulled up and the knees underneath his chin, shivering but laughing to himself" (184).

While Johnny appears as a monstrous fetus, Bruno, the writer, stands for order and profit. Bruno wants to "regenerate" Johnny, to make him abandon his intuitive cavils about time, his drugs and his visions. But Bruno's apparent good intentions conceal his desire to kill Johnny, to reduce him to that image of him which he has created in his book. Johnny's death at the end of the story appears to take place in order to round out Bruno's book:

> All this [Johnny's death] happened at the same time that the
> second edition of my book was published, but luckily I had time
> to incorporate an obituary note edited under full steam and
> inserted, along with a newsphoto of the funeral in which many
> famous jazzmen were identifiable. In that format the biography
> remained, so to speak, intact and finished. Perhaps it's not right
> that I say this, but naturally I was speaking from a merely
> aesthetic point of view. They're already talking of a new
> translation, into Swedish or Norwegian, I think. My wife is
> delighted at the news. (220)

The last two sentences, which are the conclusion of the story, indicate the
measure in which the death of Johnny also signals Bruno's defeat. The
allusion to the translations, and particularly the vagueness of the allusion,
shows to what extent the text has already been taken away from Bruno—how,
in a sense, he is out of the picture. The laconic last sentence, in its homely
triviality, reinforces this notion by showing how the pleasure generated by
these new versions of the biography is deflected away from Bruno. Like the
labyrinth, the text is empty at the end. The book has become a funeral
monument, a tomb.

But in a sense it is the whole story that reveals Bruno's defeat. In spite
of his naïve assertion that his book is "intact and finished," "The Pursuer" is
a postscript or supplement to that earlier book, and more than the story of
Johnny, it is the story of Bruno's futile attempts to commit Johnny to writing.
Bruno's writing of "The Pursuer," his return to the book that he had already
written, is like Theseus's journey into the labyrinth, the very image of self-
reflexiveness. The pursuer is Bruno, not Johnny, who on the contrary is the
epitome of hieratic immobility. Johnny lives unreflexively, a sort of
inarticulate monster who is more on the side of things than of words—his
means of expression, the saxophone, is not verbal. The rivalry between
Johnny and Bruno is apparent from the beginning in their playful banter, in
which the musician mocks the writer's practical sense. Bruno himself is aware
that his relation to Johnny is an exploitative one, that he and all the others
who hover around him are "a bunch of egotists": "Under the pretext of
watching out for Johnny what we're doing is protecting our idea of him,
getting ourselves ready for the pleasure Johnny's going to give us, to reflect
the brilliance from the statue we've erected among us all and defend it till the
last gasp" (182). Johnny's retaliation is to tell Bruno that his book has missed
the point, that the real Johnny is absent from it: "'Don't get upset, Bruno,
it's not important that you forgot to put all that in. But Bruno,' and he lifts a

finger that does not shake, 'what you forgot to put in is me'" (212). Bruno winds up writing about himself, subjecting himself to the same operation to which he submits Johnny. The text of the story is in the end Bruno's pursuit of himself, a pursuit that turns into a flight—the vanishing of infinitely receding sequences. "The Pursuer" is a postscript to Bruno's biography of Johnny, but it is also a postscript to the story that it tells, a postscript that can only be a prologue to a further story.

As in the previous texts analyzed, the hero's regressive quest leads not to individuation and difference, but to a notion of indifferentiation: empty labyrinth, desert, fire, the infinite where ends and beginnings merge and dissolve. A reflection of Bruno's brings out, in a metonymical play, this dialectic of ends and beginnings:

> It drags me to think that he's at the beginning of his sax-work, and I'm going along and have to stick it out to the end. He's the mouth and I'm the ear, so as not to say he's the mouth and I'm the ... Every critic, yeah, is the sad-assed end of something that starts as taste, like the pleasure of biting into something and chewing on it. And the mouth [Johnny] moves again, relishing it, Johnny's big tongue sucks back a little string of saliva from the lips. (167)

We shall have to look at this passage in the original, not only because the translator, Paul Blackburn, got carried away and became too explicit, but because there is in it an anagrammatic clue that is important to note:

> Pienso melancólicamente que él está al principio de su saxo mientras yo vivo obligado a conformarme con el final. El es la boca y yo la oreja, por no decir que él es la boca y yo ... Todo crítico, ay, es el triste final de algo que empezó como sabor, como delicia de morder y mascar. Y la boca se mueve otra vez, golosamente la gran lengua de Johnny recoge un chorrito de saliva de los labios.[14]

There is a complex and compelling metonymical and anagrammatic network here that leads to the notion of the mutual cancellation of Johnny and Bruno. If Johnny is the mouth and Bruno the ear, or the anus, they both stand for absences, holes, and what remains between them is the saxophone, a curved gallery of air, or, to continue the physiological metaphor, the labyrinthine digestive track (or the Eustachian tube). This imagery of absence is the same as that in Octavio Paz's poem "La boca habla," incorporated by Severo Sarduy into *Cobra*:

> La cobra
>   fabla de la obra
>   en la boca del abra
>   recobra
>   el habla:
>   El Vocablo.[15]

It is an imagery of absence conveyed by the repetition of the *o*'s, a figure of the hole, as in "El es la boca y yo la oreja, por no decir que él es la boca y yo ..." It was not reticence that kept the obvious word out, since it is more conspicuous in its absence, but the desire both to create a gap at the end of the sentence and to stop on "yo." That "yo" is already, by its very orthography, the hole, the void, the last letter of Bruno's name, but also the beginning of Johnny's—"Jo." In fact, by taking the beginning of Johnny's name and the end of Bruno's, by practicing with their names the operation that the sentence quoted suggests, we have "yo no." Ends and beginnings merge, and the result is a negation, a canceling out.

Cortázar plays this philological game, more often than has been suspected, to undermine the notion of individuality. A clear instance of this, but on another level, is Francine in *Libro de Manuel*, who so obviously stands for France and French values that she becomes an ironic abstraction. Not as obvious, though here the literary device is much more traditional, is Andrés, the protagonist of that same novel, whose name means, of course, everyman, or man in general. One might further note in this connection that the *o* plays a key role in the names of many of Cortázar's characters: Nora, Wong, Oliveira, Roland, Romero, Roberto. That *o*, or zero, is the grapheme that designates an absence, a dissolution of individuality, a sphere demarcating nothingness. In chapter 148 of *Hopscotch* Cortázar quotes one of Aulus Gellius's etymologies in which it is suggested that the origin of the word *person* is related to that *o* that occupies its center:

> A wise and ingenious explanation, by my lights, that of Gabio Basso, in his treatise *On the Origin of Words*, of the word *person*, mask. He thinks that this word has its origin in the verb *personare*, to retain. This is how he explains his opinion: "Since the mask covers the face completely except for an opening where the mouth is, the voice, instead of scattering in all directions, narrows

down to escape through one single opening and therefore
acquires a stronger and more penetrating sound. Thus, since the
mask makes the human voice more sonorous and firm, it has been
given the name *person*, and as a consequence of the formation of
this word, the letter o as it appears in it is long."[16]

The suggestion that the voice would then be the distinguishing mark is clear;
but the voice is no mark at all. In the case of Johnny, where the voice is made
firmer and more sonorous by his musical instrument, we would find the mark
in the saxophone, not in him.

But if "yo no" is the cryptic message of Cortázar's mythology of
writing, what then of our initial question about how to read an author? And
if conception denies the possibility of conception, if a cogent and
distinguishing theory of literature appears to be foreclosed by the ultimately
negative gesture of self-referentiality, how is Cortázar's literary production
held together? What can we *retain* as the distinguishing mark of his work?

It is not by accident that Cortázar's mythology of writing, as I have
represented it here, should bear a Nietzschean imprint, since it is a
Nietzschean problematic that seems to generate it. "Who writes?" is an
essentially Nietzschean question. The struggle between the Minotaur and
Theseus is analogous to that between Dionysus and Apollo in *The Birth of
Tragedy*. In "The Pursuer" this Nietzschean quality is particularly evident.
Johnny, whose musical instrument is a direct descendant of the Dionysian
aulos, exists as if in harmony with the vast forces of the universe—with truth
and actuality—and suffers as well as experiences joy for it. Bruno, on the
other hand, the Apollonian seeker of light, deals in illusions; his aim is to
domesticate Johnny's savage wisdom. The birth of tragedy, according to
Nietzsche, is generated by the confrontation of these two figures, a birth that
signaled the victory of Dionysus over Apollo, for tragedy could only emerge
when the god of reason spoke the language of the god of music. In Nietzsche
there remains a vestigial theodicy that confers meaning to the death of the
hero. It would be reassuring to be able to say the same about Cortázar. But
the analogy between the birth of tragedy and Cortázar's version of the birth
of writing can only be carried so far, and beyond that point is where Cortázar
emerges. Nietzsche, still the philologist in this early work, traces a curve that
represents the birth of tragedy and its gradual decline, a decline provoked by
the counteroffensive of Apollonian powers. Not so in Cortázar, where, as we
have seen, each confrontation leads to a mutual cancellation, each
conception carries with it its concomitant death. Writing in Cortázar must
be born anew in each text; the whole of writing must emerge with each word,

only to disappear again—not an eternal return, but a convulsive repetition of construction and deconstruction. A formal reflection of this might be found not only in the heterogeneity of Cortázar's longer texts, but also in their reliance on dialogue.[17]

Cortázar emerges, then, at the point of the cancellation, of the negation. He must therefore be read whole, establishing no generic distinctions nor privileging either the fictional or the expository texts. Each text must be read as if it were the totality of Cortázar's production, given that each begins and ends in a question so fundamental as not to be transferable from one to the other, but must rather be repeated in each text and in each reading—a kind of spasmodic eschatology. Only the double thrust of the question can be retained. Holistic criticism is not a process of accumulation whereby details are gathered, stored, to construct with them the image of an author, but instead one where the impossibility of assembling the fragments in a coherent whole can provide a glimpse of totality.

There is an ultimate meaning to Cortázar's mythology of writing that belies its negativity, one that is performative rather than conceptual. What Theseus's self-reflexive quest shows is that literature, in the long run, cannot say anything about itself. The countermodernist position that decries literature's purity, its refusal to signify something other than itself, fails to recognize that, on the contrary, literature is always having to signify something else, and to implicate someone else. And indeed here we are reading, talking, writing about Cortázar, or better yet, reading, talking, writing Cortázar. Minotaur, Theseus, Johnny, Bruno—we as readers also drift into our own textual journeys, to turn reading once more into the ritual confrontation where you and I and we share for one moment, in each other, the illusion of meaning.

NOTES

1. See Eugenio Donato, "Structuralism: The Aftermath," *Sub-Stance*, no. 7 (Fall 1973), pp. 9–26. Neither Anglo-American "new criticism" nor French structuralism really ever abandoned the notion of authorship. It is always found, albeit relegated to a self-consciously marginal position, as a rhetorical license that is tolerated but not questioned. It is only in what Donato calls the aftermath of structuralism that the notion of authorship has been subjected to a radical critique.

2. Paris, Seuil, 1966, pp. 60–61. My translation.

3. José Ortega y Gasset, *The Dehumanization of Art and Other Essays on Art, Culture and Literature*, Princeton, N.J., Princeton University Press, 1968, pp. 31–32.

4. Michel Foucault, *The Order of Things: An Archaeology of the Human Sciences*, New York, Pantheon, 1970, pp. 217–21.

5. Jean Hyppolite, *Genesis and Structure of Hegel's Phenomenology of the Spirit*, Samuel Cherniak, John Heckman, trs., Evanston, Il., Northwestern University Press, 1974, p. 160.

6. See Borges's commentary in *The Book of Imaginary Beings*, rev. & enl. ed., Norman Thomas di Giovanni, tr., New York, Discus, 1970, pp. 158–59.

7. *El individuo y el otro. Crítica a los cuentos de Julio Cortázar*, New York, La Librería, 1971, p. 34.

8. *Los reyes*, Buenos Aires, Sudamericana, 1970, p. 73.

9. Ibid., p. 49. My translation.

10. The title may come from fragment 28 of Heraclitus: "There is exchange of all things for fire and of fire for all things, as there is of wares for gold and of gold for wares." Philip Wheelwright, *Heraclitus*, New York, Atheneum, 1971, p. 37.

11. Plutarch, *The Lives of the Noble Grecians and Romans*, John Dryden, tr., Arthur Hugh Clough, ed., New York, Modern Library, 1932, p. 11.

12. *All Fires the Fire and Other Stories*, Suzanne Jill Levine, tr., New York, Pantheon, 1973, pp. 116–17.

13. *Blow-Up and Other Stories*, Paul Blackburn, tr., New York, Collier, 1968, p. 169. Subsequent page numbers refer to this edition.

14. *Las armas secretas*, Buenos Aires, Sudamericana, 1964, p. 108.

15. Buenos Aires, Sudamericana, 1972, p. 229.

16. *Hopscotch*, Gregory Rabassa, tr., New York, Signet, 1967, p. 436. Cortázar takes this excerpt from *Noches Aticas*, Francisco Navarro y Calvo, tr., Madrid, Biblioteca Clásica, 1893, vol. 1, p. 202. The relevance of Gellius's book in relation to Cortázar's novel is greater than might be suspected. In his preface Gellius says the following about the composition of his book: "In the arrangement of the material I have adopted the same haphazard order that I had previously followed in collecting it. For whenever I had taken in hand any Greek or Latin book, or had heard anything worth remembering, I used to jot down whatever took my fancy, of any and every kind, without any definite plan or order; and such notes I would lay away as an aid to my memory, like a kind of literary storehouse, so that when the need arose of a word or a subject which I chanced for the moment to have forgotten, and the books from which I had taken it were not at hand, I could readily find it and produce it." *The Attic Nights of Aulus Gellius*, John C. Rolfe, tr., Cambridge, Ma., Harvard University Press, 1970, p. xxvii. Cortázar has of course followed this same method of composition in the "dispensable" chapters of *Hopscotch*, as well as in *Libro de Manuel*. In fact, just as Ludmilla composes the *Libro* for Manuel's future enlightenment, so did Gellius assemble his "in order that like recreation might be provided for my children, when they should have some respite from business affairs and could unbend and divert their minds."

17. For further commentary on *The Birth of Tragedy* and "The Pursuer" see Djelal Kadir, "A Mythical Re-enactment: Cortázar's *El perseguidor*," *Latin American Literary Review*, 2 (1973), pp. 63–73.

STEVEN BOLDY

Libro de Manuel

INTRODUCTION

Socialism and literature: the debate

After the complex, subtle, and ultimately minority novels *Rayuela* and *62*, we are faced with a very different sort of literature in *Libro de Manuel*, published in 1973. The literary level is patently lower. The repetition of structure and character types from earlier works is mechanical; the language is often stereotyped Cortázarese bordering dangerously at times on rhetoric. It is nevertheless a brave and honest book, and is an important experiment within the political fiction which characterizes the seventies (1970, Vargas Llosa's *Conversación en la catedral*; 1974, Carpentier's *El recurso del método*; 1975, Roa Bastos's *Yo el supremo* and García Márquez's *El otoño del patriarca*; 1978, Fuentes's *La cabeza de la hidra*). Perhaps more radically if not necessarily more successfully than the authors mentioned here, Cortázar in this novel faces up to the tension between a politically committed message, and serious literary experimentation which often tends towards a relativization of any message. *Libro de Manuel* was written quickly and was designed to reach a wide reading public. It is thus unfair to judge it exclusively according to the same purely literary criteria as his other novels, or in isolation from its context.

From *The Novels of Julio Cortázar.* © 1980 Cambridge University Press.

The 'double text' of earlier works provides the structure with which he approaches the problem. A new discourse is articulated through another, more conventional one, which it uses but subverts and attempts to renew. In *Rayuela*, the alienated discourse corresponds to the conventional world of Traveler which Oliveira wants to join but must first infiltrate and modify. In *Libro de Manuel*, dogmatic Marxism and literary realism are taken as a partially alienated main discourse and vehicle, through which and against which a secondary, irrational, erotic and taboo discourse is established to liberalize and widen the first.

To understand the emphasis of *Libro de Manuel* it must be placed in the context of the debate on socialism and literature in which Cortázar was involved before its publication and which reached a crisis point with the imprisonment of the Cuban poet Herberto Padilla in 1971.

Since 1961, after a visit to Cuba, Cortázar has unequivocally proclaimed his adhesion to the cause of socialism in Latin America.[1] In *Viaje alrededor de una mesa* (1970), an account of a round table on commitment in literature, in which Vargas Llosa also participated, he forcefully criticized the attitude of many revolutionaries who, in the name of the socialist 'new man' of the future, proscribe from literature those aspects of man not directly accessible to rational analysis:

> [Neo-social realism implies] a perspective where many subjects which are delicate and equivocal but which are just as genuine a part of human personality as political faith and economic necessities (I am referring among many others to eroticism, play, imagination beyond any subject matter which can be checked out against reason or 'reality') are proscribed or mutilated in the name of a certain notion of the *hombre nuevo* which, in my opinion, would have no reason for coming into being if he were condemned to read what he is offered by those who obey similar concepts of revolutionary freedom (*VM* 28–9).

In a reply to this and other similar declarations, Miguel Alascio Cortázar, in *Viaje alrededor de una silla*, accuses Cortázar of various heresies: the irrationalism he practises leads to confusion, a state propitious to the rise of fascism;[2] his distance from social reality leads Cortázar to view any revolutionary change as spontaneous, a position which leads to *repentismo*, anathema to the classical Marxist;[3] Cortázar's claim, after Plato, that art is one of the highest forms of eroticism (*VM* 51) is countered by an assertion that Plato was essentially a reactionary whose eroticism was but an apology for the elegant vices of the aristocracy,[4] and that Cortázar's eroticism simply uses the ideal of widening the horizons of literature for the *hombre nuevo* as a pretext for writing little more than commercial pornography.[5] The Colombian Oscar Collazos, in 'La encrucijada del lenguaje', repeats many of these arguments, and suggests that the formal difficulty of texts by Cortázar and Fuentes springs from an inferiority complex *vis-à-vis* the Europeans and an attempt to prove themselves superior to the *barbarie* of Latin America: 'We can and must be capable of being superior to *our* barbarism. We too are capable of reaching the "heights" that they have achieved' (*LR* 31). Perhaps the most important accusation of Alascio Cortázar and Collazos is that Cortázar condones a dichotomy between the politics and literature of a writer, leading him to ignore reality: 'Cortázar's basic approach, reading between the lines, is simple: to authorize, to "legalize", to present this dichotomy, the split of the literary being and the political being, not only as possible, but as valid too. But also to establish a deep scorn for the reality he suspends' (*LR* 15).

Cortázar's answer to all this is that 'reality' is far more than the 'socio-historical and political context'; that any literature worth its name 'approaches man from all angles' (*LR* 65); that what is needed is writing which is revolutionary in itself rather than writing dictated by revolutionary theory ('the revolutionaries of literature rather than the literary men of the revolution' (*LR* 76)) if revolutionary language is to be cleansed of the 'rotten corpses of an obsolete social order' (*VM* 33). Repeatedly, however, he demands a great personal sense of responsibility in the writer if these ideas are not simply to embody escapism (e.g. *LR* 57). The general affirmation from the time of *Rayuela* is still basically valid: 'Historical results like Marxism or whatever you like may be achieved, but the Yonder is not exactly history' (*R* 509).

What Fuentes has called the 'tragicomic'[6] case of Padilla constitutes an important crisis in Cortázar's theoretical position. Padilla was arrested in 1971 by the Cuban authorities for anti-revolutionary attitudes: pessimism, escapism, individualism, etc. His *autocrítica* brought a strong reaction from left-wing writers in Latin America and Europe. Cortázar signed the letter of protest. Castro's reply was devastating. He would have nothing to do with 'pseudo-revolutionaries', 'bourgeois liberals' writing from the 'bourgeois salons' of Europe, unaware that the real problems of Cuba were not the temporary imprisonment of a poet, but underdevelopment, education, the real threat of invasion, the blockade. 'But as for Cuba', he concluded, 'they will never be able to utilize Cuba again, never!, not even by defending it.

When they are about to defend us we will say to them: "Don't defend us, friend, please don't defend us. We are better off without your help"' (*CP* 119–20). Cortázar was strongly affected. He did not sign the second letter of protest, but published his 'Policrítica a la hora de los chacales' (*CP* 126–30). While defending the writer's right to criticism and creative freedom, he denounced facile liberalism, and reaffirmed his adherence to the Cuban revolution:

> You are right, Fidel: only in combat do we have the right to be dis-
> [contented,
> criticism, the search for better formulae, can only come from inside,
> yes, but inside is sometimes so outside,
> and just because today I abandon for ever violet scented liberalism, the
> [signatories of virtuous texts
> be – cause – Cu – ba – is – not – that – which – their – wri – ting –
> [desk – sche – mas – de – mand,
> I know I am not an exception, I am like them, what have I done for
> [Cuba beyond love,
> what have I given for Cuba beyond a desire, a hope.
> But now I abandon their ideal world, their schemes,
> just now when
> I am shown the door of what I love, I am banned from defending it,
> *right now* I exercise my right to choose, to stand once more and more
> [than ever
> by your Revolution, my Cuba, in my own way (*CP* 128).

Such statements cannot be ignored when considering the genesis of *Libro de Manuel*, nor the fact that the royalties were given to organizations defending political prisoners in Argentina. The central mystery of the novel is a set of instructions given to the main character by a cigar-smoking Cuban which can only be known once they have been carried out. The open eyes of the corpse at the end of the novel reminded Cortázar, after the novel had been published, of those of Che Guevara.

The 'dispensable chapters' of *Rayuela*, where the readers and the characters too in many cases are exposed to the cultural context of the author, are replaced in *Libro de Manuel* by newspaper cuttings on current Latin American political issues (plus information on political violence in France and torture in Vietnam). Cortázar himself, as he says in the prologue to the novel, was rather disappointed by this experiment—he transcribed all the important news items of certain days in the hope that this somewhat aleatory way of introducing political reality into the lives of his characters would radically affect their personal trajectories (7–8).

Cortázar's somewhat contradictory attitude to his own creation cannot however be ignored. In the prologue to the novel, he announces the 'convergence' of his two roles of political essayist and novelist: 'If for years I have written texts concerned with Latin American problems, and at the same time novels and stories where those problems were absent or only came in incidentally, here and now the waters have merged' (7). In an interview given after the publication of *Libro de Manuel*, however, he admits that, due to the nature of his literary texts, his political commitment would have to find its expression in separate activity: 'I do not believe that we should falsify our goals as writers for the sake of so-called political commitment. The problem is how to insert that political commitment, if one cannot do so in the book because the book is, as you say, "hermetic", then in other lines of behaviour.'[7]

A more interesting contradiction concerns the level at which the writing of the novel is pitched. In 'Corrección de pruebas en Alta Provenza', written while proof-reading the novel, Cortázar claims that the urgency of the information contained in the novel forced him to write 'horizontally', that is, to follow a traditional, linear narrative mode, thus excluding formal innovations which take time for the reader to assimilate, a time-lag which was not important for *Rayuela*:

> But right from the start I realized that, paradoxically, if this was a book of our *here and now*, i.e. of the immediate, it did not make sense to distance it through experimentation and technique: the deepest contact would be blocked by the very methods applied to establish it (*C* 19–20).

But Cortázar later firmly rejects the possibility of lowering his standards or abdicating his literary personality in order to make his work more accessible: 'You hinted at the possibility of lowering one's tone to make literature more accessible. I am totally opposed to this option [...] because I believe that every writer has his own destiny.'[8] When taken in isolation, such statements are simply contradictory. In the novel, however, Cortázar's by now familiar use of two discourses, two 'authors', explores such contradictions thoroughly and dialectically.

Irrationalism and revolution in Libro de Manuel

Cortázar is well aware of the kind of argument which links irrationalism with totalitarianism, Nietzsche with Hitler, Unamuno with Franco. His views on the subject were well defined as far back as 1949, as can be seen in his reply to Guillermo de Torre, where he makes the point that only combined with the strictest rationalism can irrationalism become a collective danger. His views are summarized here by García Canclini:

> Reason is an ally of our aims, and it is up to us whether it is creative or destructive. Cortázar explained this intelligently in a reply to Guillermo de Torre, who held existentialist irrationalism responsible for the crimes of the Nazis. The desire for such crimes, which was an irrational impulse, would never have become a bloody reality if it had not been programmed by rigorous reason. The irrational is never a collective danger *per se*; only when organized by reason can it engender inquisitions, torture techniques and death chambers.[9]

The same idea is present throughout the work in often surprising forms. In 'Simulacros', from the 'Ocupaciones raras' section of *Historias de cronopios y de famas*, a family builds a scaffold in its front garden, but does so with the sole purpose of having dinner there and perhaps scandalizing the neighbours. The even less likely superman-like figure Fantomas repeats the point in comic-strip language: 'The world won't be destroyed by books, Steiner, but by men. Men exactly like you!' (*F* 34).

One of the most important points made in *Libro de Manuel* is that the revolution must aim to transform the whole of man, not just those aspects of him defined by Marxism. As Lonstein says, 'I'm referring to man himself, what he is and not what the others see of him from the *Capital* outwards' (226). Breton proposes a synthesis of Marx and Rimbaud ('"Transformer le monde", a dit Marx; "changer la vie", a dit Rimbaud: ces deux mots d'ordre pour nous n'en font qu'un')[10] which is taken up by Ludmilla in *Libro de Manuel*: 'I wonder if there was all that much difference between Lenin and Rimbaud' (60). A similar comment is made in *Prosa del observatorio*: 'Thomas Mann said that things would be better if Marx had read Hölderlin; but on the other hand, madam, I agree with Lukács that it would also have been necessary for Hölderlin to read Marx' (*PO* 71–2). Cortázar believes with the surrealists that there is little point in breaking the dualism capital/labour if at the same time parallel dualisms such as dream/waking life, imagination/reality, unconscious/conscious, illicit and licit sex, all variations on the same 'terrible interdit'[11] are not abolished.

Benedetti, whom Collazos quotes in order to criticize Cortázar, makes a similar point, defending the free imagination of the writer within the revolution and pointing to the convergence of imagination and revolution in the 'événements de mai '68':

> A revolution must encompass everything: from ideology to love [...]. A writer, an artist, must use his imaginative capacity to defend, within the revolution, his right to imagine more and better.
>
> It is perhaps in that word, *imagination*, where culture and revolution can really meet. 'L'imagination prend le pouvoir', read an inscription on the steps of the Faculty of Social Sciences in Paris during the recent May *revolution*.[12]

It is thus not surprising that the 'May revolution' had a strong surrealist element. Its slogan, according to Cohn-Bendit, was 'sous le pavé, la plage'.[13] What its enemies denied was 'personal liberty, the innocence of desire, the forgotten joys of creativity, play, irony, and happiness'.[14] Cortázar's own interest in these aspects of the Paris events is well documented in his 'Noticias del mes de mayo' (*Ultimo round*).

Such faith in gratuitous humour and 'pataphysical' irrationalism explains the occasionally delirious methods Cortázar has his revolutionaries use. In order to finance the kidnapping of the leader of an anti-revolutionary group presumably connected with the CIA, they smuggle counterfeit dollars into Europe in a container carrying a turquoise penguin and two armadillos, which are later to be seen walking by the Seine. In what is denominated the *pre-Joda*, they seriously shake the absolute faith of the Parisians in the infallibility of their government institutions by inserting old cigarette stubs in apparently untouched packets, violate their everyday order by effusively thanking the bus-driver for a pleasant drive,[15] standing up to eat in elegant restaurants,[16] and other similar Dadaist provocations.

'Madness', according to one character, is a way of disconcerting political enemies, as it was used by Morelli in order to *descentrar, desencasillar* the reader. But it is also a means of self-defence, a way of avoiding falling into the strategies used by the enemy and perhaps reproducing his ideology in a future socialist state: 'Binary revolutions [...] are condemned before they triumph because they accept the rules of the game. While they believe they are smashing everything, they become so deformed you wouldn't believe it. How much necessary madness, my friend, intelligent and aggressive madness to finally dislodge the ants' (200). (The 'ants', enemy agents, have connotations similar to those of the ants of previous works, minus the positive aspects.) The *pre-Joda* is thus, in general, a continuation of the provocative activity of Marrast. The madness referred to above is a development of the final madness of Hélène, itself inherited from Oliveira.

The most surprising symbol of the necessity of 'superfluous' beauty in the revolution is the mushroom for which Lonstein insistently demands such attention: 'the superfluity of certain beauties, certain toadstools in the night, all that which can make any project for a future meaningful' (183).

LONSTEIN: A NON-DUALISTIC LANGUAGE

Lonstein, in many ways the Morelli of *Libro de Manuel*, decries in the other characters the dichotomies which Cortázar tries to reconcile in the novel, the dualism between love and politics, chance and will, etc.: 'In all of you there is a binary functioning which would have sent even Pavlov to sleep watching you behave in the *Joda* or in sex' (335). He develops an ideolect, an almost private language, composed of what he calls 'fortrans', neologisms combining two normally exclusive lexical items, which are interspersed with innumerable gallicisms. The 'fortrans' point towards a new mental structure, 'a new struculture' (structure, culture) (338), which would transcend the 'binary functioning' of the others.[17]

It is highly ironical but characteristic and significant that the term 'fortran', chosen by Lonstein to express his new 'struculture', should be taken from computer technology. Throughout the novel, computers are an image of an alienated discourse: Lonstein's poem 'Fragmentos para una oda a los dioses del siglo' is described as 'cards to feed an IBM' (83); Francine, the representative of the intellectual Paris bourgeoisie in the novel, is seen as 'a little IBM machine' (131). Lonstein's attempt to 'artifucklate [*articulear*: *articular*, *culear*] the wholworld' (338) within but against an alienated language and discourse is an image of the task of the novel as a whole. It demands that the sign of this discourse should be changed from negative to positive, turned upside-down in the way Oliveira transforms the meaning of *piedad*. Like Marrast with his statue, like Jai Singh with the cold fatality of the stars in *Prosa del observatorio*, Lonstein is an 'inverter': 'but man there, the inverter, he who turns destiny upside-down, the acrobat of reality: against petrified ancestral mathematics' (*PO* 42). If the enterprise were at all successful, the 'lorpro' ('logical organization of any programme') of the deterministic world of computers (of the social novel, of fanatics) would become 'ilorpro' ('the illogical organization of any programme') (200).

Miguel Alascio Cortázar's accusing Cortázar of being a pornographer is perhaps not irrelevant to the latter's attempt in *Libro de Manuel* to treat the erotic, and especially tabooed sexuality (masturbation, sodomy), with great honesty, with 'that delirious degree of verbal nudity' that he found to be a necessary purification before any revolutionary change, 'an indispensable condition for Verrières on Friday night' (219). *El que te dije* aspires to a style which would not change key on approaching such subjects: 'The problem is closer to us: to search for something like not noticing it when we move from one area to another, and we're not capable of that yet. Paradoxically, we look on prohibited themes as special' (232). There are indications that Cortázar found such a resolution highly embarrassing at times:

> I drop my biro and pick it up again, these hairy cheeks of mine blush because I find it hard to talk about fingers up arses [...], but I pick up my biro, take the fluff off it and start writing again and feel disgusted, I've got to go and have a shower, I feel like a slug or like when you slip on a pile of shit. (233)

Lonstein, more than any other character, is aware of the censorship inherent in language and tries especially hard to talk openly about taboo subjects, those which fundamentally contradict the laws and logic of his society, such as his relationship with the corpses he washes in the morgue. It is mainly through the 'fortrans' that he attempts to solve this problem, which Andrés defines as 'naming the things that it was impossible to describe' (213). Bataille, who fought a parallel battle at the limit of language and thought, comments succinctly that 'les mots disent difficilement ce qu'ils ont pour fin de nier'.[18] One of his characters, l'Abbé C., uses a language which may well have inspired the 'fortran' in this context. He believes that the only way to express the *indicible* is in the form of an enigma: 'Il serait donc apparemment, dans la nature de cet objet de ne pouvoir être donné comme le sont les autres: il ne pourrait être proposé à l'intérét que sous forme d'énigme...'[19] The same character can only express himself to his loved one by defecating under her window and writing highly enigmatic letters to her. Both these elements are combined with a series of gallicisms in the following passage of Lonstein:

> I can't keep conjugating my boulow at Marthe's bistrow, as my coupans say, and that condemns me to silence besides which as I am a bachelor and a chastonanist I am left with no other outlet but solliloquy apart from the toiletbook where from time to time I defeposit (*defepoango*) one or two turdscripts (*sorescriptos*). (40)

Defepongo (*defecar*, *deponer*) is very similar to Bataille's 'soulépadé-pone'[20] (*souiller*, *padir*, *déposer*), which is even more disguised than Lonstein's neologism, as 'sous le petit pont'.

VERTICAL OR HORIZONTAL WRITING: THE TWO AUTHORS

Cortázar claims that in order to explore 'vertically', deeply, the experience recounted in the novel, he found himself obliged to write 'horizontally', linearly: 'And thus, through one of those curious workings of the world of communication, I realized that only by writing "horizontally" could I transmit vertical movements of meaning, a questioning of frontiers, without too much loss' (*C* 19–20).

A difficult issue is at stake in this paradoxical assertion, which is at the nerve centre of the formal tensions of the novel. Eco provides a clear introduction to the problem in his *Opera aperta*. A language is a system of predetermined probabilities.[21] Intelligibility and information (i.e. a new message) are in opposition. Any information represents an element of disorder in the established code: 'the message introduces a crisis into, the code';[22] 'the more clearly the message communicates, the less it informs'.[23] A large amount of information, a very new message, runs the risk of creating chaos, incomprehension. The only way of transmitting this message is thus a dialectic between a conventional code and the message which threatens it: 'Between the offer of a plurality of formal worlds and the offer of undifferentiated chaos, void of any possibility of aesthetic enjoyment, the distance is short: only a pendular dialectic can save the composer of an open work.'[24]

Andrés, the Oliveira-Juan of *Libro de Manuel*, and also its 'final' author, faces this problem on listening to Stockhausen's *Prozession*. He finds that he is alternately able and unable to concentrate, that he can concentrate only on the passages where the piano is used among the electronic sounds. *Prozession* had represented for him the music of the *hombre nuevo*, yet, in the midst of this new experience, 'even so the old man is still alive and remembers' (26). It becomes clear to him that although intelligibility demands the presence of the old code (of expression, of behaviour), this code is likely to project into the future the alienated structures to be transcended:

And now it is even simpler to understand how history, temporal and cultural conditioning is inevitably fulfilled, because every passage where the piano is predominant sounds to me like a recognition which concentrates my attention, wakes me up more acutely to something which is still attached to me by that instrument which serves as a bridge between the past and the future. (26)

Andrés believes that the novel will only be valid if understood: 'A bridge is a man crossing a bridge, mate' (27). The problem is thus posed of communication through a medium which implies an alien view of the world. He asks how one can 'find the way to say intelligibly, when perhaps your technique and your deepest reality are demanding the burning of the piano and its replacement by some other electronic filter' (27). His choice between the two alternatives available to him is unequivocal. He decides to trust in the comprehension of future generations, 'to build the bridge anyway and leave it there; from that suckling infant in the arms of its mother, a woman will walk away some day and will cross the bridge on her own [...]. And then the piano will not be necessary' (28). When Patricio complains that no one will ever understand the scrapbook finally compiled by Andrés, the latter answers, 'Manuel will understand, [...] Manuel will understand some day' (385)

The 'horizontality' referred to by Cortázar finds its main expression in the 'plot'. This plot is almost a commonplace: a group of revolutionaries in Paris kidnap an important official in order to secure the release of political prisoners in Latin America. The characters converge on Verrières to carry out these plans, and such a simple narrative structure and well-defined action allow and oblige Cortázar to combine the difficult symbolism of the rendezvous (as discussed in *62*) with the 'real' problems he has newly decided to approach. The plot imposes a certain discipline on material which otherwise might take on a circularity that would exclude a wider reading public.

Within this framework, there are two clearly discernible types of causality, corresponding to the two authors Andrés and *el que te dije*, which I will follow in the next two sections. The first is what might be called the mystically horizontal trajectory of Andrés from a state of uncommittedness to a participation in the events at Verrières, and reflected in his 'later' writing or rewriting of the novel. The second is the linear causality that *el que te dije* tries to impose on the lives of the characters by deterministic logic, classification and selection of the elements of the narrative. This imposition is parallel to the censorship imposed by 'my paredros' in *62*. His motivations are strictly and limitedly 'revolutionary' and his (unfinished) discourse forms the alienating and official code against which Cortázar's own causality (the writing of Andrés?) expresses itself, thus forming the *dialettica pendolare* referred to by Eco.

ANDRÉS

The dream

The position of Andrés at the beginning of the novel is much the same as that
of Oliveira in Paris. His life is plagued with dualism and he is symbolically
torn between two women: Ludmilla, like la Maga, a totally natural and 'true'
figure who 'seems to have a sort of right to violate all chronology' (15), and
Francine, like Pola,[25] middle-class, cultured and significantly the part owner
of a bookshop 'The man astride the roof trying to encompass the Ludmilla
world and the Francine world [...] and of course the continual buffeting from
the binary, the irreconcilable double view from the ridge of the roof' (167).
His attempt to break with what he considers the bourgeois institution of the
couple is only partially honest in that he takes a lover in a totally 'bourgeois'
fashion, wishing to maintain the status quo with Ludmilla. He himself
realizes the difficulty of knowing whether his choices are made freely or
dictated by unconscious taboos: 'When I choose what I believe to be a
liberating line of conduct, a widening of my world, I am perhaps obeying
pressures, coercions, taboos, or prejudices which spring precisely from the
side which I am wanting to leave behind' (168). As in the case of Oliveira,
Andrés's lucidity and intellectuality, his incapacity to choose between the
piano and the electronic filters, leads him into a state of total inactivity.

In the dream, Andrés enters a cinema to see a mystery film, which
indicates that he is a spectator in life. In the cinema, there are two screens,
an indication of the duality of his life. A waiter approaches and menacingly
informs him that a Cuban is demanding to see him. When he comes out
from the interview with the Cuban (Castro), he realizes that the scene has
been cut in the dream, that he has been given a message to deliver, a mission,
but he does not know what it is. He is now, however, both an actor in the film
and a spectator, but before he finds out the conclusion of the film (his
mission), he is woken by the postman.

The almost obligatory nature of the reference to the writing of
Coleridge's *Kubla Khan* (103) must not make one underestimate the
importance of the unconscious in the dictation of the message. The idea is
also reminiscent of other works: *El sueño de los héroes* by Bioy Casares, where
the hero has to re-enact a dream in order to find out its conclusion; García
Márquez's 'Ojos de perro azul', where the hero, on waking every day, forgets
the password by which he will recognize the 'real' lover he meets in his
dreams; in a different way Borges's 'Inferno 1, 32' from *El hacedor*.

The cut in the dream is referred to as the 'black blot' (*mancha negra*) and has extremely wide and paradoxical implications. It is censorship in that it separates Andrés from a knowledge of his destiny, and, as such, is connected with many other alienating manifestations of taboo in the novel, and thus demands destruction. It is the bulwarks cutting off access to the stern in *Los premios* and the string barrier between Oliveira and the other side of his reality, Traveler, which creates the 'black mass' in *Rayuela*. Yet at the same time, on returning to the film, there is absolutely no dualism in Andrés for the first time: 'But all this about it being double is what I say now I'm awake, there was no doubleness in the dream, I perfectly recollect that while I was returning to my seat I felt all this which I am now segmenting in order to explain it, however partially, as one single block' (103).

Paradoxically, only by doing what he has to do will he be able to know what it is: 'Rather as if only thanks to that action which I had to carry out could I find out what the Cuban had said to me, a completely absurd inversion of causality, as you can see' (103). A very similar reversal of causality was important in Oliveira's behaviour in the second part of *Rayuela*: 'I have the impression that as soon as I've got nice straight nails I'll know what I need them for'; 'First the nails and afterwards the purpose of the nails' (*R* 278). The connotations of such a reversal are complex and work on different levels. In *Rayuela*, we sensed a faith in the spontaneity prescribed by Zen, and in an impersonal causality or force which would direct Oliveira's action.

The problem becomes clearer when Andrés, after tortured attempts to penetrate intellectually the 'black blot', comes to the conclusion that 'I can no longer search with reason' (292). This is, of course, the position reached by Oliveira, largely through the example of la Maga. Intelligence is seen as accomplice of the barrier of the 'black blot', as in *Los premios*. The theorizing of Andrés leads him into a vicious circle of dualism and inactivity. The possibility of looking beyond revolutionary action to a hypothetical and very different future is considered in very similar terms in Callado's *Bar Don Juan*: 'We cannot think consecutively. We cannot manage to produce integrated analytical thought. Our barrier of guts and blood is too dense. We think with our whole body, inside the problem.'[26] Thus the 'black blot' denotes both the impossibility of thinking beyond revolutionary action towards the state such action might produce and also the necessity of renouncing a type of thought alien to the revolution.

There is also a much simpler moral side to the issue. The sort of intellectual activity symbolized by *Prozession* is a luxury which Andrés has to win the moral right to indulge in. To renounce intellectual thought in favour of pure and purifying action and violence will transform this thought in the same way as Oliveira abandons *la piedad* (conventional human sentiments) in order to return to it in a freer, less alienated form:

> Mais viendra le moment où il comprendra que pour écouter *Prozession*, il faut d'abord gagner le droit á l'écouter, et pour cela, remplir certains devoirs, accomplir certaines tâches, jouer certains jeux. Un jour, alors, oui, on peut s'asseoir dans un fauteuil et écouter *Prozession*, sans que ce soit, une fois de plus, l'égoisme, le solipsime, la solitude, l'échec.[27]

Andrés does go to Verrières and thus, symbolically, joins the revolution. The question of what sort of causality it is which leads him straight to this destination remains. His poem 'Maneras de viajar' and the fact that he travels to Verrières by underground and by train are reminiscent of the city in *62*, and suggest the passivity of an unconscious destiny. Such a destiny is reflected in a mystical faith on the part of Andrés himself: on reaching a fork in the road to Verrières, he blindly but with obvious symbolism takes the left-hand turning, exclaiming in the words of St John of the Cross ('aunque es de noche'),[28] 'Let us turn left, even though it may be night, my beloved Juan de la Cruz' (352). *El que te dije*, again quoting St John, rejects such mysticism *a priori*: 'A la caza darle alcance, etcétera. No' (13). Curiously, this same phrase, 'even though it may be night', is used by João in the novel by Callado quoted above.[29] In addition to the meaning of barrier, the 'black blot' takes on the second meaning of a 'dark night of the soul'.

A parallel could be drawn between the Cuban's message, discovered and perhaps fulfilled in the journey of Andrés, and Cortázar's concept of narrative as discussed with reference to *62*, where the *intention significative* with the mediation of *la parole* was seen to discover, by saying it, what was to be said.

One must not forget that this reversal of traditional logic also contains a clear statement on revolutionary strategy—that revolutionary praxis and theory cannot be separated. Hence Cortázar's and Andrés's mistrust of preceptive politicians as typified by Lucien Verneuil. His quotations in 'Noticias del mes de mayo' of Sartre's denunciation of the reactionary role of the Communist Party in 'mai '68', and his comments on the Cuban revolution, are relevant here: 'What is admirable about the case of Castro is that theory was born from experience instead of preceding it' (*UR* a 50). Debray in his controversial *Revolution in the Revolution?* expands this point: revolutionary theory and morality were forged not in the city by party workers, but in the *sierra*. This work would seem to be known to Cortázar. His article 'Literatura en la revolución y revolución en la literatura' is an obvious parallel to Debray's title. One should avoid confusing Cortázar's enthusiasm for the more surrealist aspects of 'mai '68' with a belief in spontaneous revolution. The lack of explicit revolutionary theorizing in *Libro de Manuel* is explained by *el que te dije* (252).

The arrival at Verrières: return to the childhood garden

Borges tells us that in 'La muerte y la brújula', a story based like *Libro de Manuel* on the ambiguity between personal motivation and destiny, he was able, through 'that voluntary dream called artistic creation',[30] to describe what he had tried unsuccessfully to describe for many years: the atmosphere of the outskirts of Buenos Aires. This he does effortlessly, for he had—consciously—tried to describe not the Androgué of his youth but the estate of Triste-le-Roy near Paris.[31] Similarly, Andrés, on arriving at Verrières, is reminded of his childhood in the Buenos Aires suburb of Bánfield

> My grandmother taught me in a garden in Bánfield,
> a sleepy suburb of Buenos Aires,
> —*Snail, snail,*
> *bring out your horns into the sun.*
> That must be why in this suburban night there are snails. (353)

For Andrés to reach Verrières is thus to return to his childhood, to his origins. The stern in *Los premios* and the blind impulse of the eels through their life cycle to their origins in the Sargasso Sea in *Prosa del observatorio* have similar connotations. The journey of the eels in this last work is as distorted by the classification and separation of the scientists as the journey of Andrés would have been by analysis and consciousness. We will later see the importance of a provincial garden in the trajectory of Oscar towards revolutionary commitment. With the importance of the origins in mind, it may well be relevant to the failure of *el que te dije* as author of *Libro de Manuel* that, on beginning to write, he turns his back on his childhood garden, on the table his grandmother has set and on the light around which the insects are flying (24), an image of the original *intention significative*. The origins will take on greater significance in our discussion of taboo.

Synthesis or schizophrenia?

The journey of Andrés to Verrières, in spite of its mystical directness, is as ambiguous as that of Julien Sorel to the Verrières of *Le rouge et le noir*. It is haunted by a duality which points either to a vital synthesis of the personal and political, or to the schizophrenia attributed to Cortázar by Collazos.

Andrés has personal, individual reasons for going to Verrières: Ludmilla is there with Marcos, the leader of the revolutionaries, whose lover she has become on leaving Andrés. It is suggested that by arriving late he brings the enemy agents, the 'ants', after him (358). One interpretation would be that it is his individualism that has introduced the 'ants', with all their connotations, into the revolutionary action. This interpretation corresponds, however, to only one reading of his relationship with Ludmilla, that is, that he is motivated exclusively by jealousy in going to Verrières. It may be licit to recall from *Rayuela* that Traveler's interpretation of Oliveira's actions in Buenos Aires, strongly coloured by jealousy, is an instance of bad faith aimed at distorting the causality which culminates in the synthesis Talita–la Maga.

But the 'ants', according to Lonstein (368), had already been hiding at Verrières four hours before the arrival of Andrés, and a very different reading becomes equally possible. Andrés's male-centred triangle had been an indication of his insincerity: 'Might not a lot of us be trying to smash the bourgeois moulds on the basis of equally bourgeois nostalgias?' (168). On going to Verrières, however, he accepts a triangle centred round Ludmilla, a far more difficult exercise for a male 'Argentinian'. This inversion of a triangle formed by one man and two women into one formed by one woman and two men constitutes an important structural link with *Rayuela*: the triangle Ludmilla–Andrés–Francine becomes Andrés–Ludmilla–Marcos in the same way as the triangle la Maga–Oliveira–Pola becomes Oliveira–Talita–Traveler.

Though the inversion of the triangle is important, the symbolic role of Ludmilla must be considered the prime factor in the deep causality of the journey of Andrés. Ludmilla is another Maga and, though the monstrous attributes of the latter are considerably sublimated in her, the spontaneity, naturalness and 'trueness' remain, as does the force of the monster. Ludmilla joins the revolution, and for Andrés to recover her or at least to rejoin her is to join the revolution, to accept its essence, the most valid forces behind it. The parallel with la Maga is absolute: Ludmilla is frustrated by Andrés, who gives her no children (92–3), is made egoistic and superficial, as reflected in her profession of actress (la Maga sings Hugo Wolf and Rocamadour is abandoned to a *nourrice*); she leaves Andrés for Marcos, whose wounds she cures (214) (la Maga looks after the sick Pola); on disappearing to join the revolution, she is purified by her new role as is suggested in the symbolic shower scene (238) (la Maga is cleansed of her 'monstrosity' by her death or disappearance); Andrés rejoins her and at the same time accepts and is integrated into the revolution (Oliveira recovers la Maga through Talita and is thus reconciled with reality, breaking the dualism which plagued his relations with it).

The synthesis achieved in *Rayuela*, symbolized and effected by the syncretism of Talita and la Maga, becomes in *Libro de Manuel* the synthesis of the individual and the universal and collective. This, for Cortázar, is the highest aim of socialism:

> Not only can society as conceived by socialism not annul this concept of the individual, but aspires to develop him to such a point that all the negativity, all his demoniacal aspects which are exploited by capitalist society, will be transformed by a level of personality where the individual and collective dimensions will cease to confront and frustrate each other. (*LR* 64–5)

Andrés, on approaching the house, cannot reconcile being an Argentinian (i.e., as in *Rayuela*, a historical individual) and being where he is, involved in revolutionary action: 'what a strange thing to be an Argentinian in this garden and at this time' (355). The paradox is expressed in the macaronically successful 'and the poor *taita* fell, the *taita* who read Heidegger' (355). The nightingale which appears just before the 'black blot' is dispelled is perhaps a symbol of the resolution of this tension. The most universal of birds is brought together with the *teros* and *bichofeos* of Andrés's youth: 'with something singing up there, perhaps the legendary nightingale, I have never heard a nightingale, being brought up on *teros* and *bichofeos* in Bánfield' (355).[32]

We will examine the effect and implications of separating the individual from the political or collective in *el que te dije*'s treatment of Oscar.

The message

The synthesis we have mentioned is further explained by the message which is revealed to Andrés as he approaches the house, and in turn helps to explain this enigmatic message. The message is 'Wake up!' (356). Our hypothesis about all the process is strengthened by Cortázar's essay 'Espeleología a domicilio', where he stresses how, in a dream, the subject and his action are not separated by the conscious mind: 'in that pure living experience where the dreamer and his dream are not distanced by categories of understanding, where every man is his dream, his dreaming of the dream and the subject of the dream' (*UR* b 50). He mentions the myth of Bluebeard's injunction to his wife not to open the door of the room where he kept the bodies of his previous, murdered wives. This door, for Cortázar, is 'underneath your eyelids' (*UR* b 50),[33] is the door which separates the conscious from the unconscious. He proposes a violation of this prohibition: 'In the light of archetypal figures every prohibition is a clear piece of advice: open the door, open it right away' (*UR* b 50). The way to open the door is 'to wake up in one's dream':

> One has only to open it [...] and the method is the following: You must learn to wake up within your dream, impose your will on that oneiric reality of which up till now you have only passively been author, actor and spectator. He who succeeds in waking up to freedom within his dream will have opened the door and gained access to a plane of being which will at last be a *novum organum* (*UR* b 50–1).

'Wake up' is thus an order to free the liberatory strength of man's other side, his oneiric world. This is none other than the surrealist programme which has always been more or less implicit in Cortázar's work. Breton talks of 'cette volonté désespérée d'aujourd'hui [...] d'opérer à chaque instant la synthèse du rationnel et du réel',[34] and describes the surrealist enterprise in the following way: 'Au point de vue intellectuel il s'agissait, il s'agit encore d'éprouver par tous les moyens et de faire reconnaitre à tout prix le caractère factice des vieilles antinomies destinées hypocritement à prévenir toute agitation insolite de la part de l'homme.'[35]

The message does not refer exclusively to the life of the individual, but also to the parallel barriers in social reality, as is suggested in a poem by Cortázar which was inspired by the graffiti and posters of 'mai '68'. One slogan demands 'be realists, ask for the impossible', to which Cortázar replies: 'We are realists, compañero, we are going / hand in hand from dream to wakefulness' (*UR* a 51).

The door of the *Ultimo round* passage is the 'black blot' of *Libro de Manuel*. The incitement to disobedience refers to prohibitions, taboos and censorship on various levels: social, in writing (the censorship of memory by *el que te dije*), and the 'door of horn and the door of ivory' (150) of sexual taboo. The rebellion and turning upside-down of *62*, closely connected with the theme of monsters, thus reappears. The monsters of *Libro de Manuel* are seen, if with less mystery, with greater clarity than elsewhere. We can now understand that the Cuban's message can only be carried out if, *at the same time* as Andrés abandons conscious thought, such prohibitions are violated in order that the repressive order they represent should not return, vampire-like, after the 'dark night' of Andrés.

EL QUE TE DIJE

Chronicler of the Joda

El que te dije is the first author of *Libro de Manuel*. His writing is, to a certain extent, a caricature of the demands from certain Marxist quarters that Cortázar should write something close to social realism, and contains a large element of an almost positivist causality. This tendency in *el que te dije*, however, though never complete or fully realized, produces the rudiments of an alienated and exclusive discourse, the code which, according to Eco and as we have seen in previous novels, is a necessary base against which a new message and causality (symbolized by the journey of Andrés) can be dialectically developed.

El que te dije is, nevertheless, a complex character and is presented with some sympathy. His personal position is very liberal. His very name suggests that he is the 'my paredros' of *Libro de Manuel*, that the other characters have delegated to him, through *pudor*, their own acts. *El que te dije* seems to mean 'the person I told you about', an ellipsis of 'it wasn't me who did it, but...'. He has at his disposal all the information on the revolutionary enterprise, registered in a chaotic pile of index cards and scraps of paper. The information is seen, as in *62* by 'my paredros', as insects flying around a light: the empty *intention signicative*. Cortázar has always demanded a 'previous opening' on beginning a novel, that the elements of the novel should generate the causality which would link them:

> One thing was clear [...]: the incapacity I still have to build a novel until the novel itself decides the process, and sometimes it finds it hard. I know that it is impossible but I also know its deep causes, the refusal of literature conceived as a humanistic, architectonic project, the need for a previous opening, that freedom demanded by everything I am about to do and, to that end, there can be no clear idea, no formal plan. (*C* 18)

Demands, however, of immediate intelligibility and clarity are made on *el que te dije* as chronicler of the *Joda*. This is the defining difference between his position and that of Andrés: 'In my case [Andrés] it was something personal and I had no need to project it onto a sort of clarity for a third party, but *el que te dije* was in a different position' (212). The personal aspects of the narration can but be neglected or distorted by *el que te dije* due to his very nature as a collective double.

Great stress is laid on the 'neutrality' of *el que te dije*'s position and narrative: 'then *el que te dije* goes to his neutral corner, which is anywhere, not necessarily in a corner' (175); 'this neutrality had led him from the start to stand sort of sideways on, always a risky operation in narrative matters' (11). Yet Andrés, getting his own back for *el que te dije*'s attacks on him, is anxious to explain that this neutrality is not at all honest: '*El que te dije* was like that, as far as he could, he dealt the cards in his own way' (48). More importantly, the ideological character of seemingly neutral concepts such as memory is carefully brought out. At first, *el que te dije* explains away the exclusion of names and passages from his narrative as a simple whim, asking 'why memory should not have its whims' (47). Later, however, after conversation with Lonstein, he realizes how memory functions as a defence of 'everyday life', that is of the 'precious daily ego': 'Forgetfulness and memory are endocrine glands just like the hypophysis or the thyroid glands, libido regulators which decree vast twilight zones and brilliantly illuminated crests so that everyday life will not bloody its nose too often' (230).

We have already noted the inseparability of personal and political motivations in Andrés. Lonstein, in his turn, stresses the importance of irrational elements (which the 'technocrats of the revolution' would consider irrelevant) in the workings of reality and consciousness: 'They are the technocrats of the revolution and think that joy, toadstools and my landlady are not part of the dialectics of history' (144). He consequently mixes together all the heterogeneous information he receives in 'one big meta-*Joda* salad' (108). Even Marcos, the leader of the revolutionaries, insists that one's personal and political lives cannot be separated, whereas this is exactly what *el que te dije* does: 'Why that obsessive habit of chopping things up as if they were salami? A slice of *Joda*, another of personal history, you remind me of *el que te dije* with his problems of organization, the poor chap does not understand and he would like to understand, he's a sort of Linnaeus or Ameghino of the *Joda*' (239).

El que te dije is not opposed to the conclusion of others such as Oscar who come to see the revolution as a wide, all-embracing movement: 'how everything tended to be the same thing, to be the *Joda* right here or far away, in Verrières or la Plata, Gladis or Silvia' (305). If he could manage not to change key when writing about erotic experiences, then 'he would begin to feel that everything is *Joda* and that there are no personal episodes between one moment and another of the *Joda*' (232).

But *el que te dije* works deductively, starting with the theory. Moreover, the pudor inherent in his constitution prevents him from writing in the way described. Consequently, at certain points, he excludes the personal analogies which are so important in the work: 'this café in the rue de Buci had nothing to do with the bar in the calle Maipú' (48). Similarly, he refuses to accept any relation between the memories of the garden of his childhood and the present: 'All this is of little relevance today, after so many years of good or bad life' (23). Hence, when he receives the trajectory of Oscar, the details of the organizational and political aspects of his involvement in the *Joda* together with seemingly frivolous newspaper cuttings which had fascinated Oscar, *el que te dije* rigorously classifies and separates it: 'one big meta-*Joda* salad which *el que te dije* had to reclassify, putting the astrological cutting from *Horoscope* and the one sent by Oscar on one side, and the problem of old Collins and the counterfeit dollars on the other side' (108).

The inadequacy of his position is finally illustrated when, confronted with the chaotic fight with the 'ants', he is overtaken by events and can only revert to a parody of the Iliad before apparently dying: 'This cannot happen like this and here and tonight and in this country and with these people; it's all over, mate (se acabó, che)' (363). His words curiously echo the last moments of Oliveira: 'paf se acabó'.

El que te dije *and Oscar*

There is in Oscar a progressive understanding of his own situation and of the forces which dictate his revolutionary action. The barriers in him which obstruct this understanding (memory, separation) are paralleled by *el que te dije's* manipulation of the facts of his life. There is an analogy between the alienated discourse which *el que te dije* attempts to impose on his material and the effect of Oscar's superego on his own consciousness. The reader is thus cleverly placed in the same position as Oscar.

El que te dije tries to explain the trajectory of Oscar in one of his many diagrams, the only virtue of which is that it explains absolutely nothing, rather like the taxonomy of Ceferino Piriz. The issue centres mainly around a newspaper article about the escape from a boarding-school in La Plata of a number of young girls, which Oscar sends before him from Argentina with a nostalgic account of his life in doña Raquela's *pensión*, of the scent of the jasmines and his amorous adventures in the light of the full moon. The press-cutting, where no mention is made of the full moon, rather of 'the shortage of light' (109), is surreptitiously introduced as 'the cutting on the full moon' (108). It immediately finds an echo in Monique, who says that 'it was perhaps the full moon as Oscar says' (110) (the reader has not yet heard Oscar's version), and recounts a parallel rebellion in a Strasbourg establishment.

As Oscar flies over the Atlantic to join the 'revolution', and tries hard to concentrate on how he is going to get the counterfeit dollars into France, he becomes increasingly obsessed by the notion of the full moon in the escape of the girls. The infiltration of the full moon into his consciousness is expressed typographically by smaller print over the main text. He has the impression that something is wrong or missing in his understanding. Whereas he himself imagines the girls scaling a wall in the light of the full moon and sexually excited by its influence, the article talks of 'a surprise black-out' (109) and claims prosaically that 'the cause of the trouble was the advertising of carnival dances by neighbouring night-clubs which craze the boarders' (110). A parallel may be drawn between the 'surprise black-out' referred to by the article and the 'black blot' of Andrés, also referred to as a 'total black-out' (267). The suggestion is that there is also some form of censorship at work in the article. To explain the reaction of the girls by the effect on them of the advertisements for dances is equivalent to limiting the motives of a revolutionary to the theory of dialectical materialism.

The full moon which impelled the young girls over the wall is the same full moon Oscar remembers from doña Raquela's boarding house. He recalls how 'in doña Raquela's patio the full moon was an imperious call, an impulse which sent out of orbit one's skin, one's [...]' (127). This image of a vital, irrational impulse is not alien to Oscar's decision to join the *Joda*. Indeed, it is suggested that such seemingly irrelevant images can dictate the whole course of a life: 'There is a sort of surreptitious recurrence of the joke or word play or gratuitous act which creeps up onto what is not a joke, onto the plinth of life, and from up there gives out oblique orders, modifies movements, corrodes customs' (125).

The separation of this motivation from his 'real' life ('the flight across the wasteland, nothing to do with this room at the other side of the world' (185)), imposed by his superego and the manipulation of *el que te dije*, leaves the revolutionary present and future he is entering empty and meaningless: 'Opening his eyes [...] tipped Oscar into something with no real hand-holds, the perfect, miniskirted and deodorized silhouette of Gladis [...], all that absolutely hollow' (128).

Gladis at this point is significantly described as being 'deodorized'. There are two very different types of 'washing' in the novel. This first instance corresponds to the sterilizing influence of the morality of Francine, which is 'as automatic as deodorant on one's armpits' (266), and to the censorship of *el que te dije*. Consequently, when Oscar finally understands his own position, his memory is like 'an odour before the shower' (164). The other type, essentially in good faith, is, for example, the shower of Ludmilla on leaving Andrés, Lonstein's and Andrés's washing baby Manuel (341), Lonstein's job of washing corpses, symbolically washing away taboo, 'the ancient, rotten corpse of time and taboos and incomplete self-definitions'. (233). There is also in *Libro de Manuel* the paradoxical washing and purification by a self-immersion in filth, corresponding to Oliveira's night with Emmanuèle, the self-burial of Heraclitus in the dungheap to cure himself of dropsy. Lonstein's dissertation on masturbation leaves him 'with his face all new and awake and as if washed' (227). Andrés's visit to the strip-club with Francine and his feeling that he ought to let a drunkard vomit on him respond to the same intention.

In his hotel room, in the state of semi-wakefulness when the 'scissors of wakefulness' (142) are relaxed, Oscar allows all the heterogeneous thoughts in his mind to mix together freely: 'It was better to go to sleep and let it all merge since there was no way of separating so many things from one's memory or from the present' (195). Listening on the wireless to Puccini's *Turandot*, he is reminded of his childhood, when he had loved this music, and at the same time of the *pensión* of doña Raquela. (A link would seem to be established between the *pensión* and his childhood.) He remembers that Puccini had died before finishing the work, that it had been completed by someone else, and muses that so many things are given a false appearance of completeness—newspaper articles, the prehistoric animals reconstructed by Ameghino from one bone. (Marcos, as we noted earlier, refers to *el que te dije* as the Linnaeus or Ameghino of the *Joda*.) His own personal version of the girls' escape is then probably right; the hole that the journalist claimed the girls had opened in the barbed wire themselves was already there: 'who knows whether the hole might not have been there already' (164). The 'previous opening' demanded by Cortázar had been there all the time, ignored by *el que te dije* in the lamp in his childhood garden. The barriers within the novel are not absolute, but created in part by the narrative itself. One is reminded of the classification of the eel's life cycle in *Prosa del observatorio*, where Cortázar asks, 'But what is the point of that "why", when all that is asked of the answer is to block off a hole?' (*PO* 41–2).

We can thus see how memories from the past, enclosing an image of the potentiality of the future, can break through the barrier of censorship. The role of analogy in the discovery of the unconscious or repressed motivating force, and in the actual functioning of this force, is essential: 'But it was not a metaphor, it came back in a different way, as if obeying an obscure likeness' (164). Its importance is also stressed in *Prosa del observatorio*:

'Tout se répond, thought Jai Singh and Baudelaire with a century between them' (*PO* 20). Here as elsewhere, the analogy often works through word play, as when Oscar is reminded of the full moon (*luna llena*) on eating a croissant (*medialuna*): 'It may only be the croissant but it is also the full moon, the implacable machine of word play opening up doors and revealing entrances in the dark' (222).

Whereas *el que te dije* understands progressively less of what is happening until his final break-down, Oscar comes to a privileged understanding of the wide, often individual and irrational motives behind his commitment. He realizes that there is absolutely no difference between the girls' scaling the school wall and his girlfriend Gladis, who loses her job as an air-hostess in order to help him, that 'everything tended to be the same thing, to be Joda right here and far away' (305). Lonstein initially asks, 'what sort of an idea do you expect Oscar himself to have about what he's doing' (105). Oscar is now in a similar position and able to assert that Lucien Verneuil, apparently the most theoretically motivated member of the group, is 'obeying obscure allegiances to what he thought was pure and practical and dialectic logic' (306).

CONCLUSION

Politics, sexual liberation and monsters

The importance of eroticism in liberation has been a fundamental theme in Cortázar's work since *Los reyes*. The issue in *Libro de Manuel* is centred round the fear of the recurrence of repressive structures in society after the revolution. The strong link between political and sexual revolution is implicitly expressed in the novel, and incorporated into the structures of its text: Andrés can only go beyond the 'black blot' to Verrières after breaking down the parallel 'black blot' of the taboo on sodomy. Sexual liberation in the novel is thus not just a luxury of the revolution, but a necessary condition to its lasting success. Though Cortázar gives few explicitly political arguments, Lonstein significantly links the mental disturbances created by taboo in the individual with the collective illnesses of society: 'the daytime harmony which so many people called morality and which then some odd day, individually, became neurosis and the analyst's couch, and which also on some odd day, collectively, became racism and/or fascism' (218). References, however, are made to Stephen Markus (170) and to Wilhelm Reich (233) who, in *The Sexual Revolution*, was probably the first to note and study the survival in post-revolutionary Russia of reactionary sexual ideas in spite of the destruction of their economic base. Pointing out the cultural backwardness of the old Russia, he stresses the need in the future for a theory of sexual revolution.[36]

The ideas of Marcuse, however, provide the most useful theoretical background to our discussion of the theme. In *Eros and Civilization*, the latter makes a fundamental development in the study of the survivals to which Reich refers. After Freud, he stresses the correspondence between the phylogenetic and the ontogenetic, the repetition in the development of the individual of the stages of the evolution of civilization. The guilt a child feels when, in the Oedipal, stage, he symbolically kills his father in order to possess his mother and rejects parental authority to seek gratification in society causes the parental values he has rejected to be reproduced in his superego, a process described as the 'return of the repressed'. Similarly, when the young men revolted against the patriarchal primal horde, where one leader held all the women yet protected the men, the dominant structures of the previous society were repeated, again through guilt, in the collective superego or superstructure. The repetition of this process from generation to generation has the effect of progressively strengthening the repressive laws of the superego.

For Freud, repression, which is used as a blanket term, is inherent in the very nature of civilization, and the process described above becomes a vicious circle. Marcuse, with his distinction between repression and 'surplus-repression', provides an insight which can break this vicious circle, if only in theory. Eros is the tendency towards complete oneness with the world, but the erogenous zones of the body (originally the whole body) have been gradually reduced to the genitals in order to leave the rest of the body free, as a tool, for the tasks of society. Marcuse argues that the scarcity which justified this repression is no longer the rule, that a high level of repression is no longer a historical necessity, but corresponds to the laws of capitalist production which demands that more and more be produced in order to maintain the money surplus. It is this no longer necessary repression that he terms 'surplus-repression.'. To present such repression as 'natural' is also to naturalize the historical state which created it. This implies that the destruction of capitalist modes of production opens up the possibility of the reactivation of 'earlier' forms of sexuality, other than the exclusively genital.

In *The Other Victorians*, from which Cortázar quotes extensively, Stephen Markus brings out the ideological connotations of various taboos—the taboo on masturbation, for example, corresponds to the mechanistic view of the world where the body was seen as a machine capable of producing only a limited amount of semen.

The fear of return of the repressed, the perpetuation of alienating structures, conveyed in the repetition of the *figuras*, has been a central theme in all the novels. We have seen that the *figuras* point to a prohibition, but indirectly indicate the liberating nature of the tabooed force, the 'monster', which can be released if the alienating and dualistic prohibition is violated, if Actaeon returns to possess Diana.

The monsters of Cortázar's previous novels are presented in *Libro de Manuel* without the mediation of literary or mythical figures, and simply embody tabooed sexual activity. Masturbation in *Libro de Manuel* is equivalent to the Minotaur in *Los reyes*. Lonstein describes the taboo on masturbation as one of 'the deep ogres, the real masters of the daytime harmony' (218). As in the case of the Minotaur, the only way to kill this ogre (to destroy its monstrosity) is to accept it. This acceptance would have the effect of turning the ogre into a prince (like the Minotaur, son of the queen Pasiphae):

> To tear Onan from the inner mass was to kill at least one of the ogres and even more, to metamorphose him by bringing him into contact with the daytime and the open, to de-ogre him, to exchange his sad clandestine coat for feathers and bells [...], the ogre which after all was a prince like so many ogres, just that you had to help him to stop being an ogre at last. (218)

Cortázar comments in the context of *Libro de Manuel* that since *Los reyes* he has taken upon himself the task of 'watching over slandered dragons' (*C* 23), the natural forces that 'the establishment defines as monsters and exterminates as soon as it can' (*C* 15). (The 'ants' significantly try to 'slander' the members of the *Joda* by killing their hostage and making it look as if the leader of the group, Marcos, had been responsible. This distortion of events is parallel to that effected by the authorities at the end of *Los premios*.)

There is the same suggestion in *Libro de Manuel* as elsewhere that the monsters preserve the memory of the origins and that only the experience of these origins can revitalize the future. For Andrés, to go to Verrières is to return to his childhood, and in the light of this return, the insistence on the pansexuality of children becomes significant. Children have been an image of the origins throughout the novels, and this novel is explicitly written for baby Manuel. The tender description of the rudimentary masturbation of Manuel is an image of the innocence lost to the guilty world-view of the adults looking on. It is a 'smack in the face (but it was also a caress) given by lost innocence to those who looked at reality in an adult fashion from the other bank, with their idiotic guilt, their stained yellow flowers from the corpses of Hindus' (90).

From the Hotel Terrass to Verrières

Libro de Manuel ends in a characteristically ambiguous and understated fashion. Perhaps it ends in a confused fashion, but then 'when there is talk of confusion, what one usually finds is confused people' (12). Without exhausting all the possible readings of the last two episodes (the 'rape' of Francine and Andrés's arrival at Verrières), I have suggested a reading involving the deep structure of recovery followed in earlier works. Though Cortázar may not consciously be proposing such a reading, only this deep structure seems able to account for the concatenation and logic of these episodes.

In the pages before the rape of Francine, the social and sexual are linked in that the 'naturalness' of the taboo on sodomy is presented as parallel to the 'naturalness' of social deprivation in the Paris slums. The taboo on sodomy is referred to as 'the truth, of course, a truth which grows in the earth of genealogical lies' (310). Francine comments on their visit to the slum areas: 'There is no need to come like a cheap doubting Thomas to check on all this inevitable filth' (278). Andrés is quick to pick up the word *inevitable*: 'You said it, my girl, everything was going all right in your speech but at the end you said that little word which is equally inevitable in your *Weltanschauung*, for your world and mine all that is always inevitable, but we are wrong' (278). In a sense, both naturalnesses are broken down when Francine admits that the sodomy has not been a rape, that 'it was not unbearable, that he was not raping her' (313): 'No, you haven't degraded me' (327).

But the experience is, at the time, presented as a partial failure in that on the following morning both feel guilty: 'Apart from the bed, we were Adam and Eve at the hour of their expulsion, something full of shadows and past, covering our faces so as not to see the daylight on the gravestones down there' (326). The reference to Eve suggests that guilt in *Libro de Manuel* retains from *62* Christian connotations. We are also reminded that it is Jehovah who strikes down Onan for masturbation (225). This failure (when the episode is taken in isolation) is confirmed when Andrés crosses the bridge back to the city, to normality. His attempt at liberation has been a 'false bridge' (290), simply a 'holiday' as against the 'work day' (329) which he rejoins in the city, restoring the old dualism. The dualism of his act, as at the same time a liberation and simple escapism, is inherent in the nature of the hotel as an institution. Its owner 'guarantees a whole lot of Judaeo-Christian values' (287), while offering the therapy of irresponsibility: 'A hotel room is a mini-therapy, unfamiliar furniture, irresponsibility [...] nobody will come and say you're a lout' (286).

But just as in *62* the rape of Celia by Hélène depends for its final value and consequences on the activity and judgements of others, the outcome of this episode is only decided by Andrés's later action. The name of the hotel, suggesting a terrace or balcony, indicates that Andrés is still a spectator, not yet an actor. Only when the two categories of spectator and actor have been brought together will the 'black blot' finally dissolve. It is the close relation in *Libro de Manuel*, as in *62*, between guilt and death which creates the deep link between the two episodes.

Andrés chooses to carry out his transgression of taboo, to rape Francine, in a room of the Hotel Terrass overlooking a graveyard, which he describes as the 'stupid perpetuation of original misery' (292), apparently a reference to original sin.[37] The graveyard signifies the death of the other half of the individual, that which lies out of bounds beyond the 'black blot'. Taboo, the rules and prohibitions of society, in the form of the penalties, fines and traffic lights of the bridge across which Andrés returns to Paris, are ironically seen as protecting the pedestrian from 'death on four wheels' (325). When Andrés 'pataphysically' shows Francine the cemetery, the 'black blot' partially and momentarily disappears: 'The black blot disappeared for one fleeting second, [...] something in me had seen across to the other side, there was a sort of final balance to the stock-taking' (293).

The cemetery forms a parallel with the morgue of Lonstein, where the corpses, despised and rejected by society, correspond to 'the ancient corpse rotten with time and taboos and incomplete self-definitions' (233). Lonstein's washing the corpses (of guilt) and caring for them (in a way which flows over into necrophilia) is presented as bringing them back to life, or at least dealing a considerable blow to death (a euphemistic rendering): 'una buena manera de darle por el culo a la pelada' (39). Both transgressions of sexual taboo in the novel are described as descents to Hades. Lonstein's discussion of masturbation is 'a grotesque saga, a descent like that of Gilgamesh or Orpheus to the hell of the libido' (218). Andrés says to Francine, 'I need to go down those steps of cognac with you and see whether there is an answer in the basement, whether you can help me to get out of the black blot' (292).

The rape of Francine is thus clearly a repetition of Oliveira's kissing Talita in the morgue of the lunatic asylum, of Hélène's raping Celia and symbolically taking her blood to the hospital morgue. The descent is always effected, as we know, to bring someone back to life. Though no one is actually dead at this point in the novel, the two characters who could be symbolically recovered are Manuel and Ludmilla. Anxiety is expressed at various points about the safety of Manuel, which links him with Jorge in *Los premios*. There are more indications, however, that Ludmilla is the person symbolically dead to Andrés. Andrés has lost Ludmilla in the same way as Oliveira loses la Maga before symbolically recovering her. Evidence from *62* points in the same direction. To go beyond the 'black blot' is equivalent to the destruction of the contents of Hélène's doll. This destruction opens up the possibility of rendezvous between Juan and Hélène, and one may assume that the disappearance of the 'black blot' in Verrières has a similar effect for Andrés as regards Ludmilla. That Ludmilla should have received him coolly is in a sense irrelevant, since what Andrés recovers is what Ludmilla represents, that is, the 'essential' Ludmilla: naturalness, spontaneity, revolution.

If at any point *Libro de Manuel* does reach the difficult 'convergence' between Cortázar's twin preoccupations, it is in these final inconclusive moments of the novel. Just as Oliveira reconciles having recovered the force of the dead Maga with going to the pictures with Gekrepken, Andrés, on joining Ludmilla, incorporates the values and force the latter has inherited from la Maga into his real, though tardy, rather superfluous, and perhaps disastrous act of adhesion to the revolution: 'Tell me where there is a gun because I may be drunk but in my time I passed all the tests at the Federal Shooting Gallery, so' (361).[38]

NOTES

1. See, for example, 'Acerca de la situación del intelectual latino-americano', in *Ultimo round*.

2. M. Alascio Cortázar, *Viaje alrededor de una silla* (Buenos Aires, 1971), 29–30.

3. Alascio Cortázar, 22.

4. Alascio Cortázar, 34.

5. Alascio Cortázar, 45

6. 'Documentos. El caso Padilla', in *Libre* I (September–November 1971), 131. Referred to henceforth as *CP*.

7. Carlos Díaz Sosa, 'Diálogo con Cortázar', in *Imagen* 101–2 (January–February 1975), 27.

8. Díaz Sosa, 'Diálogo', 27.

9. García Canclini, 29–30.

10. A. Breton, *Position politique du surréalisme* (Paris, 1972), 95.

11. A. Breton, *Les manifestes du surréalisme*, 8.

12. 'El boom entre dos libertades', in M. Benedetti, *Letras del continente mestizo* (Montevideo, 1969), 37.

13. Gabriel and Daniel Cohn-Bendit, *Obsolete Communism: The Left-Wing Alternative* (trans. A. Pomerans; Harmondsworth, 1969), 12.

14. Cohn-Bendit, *Obsolete Communism*, 31.

15. See Macedonio Fernández's 'Bobo de Buenos', in *Papeles de Recienvenido, poemas, cuentos, miscelánea* (Buenos Aires, 1967), 147, and *Museo de la novela de la Eterna*, 199ff.

16. See Juan Goytisolo, *Señas de identidad* (Mexico, 1973), 84.

17. Similar enterprises are recorded in Louis Pauwels and Jacques Bergier, *Le matin des magiciens* (Paris, 1972): the 'adjectifs à double face' of Charles Hoy Fort designed to express a 'nouvelle structure mentale', 'un troisième veil de l'intelligence' (202); an Austrian professor's 'refonte du langage occidental', where, for example, 'le retard sur l'avance que je souhaitais prendre' becomes 'l'atard' (203).

18. *L'Abbé C.*, in (*Oeuvres complètes*, III (Paris, 1971), 356.

19. *L'Abbé C.*, 339.

20. *L'Abbé C.*, 344.

21. This is also true of the literary code of verisimilitude which, as Sollers points out, is highly ideological: 'LE ROMAN EST LA MANIÈRE DONT CETTE SOCIÉTÉ SE PARLE, la manière dont l'individu DOIT SE VIVRE pour y être accepté' (*Logiques*, 228).

22. U. Eco, *Opera aperta: forma e indeterminazione nelle poetiche contemporanee* (Milan, 1971), 107.

23. *Opera aperta*, 105.

24. *Opera aperta*, 116.

25. Both women have in their names (Pola *París*, *Francine*) a reference to France, i.e. to culture and order.

26. *Bar Don Juan* (Rio de Janeiro, 1971), 13.

27. In an interview with F. Wagener, 'Marier Joyce et Mao', in *Le Monde*, 20 September 1974, 26.

28. St John of the Cross, *Obras escogidas*, 57.

29. *Obras escogidas*, 49.

30. Borges, 'El escritor argentino y la tradición', in *Discusión*, *Obras completas*, 274.

31. 'El escritor argentino', 270–1.

32. Borges makes a similar use of what is presumably the nightingale in 'Nueva refutación del tiempo' after the famous moment before the pink fence (*Otras inquisiciones*, *Obras completas*, 765).

33. Oliveira, after the syncretism of la Maga and Talita, 'emerged [...] into the world under his eyelids' (*R* 374).

34. *L'amour fou*, 106.

35. *Les manifestes du surréalisme*, 51.

36. W. Reich, *The Sexual Revolution* (London, 1969), 191.

37. In *Prosa del observatorio* (p. 67), we have the phrase, 'We have not yet learned to make love, [...] to strip death of its suit of guilt and debts.' For more discussion of transgression and death in Cortázar, see E. Rodríguez Monegal, 'Le fantôme de Lautréamont', in *Narradores de esta América*, II; S. Sarduy, 'Del Yin al Yang', in *Escrito sobre un cuerpo*; M.A. Safir, 'An Erotics of Liberation: Notes on Transgressive Behaviour in *Rayuela* and *Libro de Manuel*', in *The Final Island*.

38. Within this reading, the death of *el que te dije* would indicate the abolition of the duality between the two positions represented by himself and Andrés.

ANA HERNÁNDEZ DEL CASTILLO

Woman as Circe the Magician

The mother has from the outset a decidedly symbolical significance for a man,
which probably accounts for his strong tendency to idealize her. Idealization is a
hidden apotropaism; one idealizes whenever there is a secret fear to be exorcised.
What is feared is the unconscious and its magical influence.

—C.G. Jung
"Psychological Aspects of the Mother
Archetype," *Symbols of Transformation*

The universal goddess makes her appearance to men under a multitude of
guises; for the effects of creation are multitudinous, complex, and of mutually
contradictory kind when experienced from the viewpoint of the created world.
The mother of life is at the same time the mother of death; she is masked in the
ugly demonesses of famine and disease.

—Joseph Campbell
The Hero With a Thousand Faces

In his book on Keats, Cortázar repeatedly expresses his admiration for
Keats's capacity to respond to "the promptings of the collective
unconscious." From the ensuing discussions, however, it becomes clear that
Cortázar is mainly concerned with Keats's response to one archetype in
particular: the archetype of the Great Mother, particularly in her aspect of
Terrible Mother. In Cortázar's view, Keats becomes the fist of the Romantics
to rediscover the powerful symbolism of Mother Goddesses, whose worship

From *Keats, Poe, and the Shaping of Cortázar's Mythopoesis.* © 1981 John Benjamins B.V.

dates back to the dawn of man's consciousness. In one of the most impassioned passages of his book on Keats, Cortázar proceeds to present a "statistics" showing the recurrence of matriarchal figures and matriarchal rites in Keats's poetry,[1] emphasizing the uniqueness of Keats's poetry in the richness of its archetypal contents. He underplays, thus, the equally important role of Coleridge's "Christabel" or of the figure of Death in "The Rime of the Ancient Mariner" (Coleridge had conceived these poems in analogous trancelike states that could have been interpreted, likewise, as "seizures by the archetypes of the collective unconscious").

Cortázar's appreciation of the important role played by goddess figures in Keats's poetry, on the other hand, is not groundless or far-fetched; Walter Evert has stressed Keats's special sensitivity to the figure of the moon goddess, observing that "lunar references and encomia are abundant in his pre-Endymion poetry, and that—as one might expect from a person of Keats's sensitivity—he was moved not only by the variousness of the moon's appearances but also by the appearances of other objects touched with its light."[2] He proceeds to observe that not only in *Endymion* but also in "I Stood Tip-Toe" and others of Keats's early poems the moon receives the paean otherwise reserved for Apollo; it is she who inspires the poet, she who is associated with the principle of "light": "She has for all practical purposes become identical with him."[3] If Apollo is associated with the light of day, and thus, of intellectual pursuits, Cynthia, as ruler of the night, guides the poet into a more obscure, intuitive, and magical knowledge. Similarly, Robert Graves, in *The White Goddess*, had seen Keats as a "goddess-poet," that is, as one who is especially receptive and responsive to the numinous projections of the Feminine.[4] As his major biographers—especially Aileen Ward and Robert Gittings[5]—observe, there is an important link between Keats's difficulty in establishing relationships with "real" women and his portrayal of the goddesses around whom his major poems are built. It has been perceptively observed that there was in Keats's mind—more than in any other of the Romantic poets—a strong compulsion towards the realization of physical love which conflicted with his idealization of woman as goddess: consequently, Keats's erotic scenes either flee too far away into mythology or fall into segments of bad taste. Physical love can never be portrayed actually and directly, but must be clothed in Renaissance garb ("Isabella"), medieval lore ("The Eve of Saint Agnes"), or Greek myth (*Lamia*); a situation involving an actual woman will be bound to create a dramatic crisis.[6] Indeed, women always perplexed Keats; his attitude towards them shows a mixture of contempt for the superficiality of the "blue-stockings" and dread for the magical powers of the "Charmians."

In a letter to Bailey (22 July 1818) Keats had explored the reasons behind his feeling of uneasiness when dealing with women, attributing it to the disappointment he felt upon finding out that real women fell "so beneath my Boyish imagination.... When I was a Schoolboy I though[t] a fair Woman a pure Goddess, my mind was a soft nest in which some one of them slept, though she knew it not."[7] He reveres the ideal concept of women that he carries in his mind and feels somewhat guilty at the thought that he expects too much from the real women he meets. Moreover, he longs for the feminine presence, yet he feels extremely awkward in the company of most ordinary women he meets. Further in the same letter, he tells Bailey: "I must absolutely get over this—but how? The only way is to find the root of evil, and so cure it 'with backward mutters of dissevering Power.' That is a difficult thing; for an obstinate Prejudice can seldom be produced but from a Gordian complication of feelings, which must take time to unravell(ed) and care to keep unravelled."[8] Cortázar is right, then, when he perceives the complexity of Keats's relationship to women and establishes a connection between his "Gordian complication of feelings" regarding real women and the peculiar conception of his feminine characters. His interpretation takes a definite turn away from conventional Keatsian criticism, however, when he concentrates exclusively on the *negative* aspects of the Feminine presented in Keats's letters and works, disregarding all others.

Cortázar's study singles out the figure of Circe (*Endymion*, III) as the basic "constellation" of the Feminine in Keats's early works and as the nucleus from which the figures of "La Belle Dame sans Merci" and *Lamia* later derived. Cortázar then establishes a connection between the basic constellation of woman as "Circe the Magician" and the conflicts that characterized Keats's relationships to women. Next, Cortázar presents Keats's affair with Fanny Brawne as the poet's desperate struggle for self-preservation facing the deadly, absorbing, annihilating enemy: Woman.

Again, Cortázar's interpretation is not wholly groundless; and Keats's early critics had, in fact, literally blamed Fanny Brawne for Keats's death.[9] Before meeting Fanny Brawne, Keats apparently tended to divide women into two groups: those who were sexually attractive (the "Charmians") and those who were "good" (like Georgiana, his brother George's wife).[10] When he met Fanny he was confronting, for the first time, a woman who was both. The tragedy of Keats's passion for Fanny Brawne and its effect upon the poet's physical and mental health has been the subject of endless controversy among Keats's critics, who are often at variance in their interpretation of how "fatal" Fanny really was for Keats. It is indeed a difficult matter to deal with; for if we take Keats's last letters as the main evidence of the conflict—as

Cortázar appears to have done—the presence of Fanny appears to have been, indeed, lethal. Keats's letters to Fanny Brawne describe a kind of feeling that goes far beyond the "normal" passion of man for woman and closely approaches the devotion of a would-be saint about to be martyred for his religion. In a letter of 13 October 1819 we read:

> I cannot exist without you—I am forgetful of everything but seeing you again—my Life seems to stop here—I see no further. You have absorb'd me. I have a sensation at the present moment as though I was dissolving—I should be exquisitely miserable without the hope of soon seeing you.... I have been astonished that Men could die Martyrs for religion—I have shudder'd at it— I shudder no more—I could be martyr'd for my Religion—Love is my religion—I could die for that. I could die for you. My Creed is Love and you are its only tenet. You have ravish'd me away by a Power I cannot resist; and yet I could resist until I saw you; and even since I have seen you I have endeavoured often "to reason against the reasons of my Love." I can do that no more—the pain would be too great. My love is selfish—I cannot breathe without you. (Forman, Letter 16)[11]

Keats is "seized" by Fanny's presence, seen as "a Power I cannot resist" and as one he cannot explain away by means of reason. It is a passion that threatens with the dissolution of the self, and yet it is a state that, once known, cannot allow the poet to fall comfortably back into his former existence. He must pursue the state of ecstasy even at the cost of his own destruction. The expression "exquisitely miserable" illustrates, through the power of the opposition of feelings in it, the central nature of his experience. It is analogous to the "pleasurable pain" of the odes and of *Lamia*; it is a feeling that combines the extreme of joy with the extreme of pain, attaining a conjunction of opposites that blend as one in the instant where the self is about to dissolve.

Most of Keats's critics agree in drawing a relationship between the poet's meeting of Fanny Brawne and his conception of certain poems centering on the identification of love and death and on the appearance, in other poems, of the figure of the sorceress that provides both the acme of sensuous pleasures and the destruction of the unwary man who succumbs to her charms. The poem "Bright Star"—conceived soon after Keats met Fanny Brawne—expresses a theme destined to become almost obsessive for the later Keats: the identification of the moment of accession to the ideal with the moment of death. Only in the image of a climactic death can Keats resolve the opposing emotions aroused by Fanny: the longing to attain the most intense joy of possession, and the dread of dissolution and loss of the self in that very intensity. The erotic metaphor "to melt into" reappears in "The Eve of St. Agnes" to refer to the consummation of Madeline and Porphyro's love. The idea that the star is a poetic transposition of Woman in general and Fanny in particular seems confirmed by Keats's letter to Fanny of 25 July 1819, where he calls her "fair star."[12] But the identification between love and death, merely suggested up to this point, finds a definite expression in the haunting poem "La Belle Dame sans Merci," also written soon after Keats met Fanny Brawne. In both "La Belle Dame" and the later and longer *Lamia*, a sorceress charms an unwary dreamer, luring him away from his path and sequestering him in an "elfin grot" or an enchanted palace, away from human pursuits, and occasioning his death upon the withdrawal of her love. Both poems display the same central idea, intimately related to the feeling in the previously quoted letter from Keats to Fanny: once the heights of pleasure derived from the possession of the ideal have been tasted, a return to ordinary pursuits becomes impossible. The sorceress disappears, but her memory remains to drive her victims insane and drain the life away from them. Thus there were enough facts in Keats's letters and late poems to lay the foundations for a theory where Woman would appear as Keats's arch-enemy, and Cortázar's own experiences made him intensify this aspect of the poet's relationship with women.

Cortázar was already thirty-five, and still unmarried, when he wrote the book on Keats. According to his own declarations to Luis Harss, he was a confirmed bachelor at the time, led a secluded life, and had few friends.[13] He had lived with his mother until he was almost thirty; as previously noted, he was abandoned by his father when he was five years old and was raised by his mother and aunts in the Buenos Aires suburb of Bánfield. If—according to Cortázar—the constellation of the Feminine as Circe, magician and seductress, had been the predominant image in Keats's unconscious, the figure of Parsifal's mother seems to have arisen as the basic constellation in his own unconscious. Both in conversation and in a letter,[14] the author spoke of his identification as a youth with the hero of the Grail legend; and Austin, the youthful hero of *62*, is also likened to this hero (*62*, pp. 89, 172, 209). If the constellation of the feminine archetype serves to determine—according to analytical psychology—the nature of a man's future relationships with women, the images of Circe and Parsifal's mother will help us to define the basic difference between Keats's and Cortázar's conflicts with the Feminine.

Most of the artists best admired by Cortázar resemble him in one central, extremely important point—they were fatherless. Keats and Poe, the objects of this study, were no exceptions. However, unlike Keats, Poe—and Saki, Baudelaire, Edward Lear, René Magritte, Ambrose Bierce, and other writers with whom Cortázar liked to identify—led lives marked by incidents and relationships which were analogous to incidents and relationships in Cortázar's life, thus favoring his identification with them. Identification at the level of artistic aims was not sufficient for Cortázar; he needed to feel a more personal bond with these authors, as well, in order not only to achieve a "chameleonic" passage into their poetic selves but also to find a confirmation and reassurance of his own existence through theirs: Saki, Magritte, and Lear were also raised by spinster aunts; Baudelaire and Bierce were uncommonly and even abnormally attached to their mothers; all were pestered by asthmas, allergies, and other psychosomatic ailments associated with mother-fixation. Yet, if Poe, Baudelaire, Bierce, and Saki displayed sensitivities and aesthetic aims that were akin to Cortázar's, Keats did not. As I hope to have shown elsewhere,[15] Keats's sensitivity is so different from Cortázar's that Keats's influence appears only in the form of certain images or in general outlines of concepts that Cortázar completely reworked and transformed, even though he still referred to these as "Keats's principles." The difference between both authors' sensitivities is dramatically manifested in the contrasting constellations of the Feminine in each. Circe is basically the *sensuous* enchantress, the "young witch" whose ambivalence as gate to both positive inspiration and negative intoxication is partly linked to the hero's own attitude towards her. As previously discussed, Circe is the archetypal manifestation of the negative anima and, as such, subject to defeat by a hero capable of outwitting her or taming her *through the body*. Parsifal's mother is basically a spiritual figure; as mother—rather than anima—she inspires a greater awe and, as such, a far greater danger. Parsifal's mother— who held fast to her son, dressing him in women's clothes to prevent him from joining the knights (as her husband, Parsifal's father, had done) and from leaving her side—has the symbolic power to emasculate and nullify; she is the spiderlike, possessive, devouring Terrible Mother.[16] If Keats's early poems show woman, primarily, as the young, sensuous enchantress and the provider of pleasure, Cortázar's stories symbolically show woman as a disembodied, absorbing *presence* analogous to Poe's maelstrom, seas, and— most important—houses ("Casa tomada," "Cefalea," "Relato con un fondo de agua"), and his later tales present the towering, spiderlike Mother of "Cartas de mamá," "La salud de los enfermos," and "El otro cielo."

In spite of this basic difference in the perception of the Feminine, Cortázar seems to have compensated by emphasizing other points of contact between himself and Keats that would favor a "chameleonic" incursion into the latter's world: both were inclined to prefer the "ideal" over the "real," both came from modest backgrounds in literary milieus dominated by the upper classes, both possessed a certain unsophisticated naiveté in their early careers which often made them the objects of scorn.[17] A biographical detail provided yet another: Cortázar fell in love with Aurora Bernárdez—who became his wife in 1952—at the time when he wrote *IJK*. Through his comments on Keats, he manifested feelings which were surprisingly akin to those Keats himself had recorded on the margins of Burton's *Anatomy of Melancholy* at the time when he first felt attracted to Fanny Brawne. Cortázar's comments on Keats, like Keats's on Burton, display a violent misogynism, an intensely felt conflict between love and freedom, and a desire to reject woman for the sake of poetry.[18]

Cortázar, exercising the chameleonism of his poetic theory, attempted to place himself within Keats's self in order to absorb the vision of the Feminine that had so fascinated him. In the chapter on Fanny Brawne, Cortázar speaks, almost in the first person, from Keats's world; yet, the Keats he presents us is a new Keats, fashioned after Cortázar's own heart. For Cortázar, Keats's *affective* conflict appears as a *mental* problem; his anxiety facing women, as an insurmountable dread and a *desire to reject*. Earlier in his book, Cortázar had observed that in the sudden appearance of Miss Jane Cox, Keats had seen "al enemigo, al usurpador" who pretended to monopolize his attention and take him away from poetry. Keats's letter, however, states: "I always find myself more at ease with such a woman.... I am at such times too much occupied in admiring to be awkward or on a tremble. I forget myself entirely because I live in her."[19] But Cortázar, after describing the profound impression Miss Cox had made on Keats, states that "con la misma violencia del deseo surge el rechazo" (*IJK*, p. 169). Violent rejection? What Keats actually says is "I don't cry to take the moon home with me in my Pocket not [for "nor"] do I fret to leave her behind me."[20] Yet Cortázar claims that Keats "se alza violento contra la sospecha de que la mujer sea ese símbolo engañoso de la pluralidad en la unidad, el abregé del mundo para comodidad de poetas" (*IJK*, p. 169). What happens is, apparently, that Cortázar interpreted the reference further in Keats's letter to George and Georgiana ("Since I wrote thus far I have met with that same Lady again, whom I saw at Hastings and whom I met when we were going to the English Opera") as an allusion to Miss Cox (Charmian), and thus, he attributes Keats's repudiation of marriage in the same letter as a "violent rejection" of Miss Cox. The "lady of Hastings," however, was not Charmian, but Isabella Jones; Cortázar's mistake regarding the lady's identity is understandable enough, since "the lady of Hastings" was not identified as Mrs. Jones until 1952,[21] this is, the same year Cortázar finished his book on Keats.

However, even if we were not to suspect—as we now do—that Keats's "violent rejection" of Mrs. Jones apparently ended in the poet's affair with that lady,[22] we would still find Cortázar's interpretation of Keats's tirade about women somewhat exaggerated. Here is the passage in question:

> Notwithstanding your Happiness and your recommendation I hope I shall never marry. Though the most beautiful Creature were waiting for me at the end of a Journey or a Walk; though the carpet were made of Silk, the Curtains of the morning Clouds; the chairs and Sofa stuffed with Cygnet's down; the food Manna, the Wine beyond Claret, the Window opening on Winander mere, I should not feel—or rather, my Happiness would not be so fine, a[nd] my Solitude is sublime. Then instead of what I have described, there is a Sublimity to welcome me home—The roaring of the wind is my wife and the Stars through the window pane are my Children. The mighty abstract idea I have of Beauty in all things stifles the more divided and minute domestic happiness—an amiable wife and fine—Children I contemplate as part of that Bea[u]ty—but I must have a thousand of those beautiful particles to fill up my heart. I feel more and more every day, as my imagination strengthens, that I do not live in this world alone but in a thousand worlds.... These things combined with the opinion I have of the generality of women—who appear to me as children to whom I would rather give a Sugar Plum than my time, form a barrier against Matrimony which I rejoice in.[23]

In it, most of Keats's invectives—which are mild enough—are actually directed *against the institution of marriage*, not against women themselves, as Cortázar implies. Even the final remark about women achieves an identification between them and children—it does not liken women to Gorgons or spiders, as Cortázar's interpretation seems to suggest.[24]

Neither in his comments about Keats's meeting with Miss Cox nor in the chapter about Fanny Brawne (Isabella Jones he completely disregards) does Cortázar refer to Keats's struggle to overcome his anxieties regarding women; in Cortázar's interpretation, Keats is as blasé as Baudelaire about his misogynism. Nor does he ever allude to the positive aspects of Keats's relationship with Fanny Brawne. He observes that Keats's love for Fanny was not a passion *but a destruction*; thus, he literally interprets the bereaved and terminally ill Keats's accusations to Fanny as the poet's final statement in the affair. But he totally disregards that side of Keats's love through which the poet sought a fulfillment of his whole self. Cortázar overlooks the brighter side of Keats's love for Fanny (expressed in passages from his letters such as the following: "I never knew before what such a love as you have made me feel, was; I did not believe in it; my Fancy was afraid of it, lest it should burn me up. But if you will fully love me, though there may be some fire, 'twill not be more than we can bear when moistened and bedewed with Pleasures ...").[25] Cortázar declares that Keats retreats in horror when faced with the possibility of love: "Su gusto por las mujeres que ofrecen una misma sensualidad se ve de pronto helado ante la sospecha del encarcelamiento. ¿Y el resto del mundo? ¿Y la libertad, la poesía, *el dolce far niente*, la llave de la calle?" (*IJK*, p. 302).

A greater injustice is to be found in Cortázar's portrayal of Fanny Brawne. He presents Fanny as a vampire who will attempt—even unawares—to suck the life out of a helpless, enthralled Keats. He observes that Fanny will not be motivated to destroy Keats by any particular cruelty of her own, but by her very feminine nature: *because she is a woman*. The desire to possess, absorb, and destroy the male is, for Cortázar, the very essence of the feminine nature. And so he observes:

> El cometa Brawne entraña, más que una pasión, *una destrucción*, y no es del todo casual que la primera crisis reveladora de la enfermedad de John cerrara el año inaugural de su amor, que tan amargamente lo había hecho feliz. Sin culpa de Fanny; nada que reprocharle, pobre muchacha. En todo lo que sigue deberá entenderse que no le pido peras al olmo, y que es John quien, desesperadamente, busca ser leal a sí mismo en contra de Fanny, *busca que Fanny sea otra, sea lo que una mujer no puede ser*. (*IJK*, p. 302; my italics)

Identifying with what he sees as Keats's perception of the "evil" side of women, Cortázar discusses the poet's approach to the Feminine through mythological allusions. He embarks on a consideration of what he sees as the recurrence of matriarchal archetypes in Keats's works in an attempt to understand, absorb, and incorporate his procedures. But his discussion of archetypal figures in Keats's works follows the pattern previously established in his discussion of the role of women in Keats's life: he stresses only the *negative* aspects of the matriarchal archetype manifested in Keats's works, disregarding all others. His study focuses on those mythological figures that will later reappear as the feminine protagonists of his own novels and stories.

In Cortázar's discussion of what he sees as the martriarchal archetypes presented in Keats's works, he rightly observes that the episode of Circe's bower in Book II of *Endymion* contains the seeds of both "La Belle Dame sans Merci" and *Lamia*. Likewise, in his discussion of "La Belle Dame," he expresses the opinion that this poem contains "la horrible revelación de que la dulce y llorosa doncella que el caballero encontró a la vera del camino y llevó es Circe la eterna, es la dominación y la degradación del amante bajo los filtros de la Maga" (*IJK*, p. 219). In effect, while Book II of *Endymion* had presented the bower of Venus and Adonis as the acme of sensuous love (where a perennially childlike Adonis depended on the generous Good Mother figure of Venus [axis M+ in my Schema II]), Book III does present the contrasting bower of Glaucus and Circe, where the lover is degraded under the spell of the sorceress, as Cortázar points out. Glaucus falls in love with the nymph, Scylla, who rejects him. Seized with despair, Glaucus calls Circe to his aid. She, however, offers him her own love instead, trapping him in a net of love-dreams he cannot break away from:

> Who could resist? Who in this universe?
> She did so breathe ambrosia; so immerse
> My fine existence in a golden clime.
> She took me like a child of suckling time,
> And cradled me in roses. Thus condemn'd,
> The current of my former life was stemm'd,
> And to this arbitrary queen of sense
> I bow'd a tranced vassal ...
>
> (III, ll. 453–60)

Circe acts first as a source of inspiration—in the role of anima— provoking a state of sensuous "ecstasy" in Glaucus; however, as Cortázar stated, she soon causes the reversal of this condition by. turning the ecstasy into horror when she reveals her true face, mocking Glaucus' weakness and submission to her:

> Ha! ha! Sir Dainty! there must be a nurse
> Made of rose leaves and thistledown, express
> To cradle thee my sweet, and lull thee: yes,
> I am too flinty-hard for thy nice touch:
> My tenderest squeeze is but a giant's clutch.

So, fairy-thing, it shall have lullabies
Unheard of yet: and it shall still its cries
Upon some breast more lily-feminine.

                                                          (III, ll. 570–77)

The "reversal" or sudden overturning of ecstasy into its opposite is typical of situations where the "negative" anima is involved. As Neumann observes, sensuous ecstasy, or the ecstasy derived from drugs, alcohol, and other stimulants, is initially positive, since these substances set the unconscious in motion and may lead to transformation. Their effect easily becomes reversed, however, if the ego is overcome and "lost" in the intensity of ecstasy; if the will becomes totally extinguished, the originally positive experience leads to stupor, madness, impotence, or loss of self. The episode of Circe—which so fascinated Cortázar, so sensitive to the contradictory character of the Feminine—exemplifies the danger of loss of self implied in the abandonment to orgiastic sexuality. Glaucus, unable to keep a hold on himself, regresses to the position of the child regarding the mother, to the stage of the suckling who depends on the mother for the satisfaction of his needs. The stories in *Bestiario* were written roughly at the same time as the book on Keats; there appears to be a connection, then, between Cortázar's comments about Keats's Circe and the conception of the story he wrote under the same title. Cortázar's early story "Circe" (*Bestiario*) already displays this author's fascination with the figure of the mythical enchantress. There is a basic difference, however, between Cortázar's treatment of the sorceress and Keats's; Cortázar's Circe already displays the overlapping of the characteristics of the A– and M– sides of the archetype, as previously established. Basically, the negative anima is not a deadly figure. She is not "terrible" in the same sense as the Magna Mater; even when she seeks to destroy the male's consciousness, a positive reversal is possible, for she is always subject to defeat. As Neumann observes, "when Circe, the enchantress who turns men into beasts, meets the superior figure of Odysseus, she does not kill herself like the Sphinx, whose riddle Oedipus has solved, but invites him to share her bed" (*GM*, p. 35). Keats's Circe turns Glaucus into "an animal," but does not kill him; Cortázar's Circe, on the other hand, is deadly, displaying characteristics of the Terrible Mother, as well as the negative anima.

In Delia Mañara, the mysterious girl who kills her suitors, we find a re-creation of the myth of Circe the Magician, the Lady of the Animals who absorbs the will of men, especially younger men (Delia is 22, Mario 19), and forces them into submission. Cortázar had praised Keats for his ability to re-create the *essence* of myths; his story accomplishes precisely this. Whether in ancient Greece or twentieth-century Buenos Aires, the situation is one and the same: a young boy, Mario, is enthralled by a mysterious woman who symbolically castrates him. The description of Delia—lithe and snakelike—is meant, from the very beginning, to corroborate the identification with the mythical sorceress implied in the title: Delia "era fina y rubia, demasiado lenta en sus movimientos" (*B*, p. 92); "A veces la escuchaba reirse para adentro, un poco malvadamente y sin darle esperanzas" (*B*, p. 93). Later in the story we are told that "Todos los animales se mostraban siempre sometidos a Delia, no se sabía si era cariño o dominación" (*B*, p. 94). Moreover, the reaction of Mario is in strict accordance to the myth: he breaks all ties with family and friends and becomes completely absorbed by Delia. The means she employs to ensnare and trap her victims—magical liquors and potions she stuffs into candies and feeds to her suitors—are also in harmony with the dynamics of the archetype. Medicines as well as poisons are agents of *transformation* and manifest that process in themselves (the sequence from plant to juice, juice to elixir, etc.).[26] But there is a more "terrible" aspect in Delia that is not usually characteristic of the archetypal Circe. Circe provides her victims with the positive ecstasy of sensuality before she turns them into animals. Not so Delia, who is totally destructive and absorbing. Her own last name, Mañara, is phonetically associated with "maraña" (web) and "araña" (spider), aside from being identical with that of Don Miguel de Mañara, Valle-Inclán's diabolical Marqués de Bradomín, whose female counterpart she appears to be. The deaths of the two suitors are also in agreement with the dynamics of the archetype; the first dies of a heart attack, an accident associated with the Terrible Mother's function of "fixating" and "paralyzing," and the second becomes bereaved and drowns himself, exemplifying her power to "drown" consciousness and "absorb" the personality.

Mario, however, escapes from Circe's clutches by *seeing* and *understanding* the symbolic action she performs as a prelude to her destruction of him. He sees the family cat dying in a corner of the kitchen, its eyes perforated with wooden splinters.[27] Then he presses the chocolate Delia hands him and discovers that the attractive chocolate exterior hides a filling made of cockroaches. She pierces the cat's eyes in the same way that she intends to destroy Mario's vision, that is, his consciousness. The eye, the site of consciousness, is one of the most important weapons of the hero in his battle against the Magna Mater, whose realm is that of darkness and "blind" instinct. On the other hand, the chocolate is symbolic of Delia herself; the repulsive, parasitic insect in her hides under an attractive exterior. Mario is able to escape from Delia's clutches by understanding or "seeing" her true nature. She is returned, at the end of the story, to the character of the "defeatable" negative anima.

From the above discussion, it becomes evident that there is no actual resemblance between Keats's and Cortázar's Circe, aside from the name itself and the ambiguous feelings towards women the authors displayed through them. The influence of Keats in this instance, then, must be traced to the mere conception of the feminine figure in mythological terms, but not to the actual representation. A similar situation is presented in "El ídolo de las Cícladas" and "Las ménades," both inspired by the sacrifices in honor of the ancient Mother Goddesses. I do not know whether Cortázar's interest in sacrifices originated in connection with his study of Keats or if it anteceded it; his own statement in *IJK* suggests that there was a simultaneous interest in both and that he somehow made a connection between the two, with or without grounds. In his commentary on the ode "On a Grecian Urn" (a reworking of his 1946 article "La urna griega en la poesía de Keats"), Cortázar exhibits—perhaps more blatantly than in any other section of his book—a tendency to attribute to Keats his own reactions to certain themes. He interprets the scene portrayed on the Grecian urn as a scene of *sacrifice*, with maenads dancing around the victim; he states that Keats's susceptibility to themes connected with matriarchal rites had made him conceive of such a scene. What this comment actually reveals is *Cortázar*'s propensity to perceive the Feminine under the guise of Terrible Mother. The author's interest in ritual at the time when he wrote the book on Keats is responsible for the conception of "El ídolo de las Cícladas" and "Las ménades."

In "El ídolo de las Cícladas," Cortázar's choice of the Cycladic islands for the setting of the story is not accidental; Asia Minor is the site where the worship of a Terrible Goddess first arose. Neumann observes that these pre-Mycenean idols—dating back to 3000 B.C.—show a tendency towards abstraction that is not present in other primordial fertility goddesses and indicate "a bond between the numinous-imaginative and the realm of the spirits and the dead ..." (*GM*, p. 113). While the Great Mother in her aspect of fertility goddess tends to be characterized by a naturalistic, "sensuous" form, "her aspect as ruler over the spirits and the dead favors forms stressing the unnatural unreal, and 'spiritual'" (*GM*, p. 108). The sensuous manifestations of the goddess, predominant in Keats's works, denote an extroverted attitude, while her abstract manifestations, present in Poe's and Cortázar's, denote these writers' introverted attitudes and their tendency to identify woman with death.

Somoza, introverted and obsessive, sublimates his desire for Thérèse (his friend's wife and, as such, "taboo") by translating it into the desire to enter the world of the goddess Haghesa, whose statuette he has unearthed. But this goddess is the ruler of the dead; her rituals demand that he become her high priest, the one who will carry out the ritual sacrifices in her honor. Somoza, in his obsession, succumbs to the onrush of "ancestral memories," and gradually abandons his modern identity as he passes into Haghesa's own time. The ancient religions of Asia Minor were never fully suppressed; in the ensuing syncretism, primitive rituals were preserved. Even though Byzantium, the City of the Goddess, became Constantinople, the City of the Virgin, Byzantine priests preserved a terrible, more ancient ritual: the priest's castration in, honor of the goddess.[28] Somoza's unconscious "possession" by the spirit of the goddess has, thus, an even darker connotation. Finally, Somoza is transported to a "sacred time" and, having totally surrendered his twentieth-century self, prepares to carry out Morand's sacrifice. The latter, however, kills Somoza in self-defense, accomplishing thus the ritual to Haghesa. "Possessed," in his turn, through his active, though unpremeditated participation in the ritual, he assumes the role of sacrificial priest and lies in ambush, awaiting the arrival of his next victim: Thérèse.

"Las ménades" recreates, in a contemporary atmosphere, the ritual killing and dismemberment of the god in the primitive matriarchal rites. As Neumann states; "Death and dismemberment or castration are the fate of the phallus bearing, youthful god ... both are associated with bloody orgies in the cult of the Great Mother."[29] In this story, the "seasonal King" is the director of the orchestra, the "maenads" his public, who gather in the concert hall in the midst of an atmosphere of increasing heat and excitement. The tension builds up in a masterful *crescendo* that succeeds in involving the reader in the "ritual." At a certain point, a woman in red advances towards the stage, as if in a trance, marking the beginning of the orgy. At the end of the story, a frenzied public destroys the theater and overwhelms the conductor and the members of the orchestra. Finally, the woman in red emerges licking her lips. The motif of the enraged maenads recurs—briefly but effective—in Cortázar's last novel, *Libro de Manuel*. In it, Oscar—a younger mirror-image of the protagonist, Andrés Fava—suffers from a recurring, obsessive vision: that of the "moonstruck" girls who escape the confinement of a hospital and form what appears to be a society of enraged maenads. Although the apparent intention of this episode is to condemn society's "confining" aspect, likening it to the hospital, the vision seems to have a deeper meaning. Indeed, the whole episode has that indefinable character that marks the situations derived from the author's "archetypal" nightmares and obsessions. When described at first, the episode appears as a frightening vision: the girls escape from the hospital, gather under the moon, run half-naked and half-maddened. Oscar experiences a vague feeling of fright as he remembers his nightmare, which curiously recurs whenever he meets Gladis, with whom he is carrying on a superficial affair. If the dream simply denounces society's confining aspect, why should Oscar, one of the revolutionaries, be disturbed by the girls' flight from that confinement? Evidently, the moonstruck, nearly hysterical girls have more than a merely social symbolism. Their portrayal likens them to the legendary maenads, driven to frenzy and in pursuit of a sacrificial victim. Oscar, unconsciously afraid of Gladis, seems to fear he might be the object of the maenads' pursuit.

A more concrete evidence of Keats's influence is to be found in connection with "La Belle Dame sans Merci" and *Lamia*. The genesis of "La Belle Dame" is enveloped with an aura of mystery that must have presented a special attraction for Cortázar. Keats seems to have conceived the poem in a hypnotic mood, half asleep. The poem was written at an important point in Keats's life; his brother Tom had died shortly before, and he had recently met Fanny Brawne, who was destined to play a crucial role in Keats's life. Several sources for the poem have been pointed out; Gittings sees Burton's *Anatomy of Melancholy*—which Keats read extensively at this time—behind the portrayal of the solitary, melancholy dreamer in the poem.[30] Coleridge's "Christabel"— conceived in a similar mood—presents an analogous mysterious atmosphere where legend blends with nightmare. Moreover, the story of Tom Keats's own infatuation with the fictitious "Amena" of the love letters seems to have been in the back of Keats's mind. Keats—who had received the packet of "Amena's" letters shortly before—was convinced that this painful episode had contributed to accelerate his brother's death. But behind all these influences, there remains an unexplained element that can only be related to the archetypal roots of the story. As Robert Gittings adequately observes, none of these influences can account for "the intensity and underlying depth of a poem which brought Keats's darkest and most fundamental experiences to the surface."[31]

"La Belle Dame" presents that significant blend of characteristics from the A– and M– characters of the archetype in the previously discussed Schema II. The image we encounter at the beginning of the poem is that of the forsaken, lonely youth already smitten with a deadly "disease":

> I see a lilly on thy brow,
> With anguish moist and fever dew;
> And on thy cheeks a fading rose
> Fast withereth too.
>
> (ll. 9–12)

The cause of the disease is linked to the mysterious lady the knight has met in the meads. Her description is hallowed with the supernatural aura distinctive of all manifestations of the archetype of the Magna Mater. The lady is

> Full beautiful—a faery's child,
> Her hair was long, her foot was light,
> And her eyes were wild.
>
> (ll. 14–16)

She completely absorbs his senses ("And nothing else [the knight] saw all day long," l. 22), and keeps him in subjection by means of magical foods and drinks (ll. 25–26). By closing her eyes with "kisses four," the knight is not merely displaying a common manifestation of love, but he is performing a symbolic action whereby he "shuts her eyes" as well as his own to the reality beyond the "elfin grot." Likewise, the line "she lulled me asleep" (l. 33) possesses the connotation of a spiritual, as well as a physical, slumber and foreshadows the sleep of death that haunts the knight as we encounter him at the beginning of the poem. In the dream, the knight sees

> ... pale kings and princes too,
> Pale warriors, death-pale were they all;
> They cried—"La Belle Dame sans Merci
> Hath thee in thrall!"
>
> (ll. 37–40)

The vision of the Belle Dame's victims, appearing to him "with horrid warning" (l. 42), makes the knight realize the horror of his condition: he is asleep, blind, and under the subjection of a sorceress who will drain the life away from his body. At that very moment both lady and grot disappear, and the knight finds himself "palely loitering," forsaken and alone, as the poem returns to the setting of the opening stanzas.

As I previously observed, the Belle Dame possesses a deadly character that, transcending the qualities of the negative anima, could identify her with the archetypal Terrible Mother, whose function it is to extinguish consciousness and take back to herself, through death, that which had attempted to break away from her domination. In this poem, Cortázar saw an externalization of his own feelings towards women. We can hear echoes of this poem in several of his later creations. A noticeable parallel is to be found between "La Belle Dame" and Cortázar's story "Cuello de gatito negro," published in *Octaedro*.

Cortázar's story blends in itself characteristics from both Keats's "La Belle Dame" and the episode of Diana and Actaeon from Ovid's *Metamorphoses*. Lucho, whose name is reminiscent of Lycius, the hero in *Lamia*, finds the weeping Dina, apparently by chance, in one of his journeys in the Paris metro. The solitary mead of "La Belle Dame," the forest of *Lamia*, and the grove of Ovid's story have their modern counterpart in a tunnel of the Paris metro; though less poetic, the metro retains the characteristic aspect of "isolation" of the other settings, since it is "underground" and dark. Moreover, the train is usually associated, in Cortázar's works (let us remember the tramways in the nightmares of *62*), with the laws of chance ruling every decisive or numinous encounter. Juan, fascinated by Dina, and particularly by Dina's hands, follows her to her apartment—the modern counterpart of the "elfin grot." There, they taste the pleasures of sensuality. But soon afterwards, Dina shows her "terrible" aspect: her hands, acquiring a life of their own, pull at his penis and attempt to scratch his eyes out. At the end of the story, he stands alone in the hallway, cold, naked, pale, and confused, like the youth in Keats's poem. Cortázar's story emphasizes, much more than Keats's poem, the "terrible" aspect of the enchantress. Keats's poem merely hints at the death the knight is to suffer by presenting the Belle Dame's victims in the knight's dream; but she is never portrayed explicitly in her "terrible" manifestation. Cortázar's story, on the other hand, presents the total reversal of the shy, weeping Dina into the fierce, bloodthirsty Black Artemis. Dina's name is very similar to the name Diana; Diana's "dark" manifestation appears in Ovid's story, where the goddess, avenging herself for Actaeon's entrance into her sacred grove and his looking at her naked body, turns him into an animal and has him torn to pieces by his own mastiffs. The Terrible Diana was represented as a Black Goddess; Dina, a native of Martinique, is dark-skinned. Moreover, as in Ovid's story, Lucho looks at Dina without "seeing" her, just as Actaeon had looked at Diana's body without recognizing her divine nature. Lucho's "blindness" is symbolically alluded to in the reference to the lamp Dina unsuccessfully attempts to light, being impeded by Lucho's repeated amatory demands. Finally, Lucho breaks the lamp as she reaches for it. In the ensuing darkness, Dina turns into an aggressive maenad, attempting to blind and castrate Lucho.

The presence of Lamia can be detected behind Cortázar's best-known novels, *Rayuela* and *62*. The ambiguousness implied in the character of the Belle Dame, who represents both Love and Death, is more explicit in the character of the lamia. It has been rightly observed that the symbol of the lamia is especially attractive to Keats, since it permits him to embody the

mingled attraction and repulsion characteristic of his treatment of woman as
a love object.[32] Indeed, Lamia represents both the ideal goddess and the
dream lover that Lycius, a dreamer, had longed for. But in Lamia Keats
employs an ironic tone that was absent from "La Belle Dame." If in the latter
Keats had presented the knight's doom objectively, without attempting to
blame it on the weaknesses in the knight's character, in Lamia he seems to
adopt a critical position regarding his protagonist's attitude and, indeed,
regarding his former poetic self. Lamia belongs to a period in Keats's
development when he was trying to develop an "Apollonian" outlook to
counteract his basically "Dionysiac" nature. In *The Fall of Hyperion: A
Dream*—which also belongs to this period—he had established a
differentiation between the poet (the one who accepts his link to a specific
human group and tries to alleviate their sufferings through his art) and the
dreamer (the selfish visionary who rejects the world for the sake of his ideal
visions). By presenting Lycius as a "dreamer" and making him die at the end
of the poem, he seems to be trying to "exorcize" Lycius' attitude in himself.[33]
Keats is very much in control of this aspect of the poem's symbolism, even if
his conception of the lamia undergoes a radical metamorphosis in the course
of the poem; every element in it contributes to prepare the reader for the
final outcome.

In the initial section of the poem, Lamia is presented as the beautiful,
cruel seductress who ensnares the unwary dreamer by means of her magical
crafts; yet, there is also a mockery, on Keats's part, of the naiveté with which
Lycius succumbs to her traps. Lycius had gone to the temple of Cenchreae
to offer a sacrifice to Jove and meets Lamia on his way back from it;
apparently, he seems to have asked Jove for a happy marriage, for we read
that "Jove heard his vows and better'd his desire" (I, l. 229). Lycius, a scholar,
is so concerned with his ideal visions that he even misses the concretion of
his own desires when he passes her on the road. He had been wearied with
his companions' talk and walked alone, abandoning himself to his fantasies
without any interruption from the outside world:

> Over the solitary hills he fared,
> Thoughtless at first, but ere eve's star appeared
> His phantasy was lost, where reason fades,
> In the calm'd twilight of Platonic shades,
> Lamia beheld him coming, near, more near—
> Close to her passing, in indifference drear,
> His silent sandals swept the mossy green;
> So neighbour'd to him and yet so unseen

> She stood: he pass'd, shut up in mysteries,
> His mind wrapp'd like his mantle ...
>
> (I,ll. 233–42)

Even though Lycius is a scholar, his fantasy prevails over his reason; Lycius' reason "fades" as he is lost in nocturnal fantasies or "Platonic shades." Keats emphasizes Lycius' "blindness" when confronting the objectification of the ideal vision he longed for: Lamia stands "so neighbour'd to him, and yet so unseen"; his mind, "wrapp'd like his mantle," is so totally turned inwards that he fails to notice the presence of that "nymph" for whom he apparently longed. However, when he finally notices Lamia, he does not doubt for a second that she is a goddess sent in answer to his desires. He accepts her as such without further questioning, looking at her, "not with cold wonder fearingly / But Orpheus-like at an Eurydice" (I, ll. 247–48). The mention of Orpheus has ironic overtones, for Orpheus loses his beloved when he "looks" at her, just as Lycius will lose Lamia towards the end of the poem. Keats's ironic treatment of Lycius is sustained throughout the first part of the poem; Lycius soon forgets the goddess for the sake of the woman:

> ... gentle Lamia judg'd, and judg'd aright
> That Lycius could not love in half a fright,
> So threw the goddess off, and won his heart
> More pleasantly by playing woman's part.
>
> (I, ll. 334–37)

Absorbed in his passion for the being whom he sees as the concretion of his ideals, he appears as a ludicrous, gullible figure: "Lycius to all made eloquent reply / Marrying to every word a twinborn sigh" (I, l. 340–41). He is not even aware that Lamia has shortened the way to Corinth from three leagues to a few paces; her trick is "not at all surmised / By blinded Lycius, so in her comprized" (I, ll. 346–47).

Even though Keats portrays Lamia as a snake *travesti*, an evil creature responsible for his hero's destruction, she is not presented as a totally repulsive character. Although her cruelty is evinced by the calm premeditation with which she makes Lycius swoon by threatening him with the withdrawal of her affections (I, ll. 286–95), her love for Lycius, later in the poem, makes her surrender her supernatural powers and please Lycius by her charms as woman only. Unlike the Belle Dame, who rends her lovers and then forsakes them, Lamia submits to Lycius and remains beside him. The tragic outcome of the poem is indirectly blamed on Lycius.

Like the ecstasy Circe provided, the pleasure Lamia offers Lycius is one-sided; it is a happiness that excludes every thought of reality. Lamia had the ability "to unperplex bliss from its neighbor pain" (I, l. 192). She, a supernatural being, is capable of enjoying an undisturbed kind of happiness isolated from worldly cares; he, a human, must feel "the strife of opposites." Lycius soon tires of Lamia's unworldly bliss and longs to return to the world, for

> Love in a palace is perhaps at last
> More grievous torment than a hermit's fast:—
>
> (II, ll. 3–4)

As Lycius listens to the sounds of trumpets outside the palace, he is reminded of "the noisy world almost forsworn" (II, l. 33) and attempts to convince Lamia to leave the palace and announce their love to the rest of the world. As Lamia, grown weak and frightened at the thought of losing Lycius, pleads with him, trying to change his mind, his behavior towards her takes a sadistic turn. The initial relationship is now reversed:

> ... she nothing said, but pale and meek,
> Arose and knelt before him, wept a rain
> Of sorrows at his words; at last with pain
> Beseeching him, the while his hand she wrung,
> To change his purpose. He thereat was stung,
> Perverse, with stronger fancy to reclaim
> Her wild and timid nature to his aim:
> Besides, for all his love, in self despite,
> Against his better self, he took delight
> Luxurious in her sorrows, soft and new.
> His passion, cruel grown, took on a hue
> Fierce and sanguineous as 'twas possible
> In one whose brow had no dark veins to swell.
>
> (II, ll. 65–77)

Cortázar's comments on the above lines are very revealing; he observes that Lycius' attitude towards Lamia, in Part II of the poem, constitutes "un comportamiento de la más alta importancia" (*IJK*, p. 277). He terms this behavior "sadismo poético," stating that it constitutes a method whose aim it is to attain the ontological possession of its object (*IJK*, p. 277). According to Cortázar, the poet possesses reality by means of analogies, through metaphors that link unfamiliar objects with the familiar ones they resemble. Only contraries, those objects that possess no analogy to one another, escape the poet's tendency to embrace them in one central metaphor and must be apprehended separately. According to Cortázar, Keats felt anguished and even angered at his inability to conciliate opposites in his heart and in his mind, and he cites the "Epistle to Reynolds" as an exemplification of those feelings, adding: "Que el día no sea también la noche lo aterra y lo encoleriza; que cada cosa aprehendida presuponga su contrario remoto e inalcanzable lo humilla" (*IJK*, p. 277). Keats's answer to this schism, he continues, is expressed in a gesture that embraces opposites in a higher form of oneness. If there is no real analogy between two objects or feelings, the poet invents it; thus, Keats conceives of the expression "pleasant pain" as he solves the mystery of polarization by his *acceptance of opposites* (*IJK*, p. 277).

Most of Keats's critics would agree with Cortázar's interpretation of the expression "pleasant pain" and with his appreciation of Keats's sensitivity to polarizations.[34] His use of the term "method of poetic sadism," however, is questionable. Cortázar implies that Keats deliberately introduced the element of sadism in the poem in order to embrace, in a broader concept, the contradictory emotions love arouses. However, the very conception of a "*method* for an ontological possession of reality" (Cortázar's terminology) is alien to Keats's nature. The use of a "method" implies the preconception of a system of abstractions that is then applied to a concrete situation. It presupposes a certain distance and controlled coldness on the subject's part regarding the object of his attention. Yet abstract thinking, in the ordinary sense, was alien to Keats; as Murry observes, "the movement of his thought was richly imaged, and amazingly concrete—'sensations rather than thoughts.'"[35] I do not believe Keats's attitude in *Lamia* evinces the cool, controlled distance the use of a preconceived method would betray. The poem's ambiguousness regarding the lamia and Lycius undermines the theory that Keats was working according to a "method of poetic sadism."

The concept of "poetic sadism," in its assumption of a preconceived method, actually applies to Poe's stories better than to *Lamia*. In any case, Cortázar's reading of *Lamia* gives us an important clue for the interpretation of certain episodes in *Rayuela*, where a "method of poetic sadism" seems to be, indeed, at work.

Lamia ends with the death of Lycius as the lamia fades away under the gaze of the philosopher Apollonius. Keats had meant, apparently, to exorcize his former fascination with "ideal beauty" of an unreal kind and condemn his former pursuit of the idyllic bower. Yet he is unable to make his hero return to the claims of "reality"; Lycius dies once the lamia disappears. One might say that she appears as the archetypal Terrible Mother, who ensnares her victims to such a degree that they cannot survive the withdrawal of her affection.

The first part of *Rayuela* presents a number of parallels with both "La Belle Dame" and *Lamia*. According to Professor Barrenechea—who possesses the working notebooks for *Rayuela*—one of the first chapters originally conceived in this novel was the one that later became Chapter 123 in Part III. In it Oliveira returns to a scene of his childhood; there, he sees his sister, the garden, the house of his childhood days. Upon awakening, he is invaded by the feeling that the dream had a far greater "reality" than anything else he had later experienced; the reality of the room in Paris and la Maga's company appeared to be, indeed, the dream. From the beginning, then, Cortázar sees the character of la Maga as "unreal," illusory, the figment of imagination, or of a dream—like the lamia or the Belle Dame. Moreover, Oliveira, like Lycius and the knight, is more of a dreamer than a poet, and as such, one who "venoms all his days" and "vexes the world," rather than one who "pours a balm" on it. Like Lycius, Horacio is seen, at the beginning of the novel (if we choose the "hopscotch" way of reading and begin with Chapter 73) lost in his mental speculations. Like the knight (if we choose the "normal" way of reading and begin with Chapter 1), he wanders about, "palely loitering," searching for the ideal woman, the enchantress who has captivated his senses and then abandoned him. Just as Lycius's search for "ideal forms" finds a concrete expression in his obsession with the supernatural Lamia, so Oliveira's metaphysical longings find a concrete expression in his desire to enter la Maga's world. The Belle Dame is presented as "a faery's child"; the transformation of the lamia into the woman and the duality of her nature are presented at the very beginning of Keats's poems. La Maga is presented as a concrete woman with a good share of all-too-human stupidity; yet, the author clothes her with a supernatural aura that is many times stressed throughout the novel.

From the beginning, la Maga is presented as an elusive, mysterious female who, as "anima," entices the hero to adventure. Her description is unmistakably "unreal": we read about "su delgada cintura" and "su fina cara de transhicida piel" (*R*, p. 15). Moreover, her very name is deliberately symbolic: la Maga's name is Lucia, that is, "she who has the light"; Oliveira gives her the epithet that identifies her both with Circe and with the symbolic figure in the second mystery of the Tarot. "La Maga"—or the Archpriestess—is Isis, goddess of the night: "She is seated, holding a half-opened book in her right hand and two keys in her left, one of which is golden (signifying the sun, the work, or reason) and the other silver (the moon or imagination).... She is leaning against the sphinx of the great cosmic questions, and the floor, being composed of alternate white and black tiles, denotes that everything in existence is subject to the laws of chance and of opposites."[36] Isis, as Archpriestess and Moon Goddess, has been traditionally associated with the esoteric rites of initiation, from Apuleius' *The Golden Ass* to Godfrey Higgins' *Anacalypsis*. In Jungian theory, Isis, a representative of the Magna Mater, is identical with Ishtar of Babylonia, Astarte of Phoenicia, Kali-Durga and Anna-Purna of India, Demeter in Greece, and Themis in Asia Minor. But, most importantly, Isis is the figure that best exemplifies the triple aspect of the Magna Mater as inspiration, Good-Bad Mother, and Terrible Mother.

La Maga is also alluded to with another of the Magna Mater's names, that of the Great Whore of Babylonia: "nos fuimos a tomar una cops de *pelure d'oignon* a un café de Sèvres-Babylone (hablando de metáforas, yo delicada porcelana recién desembarcada, HANDLE WITH CARE, y ella Babilonia, raíz de tiempo, cosa anterior, *primeval being*, terror y delicia de los comienzos, romanticismo de Atalá pero con un tigre auténtico esperando detrás del árbol)" (*R*, p. 486). The presence of the baby Rocamadour, named after the French Virgin of Rocamadour, further implies an identification of la Maga with the archetypal Virgin Mother, another aspect of the Magna Mater. As Dr. Esther Harding remarks, the word "Virgin," that gives name to one of the twelve constellations of the Zodiac, did not have, for the ancients, the value it has today; it alluded to a psychological, rather than to a physical, condition. A physical virgin was called a "Virgo intacta," while the word "Virgo" itself was specifically used to designate a woman who "possessed herself" and did not cling to any particular man or demand that his relationship to her be permanent. Such a woman could be a "Virgo" whether or not she was a mother and whether her behavior was exemplary or licentious.[37]

In any case, la Maga—in spite of the numerous rapes she is subjected to—retains an oddly ascetic aura about her. The love scenes between her and Oliveira are actually rape scenes; it is in the scenes with Pola that we find more balanced erotic encounters. Pola, though far more "concrete" than la Maga, is also identified with one of the symbolic attributes of the Magna Mater: the City. As Pola-Paris she appears as the Earth, or the provider of sensuous pleasure, while la Maga-Isis appears primarily as the subject of inspiration. La Maga, as agent of transformation, performs the role of "anima"[38] through the first eight chapters in the novel. Yet even though la Maga first appears as anima, Oliveira does not succumb totally to her attraction. In fact, he appears like a forewarned Lycius, a Lycius who has read

"La Belle Dame sans Merci" and *Lamia*. While Keats's heroes lose themselves in the intensity of their passions, Oliveira remains coolly detached and suspicious. On the other hand, in spite of the initial bliss he seems to experience with la Maga, he can never abandon himself, completely to the full intensity of passion ("éramos como dos músicos," etc.), apparently from fear of being completely absorbed and lost in the world of la Maga. Like Lycius, Horacio feels he must go on to something else; unlike Lamia, la Maga offers no resistance to his desire to live his own life and engage in concerns other than herself. In fact, Oliveira is seldom presented in la Maga's company, except in the erotic scenes. Most often he is with the members of the Club, with or without la Maga, or with his other mistress, Pola, with whom he has an affair with the knowledge and apparent consent of la Maga. As Oliveira feels the call of the outside world, from which he fears la Maga will separate him, he resorts to a sadistic behavior against her, just as Lycius had regarding Lamia. Yet their perverseness is, essentially, of a different nature. In Keats's poem, perverseness appears as an amplification of the concept of love that includes suffering as well as joy; it explores a new aspect of Lycius' relationship to Lamia (Lycius takes delight in her sorrows, "soft and *new*"). Oliveira's cruelty towards la Maga, on the other hand, seems to respond, indeed, to what Cortázar termed a "method of poetic sadism" in his discussion of *Lamia*. Oliveira's cruelty is cold, even premeditated and objective. Its chief object seems to be *Oliveira's self-defense*, and the preservation of his identity in the face of the mounting threat posed by la Maga. As in Poe's stories ("Berenice," "The Fall of the House of Usher," "The Oval Portrait," "The Black Cat"), the hero paradoxically expresses his love through the destruction of its object, thus freeing himself from the manic states and the anxiety neuroses provoked by the object of his love. Just as Egaeus' love for Berenice increases as the heroine sickens and is on the verge of death, and just as Roderick Usher's love for his sister Madeline finds its extreme expression in the entombment of his live sister in a crypt while she is under the effects of a cataleptic seizure, Oliveira's love increases with la Maga's sorrows, and his highest expression of love is manifested in his desertion of la Maga after the death of her child. If we attribute what Cortázar calls a "method of poetic sadism" to Cortázar's own works, the reason for Oliveira's behavior becomes clear. According to this declaration, the author wishes to burst through the usual demarcations and definitions of "love" and "hatred" by presenting a situation that encompasses both. Such had been the effect attained by Keats in *Lamia*. But in *Rayuela* the author's overt intention seems too noticeable, and moreover, we seem to detect a more subtle and unconscious force below the surface. That "hidden force" seems to be the hero's desire to protect himself from the devastating effect of passion: the dissolution of the self. The dread of the "devouring" female is, as we have seen, an important theme in Cortázar's works from the very beginning, and it had played a central role in his two preceding novels, *El examen* and *Los premios*. *Rayuela* is the work where it is first openly confronted and portrayed; the author has brought himself to a point where he attempts to dissect the relationship between his hero and heroine, yet fears to carry the "operation" to its utmost conclusions.

If in *Lamia* and "La Belle Dame" the sorceress abandons the hero, here it is Oliveira who first leaves la Maga on the night of the baby Rocamadour's death; when she later leaves the apartment, it is because he has indirectly ordered her to do so. Yet, as soon as she leaves, Oliveira literally falls apart, expressing his longing for her. If the knight in "La Belle Dame" has the mark of death on his brow and cheeks after the sorceress deserts him and Lycius collapses dead on the point of Lamia's disappearance, Oliveira becomes progressively weakened throughout the second part of the novel, but the final outcome is the same as in Keats's poems. Even though Oliveira originally intended to desert la Maga in order to preserve his freedom and pursue his literary ambitions, after she leaves he betrays that very freedom by setting up housekeeping with the foolish Gekrepten and nearly abandons all literary concerns, absorbed by the haunting memory of la Maga. Once his defense system is thoroughly broken (after the episode in the morgue, where he "accepts" la Maga in Talita's person), he faces three possible destinies: madness, suicide, or symbolic castration through his subjection to the motherly Gekrepten. Various critics and the author himself have claimed that the novel has an "open ending" and that Oliveira's future has endless possibilities. I believe, however, that we must limit ourselves to what is expressed in the text itself. And the text offers only these three possibilities, all of which imply a dissolution of the self, an overturning of the mind that is the archetypal outcome of an encounter with the Terrible Mother, as has been exemplified in our analysis of both of Keats's poems.

Even though the "terrible" side of la Maga is merely hinted at in the episode involving her spell on Pola, her nature is known through the effect she provokes on Horacio; the novel, thus, presents an ideal case of negative anima projection, since the heroine is not objectively presented as a wicked sorceress but is mostly known to us through the effects she has wrought on Oliveira. There is, however, another indirect allusion to la Maga's "terrible" aspect in the second part of the novel: the references to "el perro." The references to "the dog" first appear towards the end of the novel, soon before Oliveira's encounter with the ghost of la Maga in the asylum's morgue. As the asylum is transferred to a new owner—the former director of the circus—the patients are asked to sign the deed signifying their consent in order to legalize the transaction. The patients, however, demand the death of a dog as a necessary condition before they grant approval. No further explanations are given; "the dog" remains a cryptic allusion that gains an ominous aura as it is reiterated. Dogs are a symbol of the Terrible Mother and are associated with the "tearing to pieces" symbolic of madness and dissolution of the self through the fragmentation of the personality. Diana's dogs tear Actaeon to pieces in revenge for his having looked at her without seeing her. Dogs are also the companions of Hecate, identified with Artemis in Greek syncretism and, in fact, Artemis' "dark" aspect. "El perro" can be interpreted, then, as an objectification of Oliveira's dread of la Maga's return, and of the fragmentation of his consciousness through the shock occasioned by that return. This is, actually, what happens at the end of the novel; and the references to "the dog" act, then, as a premonition. The symbol of the dog reappears in Cortázar's next novel, *62: Modelo para armar*, where the archetype of the Terrible Mother is further elaborated.

The character of Hélène holds a greater direct affinity with the lamia and the Belle Dame. Firstly, both heroines are associated with the mythical figure of the vampire and with Hecate, the "dark" Moon Goddess, ruler of the underworld, witchcraft, madness, and death. That Lamia and Hélène both represent the "spook" Moon Goddess Hecate—traditionally associated with witches, phantoms, and vampire. (cf. Schema 11 above)—can be confirmed by recalling Hecate's traditional attributes: "As an incubus or vampire she [Hecate] appears in the form of Empusa, or as a man-eating lamia, or again in that more beautiful guise, the 'Bride of Corinth.'"[39] Lamia is, concretely, the "Bride of Corinth," whose story, derived from Philostratus' *Life of Apollonius of Tyana*, Keats found in Burton's *Anatomy of Melancholy*; Hélène, who lives in the rue de la Clef, possesses "the key," one of Hecate's traditional attributes, together with the torch and the dog.[40] Both are, thus, identified as vampiresses, as man-eating lamiae.

Cortázar confirms the identification of Hélène with the "terrible" side of the Moon Goddess further in the novel. Juan, who had called Hélène "a basilisk" (a variation of the vampire), also identifies her with Diana. On the night of their encounter, Juan tells Hélène: "Siempre me tuviste rencor, siempre te vengaste de alguna manera. ¿Quieres saber cómo me llamó un día mi paredro? Acteón" (*62*, p. 235). Later, she tells him:

> Vaya a saber si Diana no se entregó a Acteón, pero lo que cuenta
> es que *después le echó los perros* y probablemente gozó viendo como

lo destrozaban. No soy Diana *pero siento que en alguna parte de mí hay perros que esperan*, y no hubiera querido que te hicieran pedazos. (*62*, p. 238; my italics)

If the relationship between "el perro" and the Terrible Mother aspect in la Maga had been merely suggested in *Rayuela*, it becomes explicit—as the preceding quotation demonstrates—in the case of Hélène. Like la Maga in the second part of *Rayuela*, Hélène seems to be motivated by a vague desire for *revenge*.

Like Lycius, Juan is manipulated by forces he can neither understand nor control. He tries to find sensuous oblivion through his relationship with Tell and attempts to "blur his vision" through constant drinking (we never see Juan without a drink in his hands—Campari, whiskey, slivovitz, Médoc, Sylvaner ...). Juan is in love with a symbol: the petrified and petrifying beauty of the Medusa, Empusa Hélène, the evasive anesthetist of the rue de la Clef. Juan's monologues stress Hélène's unreal nature from the very beginning; he says: "¿Estabas en la zona o te soñé? ... Pero tú, Hélène, ¿habrás sido una vez más un nombre que levanto contra la nada, el simulacro que me invento con palabras ...?" (*62*, p. 21). Later, we realize that, unlike Lycius, Juan does not want Hélène "to throw the goddess off"; in fact, he loves her *as goddess*, precisely because of her evasiveness and coldness: "Hélène Arp, Hélène Brancusi, ... fría astuta indiferente crueldad cortés de infanta entre suplicantes y enanos ... (La sombra de Hélène es más densa que las otras y más fría; quien posa el pie en sus sargazos siente subir el veneno que lo hará vivir para siempre en el único delirio necesario) ..." (*62*, pp. 76–77). Even though he suspects Hélène's true nature, Juan *does not want to face it*; at the end of the novel we read: "... te quería demasiado para aceptar esa alucinación en la que ni siquiera estabas presente ... llegué al borde y preferí no saber, consentí en no saber aunque hubiera podido ..." (*62*, p. 262).

Like Lycius, Juan becomes obsessed with his vampiress, almost disregarding the rest of the world. Both heroes, however, really succumb to the destructiveness of *their own* passions, rather than to an innate perfidy on the part of the beloved. Just as Lamia, the "cruel lady" of the opening scenes, becomes tame and submissive as the poem progresses, and she seems to have become truly human through her love for Lycius, so Hélène displays at least a desire to become "human" on the night of her encounter with Juan: she obsessively wipes her face as if trying to remove a mask (*62*, p. 237), and she asks Juan to change her, if he can (*62*, p. 238). Neither Keats nor Cortázar succeeds in presenting the heroine as a truly repulsive creature (in spite of the explicit identification of the heroine with the snake and the vampire, respectively) because each author seems to place a great part of the blame on the hero himself; he does not love the woman but the dream, and by rejecting the real for the sake of the ideal vision, he succumbs under the weight of the reality he was unwilling to face, once the object of his fantasy disappears. Lycius asks the gods for a dream woman; once his wish is granted, he wants to impose his dream on the diurnal world and is destroyed by his folly. Juan, likewise, want; to love his own Hélène, and thus provokes her wrath when he unwittingly refuses to see her "unmasked" face (*62*, p. 262).

As is always the case when the hero "turns away" from an archetype arising from his disconcerted psyche, the refusal of the archetype's summons turns the adventure into a negative one. Rather than being saved, the hero becomes doomed; all he can do is await the process of his disintegration. The hero refuses to give up his present dreams and ideals, for he sees the future not as a process of growth, but as an indefinite prolongation of his present state; hence, he becomes imprisoned in his infantile ego, unable to make the passage from his inner world to the world outside. His former "dream vision" becomes a monster that will constantly haunt him; his very house, a house of death.

NOTES

1. *IJK*, pp. 266–70.
2. Walter Evert, *Aesthetic and Myth in the Poetry of Keats* (Princeton: Princeton University Press, 1965), p. 91.
3. Evert, p. 91.
4. Robert Graves, *The White Goddess* (New York: Macmillan, 1972), pp. 427–33.
5. Aileen Ward, *John Keats: The Making of a Poet* (New York: Compass-Viking, 1967), pp. 312–13; Robert Gittings, *John Keats* (Boston: Atlantic-Little, Brown, 1968), pp. 358–61.
6. Allen Tate, "A Reading of Keats," *The American Scholar*, 15 (Winter–Spring 1945–46), 62.
7. Rollins, I, 341.
8. Rollins, I, 392.
9. In *Keats and Shakespeare* (London: Oxford University Press, 1926), John Middleton Murry had stated that "Fanny Brawne killed Keats," although he later recanted his idea in *The Mystery of Keats* (see Bibliography). Both works were included in Cortázar's bibliography for *IJK*; but he seems to have stuck to Murry's earlier belief.
10. Rollins, I, 391–92, 394–96; "As a Man in the world I love the rich talk of a Charmian; as an eternal being I love the thought of you [Georgiana Keats]. I should like her to ruin me, and I should like you to save me..." (p. 396).
11. Rollins, II, 223–24. The letter of 19 October 1819 expresses a similar feeling: "I must impose chains upon myself—I shall be able to do nothing—I shold [sic] like to cast the die for love or death—I have no Patience with anything else—if you ever intend to be

cruel to me as you say in jest now but perhaps may sometimes be in earnest be so now—and I will—my mind is in a tremble, I cannot tell what I am writing" (p. 224).

12. Rollins, II, 133.

13. Luis Harss and Barbara Dohmann, *Into the Mainstream* (New York: Harper & Row, 1967), pp. 214–15.

14. Letter received from Julio Cortázar, 19 July 1974.

15. Hernández, "Camaleonismo y vampirismo."

16. Emma Jung and Marie Louise von Franz, *The Grail Legend*, trans. Andrea Dykes (New York: G.P. Putnam's Sons for the C.G. Jung Foundation for Analytical Psychology, 1970), pp. 40,43–44.

17. See, for instance, Cortázar's own account of the critics' reaction to *IJK* (*VDOM*, p. 209). As for Keats, the negative reception of *Endymion* has become legendary.

18. For a discussion of Keats's annotations on the margins of the *Anatomy*, see Gittings, *John Keats*, pp. 323–24, 345, and Ward, pp. 312–13.

19. Rollins, I, 395.

20. Rollins, I, 395.

21. In Joanna Richardson, *Fanny Brawne* (London: Thames & Hudson, 1952), pp. 20, 172, and Gittings, *John Keats: The Living Year* (New York: Barnes & Noble, 1968), pp. 3–33, 59–60, 230–35 (this is the sole reference to this Gittings work).

22. Walter Jackson Bate, *John Keats* (New York: Oxford University Press, 1966), pp. 167–68; Ward, pp. 121–22; Gittings, *John Keats*, pp. 139–40; Murry, *Keats* (New York: Minerva Press, 1968), p. 123. These critics speculate about such a possibility.

23. Rollins, I, 403–04.

24. None of Keats's later critics has been so totally negative when interpreting the Fanny Brawne affair. See, for instance, Murry, *Keats*, pp. 19–81; Ward, pp. 292–324; Gittings, *John Keats*, pp. 327–30.

25. Rollins, II, 126.

26. "Medicines as well as poisons are numinous contents that have been acquired and communicated in mysterious wise. The communicators and administrators of this aspect of the Feminine—originally almost always women—are sacral figures, i.e., priestesses—" (*GM*, p. 60).

27. Freudian psychology generally establishes a connection between the eyes and the male genitalia. Thus, Oedipus' self-blinding is seen as punitive castration. In Ancient Greece, the interpreters of the oracle of Themis were blinded and had been castrated in honor of the goddess; in this case, blindness appears as a symbolic surrendering of the male realm, that of "visionary reason," in favor of the feminine realm, that of "blind intuition." Also, see note 28 below.

28. "For a boy to be really successful, it might be wise to castrate him; for Byzantium was the eunuch's paradise. Even the noblest parents were not above mutilating their sons to help their advancement.... A large proportion of the Patriarchs of Constantinople were eunuchs; and eunuchs were particularly encouraged in the Civil Service, where the castrated bearer of a title took precedence of his unmutilated compeer and where many high ranks were reserved for eunuchs alone"—Steven Runciman, *Byzantine Civilization* (New York: Meridian, 1956), pp. 162–63.

29. Erich Neumann, *The Origins and History of Consciousness*, trans. R.F.C. Hull, Bollingen Series XLII (Princeton: Princeton University Press, 1971; first ed. 1949), p. 58.

30. Gittings, *John Keats*, p. 303.

31. Gittings, *John Keats*, p. 303.

32. "The symbol inherently contains the repulsive element, but keeps it at a distance, so that he [Keats] does not have to face it in terms of a common experience, his own...." (Tate, p. 62).

33. Cf. Murry, *Keats*, p. 237; Gittings, *John Keats*, pp. 338–41.

34. Gittings, *John Keats*, p. 301: "Keats was living out the diversities of love which had formed part of his satisfaction with his treatment of *Lamia*, a love which included every possible element"; Morris Dickstein, *Keats and His Poetry* (Chicago: University of Chicago Press, 1971): "Love, possession and sadistic desire for domination intermingle here, under the significant banner of Keats's old ideal of 'luxury'"; Murry, *Keats*, p. 237: "'Light and shade,' 'pro and con,' are in Keats's experience the very law and principle of life—and death."

35. Murry, *Keats*, p. 231.

36. J.E. Cirlot, A *Dictionary of Symbols*, trans. Jack Sage (New York: Philosophical Library, 1962), pp. 127–28.

37. M. Esther Harding, *Woman's Mysteries, Ancient and Modern*, 2nd ed. (New York: G.P. Putnam's Sons for the C.G. Jung Foundation for Analytical Psychology, 1971; first ed. 1935), pp. 103–04.

38. Cortázar has observed as follows:

> El capítulo del "anima" es muy hermoso, y creo que tienes toda la razón al ver así a la Maga. Eres la primera en asimilarla a esta concepción de Jung, y creo que tu interpretación echa por tierra muchas otras que andan por ahí. Ahí sí entro de lleno en tu campo, sin el menor esfuerzo; porque yo mismo siento, retrospectivamente, las fuerzas que me impulsaron y me compulsaron cuando escribí ese libro; no tenían nombres ni parámetros psicoanalíticos, pero yo las sentía, desde el tablón inicial (y bien que lo citas) hasta el final del libro. Sólo en algunos momentos de *62* he vivido tan sometido a esas potencias que tiran y empujan desde abajo, si abajo quiere decir alguna cosa. Y a propósito de *62*, me deslumbró que vieras en Hélène un complemento de la Maga; eso me aclara muchas cosas, mi fascinación personal por Hélène, vagamente basada en una mujer que sólo vi dos o tres veces y a quien hubiera querido conocer íntimamente: lesbiana (no tengo pruebas), misteriosa, esquiva, cruel, bella, distante, y a la vez irradiando una atracción permamente: de ahí nació Hélène, y es cierto que es la otra mitad, por decirlo así, de la Maga. (Letter received from Julio Cortázar, written at Saignon, 30 June 1973.)

39. C.G. Jung, *Symbols of Transformation*, trans. R.F.C. Hull, 2nd ed. Vol. V of *The Collected Works of C.G. Jung*, Bollingen Series XX (Princeton: Princeton University Press, 1970), p. 370.

40. Jung, *Symbols of Transformation*, p. 369.

GORDANA YOVANOVICH

An Interpretation of Rayuela Based on the Character Web

Although on one level the characters in *Rayuela* are autonomous, on a different level they imply a unified, single fictional world. The great art of Julio Cortázar's novel is his creation of this unified world out of a fragmented text; he has invented characters who, while retaining their identity, form part of the author's and the reader's single consciousness.

The difficult interpretation of the whole of *Rayuela* requires great participation by readers. The meaning resides in the articulation of what is between the signs; always, of course, starting from the sign. Jean-Paul Sartre writes: 'The literary object, though realized *through* language, is never given *in* language ... Nothing is accomplished if the reader does not put himself from the very beginning and almost without a guide at the height of this silence.'[1] According to Kathleen Genover, *Rayuela* should be interpreted 'del mismo modo que las alegorías medievales'[2] / 'in the same way as the medieval allegories.' Genover's statement is true only because the story and the discourse in *Rayuela* are not equivalent. However, the analogy between the meaning and the text is not a simple one, since in *Rayuela* there is no pre-existing reference to serve as the basis of allegory—no reference comparable, for example, to the Bible's place in Edmund Spenser's *The Faerie Queene*.

A study of the names of the characters in *Rayuela* shows that even though there are examples of allegory, the novel as a whole is not allegorical.

From *Julio Cortázar's Character Mosaic*. © 2003 Gordana Yovanovich.

The name 'La Maga' may relate to imagination, especially because the character is a dreamer. 'Horacio' certainly brings to mind the name of Horace, the Latin poet, and 'Traveler' associates the character with a person on the move (ironically, because Traveler never travels). Names such as these certainly suggest correlated order but, despite their symbolic qualities, they do not, taken together, form a single system. In other words, the novel as a whole does not bring in another correlated order in the same way that George Orwell's *Animal Farm*, for example, consistently alludes to the Russian revolution.

Many names in Cortázar's novel do not have an allegorical dimension—for example, Rocamadour, Ronald, Babs, and Gregorovius. Readers are therefore not encouraged to interpret the novel on the basis of a pre-existing reference related to the novel through characters; the names of characters in *Rayuela* are not a link between its sense and its reference. The names of La Maga and Horacio encourage readers to look for secondary meaning, while names such as Rocamadour and Gregorovius remind us that the secondary meaning is not to be found in the outside world.

The organizing principle in *Rayuela* is a metaphor rather than allegory. Mario Valdés, using an example from García Lorca's poetry, explains how metaphor involves the reader in an interpretation:

> The range of expression through metaphor is only limited by the reader's ability at imaginative association and transference of characteristic. Consider the following line: 'El mar baila por la playa / un poema de balcones' ... The meaning of the line is so much more than the subject matter. It is evident that the reference is to the sea breaking on the beach, but the metaphorical element is the essential expansion which takes place due to the juxtaposition of the extraneous objects and activities of 'poema,' 'balcones,' and 'bailar.' Consequently the metaphoric meaning includes the transference of characteristics in the mind of the reader; thus, we have an expanded and expanding consciousness where the sea is merely the starting point.[3]

A metaphoric mode of expression implies new relationships among normally extraneous objects. These new connections are usually found more easily in a poem than in a novel, simply because a poem is shorter. In *Rayuela* the problem is simplified because readers are not expected to juxtapose all of the words in the text; the characters and their worlds function in the same way that individual words do in poetry. Oliveira explains the relationship between characters and words: characters are both human beings and symbols of different semantic fields or fictional worlds. A reader's realization, as Iser would say, of the characters' relationship, as an explanation of the relationship of words in poetry, reveals the meaning of the novel.

Cortázar's own ideas, as expressed in the writings of his character Morelli, are important clues in the interpretation of the novel; they are a model for *Rayuela*. Morelli's book is made up of different notes combined according to the rules of chance; he does not believe that any logical organization is representative of life. This does not mean that there is no unity in his text. In chapter 109 one of the members of the club who has read Morelli's work says:

> Leyendo el libro [de Morelli] se tenía por momentos la impresión de que Morelli había esperado que la acumulación de fragmentos cristalizara bruscamente en una realidad total.   (647)

> Reading the book, one had the impression for a while that Morelli had hoped that the accumulation of fragments would quickly crystallize into a total reality.   (469)

After many readings, the reader gets the same impression about *Rayuela*. Cortázar's novel is rich in unconnected details, but it simultaneously seeks the unified 'cosmovision' sought by the surrealists. It wishes to synthesize all elements of life. Evelyn Picón Garfield shows that Cortázar does share the basic idea of surrealism defined by André Breton, whom Picón Garfield quotes in her book:

> Todo induce a creer que en el espíritu humano existe un cierto punto desde el que la vida y la muerte, lo real y lo imaginario, el pasado y el futuro, lo comunicable y lo incomunicable, lo alto y lo bajo, dejan de ser vistos como contradicciones.[4]

> Everything leads us to believe that in the human spirit there is a point where life and death, the real and the imaginable and the incommunicable, the high and the low, stop being seen as contradictions.

Single elements form a unity, as in a mosaic where a single picture is formed by the fragments; but the fragments also stand as individual pieces, with a noticeable space between them.

Mikhail Bakhtin's notion of the polyphonic novel is of great assistance
in understanding Cortázar's complicated novel. Bakhtin explains how writing
can achieve the simultaneity of coexisting forces. This is nothing new, as
Bakhtin points out, because it was achieved by Cervantes, Shakespeare, and
Rabelais, but 'its germs ripened in the novels of Dostoyevky.'[5] Bakhtin
explains the basic nature of Dostoyevsky's novel and, by inference, of
Cortázar's *Rayuela*:

> The essence of polyphony is precisely in the fact that the voices
> remain independent and, as such, are combined in a unity of a
> higher order than a homonymy. These independent voices are
> the voices of the characters in the novel. Their independence and
> freedom are a part of the author's plan which, as it were,
> predestines them to be free (relatively speaking of course) and
> introduces them, as free men into the strict and calculated plan of
> the whole.[6]

Since the independence of the voices is the most apparent characteristic of
Dostoyevky's novel (and Cortázar's), the 'calculated plan of the whole' is to
be found in the second level of narration. Even then it is very difficult to
grasp the totality because the relationship between the parts and the whole
in *Rayuela* is much more complex than it is in medieval allegory.

In the very first chapter (73) of the suggested reading, Cortázar warns
his readers that sense and reference in his novel are not divorced and that the
novel must be understood in the same way a metaphor is understood: even
though its tenor and its vehicle are different, they combine in a single unit,
the metaphor. Cortázar illustrates this through a commentary on a particular
interpretation by Morelli. In one of his books Morelli talks about a
Neapolitan who spent years sitting in the doorway of his house looking at a
screw on the ground. The fellow dropped dead of a stroke and as soon as the
neighbours arrived the screw disappeared. One of them has it now. Morelli
suggests that perhaps the neighbour takes it out secretly, puts it away again,
and goes off to the factory, feeling something that he does not understand,
'una oscura reprobación' (545) / 'an obscure reproval' (384). Morelli's
interpretation is that the screw must have been something else, 'un dios o
algo así' (545) / 'a god or something like that' (384). The narrator, who is
probably Oliveira, comments: 'Solución demasiado fácil' (545) / 'Too easy a
solution' (384).

Morelli's interpretation, to which Oliveira objects, has a long history in
literature. Critics have frequently interpreted literary works by relating them

to what Hegel called 'the spirit of the age,' or to existing historical conditions, putting their emphasis on what was already familiar to them. In doing this they undermine the work itself, or a smaller sign within a work. Oliveira wishes to look at the screw as a screw first, and only then to perceive it as a symbol of something else.

The interpretation of the novel, 'the plan of the whole,' stands above the text but is not divorced form it. Etienne, who reads Morelli's text with Oliveira, tells him: 'Race rato que mucha gente sospecha que la vida y los seres vivientes son dos cosas aparte' (314) / 'It's been some time now since people have suspected that life and living things are two completely different things' (164). They are different and one at the same time. Oliveira explains this paradox in his understanding of La Maga, who is simultaneously a person and a poetic image. He says:

> Así la Maga dejaría de ser un objeto perdido para volverse la imagen de una posible reunión—pero no ya con ella sino más acá o más allá de ella; por ella pero no ella.   (451)

> In that way La Maga would cease being a lost object and become the image of a possible reunion—no longer with her but on this side of her or on the other side of her; by her, but not her.   (292)

The meaning of the text is not something that stands above the text; rather, it is created through—'por'—the text. It is to be found in the reader's response, which has been stimulated by the text. Etienne explains:

> ... la verdadera realidad que también llamamos Yonder ... esa verdadera realidad, repito, no es algo por venir, una meta, el último peldaño, el final de una evolución. No, es algo que ya está aquí, en nosotros. Sula siente, basta tener el valor de estirar la mano en la oscuridad.   (618)

> ... the true reality that we also call Yonder ... that true reality, I repeat, is not something that is going to happen, a goal, the last step, the end of an evolution. No, it's something that's already here, in us. You can feel it, all you need is the courage to stick your hand into the darkness.   (445–6)

In *Rayuela*, it is important to remember, what is said about life is relevant for literature, and vice versa. Cortázar points out many times in

Rayuela his dislike for literature that is only 'literatura,' an empty rhetoric with little bearing on life itself. Consequently, the place of the reader becomes similar to that of a character. If Etienne looks for the 'Yonder' in himself, readers must also look for an interpretation in the text and through the text as the text becomes a part of them.

COMMUNICATION THROUGH FORM

Alfred J. MacAdam points out that there is not yet an interpretation of *Rayuela* as a whole in which the reader distances himself or herself after having analysed each individual part of the novel. 'The sad reality of most of Cortázar's criticism is its pious repetition of what the author or his surrogate [Morelli] says about literature.'[7] What is most important is to see the novel as a whole. One of the outstanding characteristics of Cortázar's novel is that there is no extraneous material; everything functions in relation to everything else, and Cortázar often gives explicit clues as to how readers should interpret the novel. He tells us that Gregorovius and Traveler are Oliveira's doubles. Furthermore, he tells us that La Maga and Pola complement each other in their relationship to Oliveira. Readers soon realize that not only these but all of the characters function together; they form a picture of a complete human being, and reveal the relationship between an individual and the human collective. The form of the novel complements the content. Cortázar creates the character of Oliveira not as something independent, but as a commentary on what other characters are or are not. Without the others Oliveira is nothing; without him they are incomplete. Their interrelationship can best be seen in the board scene.

The board scene, in the middle of the novel, is the seed from which the novel *Rayuela* grew. Like James Joyce, who wrote *Ulysses* from a short story, Cortázar built his novel from the nucleus of a single scene. He has said that '*Rayuela*, for example, began in the middle. The first chapter I wrote was about Talita aloft on the boards. I hadn't the least idea of what I'd write before or after that section.'[8] In this scene Oliveira wants Traveler, in an apartment opposite his, to send over some nails and *mate* leaves to him. Oliveira does not need the nails for any specific purpose; he wants them because he cannot tolerate the crooked ones he already has. The conventional, normal, way to get the package is to go downstairs, cross the street, and climb up to Traveler's room at the same level in the other apartment building. But this route is too long; furthermore, it is meaningless because it has been repeated too often. Consequently, Oliveira and Traveler, his double, invent a new, logical, and entertaining way to do the job: they each put a board out of their windows so the two boards meet in the middle. The men then hold the boards and Talita, with nails and *mate* in her pocket, crosses over by crawling on her stomach. The act is adventurous and bold, but not foolish, because Oliveira and Traveler do everything possible to secure Talita's passage. They even give her a hat so that she will not get sunstroke. The activity scandalizes the women who watch them from below, even though there is no reason for complaint: their three young neighbours are having fun at nobody's expense. In fact, they provide entertainment for the women, who function as their audience.

At the end of the episode Oliveira tells Traveler, 'Somos el mismo, uno de cada lado' / 'We are the same, one from each side.' They are, in fact, one unity. Holding the boards on each side, they are in physical contact and create a meaningful unit called 'the bridge.' On a higher level, they are also one because they merge in their love for Talita, who lies on the boards. In chapter 43 Oliveira explicitly tells Talita 'Sos nuestra ninfa Egeria, nuestro puente mediúmnico. Ahora que lo pienso, cuando vos estás presente Manú y yo caemos en una especie de trance' (423) / 'You're Egeria, our nymph, our bridge, our medium. Now that I think of it, when you're present Manú and I fall into some sort of trance' (265). Cortázar then takes his readers one step further. Talita, the link between the two opposites, becomes a catalyst. She is important not only in herself, but also as an agent that speeds up a chemical reaction between the two men. Talita realizes that they look beyond her, and says, 'Estos dos han tenido otro puente entre ellos ... Si me cayera a la calle ni se darían cuenta' (404) / 'Those two have got another bridge working between them ... If I were to fall into the street they wouldn't even notice it' (247). She knows that she is and is not a bond, because Oliveira and Traveler begin with her but transcend her. 'Hablen de lo que hablen,' she says, 'en el fondo es siempre de mí, pero tampoco es eso, aunque es casi eso' (405) / 'no matter what they talk about, it's always about me in the end, but that's not what I really mean, still it's almost what I mean' (248). She inspires love; love is not only in her, but also in the subject who loves. Oliveira and Traveler meet in her but also above her. In *Libro de Manuel* the narrator says, 'Un puente es un hombre cruzando el puente, che'[9] / 'A bridge is a man crossing a bridge, by God.'

The important point here is that relationships (as well as the text of the novel) encompass a hierarchy of meaning, and in the final phase form a complete synthesis. People are complicated beings who in their depths possess undiscovered and unrealized layers of personality. Oliveira shows this in his conversation with La Maga. When La Maga tells him that they are two very different people, that he is a 'Mondrian' and she is a 'Vieira da Silva,'

Oliveira asks her, '¿Y no se te ha ocurrido sospechar que detrás de ese Mondrian puede empezar una realidad de Vieira da Silva?' (212) / 'And didn't it occur to you that behind this Mondrian there might lurk a Vieira da Silva reality?' (76). The answer is in the affirmative. Each person is able to be in contact with the other because people are a sum of possibilities. Oliveira sees in everything the potential for a different way of life, and he longs for this completeness:

> Si hubiera sido posible pensar una extrapolación de todo eso, entender el Club, entender 'Cold Wagon Blues', entender el amor de la Maga, entender cada piolincito saliendo de las cosas y llegando hasta sus dedos, cada títere o a cada titiritero, como una epifanía; entenderlos, no como símbolos de otra realidad quizá inalcanzable, pero sí como *potenciadores* (qué lenguaje, qué impudor), como exatamente líneas de fuga para una carrera a la que hubiera que lanzarse en ese momento mismo.
>
> (206, emphasis added)

> If he could have conceived of an extrapolation of all this, understanding the club, understanding the *Cold Wagon Blues*, understanding La Maga's love, understanding everything every thread that would become unravelled from the cuff of things and reach down to his fingers, every puppet and every puppeteer, like an epiphany; understanding them, not as symbols of some other unattainable reality perhaps, but agents of potency (such language, such lack of decorum), just like lines of flight along the track that he ought to follow at this very moment.   (72)

Each character offers a possibility of escape. Oliveira accepts some of their characteristics and tendencies and subtly criticizes others. The way in which Cortázar delineates his protagonist's search is similar to the way in which Cervantes illustrates the development of Don Quixote; Cortázar does not describe the development directly but leads the hero through different contexts. In *Rayuela* these contexts are the worlds of different characters. Each of them represents a different quality of life. Oliveira's contact with them modifies and enriches his character.

Cortázar uses irony as a predominant technique to create the character of Horacio Oliveira. This ironic mode of expression in Cortázar's novel, like the metaphoric mode of expression, also requires great participation by readers. 'The reconstructions of irony,' Wayne Booth points out, 'are seldom if ever reducible either to grammar or semantics or linguistics.'[10] Readers begin from the language, but search for the meaning beyond language—in the relationship of contexts. According to Booth, in an ironic text the deception of readers is a precondition:

> The essential structure of irony is not designed to 'deceive some readers and allow others to see the secret message' but to deceive *all* readers for a time and then require *all* readers to recognize and cope with their deception.[11]

In *Rayuela* secondary characters claim moral superiority and explicitly scorn Oliveira for his immoral deeds. In the course of the novel the readers, who originally share the views of the secondary characters because their views are the dominant ethics of society, realize that they are being deceived by the author and above all by society. In the section entitled 'Del lado de acá' / 'From This Side' the character who is presented in this manner is Ossip Gregorovius, who helps most to build the character of Oliveira. In *Rayuela* Gregorovius has the role of a humanist. When Babs accuses Oliveira of heinous crimes, Oliveira does not answer her but secretly looks at Gregorovius, knowing that Gregorovius is a symbol of such views, a person who often uses such moral arguments as ammunition against Oliveira. Readers side with Babs and Gregorovius because Oliveira leaves La Maga at the moment of her son's death. Desertion at such a time is a horrible deed; a woman in this situation should be helped, not abandoned. Oliveira, who does not deny that he should be with La Maga, only points out that if he went to her, he would do so for himself and not for her.

> Oliveira se dijo que no sería tan difícil llegarse hasta la cama, agacharse para decirle unas palabras al oído a la Maga. 'Pero eso yo lo haría por mi', pensó. 'Ella está más allá de cualquier cosa. Soy yo el que después dormiría mejor, aunque no sea más que una manera de decir. Yo, yo, yo. Yo dormiría mejor después de besarla y consolarla y repetir todo lo que ya le han dicho éstos.'   (320)

> Oliveira told himself that it would not be so difficult to go over to the bed, squat down beside it and say a few words in La Maga's ear. 'But I would be doing it for myself,' he thought. 'She's beyond anything. I'm the one who would sleep better afterward, even if it's just an expression. Me, me, me. I would sleep better

after I kissed her and consoled her and repeated everything these
people here have already said.'   (170–1)

The critic Graciela de Sola has stated that Gregorovius is a European
Oliveira.[12] Oliveira himself realizes that he and Gregorovius are very similar:
'Vos sos como yo' (324) / 'You're like me' (174). They are alike because they
are both highly educated, intelligent men. Gregorovius is often reading or
carrying books, and from various discussions in the club it becomes obvious
that he reads the works of Pascal, Wittgenstein, and many other thinkers
who are also known to Oliveira. Like Oliveira, Gregorovius is not sure where
he comes from or where he is going. They both live on borrowed money and
search for some meaning in their existence. There are important differences
between them, however. Here Cortázar creates a hierarchy, which readers
dramatize and use to draw important conclusions. Brita Brodin agrees with
Graciela de Sola that Gregorovius is the 'Oliveira europeo' who is left behind
when Oliveira begins to search actively for La Maga.[13] This may be true, but
it has to be explained. Oliveira never rejects his knowledge and erudition.
What he rejects is Gregorovius's hypocrisy.

As we have seen in the first chapter, Cortázar shows Gregorovius, the
moralist, to be La Maga's psychological rapist. Oliveira makes Gregorovius
admit that his charity towards La Maga during Rocamadour's funeral is not
as great as it appears. When he asks Gregorovius, '¿Y estuviste aquí todo el
tiempo? CARITAS' / 'And you were here all the time? CARITAS' he admits that
he stayed in La Maga's apartment because he hoped to keep it now for
himself: 'No era por eso, tenia miedó de que alguno de la casa aprovechara
para meterse en el cuarto y hacerse fuerte' (322) / 'That wasn't why. I was
afraid somebody from the landlady might use that time to get in here and
cause trouble' (172). More important, however, Oliveira insinuates that
Gregorovius stayed with La Maga for sexual pleasure. A careful reader links
the two important scenes because Oliveira comments on both in a similar
fashion. When La Maga tells Oliveira about the lovers who had taken
advantage of her, the conversation runs in the following way:

—Sí—dijo la Maga, mirándolo—. Primero el negro. Después
Ledesma.
—Después Ledesma, claro.
—Y los tres del callejón, la noche de carnaval.
—Por delante—dijo Oliveira, cebando el mate.
—Y monsieur Vincent, el hermano del hotelero.
—Por detrás.

—Y un soldado que lloraba en un parque.
—Por delante.
—Y vos.
—Por detrás. Pero eso de ponerme a mí en la lista estando yo
presente es como una confirmación de mis lúgubres
premoniciones.   (218–19)

> 'Yes,' La Maga said, looking at him. 'First the Negro. Then
> Ledesma.'
> 'Then Ledesma, of course.'
> 'And the three up the alley, on carnival night.'
> '*Por delante*,' said Oliveira, sipping his *mate* ...
> 'And Monsieur Vincent, the hotel keeper's brother.'
> '*Por detrás*.'
> 'And a soldier who was weeping in a park.'
> '*Por delante*.'
> 'And you.'
> '*Por detrás*. But the idea of putting me on the list in my
presence just bears out my gloomiest premonitions ...'   (82–3)

When Gregorovius describes Rocamadour's funeral, Oliveira comments
supportively. He repeats the words 'por delante' / 'from the front' and 'por
detrás' / 'from the back,' making the two scenes similar. Gregorovius begins:

> —Sí, él [Ronald] y Perico y el relojero. Yo acompañaba a Lucía.
> —Por delante.
> —Y Babs cerraba la marcha con Etienne.
> —Por detrás.   (327)

> 'Yes, he and Perico and the watchmaker. I went with Lucía.'
> '*Por delante*.'
> 'And Babs brought up the rear with Etienne.'
> '*Por detrás*.'   (177)

Gregorovius looks for an advantage in everything, which inspires Oliveira's
description of him as 'una especie de lameculos metafísico' (324) / 'a kind of
metaphysical ass-kisser' (174). He does not criticize Gregorovius's education
but attacks his tendency to moralize and to indulge in immoral behaviour.

Oliveira's position is further crystallized when he is juxtaposed with
Etienne. Through an interaction of contexts Cortázar develops the character

further. Unlike Gregorovius, Etienne wishes to break away from European social norms. Oliveira takes him to visit Morelli, with whom the two young intellectuals share ideas about art. They all wish to break away from empty rhetoric and to communicate through form:

> [La Maga] admiraba terriblemente a Oliveira y Etienne, capaces de discutir tres horas sin parar. En torno a Etienne y Oliveira había como un círculo de tiza, ella quería entrar en el círculo, comprender por qué el principio de indeterminación era tan importante en la literatura, por qué Morelli, del que tanto hablaban, al que tanto admiraban, pretendía hacer de su libro una bola de cristal donde el micro y el macrocosmos se unieran en una visión aniquilante.   (150)

> [La Maga] was terribly in awe of Oliveira and Etienne, who could keep an argument going for three hours without a stop. There was something like a circle of chalk around Etienne and Oliveira and she wanted to get inside, to understand why the principle of indetermination was so important in literature, why Morelli, of whom they spoke so much, whom they admired so much, wanted his book to be a crystal ball in which the micro- and the macrocosm would come together in an annihilating vision.   (25)

For Etienne, as for Morelli and Oliveira, art is the giver of meaning. Etienne says, 'Pinto, ergo soy' echoing Descartes's 'I think; therefore I am.' Etienne searches for complete liberation, and in his way is very similar to Oliveira. None the less, art does not have a deeper meaning for Etienne because he is concerned only with form and his own pleasure. When Wong shows pictures of torture victims Oliveira comments, 'Por más que me pese nunca seré un *indiferente como Etienne* ... Lo peor era que había mirado fríamente las fotos de Wong, tan sólo porque el torturado no era su padre, aparte de que ya hacía cuarenta años de la operación pekinesa' (188, emphasis added) / 'No matter how it hurts me, I shall never be indifferent like Etienne ... The worst was that he had looked at Wong's picture with coldness because the one they were torturing had not been his father, not thinking about the forty years that had passed since it all took place in Peking' (57). Etienne is obviously not as interested as Morelli and Oliveira in universal justice for humankind. Oliveira repeats again that Etienne is an egoist, and compares him to La Maga:

> La Maga jamás ha sido capaz de entender las cuestiones morales (como Etienne, pero de una manera menos *egoísta*; simplemente porque sólo cree en la responsabilidad en presente, en el momento mismo en que hay que ser bueno, o noble; en el fondo, por razones tan hedónicas y egoístas como las de Etienne). (710, emphasis added)

> [La Maga] has never been able to understand moral questions (just like Etienne, but less selfishly; just because the only responsibility she believes in is of the present, the very moment when one must be good or noble; underneath it all, for reasons just as hedonistic and selfish as those of Etienne's).   (527–8)

Oliveira rejects the moral concerns of Gregorovius and censures Etienne for his amoral attitude to life. This does not mean that he is contradicting himself, if we keep in mind that *Rayuela* is structured on the principle of metaphor. In both instances Oliveira criticizes self-interest and pure egoism, and he rejects moral, ethical norms not for the sake of amorality but in the hope of creating a new moral order.

In their attempt to revolutionize the world, Etienne, Oliveira, and Morelli emphasize the importance of form. None the less, formal experimentation for its own sake is not the goal of *Rayuela*. Through the example of Berthe Trépat, Cortázar shows what he wants by explaining what he does not want. Like Morelli, who wishes to revolutionize literature, Berthe Trépat attempts to revolutionize music. She is introduced as an avant-garde composer whose 'Síntesis Délibes-Saint Saéns' represents one of the most profound innovations in contemporary music, something Trépat calls 'Sincretismo fatídico.' Oliveira is interested in her arrangement, but quickly becomes disappointed because 'el sincretismo fatídico no había tardado en revelar su secreto' (250) / 'the prophetic syncretism was not long in revealing its secret' (107). She took four chords from well-known works and alternated them. Cortázar ridicules the lack of a true synthesis on a different level through her grotesque presentation and the behaviour of her audience, who gradually leave. Readers, necessarily comparing her to Morelli, deduce that a revolution is fruitful only if it creates a new order in which there is a true and complete union of parts. This point becomes even more clearly established in a juxtaposition of the members of the Club de la Serpiente and 'el viejo de arriba,' the old man who lives above La Maga's apartment.

The members of the club and the old man are social outcasts. (Babs points out that their neighbours suspect them of smoking marijuana even when they are only making goulash.) Despite this similarity, the members of the Club de la Serpiente, to which Oliveira belongs, are very different from the old man. 'El viejo de arriba' is driven by hate; the nailed shoe and other strange objects on his door reflect decadence and madness. He complains whether or not he has a valid reason. In other words, he is different from his society not for any valid reason but because he is a difficult, obstinate individual. The members of the club, in contrast, reject social norms in favour of a higher order; the atmosphere at the club is warm and friendly. During one of their 'discadas' or record-playing parties, inspired by the freedom of jazz, the members create chaos: at one point La Maga weeps, Babs is very drunk, Etienne, Wong, and Ronald argue over what record to play, Guy remembers his ex-girlfriend, and Oliveira, who observes all of them, thinks:

> Y todo eso de golpe crecía y era una música atroz, era más que el silencio afelpado de las cosas en orden de sus parientes intachables, en mitad de la confusión donde el pasado era incapaz de encontrar un botón de camisa y el presente se afeitaba con pedazos de vidrio a falta de una navaja enterrada en alguna maceta, en mitad de un tiempo que se abría como una veleta a cualquier viento, un hombre respiraba hasta no poder más, se sentía vivir hasta el delirio en el acto mismo de contemplar la confusión que lo rodeaba y preguntarse si algo de eso tenía sentido. Todo desorden se justificaba si tendía a salir de sí mismo, por la locura se podía acaso llegar a una razón que no fuera esa razón cuya falencia es la locura.   (210)

> And suddenly from all this there came some horrid music, it was beyond the felted order of homes where untouchable kin put things in order, in the midst of the confusion where the past was incapable of finding a button on a shirt and the present shaved itself with pieces of a broken bottle because it could not find a razor stuck away somewhere in some flowerpot, in the midst of a time which opened up like a weather vane to whatever wind was blowing, a man breathed until he could no longer do so, he felt that he had lived until he reached the delirium of the very act of taking in the confusion which surrounded him and he asked himself if any of this had meaning. All disorder had meaning if it seemed to come out of itself, perhaps through madness one could arrive at that reason which is not the reason whose weakness is madness.   (75)

While the old man stays at the level of 'locura,' or insanity, the club attempts to transcend madness and create a new order. This new order is beyond common experience, and Cortázar describes it only elliptically by juxtaposing two social outcasts and then insinuating their differences.

Each member of the Club de la Serpiente contributes something to the creation of the new order. Oliveira observes and appropriates these different facets, in the end creating his own new order and new union with the other, 'el otro,' thanks to lessons learned in the club. This is also true for readers. From experience readers know that when different characters represent different qualities the author has a specific purpose in creating each of them. Readers also know that the only way to understand something completely is to try to knit all of its parts together. They observe each character and then form a synthesis. Wong, for example, representing the ceremonial aspect of life, studies oriental ways of torture, and often carries photos of torture victims, which he shows in the club. This in itself is a negative quality. Despite the obvious cruelty that can be seen in his pictures, there is also a certain mysticism in the way the tortures are performed. The mystery softens the horror, making death seem less bleak and tragic. Cortázar also softens the criminal aspect by making Wong an attractive character. Brita Brodin lists all the adverbs, adjectives, and nouns that describe Wong: sonriendo / smiling, sonrisa / smile, reverencia / reverence, ceremonioso / ceremonious, and ceremoniosamente / ceremoniously.[14] Wong's nature, together with the ceremony with which the victims are tortured, changes the picture of death for the members of the club and for readers. La Maga, a sensitive person for whom 'morir era la peor ofensa, la estupidez más completa' (193) / 'to die would have been the worst offense, the most complete stupidity' (61), thinks of Wong fondly. When he brings coffee she thinks: 'Ah, olor maravilloso del café, Wong querido, Wong Wong Wong' (197) / 'ah, a wonderful smell of coffee, dear Wong, Wong Wong Wong' (65). In addition to being a warm person, Wong always looks for a humorous aspect of life. He adorns bare, meaningless reality with unusual objects. Oliveira says to Ronald:

> Acércate aquí. Vas a estar mejor que en esa silla, tiene una especie de pico en el medio que se clava en el culo. Wong la incluiría en su colección pekinesa, estoy seguro.   (302)

> Come on over here ... You'll be more comfortable than in that chair, it has a kind of point in the middle of it that pricks your ass. Wong would include it in his Peking collection if he knew about it, I'm sure.   (153)

Wong needs to be imaginative and creative in both the practical and the theoretical sense. Speaking about the fact that Etienne and Wong have seen Oliveira with Pola, Gregorovius tells La Maga: 'Wong se aprovechó más tarde para edificar una complicada teoria sobre las saturaciones sexuales' (282) / 'Wong used all this later on to work out a complicated theory on sexual saturation' (135). Wong's approach to life is important for the development of *Rayuela*. When Guy Monod, a minor character, attempts to commit suicide, Oliveira calls him stupid. In other words, death is completely ruled out as a possibility in Oliveira's search. Since death is none the less present literally and symbolically, Cortázar shows Wong's approach to life—ceremony—as a possible way to escape both boredom and death. This becomes particularly obvious in comparison with the lives of Traveler and Talita. For the two Argentinians, games and ceremony are a way of conquering the absurd and the important factors in relationships.

Babs and Ronald's relationship, strengthened by a naïve enjoyment of music, is important for the rendering of the character of Oliveira and in the development of the novel as a whole. Oliveira, with his predominantly intellectual approach to life, is incapable of identifying completely with music or anything else.

> Por más que le gustara el jazz Oliviera nunca entraría en el juego como Ronald, para él sería bueno o malo, hot o cool, blanco o negro, antiguo o moderno, Chicago o New Orleans, nunca el jazz, nunca eso que ahora eran Satchmo, Ronald y Babs, 'Baby don't you play me cheap because I look so meek', y después la llamada de la trompeta, el falo amarillo rompiendo el aire y gozando con avances y retrocesos y hacia el final tres notas ascendentes, hipnóticamente de oro puro, una perfecta pausa donde todo el swing del mundo palpitaba en un instante intolerable, y entonces la eyaculación de un sobreagudo resbalando y cayendo como un cohete en la noche sexual, la mano de Ronald acariciando el cuello de Babs y la crepitación de la púa mientras el disco seguía girando y el silencio que había en toda música verdadera se desarrimaba lentamente de las paredes, salía de debajo del diván, se despegaba como labios o capullos.   (182)

> As much as he liked jazz, Oliveira could never get into the spirit of it like Ronald, whether it was good or bad, hot or cool, white or black, old or modern, Chicago or New Orleans, never jazz, never what was now Satchmo, Ronald, and Babs, 'So what's the

use if you're gonna cut off my juice,' and then the trumpet's flaming up, the yellow phallus breaking the air and having fun, coming forward and drawing back and towards the end three ascending notes, pure hypnotic gold, a perfect pause where all the swing of the world was beating in an intolerable instant, and then the supersharp ejaculation slipping and falling like a rocket in the sexual night, Ronald's hand caressing Babs's neck and the scratching of the needle while the record kept on turning and the silence there was in all true music slowly unstuck itself from the walls, slithered out from underneath the couch, and opened up like lips or like cocoons.   (512)

This passage suggests that there is an absolute equality between music and love-making. Cortázar, like Oliveira and Morelli, searches for a similar but even more complex union in life. At that moment Oliveira cannot surrender himself to the music and allow it to awaken feelings that might integrate different experiences. Ronald and Babs are capable of this, but unfortunately lack the ability to comprehend the experience and therefore cannot change a naïve identification into a meaningful progress in life. Oliveira, who envies Ronald's ability to become music, shows Ronald's limitations at the same time. When Ronald says, 'Estoy de acuerdo en que mucho de lo que me rodea es absurdo, pero probablemente damos ese nombre a lo que no comprendemos todavía. Ya se sabrá alguna vez' / 'I agree that a lot of what is around me is absurd, but we probably call it that because that's what we call anything we don't understand yet. Someday we'll know,' Oliveira comments, 'Optimismo encantador' (314) / 'Charming optimism' (164). Ronald identifies with music but does not search for the meaning of life in music as Johnny Carter, for example, does in the short story 'El perseguidor.' Oliveira, however, wants to see jazz as an absolute freedom that he both feels and understands. Cortázar has said that

> Johnny y Oliveira son dos individuos que cuestionan, que ponen en crisis, que niegan lo que la gran mayoría acepta por una especie de fatalidad histórica y social. Entran en el juego, viven su vida, nacen, viven y mueren.[15]

> Johnny and Oliveira are two individuals who question, create a crisis, deny what a great majority accepts as a type of historical and social fate. They enter the game, live their life, are born, live and die.

Ronald and Babs die in music, but they are not able to be reborn; this is something Oliveira attempts to do not just in music but in all spheres of life. A precondition for this rebirth is the experiencing of different aspects of life. This is why Oliveira must be put in contact with all members of the club before he can make the final leap in his relationship with Traveler and Talita. Like La Maga in the poetic world, and like Ronald and Babs in the world of music, Oliveira must identify with the objects observed or listened to as if he were making love to them. Like Wong, he must, through imagination and ceremony, overcome death and the uglier aspects of life. And like Etienne, he must look for the meaning of life not in the outside world but in his art and games. In this attempt he must avoid the hypocrisy of Gregorovius and Perico Romero by focusing on the other and not on himself.

There is one more character in the first part of the novel, Pola, who, though not a member of the club, contributes significantly to the rendering of Oliveira's character and to the development of the theme. At the beginning of the novel Oliveira is described as a man who perceives the world intellectually; his relationship with Pola develops this idea. La Maga believes that Oliveira left her for Pola because Pola knows how to think. While Oliveira does wish that La Maga knew how to think, he does not give priority to reason and the ability to think logically. The narrator, who adopts Oliveira's point of view says:

> Fracasar con Pola era la repetición de innúmeros fracasos, un juego que se pierde al final pero que ha sido bello jugar, mientras que de la Maga empezaba a salirse resentido, con una conciencia de sarro y un pucho oliendo a madrugada en un rincón de la boca.
> (588)

> Failure with Pola was the repetition of innumerable failures, a game that ultimately is lost but was beautiful to play, while with La Maga he had begun to come out resentful, with a taste of tartar and a butt that smelled of dawn in the corner of the mouth.
> (422)

What attracts Oliveira to Pola is her schizophrenia. During the daytime she lives in a perfectly ordered apartment and she depends on the objects around her to confirm her existence. Oliveira tells her ironically,

> Enumerá, enumerá. Eso ayuda. Sujetate a los nombres, así no te caés. Ahí está la mesa de luz, la cortina no se ha movido de la

ventana, Claudette sigue en el mismo número, DAN-ton 34 no sé cuántos, y tu mamá te escribe desde Aix-en-Provence. Todo va bien.   (527–8)

Name them, name them. That helps. Give them names, then you won't fall. There's the night-table, the curtain hasn't run away from the window, Claudette is still at the same address, DAN-ton *34* I can't remember the rest, and your mother still writes to you from Aix-en-Provence. Everything's fine.   (366–7)

Simultaneously, in her sexual behaviour Pola leads Oliveira into the realm of the forbidden, and experiences life without any control. What she cannot do, however, is unite her daytime activities with her nighttime activities. Oliveira attempts to show her that they are closely related and that the order and disorder mutually presuppose each other. While they walk through the streets of Paris, Oliveira points out to Pola that the classical paintings on the sidewalk have to be erased at night in order to be repainted in the morning; creation and destruction, her perfection and her pornography; are two sides of the same coin. Pola, who fears that her daily security is not as stable as it was before she met Oliveira, tells him, 'Me das miedo, monstruo americano' (528) / 'You make me afraid, you South American monster' (367). The same night Oliveira kisses her breast and becomes aware of himself only through the kiss. The two reach a union through the realization that life is based on paradox. Unlike Pola, La Maga can never reach this conclusion; she can feel it, but she cannot understand it. Pola is capable of understanding metaphysical questions in the same way Oliveira understands them. Because of this the two women complement each other, and Oliveira loves them both at the same time. Oliveira's relationship to Pola is important not because she teaches him anything new, but because it shows that reason is also a form of union between people. Oliveira becomes the kiss itself after their intellectual conversation about the paintings on the sidewalk.

In the section entitled 'Del lado de acá' / 'From This Side,' Oliveira acquires one more important characteristic: in his contact with Traveler he is forced to participate actively in life. In the very first chapter of 'Del lado de acá' Traveler is described in the following way: 'A falta de lo otro, Traveler es un hombre de acción' (377) / 'Since he doesn't have this otherness, Traveler is a man of action' (223). In keeping with his usual practice, Cortázar first provides us with the basic characteristic of his hero and later elaborates on it through the hero's juxtaposition with other characters. Traveler is a man of action because he often changes jobs, throws water in his boss's face as a sign of protest, makes Talita explain to him how to use medication, how exactly to put it in his rectum, and so on. However, his action acquires serious meaning only when he comes in contact with Oliveira—not because he changes his activities, but because he changes his attitude towards what he does.

Before Oliveira's arrival Traveler had reacted against the stupidities of the established order, but he did not foresee that a new order could be created. He complains that he is unable to travel, in a metaphysical rather than a literal sense, and sees this as his personal failure:

> Una cosa había que reconocer y era que, a diferencia de casi todos sus amigos, Traveler no le echaba la culpa a la vida o a la suerte por no haber podido viajar a gusto. Simplemente se bebía una ginebra de un trago, y se trataba a sí mismo de cretinacho.   (374)

> One thing had to be recognized and it was that unlike almost all her other friends, Traveler didn't blame life or fate for the fact that he had been unable to travel everywhere he had wanted to. He would just take a stiff drink of gin and call himself a boob.
>
> (219)

He knows that it is up to him to change his life, but he fails to act because he does not believe he can accomplish anything. Oliveira, however, strongly believes that there is a way to travel to different lands, and that this will replace the boredom of everyday habits. Oliveira asks Traveler, '¿No sos capaz de *intuir* un solo segundo que esto puede no ser así?' (505, emphasis added) / 'Aren't you capable of sensing even for a single second that this. might not be like that?' (344). Traveler knows that life has its own course and is willing to accept it without struggle, while Oliveira struggles to incorporate himself into the current. Oliveira has the will to go beyond everyday reality but fails to act. Traveler acts, but lacks the ease with which Oliveira makes his action meaningful. For this reason the two men are 'doppelganger, uno de cada lado' (504) / 'doppelganger, one from each side' (344).

In their relationship Traveler always creates the situation in which Oliveira is forced to act. He waits for Oliveira at the harbour and thereby renews their relationship. He introduces Talita to Oliveira. In the board scene Traveler suggests that they build the bridge, and he volunteers Talita to take the nails and *mate* leaves over to Oliveira, despite the actual and implied dangers. Furthermore, despite his knowledge that a relationship is beginning to develop between Talita and Oliveira, Traveler finds Oliveira a job in the circus where he and Talita work. At this point Traveler initiates all the actions that force Oliveira to participate actively in life.

The relationship between Traveler and Oliveira is significant not only because it influences Oliveira to act but also because it sums up all the aspects of life discussed until now, and, more important, because of its intensity. Like Oliveira, Etienne, and Morelli, Traveler does not wish to follow the existing order. His chief entertainment is to ridicule the old women in his neighbourhood—the representatives of social order. Like Wong, Traveler plays games with Talita in an attempt to conquer the boredom and absurdity of everyday reality. Like Pola, Traveler comes to understand Oliveira's metaphysical preoccupations; at the end of the novel the two achieve absolute understanding. Unlike the characters in Paris, they succeed not only in understanding each other but also in feeling their understanding, a quality embodied in La Maga.

The relationship between Traveler and Oliveira begins from the liberation of the social order and moves upwards. When Traveler finds Oliveira a job despite the fact that Oliveira is a threat to his marriage, Oliveira is unhappy.

> A Oliveira no-se-le-escapaba que Traveler había tenido que hacer un-esfuerzo-heroico para convencer al Dire, y que lo había convencido más por casulidad que por otra cosa.   (420)

> Oliveira had-not-failed-to-notice that Traveler had had to make a-heroic-effort to convince the Boss, and that he had convinced him more by chance than for any other reason.   (262)

The ironic adjective 'heroico' / 'heroic' reminds the reader of Morelli's and Oliveira's goal to search for the new man without being a hero. They search for the man who completely ignores the social norms and acts according to his inner drives. Traveler has not yet reached this stage.

Traveler's actions begin to be meaningful when he becomes jealous of Oliveira, when, despite sleepless nights, he chooses to continue in the union because he feels that there is a higher order that makes sense:

> Había noches en que todo el mundo estaba como esperando algo. Se sentían muy bien juntos, pero eran como una cabeza de tormenta ... Al final se iban a la cama con un malhumor latente, y soñaban toda la noche con cosas divertidas y agradables, lo que más bien era un contrasentido.   (387)

There were nights when everybody seemed to be expecting
something. They felt very good together, but it was like the eye
of a hurricane ... Finally they would go to bed with latent ill-
humour, and spend the whole night dreaming about happy and
funny things, which was probably a contradiction of terms. (231)

What inspires Traveler to continue acting is a sense of being alive, which
expresses itself through jealousy, fear, compassion, and similar feelings.
Movement is a necessity. Traveler explains to Talita that it is not Oliveira
who disturbs their relationship, but something more profound.:

No es por Horacio, amor, no es solamente por Horacio aunque
él haya llegado como una especie de mensajero. A lo mejor si no
hubiese llegado me habría ocurrido otra cosa parecida. Habría
leído algún libro desencadenador, o me habría enamorado de otra
mujer.   (429)

It isn't because of Horacio, love, it isn't only because of Horacio,
even though he may have come like some sort of messenger. If he
hadn't come, something else like it would have happened to me.
I would have read some disillusioning book, or I would have
fallen in love with some other woman.   (271)

Oliveira knows from the very beginning not only that this is one of the
rules of life, but also that a man himself can and should create a situation in
which he will have the opportunity to experience such feelings. Like Wong,
he therefore creates a situation that makes him experience feelings; because
of Talita, he is afraid of Traveler; 'el pobré infeliz tenía *miedo* de que él
[Traveler] lo matara, era para reírse' (703, emphasis added) / 'so the poor
devil was afraid he [Traveler] would kill him, it was laughable' (522). In
reality Oliveira knows that Traveler does not plan to kill him. He creates a
situation in which the attack and the defence are a pretence to escape the
deadly atmosphere of everyday life. He explains to Traveler, 'A veces siento
que entre dos que se rompen la cara a trompadas hay mucho más
entendimiento que entre los que están ahí mirando desde afuera' (437) /
'Sometimes I feel that there's more understanding between two people
punching each other in the face than among those who are there looking on
from outside' (279). Oliveira intuits violence in Traveler's words to Talita:
'Apurate. Talita. Rajale el paquete por la cara y que nos deje de joder de una
buena vez' (405) / 'Hurry up, Talita. Throw the package in his face so he'll

stop screwing around with us once and for all' (249), and chooses to play the game until the end. On the night of the pretended murder Talita says of Oliveira, 'Está tan conento de tener *miedo* esta noche, yo sé que está contento en el fondo' (703, emphasis added) / 'He's so happy to be afraid tonight, I know he's happy' (522). Both Oliveira and Traveler live this game intensely. Oliveira tells him, 'Por lo parte no me vas a negar que nunca estuivste tan despierto como ahora. Y cuando digo despierto me entendés iverdad?' (505) / 'For your part you can't deny that you were never as awake as right now. And when I say awake you understand, right?' (344). Traveler is awake not because he is afraid for himself but because he has identified with Oliveira in the game, and he fears for Oliveira's life. This action, together with the characters' intelligence, willingness to play, and genuine concern for each other, leads to an intensive feeling of life. Traveler inspires Oliveira to act: at the level of everyday reality, on the level of the dirty sidewalk, as Cortázar expresses it, playing rayuela / hopscotch together, Oliveira and Traveler attain what is symbolized by the word 'cielo' / 'heaven.'

Cortázar's goal in *Rayuela* is to awaken the characters and the readers. The fragmentation of the text has this precise purpose. It is a goal that Cortázar shares with many writers of the twentieth century. The absurdists, such as Samuel Beckett or Franz Kafka, exhibit not only the aimlessness and impotence of their heroes, but also their inability to feel that they are alive at all. Others, such as Miguel de Unamuno and Cortázar, use the absurdity of life as a point of departure, and suggest possible ways to avoid the fate of Kafka's hero Joseph K. For Unamuno, to doubt means to live. For Cortázar, the driving forces of life are the conscious, rejection of the established order, the invention and creation of games, and the identification with the other. In their game, in which they are completely involved, Traveler and Oliveira experience life intensely.

Another character, Gekrepten, is the opposite of Talita and has no influence on the development of the character of Oliveira. The rest of the secondary characters in 'Del lado de acá' / 'From This Side' have the same function as the old man who lives above La Maga's apartment; the patients in the mental hospital point out what Oliveira is not—that he is not crazy—and the hospital officials and the neighbours represent the social norm. Some critics (for example, Robert Brody) believe that Oliveira's search ends in madness:

> Oliveira becomes completely insane at the end of the novel when, convinced of Traveler's desire to kill him, he sets up an elaborate protective maze of string and ball bearings and threatens suicide.

Oliveira's quest ends in failure, since he finds neither la Maga nor his 'centro,' 'kibbutz del deseo,' 'absoluto,' 'reino milenario,' all of which may be placed in the final Heaven Section of the hopscotch design.[16]

Cortázar attempted to prevent the reader from drawing a similar conclusion; to show that Oliveira's actions are not ordinary madness, Cortázar puts his protagonist in a hospital with the true lunatics, with whom Oliveira his little in common. In contrast to them, and in contrast to the officials, Oliveira's situation becomes a reality of a higher order. Talita indicates this in her response to Cuca, who treats Oliveira as if he were a child or one of her patients. She offers to make some coffee hoping that Oliveira will come down.

> —Con medialunas fresquitas. ¿Vamos a preparar el café, Talita?
> —No sea idiota—dijo Talita, y en el silencio extraordinario que siguió a su admonición, el encuentro de las miradas de Traveler y Oliveira fue como si dos pájaros chocaran en pleno vuelo y cayeran enredados en la casilla nueve.   (508)

> 'With nice hot croissants. Shall we go make some coffee, Talita?'
> 'Don't be an ass,' Talita said, and in the extraordinary silence that followed her admonition, the meeting of the looks of Traveler and Oliveira was as if two birds had collided in flight and all mixed up together had fallen into square nine.   (348)

Clearly, the novel does not end on a negative note. There is an 'encuentro'—'a meeting' between Oliviera, Traveler, and Talita that lies beyond the possible manipulation of reason. When the mental patients are asked to sign the hospital over to the new owners, they are bribed in the same way Cuca attempts to bribe Oliveira. While the patients do not have the intelligence to resist the deception, Talita, Traveler, and Oliveira certainly do. Oliveira's lucidity is seen in his conversation with Traveler a moment before Cuca's offer, in which he tells Traveler that he saw La Maga:

> —No es la Maga—dijo Travele.—Sabés perfectamente que no es la Maga.
> —No es la Maga—dijo Oliveira—Sé perfectamente que no es la Maga. Y vos sos el abanderado, el heraldo de la redición, de la

vuelta a casa y al orden. Me empezás a dar pena, viejo. (503)

> 'It's not La Maga,' Traveler said. 'You know perfectly well it's not La Maga.'
> 'It's not La Maga,' Oliveira said. 'I know perfectly well it's not La Maga. And you're the standard-bearer, the herald of surrender, of the return to home and order. You're beginning to make me feel sorry, old man.'   (343)

Oliveira is beyond both the simple reasoning of the officials of the hospital and Traveler's reasoning. He is conscious of reality, but transcends it by living like the patients yet differently from them.

In *Rayuela* Cortázar says very little about Oliveira directly. However, Oliveira is the protagonist of the novel; his character exhibits depth and a wide vision of the world. Cortázar creates and develops him through his relationship with other characters. Readers who fill in the gaps do not passively follow Oliveira in his search, but search with him, enriching their own personalities. Cortázar leads readers through multiple interruptions to make them think about what they read. Through the use of juxtaposition and irony Cortázar implies a new order that the reader can reconstruct. From the formal aspect of the novel readers conclude that everything is related to everything else. The richer the contact between Oliveira and people and the world around him, the richer Oliveira's personality becomes. This has important implications. Georgy Lukács quotes Marx as saying that 'the real spiritual wealth of the individual depends completely on the wealth of his real relationships.'[17] In *Rayuela* Oliveira forms no long, meaningful relationships. However, his personality, in contact with other characters, achieves a high level of evolution—liberates itself of its egoism—and, at least for a moment, engages in a complete communication with Traveler and Talita.

The social implications of Oliveira's search are a new step within socialist thinking; Cortázar does not concentrate on the dialectics caused by the progress of history. He believes in the idea of an individual's enrichment, which leads automatically to the formation of the human collective. In this respect Cortázar's novel offers an important contribution to the study of the individual and the social order. The form of the novel tells us that an individual, Oliveira, is himself plus all the people he comes in contact with. In humanity's evolution towards a truly integrated collective, the main obstacle is the egoism that is the product of existing social norms. Oliveira liberates himself from his social 'yo,' not alone but in union with others. Readers who actively accompany Oliveira through *Rayuela*, which constantly demands keen participation and interpretation, learn much about their own abilities to reconstruct social involvement.

THE BRIDGE THEME

A la mano tendida debía responder otra mano desde el afuera, desde lo otro.   (140)

The outstretched hand had to find response in another hand stretched out from the beyond, from the other part.   (99)

In addition to its formal aspects, which juxtapose and unite characters, *Rayuela* contains two important themes that further explain the union between an individual and others—the bridge theme and the pity theme. For Cortázar a bridge is not an artificial link, but an image that illustrates a complete union between people. In Cortázar's short story 'Lejana' ('The Distances') the bridge is a symbol of the search for a complete being. Alina Reyes thinks, 'Más fácil salir a buscar ese puente, salir en busca mía y encontrarme'[18] / 'Easier to go out and look for that bridge, to go out on my own search and find myself.' On the bridge in Budapest Alina embraces her double, a beggar, liberating herself from social values. Jaime Alazraki says, '[In the criticism of Cortázar's works] it is necessary to follow a course opposite to the one adopted until now—not so much to explain the text through the double, but to explain the double through the text in which it has been inserted as an answer to questions and problems posed by the text.'[19] In the board scene Talita changes from a woman standing on two boards to the uniter of Traveler and Oliveira. Through her we understand the type of relationship that binds the three of them together. Cortázar introduces the idea of a bridge in three important instances in *Rayuela*. Oliveira meets La Maga on the bridge; he spends the night with the *clocharde* under the bridge; and Talita is the bridge between him and Traveler. In these three instances Oliveira searches for union with the other, and La Maga seems to be the most distant from him. None the less, Oliveira meets with her through the other two women; she is a friend of the *clocharde*, and Talita reminds Oliveira of La Maga. What is the real relationship between these women and Oliveira? It seems that La Maga is too high to reach, that the *clocharde* is too difficult a companion, and that Oliveira finally reaches the heaven of hopscotch only with and through Talita.

Brita Brodin, along with other critics, points out that La Maga is the poetic ingenuity. Oliveira loses her so that she may be reborn in the image of Talita. Using Cortázar's essay 'Para una poética' ('Towards a Poetics') as a reference point, Saúl Sosnowski explains the relationship between poetic intuition and the poet:

> Según Cortázar, la intuición del hombre es la manifestación de ese estrato 'más real' que trata de poseer. Se establece así una dialéctica poemáctica entre el poeta y esa realidad trans-racional que llamamos 'supra-realidad.' El poeta busca ser, 'quiere poseer la realidad al nivel ontológico, al nivel del ser' y esta supra-realidad trata de manifestarse por medio de la sensibilidad del ser del poeta ... La intuición inicial lleva al poeta a sentir un mundo que no es el hombre pero del cual participa. Es esa supra-realidad que lo usa como MEDIUM, 'ser' es el principio unificado de todo.[20]

> According to Cortázar, a man's intuition is the manifestation of the 'more real' layer which he attempts to possess. In this way a poematic dialectic is established between the poet and this transrational reality which we call 'super-reality.' The poet wishes to be, 'wants to possess the reality on the ontological level, on the level of being' and this super-reality attempts to manifest itself through the sensitivity of being of the poet ... The initial intuition leads the poet to feel a world which is beyond man but in which he participates. It is this super-reality that uses him as a MEDIUM; 'being' is the unifying principle of everything.

If Oliveira is the poet, and La Maga the other reality he attempts to possess, we see that she is not equal to poetry, but only to the 'initial intuition' that is the first step in Oliveira's development. The poet is not only a 'medium,' as Sosnowski believes, because he is not completely passive; he chooses what to accept from the outside world (inspiration). Oliveira wants to possess some of La Maga's characteristics and reject others. He respects her ability to move through life spontaneously, as the current carries her:

> La Maga no sabía demasiado bien por qué había venido a París, y Oliveira se fue dando cuenta de que con una ligera confusión en materia de pasajes, agencias de turismo y visados, lo mismo hubiera podido recalar a Singapur que en Ciudad de Cabo; lo único importante era haber salido de Montevideo, ponerse frente a frente con eso que ella llamaba modestamente la vida.   (146)

> La Maga didn't really know why she had come to Paris, and
> Oliveira was able to deduce that with just a little mixup in tickets,
> tourist agents, and visas she might just as well have disembarked
> in Singapore or Capetown. The main thing was that she has left
> Montevideo to confront what she modestly called 'life'.   (22)

Because of this quality La Maga is an important influence on Oliveira. Soon
after meeting her he tells her, 'Parto del principio de que la reflexión debe
proceder a la acción, babalina' (144) / 'I believe in the principle that thought
must precede action, silly' (20). After spending time with her and then losing
her he approaches life in a different fashion. He thinks, 'Te sentí *previa a
cualquier organización mental*' (532, emphasis added) / 'I sensed you ahead of
any mental organization' (371). This is La Maga's most important effect on
Oliveira. Nothing else about her is strong. Because she is not a rational
being, she allows weeping soldiers and other destructive people to take sexual
advantage of her. She inspires life, but she is not able to protect it. She allows
her son to die because she cannot overcome her intuitive dislike of 'esa cara
de hormiga' (273) / 'that ant-faced doctor' (128). Oliveira also points out that
she is a poor companion in everyday situations: 'Lo horrorizaba la torpeza de
la Maga para fajar y desfajar a Rocamadour [y] sus cantos insoportables para
distraerlo' (230) / 'He was horrified by La Maga's laziness in diapering and
undiapering Rocamadour, the way she would sing at him to distract him'
(77). Oliveira has to ask her to wash her hands after she changes
Rocamadour's diapers, and she annoys him when she spoils his *mate* because
she does not know how to move the *bombilla*.
    So it becomes clear why Oliveira meets La Maga on the bridge. She is
above everyday life, and the two characters need a link between them. To
follow Sosnowski's metaphor, without the poet's firm 'ser' / 'a sense of being'
to filter her through reason, she is easily destroyed. Figuratively, Oliveira has
to bring her down and incorporate her into everyday reality. In Cortázar's
understanding, as in the writings of many other Latin American writers such
as Borges and García Márquez, the fantastic, or the intuitive form, is not a
break with historical reality. As Jaime Alazraki explains, the form is a
realization of what appears to be unreal within our casual contexts.[21]
    Unlike La Maga, who is above life, the *clocharde* is a symbol of survival.
She provides Oliveira with three basic things: heat, food, and sex. More
important, she shows Oliveira how to defy death and conquer nothingness.
When Oliveira spends the night with her he has nothing: he has just broken off
his relationship with La Maga and the members of the club, Pola is dying of
cancer, and he has no apartment, no profession, nothing to eat. Because of the

cold, he is forced to sit close to the stinking Emmanuèle and to drink from the bottle covered with her lipstick and saliva. In short, he has none of the resources Westerners have invented as an escape from nothingness. In loneliness and filth, in his primitive state for the first time, he becomes conscious of himself. There is only one option left for him, his own conscious beginning: 'Deseducación de los sentidos, abrir a fondo la boca y las narices y aceptar el peor de los olores, la mugre humana' (361) / 'Untrain the senses, open your mouth and nose wide and take in the worst of smells, human funkiness' (209). This acceptance of the battle is equivalent to the retreat of Sisyphus; it is a moment of lucidity in which a character willingly accepts fate, which thus stops being fate. In the police car, a symbol of the social order; Emmanuèle consciously throws herself on the floor and chooses to ignore the world around her. In her singing, Oliveira intuits the happiness of being human.

> Y por los mocos y el semen y el olor de Emmanuèle y la bosta del Oscuro se entraría al camino que llevaba al Kibbutz del deseo, no ya subir al Cielo (subir, palabra hipócrita, cielo, flatus vocis), sino caminar con pasos de hombre por una tierra de hombres hacia el kibbutz allá lejos pero en el mismo plano, como el Cielo estaba en el mismo plano que la Tierra en la acera roñosa de los juegos, y un día quizá se entraría en el mundo donde decir Cielo no sería un repasador manchado de grasa, y un día alguien vería la verdadera figura del mundo, patterns pretty as can be, y tal vez, empujando la piedra, acabaría por entrar en el kibbutz.   (369)

> And through the snot and semen and stink of Emmanuèle and the shit of the Obscure one you would come onto the road leading to the kibbutz of desire, no longer rising up to Heaven (rise up, a hypocrite word, Heaven, flatus vocis), but walk along with the pace of a man through a land of men towards the kibbutz far off there but on the same level, just as Heaven was on the same level as Earth on the dirty sidewalk where you played the game, and one day perhaps you would enter that world where speaking of Heaven did not mean a greasy kitchen rag, and one day someone would see the true outline of the world, patterns pretty as can be, and, perhaps, pushing the stone along, you would end up entering the kibbutz.   (216)

Emmanuèle is the awareness of self, while La Maga is selfless inspiration, a fantastic reality. Together these two women produce a complete picture of life which is wholly expressed through the character of Talita. Talita possesses La Maga's intuition and mystery, and like Emmanuèle struggles for the survival of self through consciousness. If La Maga represents poetic inspiration, Talita, being more earthy, is an incarnation of poetry and of true human life. Like La Maga, she inspires the world beyond reality. Traveler tells her that Oliveira does not want her but something beyond her, something through her ('no ella, pero por ella'). Traveler says to Talita, 'El no to busca en absoluto ... Es otra cosa. ¡Es malditamente otra cosa, carajo' (430) / 'He's not after you in the least ... It's something else ... It's something fucking else, God damn it' (271). Talita is aware of this; when Oliveira kissed her in the morgue she realized he was in an exalted state:

> Nunca lo había visto sonreír así, desventuradamente y a la vez con toda la cara abierta y de frente, sin la ironía habitual, aceptando alguna cosa que debía llegarle desde el centro de la vida.   (481)

> She had never seen him smile like that, faintheartedly and at the same time with his whole face open and frontward, without the usual irony, accepting something that must have come to him from the centre of life.   (321)

Talita is capable of taking Traveler as well as Oliveira on a journey beyond everyday reality. She tells her neighbour about Traveler:

> Por supuesto yo soy el mejor de sus [Traveler's] viajes. Pero es tan tonto que no se da cuenta. Yo, señora, lo he llevado en alas de la fantasía hasta el borde mismo del horizonte.   (374)

> Of course, I have been his best trip ... but he's so silly that he doesn't realize it. I, my dear, have carried him off on the wings of fantasy to the very edge of the horizon.   (219)

Like La Maga, Talita has a childlike, imaginative attitude towards life; while La Maga invents 'glíglico,' Talita plays games with Oliveira and Traveler. There is an important difference between the two women, however. La Maga is inventive but not especially intelligent; she keeps her game at a very simple level, and Oliveira complains: 'Me aburre mucho el glíglico. Además vos no tenés imaginación, siempre decís las mismas cosas. La gunfia, vaya novedad' (221) / 'I'm getting sick of Gliglish. Besides, you haven't got any imagination, you always say the same things. Gumphy, that's some fine invention' (85). Talita, in contrast, is an equal partner to Oliveira in 'sementerio' and 'preguntas balanza.'

Unlike La Maga, Talita is a woman who knows how to think; like Emmanuèle, she struggles to maintain her identity. Her games are not only entertainment but also a search for meaning in life. Since Talita and Traveler know that life is absurd, they attempt to conquer the absurd through humour.

> A Talita le hacía poca gracia la idea del manicomio, y Traveler lo sabía. Los dos le buscaban el lado humorístico, prometiéndose espectáculos dignos de Samuel Beckett.   (426)

> Talita didn't find the idea of the mental hospital very funny, and Traveler knew it. The two of them tried to find the humorous side, promising themselves spectacles worthy of Samuel Beckett.
>   (268)

For the same reason, Traveler hides in the bathroom with a cloth over his mouth 'para escuchar como Talita hacía hablar a las señoras' (374) / 'listening while Talita got the ladies to talk' (220). Together with Oliveira they stretch the boards from one window to the other, giving some life to the dead hours of a summer afternoon. That scene is from the theatre of the absurd; to paraphrase Oliveira, they understand that only by living absurdly is it possible to break out of infinite absurdity.

Talita attempts to conquer absurdity and despair through games and through small domestic activities. With her cooking Talita answers some of Traveler's needs and makes him relatively happy.

> Cuando Traveler está triste y piensa que nunca ha viajado (Talita sabe que eso no le importa, que sus preocupaciones son más profundas), hay que acompañarlo sin hablar mucho, cebarle el mate, cuidar de que no le falte tabaco, cumplir el oficio de mujer cerca del hombre pero sin taparle la sombra.   (376)

> When Traveler gets sad and thinks about the fact that he has never travelled (and Talita knows it's not that that bothers him, that his worries are much deeper), she has to go along with him and not say very much, prepare his *mate*, make sure that he never runs out of tobacco, do her duty as a wife alongside her husband but never casting a shadow on him.   (222)

La Maga never possessed these skills. In fact, she often annoyed Oliveira with her clumsiness. She embarrassed the members of the club in a restaurant because she did not know how to use a fork, and she particularly disgusted Etienne with her ignorance. Talita, though, is always a congenial companion.

To show how Talita's small gestures are a form of special communication, Cortázar juxtaposes Gekrepten with Talita. Gekrepten cooks as well as Talita, and as a 'faithful Penelope' makes an effort to please Oliveira. She fails, however, and becomes a grotesque figure because her actions are mechanical. Her stories about visiting a doctor are humorous mainly because they are out of context. Gekrepten does not listen to Oliveira, Traveler, and Talita. Even if Oliveira needed her, she would not be able to perceive it, because she acts only according to a sense of wifely duty.

In her search for meaning Talita is also fighting to maintain her identity—a quality absent in the character of La Maga. When Oliveira tells Talita that she looks like La Maga, Talita says, 'Pero no to fabriques una de tus teorías de posesión, yo no soy zombie de nadie' (477) / 'But don't you go making up one of your theories about my being possessed, I'm nobody's zombie' (317). She also tells Traveler, 'Ustedes [Traveler y Oliveira] están jugando conmigo, es como un partido de tenis, me golpean de los dos lados, no hay derecho Manú, no hay derecho' (429) / 'You two were playing with me, like a tennis ball, you hit me from both sides, it's not right, Manú, it's not right' (270. La Maga does not fight for justice or for herself, though almost everyone wrongs her.

While La Maga becomes the object she observes or experiences, Talita retains her individuality in her awareness of being the observing object that is becoming the object itself. In a taped monologue, Talita, for example, realizes that she is beginning to fall in love with Oliveira. She struggles:

> Soy yo, soy él. Somos, pero soy yo, primeramente soy yo, defenderé ser yo hasta que no pueda más. Atalía, soy yo. Ego. Yo. Diplomada, argentina, una uña encarnada, bonita de a ratos, grandes ojos oscuros, yo. Atalía Donosi, yo. Yo. Yo-yo.   (442)

> I am I, I am he. We are, but I am I, first I am I, I will defend being I until I am unable to fight any longer. I am I ... Atalía Donosi, I. Yo. Yo-yo.   (283)

Talita does not mind that she is he, and that they are one, but she wishes first to be herself. Her 'yo' is different from the 'yo' of Oliveira's uncles in Buenos Aires, which Oliveira ridicules earlier in the novel. Since Talita is not a selfish person, her 'yo' is not a result of social conditioning. Instead, it is a struggle for identity, against nothingness, Her 'yo' is a centre giving unity to everything around her and in her. She is the 'I' of a poet, or, as Sosnowski says, '"ser" es el principio unificador de todo'[22] / '"being" is the unifying principle of everything.'

Talita's struggle is existential in nature: her main question is, Who am I? Her struggle is not purely intellectual, however. Victor Brombert reproduces a typical monologue of the existentialist hero: 'I am, I exist, I think therefore I am; I am because I think; why do I think? I no longer want to think; I am because I think that I do not want to be; I think that I ... because pou ah!'[23] While existentialist heroes attempt to find themselves in their thinking, Talita is satisfied with an almost childlike proof of her existence. Her questioning is complicated, yet it does not reach pure abstraction; she attempts to find an answer in ordinary things. The insecurity of her existence does not put her in a mood that is as serious as the one created by the existentialist hero. She gives her struggle a humorous tone through the repetition of the pronoun 'yo,' which in the end becomes 'yo-yo,' a toy. Cortázar often inserts English phrases in *Rayuela*, and the pun is obviously intentional.

Rather than concentrating on intellectual certainty, Talita shows openness towards life. Even though she objects to being La Maga, in an important moment she admits that on a different level she may be someone else. She does not object when Oliveira tells her:

> —Y vos—dijo Oliveira, apuntando con el dedo—tenés cómplices.
> —¿Cómplices?
> —Sí, cómplices. Yo el primero, y alguien que no está aquí [la Maga].   (424)

> 'And you two,' Oliveira said, pointing his finger at her, 'have accomplices.'
> 'Accomplices?'
> 'Yes, accomplices. First me, and then someone who's not here [La Maga].'   (266)

Even when she tells Oliveira that she is not 'el zombie de nadie' / 'anybody's zombie,' she admits that she thought herself to be La Maga when playing hopscotch. 'Tenés razón. ¿Por qué me habré puesto? A mí en realidad no me gusto nunca la rayuela' (477) / 'You're right. Why did I? I never really did care for hopscotch' (317). Talita feels that she belongs to a world larger than herself, but at the same time she is conscious of her identity.

The struggle expressed in the words 'soy yo, soy él' is also Oliveira's struggle. At the beginning of the novel he was unable to become the other, and he envied La Maga's ability to grasp—to take in—the world around her. Later in the novel he is able to become the other because Talita and Traveler make it easier for him to possess them. When Oliveira left La Maga he said, 'Desde la mano tendida debia responder otra mano desde el afuera, desde lo otro' (240) / 'the outstretched hand had to find response in another hand stretched out from the beyond, from the other part' (99). Talita, being similar to him and consequently (unlike La Maga) able to understand him, offers him a hand from the outside. In becoming Talita and simultaneously remaining himself, Oliveira sets his life in motion in the way Cortázar describes it in Ultimo Round:

> Hay que aprender a despertar dentro del sueño, imponer la voluntad a esa realidad onírica de la que hasta ahora sólo se es pasivamente autor, actor y espectador. Quien llegue a despertar a la libertad dentro de su sueño habrá franqueado la puerta y accedido a un plano que será por fin un NOVUM ORGANUM.[24]

> One must learn to wake up within the dream, to impose one's will on the oneiric reality of which, until now, one is only a passive author, actor, and spectator. The one who succeeds in waking up to freedom in his dream will open the door and accede to a level which finally will be a NOVUM ORGANUM.

In his relationship with La Maga, Oliveira learns to enter the world of dreams. With the *clocharde* he learns both to wake up and to be conscious of himself dreaming. His relationship with Talita gives expression to both these states in an experience equivalent to poetry. Another Argentinian writer, Ernesto Sábato, explains the distinction between dreams and poetry:

> El arte y el sueño tienen un principio común, a mi juicio. Pero en el arte hay salida y en el sueño no. El arte se sumerge, en un primer momento, en el mundo de su inconsciencia, que es el de la noche, y en eso se parece al sueño. Pero luego vuelve hacia fuera, es el momento de la ex-presión, despresión hacia fuera. Es entonces cuando el hombre se libera. En el sueño todo queda adentro.[25]

In my opinion, art and a dream have a common beginning. However, in art there is a way out and in a dream there is not. The art submerges itself, at the first moment, in the world of the unconscious, which belongs to night, and in this it is similar to a dream. But then it comes back out, it is the moment of expression, depression outward. It is then that the person is liberated. In a dream everything remains inside.

The three women Oliveira meets *on*, *under*, and *in* the bridge explain Oliveira's gradual liberation from the social 'yo' to the creation of a poetic 'I.' The relationship between the 'I' and the external world, the other, is also a key to Cortázar's second theme, that of pity. The relationship—'soy yo, soy él'—reveals that Talita's struggle is also Oliveira's.

THE THEME OF PITY

Thou art the thing itself, unaccommodated man is no more but such a poor, bare, forked animal.
                                                                —Shakespeare, *King Lear*

Through *Rayuela*'s constant juxtaposition and question-raising, readers come to discover the importance of a word that recurs like a leitmotiv throughout the novel. The word 'lástima' / 'pity' is repeated in Oliveira's relationship with Berthe Trépat, with La Maga, with Traveler, and with Talita. In the first two instances Oliveira rejects the feeling of pity because it does not arise out of a genuine and equal relationship. In the last two he accepts it because it is a product of authentic togetherness. Readers draw their own conclusions and probably wonder why the same feeling is accepted in one situation and rejected in another.

The ability to feel pity is, for Oliveira and Cortázar, a sign of life; a meaningful, intense life is possible only in a relationship with the other. The theme of pity, the theme of the bridge, and the development of the protagonist in relation to other characters in the novel combine to generate an important philosophy of life. Cortázar was often criticized for taking an irresponsible attitude towards his society at a time when his country, as well as the whole of Latin America, was in a state of economic and political crisis. Many critics did not realize that Cortázar had his own profound view of this struggle. In fact, he advocates revolution in his novel—a revolution not only artistic but also subtly political.

> Political preoccupation in no way imposes a limitation of the
> artist's creative value and function; rather, his literary or artistic
> creation develops within a context that includes the historical
> situation and its political options, which, in a subtle or direct
> manner, will be reflected in the most vital aspect of his work.[26]

Cortázar does not write 'proletarian literature,' as he calls the literature of socialist realism, which deals with social problems in the form of propaganda. He believes that a revolution can be successful only if it starts from the very essence of individual people and moves out towards a larger context. In this he differs from most socialist writers. Brecht, for example, says in his *Organon* that 'we must not start with the individual but work towards him.'[27] Cortázar's goal in *Rayuela* is 'establecer una verdadera comunicación del hombre consigo mismo, con los demás y con el mundo que lo rodea'[28] / 'to establish a true communication of man with himself, with others and with the world that surrounds him'. In his novel Cortázar defines man not as an individual but as someone with a relationship to the world and to people around him. In this approach Cortázar produces a double effect: he exhibits the hypocrisy of the old society and shows how a new, more honest and natural society creates itself. Once liberated from the egoism and hypocrisy taught in the existing world, people can rediscover natural links with their fellow human beings. Culture, which provides no answers to these new people, functions only as a game.

Cortázar introduces the theme of pity in *Rayuela* through Oliveira's relationship with Berthe Trépat. After he tells La Maga that he does not wish to stay in the same apartment with her because her son Rocamadour disturbs him, Oliveira, having nothing better to do, goes to a concert given by Berthe Trépat. All the spectators leave because the concert is as grotesque as the woman giving it; but Oliveira stays because 'le hizo gracia esa especie de *solidaridad*' (249, emphasis added) / 'he was amused by this bit of solidarity' (107). From the psychological point of view it is possible that Oliveira, feeling guilty because he cannot tolerate the presence of an innocent baby, attempts to assuage his guilty conscience with this act. His staying until the end of the concert is perhaps analogous to the act of giving alms in expiation for some horrible deed. If this is the case, it is only one of the reasons for the scene that follows the concert. There is a still more important message: if it is imbued with self-interest, pity can lead to a more serious and more embarrassing situation. Oliveira waits for the pianist after the concert and offers to see her home. When they arrive at her house Valentín, the pianist's boyfriend, will not let her in. Oliveira then offers to pay for a hotel room with his last franc and to accompany her to a bar, or to go and talk to Valentín.

At this point readers are caught in a trap. Oliveira's offers seem serious, and Berthe Trépat's stories about Valentín make her definitely Valentín's victim. Readers begin to feel that Oliveira is a nice fellow who is fulfilling his duty as a good citizen by helping a poor woman. But Cortázar's use of irony dramatically alters these assumptions. Cortázar ridicules not the basic need to help the other, but the reason the help is given. Oliveira does not help Berthe Trépat just because he truly understands or likes her. He has ulterior motives:

> Es demasiado idiota, pero hubiera sido tan bueno, subir a beber una copa con ella y con Valentín, sacarse los zapatos al lado del fuego. En realidad por lo único por que yo estaba contento era por eso, por la idea de sacarme los zapatos y que se me secaran las medias ... Era para reírse.   (269)

> It's all been too nutty, but it would have been nice to have gone upstairs and had a drink with her and with Valentín, taken off my shoes next to the fire. Actually, that's all I ever wanted to do, the idea of taking off my shoes and drying my socks ... It was enough to make you laugh.   (124)

Oliveira exhibits selfishness in the act of giving, but the pianist also uses him for her own purposes. When he offers to pay for her hotel room she slaps him across the face, not because she believes that he wants to sleep with her but because she needs to regain her self-esteem on the pretext of asserting her moral and sexual purity. She hits him, and speaks very loudly when she hears her neighbours coming downstairs. In both instances the subject is only conscious of his or her own need; the object, the other, is completely foreign.

Oliveira's behaviour with Berthe Trépat is not an isolated example. Oliveira says that he, like Gregorovius, feels pity for La Maga. Looking at Gregorovius, who is stroking La Maga's head after she has told him her rape story, Oliveira thinks:

> Y le tenemos *lástima*, entonces hay que llevarla a casa, un. poco bebidos todos, acostarla despacio, acariciándola, soltándole la ropa, despacito, despacito, cada botón, cada cierre relámpago, y ella no quiere, quiere, no quiere, se endereza, se tapa la cara, llora,

nos abraza como para proponernos algo sublime, ayuda a bajarse
el slip ... Te voy a tener que romper la cara, Ossip Gregorovius,
pobre amigo mío.   (177–8, emphasis added)

We feel sorry for her and we have to take her home, all of us a
little tight, and put her to bed, petting her gently as we take off
her clothes, slowly, button by button, every zipper, and she does
want to, wants to, doesn't want to, straightens up, covers her face,
cries, hugs us as if suggesting something sublime, wiggles out of
her slip ... I'm going to have to bust you in the face, Ossip
Gregorovius my poor friend.   (47–8)

La Maga is in one world while they are in another. The pity they feel is obviously
not the way to a complete communication, even if she does respond to them slightly.
     When Rocamadour dies and La Maga is in a similar situation, Oliveira
avoids this hypocrisy. Even though it appears cruel to the members of the
club, who judge him by the old existing criterion, Oliveira chooses not to stay
with La Maga for the following reasons:

Oliveira se dijo que no sería tan difícil llegarse hasta la cama,
agacharse para decirle unas palabras al oído a la Maga. 'Pero eso
yo lo haría por mí', pensó. 'Ella está más allá de cualquier cosa.
Soy yo el que después dormiría mejor, aunque no sea más que una
manera de decir. Yo, yo, yo. Yo dormiría mejor después de besarla
y consolarla y repetir todo lo que ya le han dicho éstos.'   (320)

Oliveira told himself that it would not be so difficult to go over
to the bed, squat down beside it and say a few words in La Maga's
ear. 'But I would be doing it for myself,' he thought. 'She's
beyond anything. I'm the one who would sleep better afterward,
even if it's just an expression. Me, me, me. I would sleep better
after I kissed her and consoled her and repeated everything these
people have already said.'   (170–1)

In this case Oliveira rejects self-interest as well as hierarchy among people.
In another example, at a time when La Maga feels pity for Oliveira, she has
no self-interest. None the less, she feels superior to Oliveira—a feeling that
is also unacceptable because it shows a lack of understanding. The following
conversation takes place between La Maga and Oliveira:

—Te tengo tanta lástima, Horacio.

—Ah, eso no. Despacito, ahí.

—Te tengo *lástima*—insistió la Maga—. Ahora me doy cuenta. La noche que nos econtramos ... Si te dijera que todo eso lo hice por *lástima*.

—Vamos—dijo Oliveira, mirándola sobresaltado.

—Esa noche vos corrías peligro. Se veía, era como una siren a lo lejos ... no se puede explicar.   (225–6, emphasis added)

'I feel so sorry for you, Horacio.'

'Oh no; hold it right there.'

'... I feel sorry for you.' La Maga repeated. 'I can see now. That night we met ... If I were to tell you that I did it all out of pity.'

'Come off it,' Oliveira said, looking at her with surprise.

'You were in danger that night. It was obvious, like a siren in the distance ... I can't explain it.'   (89)

If Oliveira is in any danger, he tells her, his danger is of a metaphysical nature. But since she does not understand metaphysics, she does not understand him. Her feeling of pity, therefore, is not based on understanding, and her love-making with him, a form of charity, does not solve any of his problems.

Understanding is an important factor for Oliveira. He says about his experience with two of his ex-girlfriends:

En dos ocasiones había estado a punto de sentir *lástima* y dejarles la ilusión de que lo *comprendían*, pero algo le decía que su *lástima* no era *auténtica*, más bien un recurso barato de su egoísmo y su pureza y sus costumbres.   (484, emphasis added)

On two occasions he had been at the point of feeling pity and letting them keep the illusion that they understood him, but something told him that his pity was not genuine, it was more a cheap trick of his selfishness and his laziness and his habits.

(419–20)

What Oliveira searches for is an authentic pity, a true sign of life.

Y con tanta ciencia una inútil ansia de tener *lástima* de algo, de que llueva aquí dentro, de que por fin empiece a llover, a oler a tierra, a cosas vivas, sí, por fin a cosas vivas.

(235, emphasis added)

And with so much knowledge a useless anxiety to pity something,
to have it rain here inside, so that at long last it will start to rain
and smell of earth and living things, yes, living things at long last.

(96)

The feeling of pity that Oliveira longs for here is very similar to La
Maga's experience of the world: the ability to rejoice at the smallest detail, to
be happy because she finds a piece of red cloth on the street. While he stayed
with her Oliveira was no more able to join La Maga in this enjoyment than
she was able to join him in his metaphysical quest. By the end of the novel,
however, Oliveira is able to experience life fully in his friendship with
Traveler and Talita.

When thinking about his relationship with Traveler and Talita,
Oliveira remembers the incident with Berthe Trépat: There is a superficial
similarity to that grotesque scene, but the new situation develops very
differently. Oliveira compares Traveler's kindness in finding him a job in the
circus with his own seemingly kind treatment of Berthe Trépat: 'En ese caso
apiadarse hubiera sido tan idiota como la otra vez: lluvia, lluvia. ¿Seguiría
tocando el piano Berthe Trépat?' (451, emphasis added) / 'In that case it
would have been just as idiotic as the other time: rain, rain. I wonder if
Berthe Trépat still plays the piano?' (292). Oliveira accepts the job because in
this situation Traveler does not demonstrate either his superiority or self-
interest. He accepts him as an equal rival and invites him to fight. Similarly,
when Talita asks Oliveira to leave the morgue he accepts her hand even
though he again recalls Berthe Trépat:

> Estaba viendo con tanta claridad un boulevard bajo la lluvia, pero
> en vez de ir llevando a alguien del brazo, hablándole con *lástima*,
> era a él que lo llevaban, *compasivamente* le habían dado el brazo y
> le hablaban para que estuviera contento, le tenían tanta *lástima*
> que era positivamente una delicia ... Esa mujer jugadora de
> rayuela *le tenía lástima*, era tan claro que quemaba.

(480, emphasis added)

He could see with great clarity a boulevard in the rain, but instead
of leading somebody along by the arm, talking to her with pity,
he was being led, they had given him a compassionate arm and

they were talking to him so that he would be happy, they had so
much concern for him that it was absolutely delightful ... That
woman who played hopscotch had pity on him, it was so obvious
that it burned.   (320)

At this point readers have to ask, Why is pity ridiculed in one instance and
accepted with enthusiasm in another? The answer lies in the relationship of
equality between Oliveira and Traveler and Talita. Traveler and Talita pity
Oliveira because they understand him and feel that his situation is also theirs.
Traveler feels that there is a mystical bond that ties them together. He tells
Talita:

> Increíble, parecería que cuando él [Oliveira] se junta con nosotros
> hay paredes que se caen, montones de cosas que se van al quinto
> demonio, y de golpe el cielo se pone fabulosamente hermoso, las
> estrellas se meten en esa panera uno podría perlarlas y
> comérselas.   (430)

> It's incredible, when he's with us it's as if walls collapsed, piles of
> things all going to hell, and suddenly the sky becomes
> fantastically beautiful, the stars come out on that baking dish, you
> can skin them and eat them.   (272)

Oliveira feels the same way. He tells Traveler and Talita:

> Me da por pensar que nuestra relación es casi química, un hecho
> fuera de nosotros mismos. Una especie de dibujo que se va
> haciendo.   (439)

> It makes me think that our relationship is almost chemical,
> something outside of ourselves. A sort of sketch that is being
> done.   (281)

Their relationship has an element of mysticism and mystery, something
similar to the quality that La Maga represented. It also has the sense of
ceremony embodied in the character of Wong. Oliveira, Traveler, and Talita
spend most of their time playing games in an attempt to overcome the
boredom of their job and their neighbourhood. Like Etienne and Morelli,
they break away from the traditional way of living to create a new order.
Traveler forces Oliveira to stay with them, even though he is jealous and

knows that there is an attraction between Oliveira and Talita. In this rivalry
a certain fear is awakened in both men, giving them the sense that they are
living fully. Like Babs and Ronald, the Argentinian threesome is able to
experience a childlike identification with the world around them. When
Oliveira threatens to commit suicide, Traveler reacts emotionally: 'Traveler
lo miraba, y Oliveira vio que se te llenaban los ojos de lágrimas. Le hizo un
gesto como si le acariciara el pelo desde lejos' (507) / 'Traveler looked at him,
and Oliveira saw that his eyes were filling with tears. He made a gesture as if
to stroke his hair from a distance' (346). Talita also loses herself in her
feelings for Oliveira. Oliveira comments at the end of the novel: 'Se sacrificó
por mi—dijo Oliveira—. La otra no se lo va a perdonar ni en el lecho de
muerte' (509) / '"She sacrificed herself for me," Oliveira said. "The other one
is never going to forgive her, not even on her deathbed"' (348). The reason
La Maga will not forgive Talita is that Oliveira's relationship with Talita (and
Traveler) is much stronger because it is more complete. It has most of the
qualities of life that Oliveira defines in his relationship with the members of
the Club de la Serpiente. At the same time, Talita has similar characteristics
to both La Maga and the *clocharde*. The combination of these qualities
spontaneously creates an intense and complete unity among Oliveira and his
two Argentinian friends.

To show the seriousness and the difficulty of the struggle to achieve
this union, Cortázar's novel does not end like a fairy tale—'and they lived
happily ever after'—but puts Oliveira in an absurd situation in which he is
fed by his ridiculous girlfriend Gekrepten. Many critics have therefore
concluded that *Rayuela* ends in madness, and that Cortázar is a nihilist. For
those who have closely followed the account of Oliveira and his rewarding
union with Traveler and Talita, this last scene is similar to Oliveira's descent
to the filthy world of the *clocharde*. It gives Oliveira strength to get up and
continue the larch for La Maga, who has become the lighthouse towards
which he moves.

As a mimetic novel, *Rayuela* has to end on a negative note. Any quick
change for the better either in Oliveira or in his outside world would be
artificial. In spite of this, the novel as a whole is positive. Readers are shown
the possibility of human evolution (even though it points backwards towards
the original self) and a route to a more natural human collective. Steven
Boldy observes:

> Oliveira rejects the whole world of history and politics, 'not
> because of Eden, not so much because of Eden itself, but just to
> leave behind the jet plane, the face of Nikita or Dwight or

Charles or Francisco.' Thus he condemns oppressive Russian communism, American imperialism, French nationalism, Spanish fascism, not for any other political position, but for what they have in common, their negation of man. It is the whole system of thought in the West that he attacks: 'since the Eleatics to the present day, dialectical thought has had plenty of time to yield its fruits. We are eating it, it's delicious, it is boiling with radioactivity.' Thus until man's whole way of thinking is changed, any political action will simply be a perpetuation of the same state of affairs.[29]

Cortázar's contribution to humanity and social development in *Rayuela* becomes especially obvious in the context of the works of those Russian and East European writers who disagree with the political reality in their countries and are fighting for a better model of socialism. These writers believe that the main failure of the social revolution in Eastern European countries lies in its preference for the collective to the exclusion of the individual. In *Doctor Zhivago* Boris Pasternak does not object to revolution as such, but to the preference for ideas and people as a general concept over human life and the individual. His hero Zhivago ('Zhivago' in Russian means 'alive') is destroyed by fanatics and opportunists who fight for revolutionary ideas rather than for human life. In *Rayuela* human life is of supreme importance. Cortázar, like Pasternak, believes the individual must not be sacrificed for the collective. In *Doctor Zhivago* Tonya's father, an honest pre-revolutionary aristocrat, returns to his house and finds that it is no longer a home for him and his family. When he is told that his house was taken for the people, he asks, 'Are we not people?' In Cortázar's revolution, there is no need for such a question; a person is as important as people. People are an amalgamation of honest, intelligent, educated, and imaginative men and women.

Dobrica Chosich, a contemporary Yugoslavian writer who fought for the socialist revolution beside Tito, asks a question similar to Pasternak's. In Chosich's novel *The Sinner* his heroine Milena leaves her bourgeois home to fight for the revolution alongside her husband. She suffers imprisonment with him without a trace of fear or disappointment. Her husband, however, leaves her in order to belong totally to the Komiterna and communism. Milena's question to his friend Peter is the key question in the novel: 'What kind of a communist are you, Bogdan, if you are unable to love a woman?'[30] Unlike Chosich's heroes, Talita, Traveler, and Oliveira form a collective firmly based on human emotion and understanding. They are Cortázar's models for the reader in the struggle for the new human being and for future, true revolutions.

Cortázar is a socialist writer whose work is extremely important to the development of socialism. A supporter of the Cuban revolution, he wrote to Fernández Retamar:

> Jamás escribiré expresamente para nadie ... Y sin embargo hoy sé que escribo para, que hay una intencionalidad que apunta a esa esperanza de un lector en el que reside ya la semilla del hombre nuevo.[31]

> I will not write explicitly for anyone ... Nonetheless, today I know that I write for, that there is an intention which aims at the hope of a reader in whom resides a seed of the new man.

Cortázar writes with a certain intention in mind: completeness of being and the human collective. The form of the novel gives evidence of this thematic aspect. Cortázar's characters are simultaneously autonomous characters and part of a single author's plan, a plan which considers the nature of a person and the union with the other. The dialectics of the novel arise from the tension between awareness of one's self and a belonging to something else. Talita's struggle—'soy yo, soy él'—is a nucleus of the struggle in the novel as a whole.

In *Rayuela* Cortázar searches for a complete liberation and complete involvement. Honesty leads his characters, particularly La Maga, away from social lies and allows the characters to possess the world around them. Imagination and games, represented by Wong, Traveler, and Talita, complement Ronald's and Babs's complete identification, and lead to a rebirth. Games in *Rayuela* have the same function as rituals in primitive times. Octavio Paz explains:

> The fiesta is not only an excess, a ritual squandering of the goods painfully accumulated during the rest of the year [as certain French sociologists had claimed]; it is also a revolt, a sudden immersion in the formless, in pure being. By means of the fiesta society frees itself from the norms it has established. It ridicules its gods, its principles, and its laws; it denies its own self ... The group emerges purified and strengthened from this plunge into chaos. It has immersed itself in its own origins, in the womb from which it came.[32]

Cortázar's anti-novel *Rayuela* is for the reader exactly this: a fiesta leading to a rebirth.

Rayuela is also a polyphonic novel that rebels against any logical simplification; it emphasizes the individuality of its elements while searching at the same time for their synthesis. The clue to the synthesis, and to the understanding of the novel, is to be found in the relationship of characters, in the character web. Cortázar constructs his novel on the principles of metaphor and irony—two similar modes of expression, according to Wayne Booth:

> In reading any metaphor or simile, as in reading irony, the reader must reconstruct unspoken meanings through inferences about surface statements that for some reason cannot be accepted at face value; in the terminology made fashionable by I.A. Richards, there is a *tenor* (a principal subject) conveyed by a vehicle (the secondary subject). It is not surprising, then, that many casual definitions of irony would fit metaphor just as well, and that the two have sometimes been lumped together in criticism.[33]

While irony deceives readers and makes them reconsider their original understanding of the text and issues, metaphor requires a complete synthesis of different semantic fields (worlds) and a formation of a new, all-encompassing field (world). In *Rayuela* different characters are carriers of different semantic fields, or different philosophical ideas. The osmosis of the secondary characters by the protagonist produces the character of Horacio Oliveira, the constant point of reference in the interpretation of the novel. In *Rayuela* the main question is, What is a human being? The 'yo' of Cortázar's principal character differs from the 'yo' of the Romantic hero because in Oliveira's case the subjective 'I' is inseparable from the outside world.

The relationship between the 'I' of Cortázar's hero and his 'circumstances' must first be examined from the existentialist point of view; only then can we deduce the social, political, and other implications. Cortázar's man is conscious that he is himself and the world around him. This is well illustrated in Talita's taped monologue which begins, 'Soy yo, soy él.' In the novel as a whole Oliveira struggles against the egoism, or emphasis on individuality, that is encouraged by Western thought. With the help of La Maga, who lacks the awareness of self but is able to become the object observed, he succeeds in bridging his concerns for self-awareness and La Maga's intuitive grasp of the world around her. Oliveira's struggle is equivalent to the poetic experience of the world in which the poet synthesizes his I, his consciousness, with the poetic inspiration, an emotional and illogical aspect of life.

Cortázar's development of the theme of pity makes evident his intention with respect to the further implications of this question. Pity in *Rayuela* is synonymous with understanding. Pity is not pity as we normally conceive it but, as with César Vallejo, a sense of solidarity that requires liberation from social prejudices, and egoism, and an openness towards life (the other). It also requires an imaginative, active participation, as in a game, and an awareness that the absurd can be conquered only by a decision of the sort made by Sisyphus not to avoid his destiny but to participate willingly in an absurd situation. In other words, a feeling of pity arises out of our decision to search for meaning in union with the world and the people around us. Oliveira's happiness at the end of the novel is like that expressed by the Spanish poet Vicente Aleixandre:

> Hermoso es, hermosamente humilde y confiante
> vivificador y profundo,
> sentirse bajo el sol, *entre los demás*.[34]

> It's beautiful, beautifully humble and trusting,
> exhilarating and profound,
> to feel yourself under the sun with others.

The union with the other in *Rayuela* is not an artificial union but arises from humanity's essential need to surpass its own limited sphere. By writing the novel Cortázar shows us a struggle for a true socialism.

The artistic and educational strength of Cortázar's *Rayuela* lies in its ability to engage readers and make them arrive at their own conclusions. The possibility of multiple interpretations arises from Cortázar's metaphor, which suggests new relationships. He writes economically about the essential problems, leaving the rest of the explication up to the readers. The characters in the novel are important stimuli because readers easily relate to other human beings. The identification with the character, an important aspect of literature, is only the first step in the interpretation of the novel. *Rayuela* requires a perceptive, imaginative, and informed reader. The relationship between the characters in the novel and between the characters and readers has two main functions: to stimulate the readers' identification and to guide them in the interpretation. Given *Rayuela*'s fragmentary nature, readers must understand its characters in order to interpret its meaning. The characters are not superimposed on the text; the text is the stuff of which they are made. Cortázar has earned a special place in the development of the modern novel because he creates multidimensional characters while carrying out intellectual and stylistic experimentation.

NOTES

1. Sartre, *What Is Literature?* 38
2. Genover, *Uno novelística existencial*, 57
3. Valdés, *Shadows in the Cave*, 102
4. Picón Garfield, *¿Es julio Cortázar un surrealista?* 70
5. Bakhtin, *Dostoyevsky's Poetics*, 28
6. Ibid., 17
7. MacAdam, *Modern Latin American Narrative*, 54
8. Picón Garfield, 'Interview with Julio Cortázar,' 9
9. *Libro de Manuel*, 27; *A Manual for Manuel*, 23
10. Booth, *A Rhetoric of Irony*, 43
11. Ibid., 106
12. Sola, *El hombre nuevo*, 122
13. Brodin, *Criaturas ficticias*, 33
14. Ibid., 45
15. Picón Garfield, *Cortázar por Cortázar*, 20
16. Brody, *Julio Cortázar*, 20
17. Lukács, *European Realism*, 143
18. Cortázar, 'Lejana,' in *Bestiario*, 44
19. Alazraki, '"Lejana" Revisited,' 73
20. Sosnowski, *Julio Cortázar*, 12
21. Alazraki, *En busca del unicornio*, 75
22. Sosnowski, *Julio Cortázar*, 12
23. Brombert, *The Intellectual Hero*, 181
24. Cortázar, *Ultimo Round*, 50, planta baja
25. Sábato, 'Borges-Sábato,' 23
26. Cortázar, 'Politics and the Intellectual,' 42
27. Quoted in Dickson, *Towards Utopia*, 46
28. Genover, *Una novelística existencial*, 72
29. Boldy, *Novels of Cortázar*, 44
30. Chosich, *Greshnik*, 442. The translation is mine.
31. Cortázar, 'Carta a Retamar,' 86
32. Paz, *Labyrinth of Solitude*, 51
33. Booth, *A Rhetoric of Irony*, 22
34. Aleixandre, 'En la plaza,' in *Historia del corazón*, 209

DORIS SOMMER

Grammar Trouble:
Cortázar's Critique of Competence

From the opening lines in "The Pursuer" (1959), Julio Cortázar's narrator seems uneasy.[1] Bruno is a jazz critic, respected among Parisian publishers and academics, but surprisingly out of phase from the very beginning of his story.[2] By contrast, the disarmingly lucid character here is a drug-dependent saxophonist who stands in for Charlie Parker. Any jazz buff would recognize him from the biographical dates and details that follow, and maybe even from the title and our first glimpse of a self-destructive and arrogant "Johnny Carter," but Cortázar makes sure we get the reference from his dedication to Parker in memoriam. The narrating critic, as I said, shows signs of awkwardness even before Johnny greets him sardonically—"Faithful old buddy Bruno, regular as bad breath" [161].[3] Not that Bruno justifies Johnny's distasteful reception, as if faithfulness were any reason for embarrassment. On the contrary, Bruno assumes no responsibility for Johnny's bad mood. Why should he, when the loyal friend had rushed to the musician's cheap hotel room to rescue him—once again—from the childish irresponsibility that only artists get away with? This time Johnny had forgotten his saxophone under the seat of a subway car and Bruno offered to replace it. The rescuer's condescending concern obviously grates on the black musician, who seems helpless, sweating, and shivering after some forbidden drug-induced high. Patronized and misprized, Johnny surely knows the self-

---

From *Diacritics* vol. 25, no. 1 (Spring 1995). © 1995 The Johns Hopkins University Press.

serving motives for solicitude, and he probably dismisses Bruno's genuine concern for the man wasting his talent and his life, just as Charlie Parker was said to dismiss his own friends and fans.[4] Bruno's objection to heroin means, for Johnny, a determination to cancel the trips that take him away from work. Johnny's work is, after all, the necessary condition for Bruno's success. "I'm thinking of the music being lost, the dozens of sides Johnny would be able to cut, leaving that presence, that astonishing step forward where he had it over any other musician" [167].[5] The poor "savage monkey" of a musician is not only the object of Bruno's own, casually racist dismissals [see 258, 263, 288, 291, 299; English 164, 174, 179,199]; he is also the subject of the critic's authoritative biography. Johnny plays the alto sax as "only a god can play" [251; 163], and he continues to be the capital for Bruno's critical purchase. But Johnny is precarious capital, because—as Bruno frets toward the end— he might publicly contradict the interpreter, or simply leave him behind in the wake of musical and personal mischief.

COMMAND PERFORMANCE

Bruno has good reason to fret, while his professional identity and public worth wither from exposure to questions of competence. For Bruno to admit that the biographer doesn't really know his subject, that the critic can't quite keep time to the music, is to admit defeat in criticism and to de-authorize himself. Critics are supposed to know better, and Bruno can stand in for so many professional readers in Cortázar's narrative commentary, as well as in the following abbreviated discussion about critical deafness to textual refusals of cooperation.[6] We are far more likely to treat a text as a command performance; it happens thanks to our attention. Ever since interpretation freed itself from its origins in pious exegesis, which could remain open to wonder and awe, critics have tended to take the responsibility, and the credit, for understanding art better than the artist. "Don't ask a writer to interpret his own work" is the common caution, as if writers, or musicians, were inspired but not very smart people. Even in the improvisational styles of today's critical riffs, where striking the right note is far less interesting than playing on variations, and where "correct" interpretation fragments and multiplies into a range of competing takes, critics continue to assume that they know the score.

Years of privileged literary training understandably add up to a kind of entitlement to know a text, possibly with the possessive and reproductive intimacy of Adam who knew Eve. As teachers and students we have until now welcomed resistance as a coy, teasing invitation to test and hone our mastery.

We may pick up a book because we find it attractive—or because of mimetic desire through (for) a model reader, the real object of our murderous desire to displace her. We always assume, in our enlightened secular habits, that the books are happy to have our attention, like so many wallflowers lined up to be selected for a quick turn or an intimate tête-à-tête. If the book seems easy, if it allows possession without a struggle and cancels the promise of self-flattery for an expert reading, our hands may go limp at the covers. Easy come, easy go. The more difficult the book the better. Difficulty is a challenge, an opportunity to struggle and to win, to overcome resistance, to uncover the codes, to get on top of it, to put one's finger on the mechanisms that produce pleasure and pain, and then to call it ours. We take up an unyielding book to conquer it and to feel grand, enriched by the appropriation and confident that our cunning is equal to the textual tease that had, after all, planned its own submission as the ultimate climax of reading. Books want to be understood, don't they, even when they are coy and evasive? Evasiveness and ambiguity are, as we know, familiar interpretive flags that readers erect on the books they leave behind. Feeling grand and guiltless, we proceed to the next conquest.

"I am only interested in what does not belong to me. Law of Man. Law of the Cannibal" [35] is the gluttonous way Oswald de Andrade inflected this desire to conquer difference. Appropriation of the other is what our New World cultures feed on, according to the Brazilian modernist, as long as the other offers the spice of struggle. Cannibals reject the bland meat easily consumed, in this digestion of Montaigne's essay.[7] Europe, apparently, was also constituted by ingesting its others. And Andrade's point is, after all, that cannibalism is what makes us all human, or at least participants in an extended occidental culture nourished on novelty. His manifesto is intentionally provocative; it makes outrageous theater of more contrite admissions of plunder.

But how much less provocative is Roland Barthes's *Pleasure of the Text*? It pushes the engagements of reader-response theory to their eroticized limits, to a knowing note of triumph over the text. He takes for granted that texts exist to give him pleasure, that in fact he is their reason for being: "The text is a fetish object, and *this fetish desires me*" [27]. The reader as object of desire, the solicited partner for an intimate entanglement, Barthes performs tirelessly in his extended essay to reciprocate. The result is a book composed of flirtatiously neurotic [6] intermittence, deliciously anticipated but unpredictably timed interventions at gaps in the body of conventional criticism. This boldly self-celebratory role for the reader sounds almost scandalous against the drone of academic theories; and it rubs dangerously against the sensitive skin of sexually correct comportment in today's American academy. But I wonder how fundamentally different it is from other strains of reader-response theory that also flatter readers by locating them as objects of textual desire and elevating them from the perverse role of voyeur to the category of partner, collaborator, co-author.

In critics as different from one another as Georges Poulet is from Wolfgang Iser, the focus is on the agency of readers. Whether agency is understood as interiorizing (not to say cannibalizing) instead of talking back to a text (in Poulet's version), or as putting the text into dialogic motion (as in Iser's classic and familiar studies),[8] readers are necessary and equal partners in the shared pleasures of aesthetic production. Poulet's claims selflessly to "accede" to a text can prove the outlying example of an inclusive culture of criticism.[9] He protests against modest passivity only after initiating his own surrender to helplessly dependent objects that crave his attention:

> Books are objects. On a table, on shelves, in store windows, they wait for someone to come and deliver them from their materiality, from their immobility. When I see them on display, I look at them as I would at animals for sale, kept in little cages, and so obviously hoping for a buyer. For—there is no doubting it— animals do know that their fate depends on a human intervention.... Isn't the same true of books? ... They wait. Are they aware that an act of man might suddenly transform their existence? They appear to be lit up with that hope. Read me, they seem to say. I find it hard to resist their appeal. [56]

Once Poulet, the reader-prince, commands a performance and succumbs to his own sensitivity to the text's charming eagerness for a kiss, the rest of his essay follows the flirtatious rhythm of reciprocal possession. The analogy between bookshops and pet stores is a provocatively flimsy cover-up for love for sale.[10] The first move is to purchase a partner and to feel chosen by the book; the next is to appreciate its "offering, opening itself.... It asks nothing better than to exist outside itself, or to let you exist in it. In short, the extraordinary fact in the case of a book is the falling away of the barriers between you and it. You are inside it; it is inside you" [57]. As the entanglement proceeds, Poulet manages some distance; he takes a breath of reflection on such breathless activity. ("On the other hand—and without contradiction—reading implies something resembling the apperception I have of myself.... Whatever sort of alienation I may endure, reading does not interrupt my activity as subject" [60]. But the repeatable rhythm of contact and consummation concludes by celebrating abandon to the writer who "reveals himself to us *in* us" [61]. Perhaps celebration is in order because abandon, far from diminishing the reader as ventriloquist and vehicle, returns him to princely primacy. "The work lives its own life within me; in a certain sense, it thinks itself, and it even gives itself a meaning within me" [62], a universal meaning that finally does not belong to a particular work. It is a haunting "transcendence" that is perceptible when criticism can "annihilate, or at least momentarily forget, the objective elements of the work, and to elevate itself to the apprehension of a subjectivity without objectivity" [72].

If Poulet's finally immodest and mutually penetrating dance with the death of authorship can suggest one kind of border in reader-response criticism, the frontier between unabashedly self-centered unscientific ludicism and the philosophically cautious grounding in the reality of reading as an activity, a different border is the site of equally serious trouble. It is the promising but underdeveloped place where reader response meets political imperatives, the critical place marked in Cortázar's story by a racial difference that complicates the question of competence. The trouble brewing there is, to a great degree, Bruno's nervousness about the self-authorizing assumptions common to professional readers. He remains unconvinced of his own competence and is therefore unrecognizable as a critic. Since when have educated readers recognized themselves as the possible targets of a text, as incompetent voyeurs? Perhaps it is time that we learn to do so.

One notable case of missing the aggressive point is Ross Chambers's *Room for Maneuver: Reading (the) Oppositional (in) Narrative*. Beginning with an admirably ethical inspiration, the study is plainly a program for politically productive reading; "Changing the World" is the first heading of the introductory chapter. Chambers is therefore at pains to open a space beyond the action/reaction dynamic that reads resistance in a Foucauldian spiral of power and dissent which reinforce one another. He pries the dead-end dyad of opposition open to real resistance; the fulcrum, the third term, is the reader as a neatly dialectical solution to unproductive tensions. "The communicational relationship between text and myself, as *reader*, is of a different kind, and positions me in such a way that I coincide fully neither with 'Paddy' [narrator] nor with 'Stephen' [narratee] but find myself in a triangulated relationship in which the third position (mine) is, with respect to the textual relationships, both that of *tiers exclu*—the excluded third party—and that of *tertius gaudens*, the third who enjoys or profits" [24]. The reader, as the indirect object of discourse, the redeemable viewer of discord, is available for the kind of sentimental re-education that could amount to the social condition for political changes of heart.

To do justice to Chambers's important move here is to acknowledge the stages of reader response that lead to the narrative's "influencing the desires and views of readers" [12]. The first is an identification between powerful narratee and privileged reader. The reader "slips into the slot furnished— often as a vacancy—in the text as that of the narratee, and becomes the object of the narrator's seduction" [32]. But because Chambers assumes that the reader is excluded from the oppositional act directed at the narratee (or that he should exclude himself thanks to the distance vouchsafed as voyeur), a triangulated reading becomes possible in which the opposition is given the visibility [33] that amounts to the reader's collaborative operation with the text. "For my role as reader of a text is not so much to receive a story (identifying with the narratee position) as to collaborate with the text in the production of meaning, a task that redistributes—perhaps equalizes—the power relationship, and certainly dissolves the simplistic distinctions of self and other, sender and receiver that are inherent in the concepts of narrator and narratee" [26].

The danger may be evident in this bloodless *Aufhebung* of narratee stand-in into the oppositional narrator's ally. By excluding ourselves from the struggle we get away unscathed, possibly with our retrograde desire still in place. Despite the best intentions of Chambers to describe desire in politically altered states, thanks to sensitive and self-critical readings, our self-appointed role as co-author/collaborator remains, for example, unchallenged. And the possibility of sustained hostility toward the reader vanishes in the dialectical magic of helping hands. It is not that Chambers ignores that initial tension, but that he decides too quickly perhaps that it is a dead end, that readers are capable of self-criticism without enduring redundant reminders of complicity.

We have almost lost the trail of a truly humbling exercise that Stanley Fish might have taught us in *Surprised by Sin*. This early (and outlying) book focuses on the reader's role in Milton's *Paradise Lost*, but certainly not to illustrate any possible co-authorship or complicity, no eroticized pas de deux or transcendental erasure of the text. Instead, Milton is shown to set his reader up at every point, to cajole him into thinking he has understood something of God's divine pattern only to dash the reader's presumptuous satisfactions. The true Christian should know that God is unknowable, and the text plays on our stubbornly earthly expectations of enlightenment in order to counter them abruptly, aggressively, repeatedly.

This is the track we might tread again when we learn to listen to the nervousness in Bruno's narrative. Like Fish's Milton, Cortázar may also be playing on the expectations of enlightened modern readers for whom the amount of energy expended should predict the level of mastery gained. But labor theories of readerly value will miss the specific use value of Bruno's frustrating efforts. Milton's poem refuses workerly improvements because they are arrogant examples of the work's main point: the mortal reader's incorrigible incompetence. Without making transcendent claims for Johnny's music, and arguing more modestly that his particularly positioned life defies easy universalizing and transcendent appropriations that would allow readers to assume some ultimate knowledge of him, he too discounts the unsolicited labor of Bruno, the self-defined collaborator. Like Milton, Johnny insists repeatedly that we miss the point by striving for it so confidently.

Some lives, and books, resist the competent reader, intentionally. Cool before the Whitmanian heat that would melt down differences, as if difference obstructed democratic vistas, unyielding texts erect signposts of impassable terrain. They raise questions of access or welcome to produce a kind of readerly "incompetence" that more reading will not overcome. I am not referring to the ultimate or universal impossibility to exhaust always ambiguous literature through interpretation. Ambiguity, unlike the resistance that interests me here, has been for some time a consecrated and self-flattering theme for professional readers. It blunts interpretive efforts, and thereby invites more labor, so that ambiguity allows us to offset frustrated mastery with a liberating license to continue endlessly.[11]

The point is rather that certain textual strategies announce limited access to interpretation, whether or not information is really withheld. In fact, Bruno has lots of information; he understands Johnny and his music far better than the musician wants to acknowledge. But Johnny's refusal to acknowledge Bruno is the sticking point. Resistance does not necessarily signal a genuine epistemological impasse; it is enough that the impasse is claimed in this ethico-aesthetic strategy to position the reader within limits.[12] The question, finally, is not what "insiders" can know as opposed to "outsiders"; it is how those positions are being constructed as incommensurate or conflictive. And Cortázar's particular constructions, as he pursues and performs textual refusals of interpretation, are worth tracing in some detail.

Pursuing a Perfect Present

Bruno, as I said, has good reason to fret. Rather, he has two good reasons. One is his self-doubt, of course; the other is knowing himself to be a target of Johnny's hostility. The new jazzmen of the 1940s and early '50s were notorious for psychologically harassing those who couldn't keep up, meaning other musicians as well as a public still avid for the musical Uncle Toms who played the sensual sounds of "hot" music.[13] Louis Armstrong was probably the most visible target, and his characteristic courtesy to other jazzmen cracked with the boppers: "they want to carve everyone else because they're full of malice, and all they want to do is show you up," he complained. "So you get all them weird chords which don't mean nothing ... and you got no melody to remember and no beat to dance to" [2]. Sometimes literally turning its back on the audience, "cool" jazz refused to pander. Instead of tortured and passionate, repeatable songs, cool "bebop" delivered an oblique sense of melody, a deliberate exploration of unsuspected harmonies and rhythms. Bruno fancies himself a "hipster" on the inside of innovation, but he can feel the chill of being left out (*"And furthermore, cool doesn't mean, even by accident ever, what you've written,"* Johnny would accuse him [208; 300]. So Bruno worries about a possible professional shaming.

> Honestamente, ¿qué me importa su vida? Lo único que me inquieta es que se deje llevar por esa conducta que no soy capaz de seguir (digamos que no quiero seguir) y acabe desmintiendo las conclusiones de mi libro. Que deje caer por ahí que mis afirmaciones son falsas, que su música es otra cosa.   [303–04]

> [To be honest, what does his life matter to me? The only thing that bothers me is that if he continues to let himself go on living as he has been, a style I'm not capable of following (let's say I don't want to follow it), he'll end up by making lies out of the conclusions I've reached in my book. He might let it drop somewhere that my statements are wrong, that his music's something else.]   [211]

That "something else" haunts Bruno, when he's in Johnny's company. Brooding about getting it all wrong (Johnny, his music, his biography), Bruno knows the pain of writing it anyway. He also knows, and tells us early on, that his pathetic insufficiency is its own paradoxical license to narrate. Because he admits his own shortcomings, Bruno can become strangely trustworthy as a critic of what continues to elude him. (Were it not for this paradox, how could any reader dare to comment on this story by Cortázar, on his pursuits and accomplishments?)

Soy un crítico de jazz lo bastantesensible comopara
comprendermis limitaciones, y me doy cuenta de que lo que estoy
pensando está por debajo del plano donde el pobre Johnny trata
de avanzar con sus frases truncadas, sus suspiros, sus súbitas rabias
y sus llantos. A él le importa un bledo que yo lo crea genial, y
nunca se ha envanecido de que su música está mucho más allá de
la que tocan sus compañeros. Pienso melancólicamente que él
está al principio de su saxo mientras yo vivo obligado a
conformarme con el final. El es la boca y yo la oreja, por no decir
que él es la boca y yo ...   [256]

[I'm sensitive enough a jazz critic when it comes to understanding
my limitations, and I realize that what I'm thinking is on a lower
level than where poor Johnny is trying to move forward with his
decapitated sentences, his sighs, his impatient angers and his
tears. He gives a damn where I think everything ought to go easy,
and he's never come on smug that his music is much farther out
than his contemporaries are playing. It drags me to think that he's
at the beginning of his sax-work, and I'm going along and have to
stick it out to the end. He's the mouth and I'm the ear, so as not
to say he's the mouth and I'm the ...]   [167]

Self-awareness, though, does not mean that Bruno is resigned to the
aesthetic and intellectual asymmetry. The limitations that he confesses,
together with Johnny's relentlessly searching talk, evidently make the critic
anxious. The very next thing Johnny says, in fact, sounds like a reproach:
"Bruno, maybe someday you'll be able to write.... Not for me, understand,
what the hell does it matter to me" [167].[14] Bruno feels diminished in
Johnny's presence, both because he has trouble following the musicians'
verbal improvisations and because he may be serving as Johnny's instrument
to be played on and with. "[A]fter the wonder of it's gone you get an
irritation, and for me at least it feels as though Johnny's been pulling my leg"
[173].[15] In either case, Bruno can't wait to leave the hotel room, so that
Johnny's troubling text can safely unravel into commonplaces. "I smile the
best I can, understanding fuzzily that he's right, but what he suspects and the
hunch I have about what he suspects is going to be deleted as soon as I'm in
the street and've gotten back into my everyday life" [173].[16]

　　The layered relationship that Cortázar manages to portray in this
initial scene would be admirable enough: Bruno's vexed reverence for the
"childish" genius who makes the mature critic feel stupid; Johnny's reluctant

respect for the interpreter who gets more right than is safe to say, and who listens well enough to keep Johnny talking. (In fact experimental jazz was indebted to European, even academic, influences.)[17] But the story is admirable beyond the probing dialogue and reflection, just beyond, in the subtly disquieting performance of the narrative passages that frame the encounter. From the first lines, as I said, while the narrator still casts himself as blameless and forebearing, before acknowledging any uneasiness at the level of story, his plight is *felt* in the grammar.

To be precise, Bruno's nervousness comes out in his obsessive recourse to the present perfect tense. The very term "present perfect" is oxymoronic, unstable, dislocating, with one foot in the past and the other in the present. Its function is logically pivotal, providing a point of departure from one component tense to the other. But Bruno's compound tense doesn't resolve itself into either the past or the present; instead it stays deadlocked and dizzying in its own repeated contradiction. Fourteen present perfect verbs cluster on the first full page of text. "Dédée me ha llamado ... *yo* he ido ... Me ha bastado ... he encontrado ... ha dicho ... he sacado ... no he querido ... he preguntado ... se ha levantado y ha apagado ... nos hemos reconocido ... ha sacado ... he sentido ... ha dicho ... Me ha alegrado."

Dissonant, almost shrill from repetition, the present perfect tense becomes a structural feature of Bruno's writing. It is as if the writing refused to fit into time, the conventional grammatical time that opposes past to present in neat, mutually exclusive categories. The present perfect scrambles categories. It straddles between excess and inadequacy, too much time and too little. Does a present perfect action spill over from past to present, an exorbitance and difference carried in a single composite tense? Or does the action fit nowhere, already exiled from the past and not quite surviving into the present? The specific problem for Bruno is that Johnny is unstable, exorbitant as the subject of a definitive biography. He is still alive and willful, too present and palpable to be the manageable material of an informative story. Alive, he is not really perfect, a term that I take here in the grammatical sense of finished, past. Only at the end of Bruno's long struggle in the disturbingly present perfect of Johnny's life, after 63 closely written pages, does the biographer finally put a full stop to his work in simple, perfect grammar. Johnny dies, Bruno reports with some relief and no less bad faith, "as he really is, a poor sonofabitch with barely mediocre intelligence ..." [218].[18] And the story achieves the finality of a simple past tense that can be superseded by the repose and plenitude of a perfectly simple present.

Todo esto coincidió con la aparición de la segunda edición de mi libro, pero por suerte tuve tiempo de incorporar una nota necrológica redactada a toda máquina, y una fotografía del entierro donde se veía a muchos jazzmen famosos. En esa forma la biografía quedó, por decirlo así, completa. Quizá no está bien que yo diga esto, pero como es natural me sitúo en un plano meramente estético. Ya hablan de una nueva traducción, creo que al sueco o al noruego. Mi mujer está encantada con la noticia.

[313]

[All this happened at the same time that the second edition of my book was published, but luckily I had time to incorporate an obituary note edited under full steam and inserted, along with a newsphoto of the funeral in which many famous jazzmen were identifiable. In that format the biography remained, so to speak, intact and finished. Perhaps it's not right that I say this, but naturally I was speaking from a merely aesthetic point of view. They're already talking of a new translation, into Swedish or Norwegian, I think. My wife is delighted at the news.]   [220]

Presumably the verbs were always simple in the biography, even in the first edition, but now there are comforting grounds for simplicity. Real death, mercifully for Bruno, has stabilized the virtual loss that biography effects into loss, pure and simple. The very genre that presumes to preserve a life defaces it, as Paul de Man argues so poignantly, because biography petrifies living movement into a monument, spirit into letter. Here the hardening takes the form of fixing an unstable present perfect tense into a solidly perfect past. Until that final page, though, Johnny's vitality has been outstripping Bruno's best biographical efforts to control it. The biographer would reduce the complexity of his subject's relationships to an orderly report of information. The violence of that project should be clear. It collapses the obliging and ensnaring discourse of *sociability* into the unencumbered, antiseptic language of *knowledge*, to use Emmanuel Levinas's terms.[19] In the place of a social subject who makes claims on his interlocutors, Bruno prefers the unfettered objective hero, a cluster of data available for bloodless exchanges among music mavens.

But Bruno can't seem to package the narrative interlude we are reading now, the story that comes between the official editions of Johnny's life. Bruno's writing in "The Pursuer" doesn't cooperate with marketing demands. As if to call attention to his performance in an anxious present perfect tense, the narrative voice pauses after a first page. The writing is, in fact, so apparently clumsy that Paul Blackburn's overly graceful English translation refuses to respect the redundant awkwardness. The English version presumes to correct Cortázar's purposefully unpleasant Spanish with the predictable elegance of variety that good taste dictates. For example, the first two Spanish verbs ("Dédée me ha llamado ... yo he ido"), which set the dissonant tone and timing for Bruno's nervous style, are fixed in the translation into easily chronologized past perfect conjugations: "Dédée had called me ... and I'd gone." Johnny, we know, reviles conventional "good taste"; and perhaps surprisingly, respectable Bruno seems incapable of practicing it.

The attention-getting pause after that first narrative page is a short dialogue about timing, the very feature that has presented a problem. Bruno begins with a conventional comment about how long the friends had not seen one another. That triggers Johnny's objection to Bruno's penchant for putting everything into orderly, linear time. The irony, of course, is that the page we have just seen, but that Johnny has not, can hardly keep things straight. And Bruno's messy compound tense continues to narrate in the frame of the dialogue. "'We haven't seen one another for a while,' I [*have*] said to Johnny. 'It's been a month at least.' 'You got nothin' to do but tell time,' he [*has*] answered in a bad mood. 'The first, the two the three, the twenty one. You, you put a number on everything'" [162, my insertions and emphasis].[20]

Johnny's objection is to counting, to marking time in foreseeable sequences. Were his emphasis on time understood differently, it would point to his own obsession as well. "Johnny ... kept on referring to time, a subject which is a preoccupation of his ever since I've known him. I've seen very few men as occupied as he is with everything having to do with time" [164].[21] Among those rare obsessives is the narrator Bruno himself. Johnny noted as much, but too impatiently, perhaps because he is not reading the text before us. In it Bruno's discordant performance in the present perfect is unmistakably doubled. While it seems to comment coolly on the confusing temporality of the jazz musician, the narrator's timing is in fact contaminated by Johnny's own experiments with music. This slippage between musical timing and verbal tenses works in both directions; this is particularly plain when Johnny's drive to get beyond convention finds textual representation in oxymoronic verbs. Consider the way he forces the present progressive or the simple past to perform in the future. "I am playing this tomorrow," Bruno remembers him complaining during a rehearsal years earlier. "I already played this tomorrow, it's horrible, Miles, I already played this tomorrow"

[164].[22] And Bruno himself will play an extended variation, when he takes a break from the present perfect and narrates the recent past (or the present?) in a consistent future tense [201–04; 293–95].

By making his agonists share a preoccupation with time, Cortázar is evidently deconstructing the difference between Bruno's intellectual work and Johnny's artistic genius. Bruno should logically be talking about artistic challenges; instead he performs them. And Johnny should be pursuing his speculations through performances, musical rather than verbal; yet he talks far more than he plays. Like Charlie Parker's critics—who acknowledge his superior intelligence and technical appreciation for his own work—Bruno is careful to let Johnny talk, always quoting rather than reporting his textual riffs.[23] This slippery difference between art and critique has at times, of course, been taken to be a more stable opposition. It was, for instance, fundamental to a fascist aesthetics that distinguished radically between two types of writers: the pedantic *Schriftsteller* and the inspired *Dichter*. The opposition is unhinged by Cortázar's own variegated virtuosity, combining inspiration and intellection as a continual challenge to his own critics. Readers usually develop along with Cortázar's experimental writing, but more slowly.

His accomplishment in "The Pursuer," it would seem, both depends on and overrides a naïve reading that would simply oppose Bruno to Johnny. To appreciate the deconstructive turn is also to acknowledge its polarized pretext as a simple reading that would make the title refer only to Johnny. He "was no victim, not persecuted as everyone thought, as I'd even insisted upon in my biography of him.... Johnny pursues and is not pursued" [196].[24] Only this disingenuous interpretation could mistake Johnny as the sole medium of the story's almost mad metaphysical desire to beat down the doors of arbitrary limits. Only willful simplicity could demote Bruno to the prosaic condensation of everything Johnny resists. It would draw a stark contrast between the castrating conventionality of Bruno's language and the liberating trespasses of Johnny's music.

A conclusion, logically, would be that Cortázar is celebrating the superiority of extralinguistic and nonintellectual communication. This is not the only story where nonliterary arts seem to compensate Cortázar for the limitations of his medium. (See "Apocalypse in Solentiname," in which viewing his own slides of naïve Nicaraguan paintings shocks the narrator into finally seeing Somoza's official terror; "Return Trip Tango," where the recursive rhythm of urban music provides the logic of human disencounters; and "Graffiti," where an academic painter wakes up to political repression through an amorous dialogue of public drawings.) The examples come readily to mind, and Cortázar's borrowings from the visual and performing arts are already the topic of important studies [see, for example, Zamora; Luli]. But the borrowings should not obscure the obvious fact that Cortázar's own pursuit is rendered in the apparently disdained medium of literature. In other words, a simple reading that would diminish the value of Bruno's probing literary styles in order to exalt the spontaneity of experimental music misses the charm of this story: "The Pursuer" manages to accomplish those winning experiments through writing. Even Johnny's putative superiority is, after all, an effect of his own evasive words and of Bruno's tortuous, tense-troubled responses. Bruno's haunted memory "insists and insists on Johnny's words, his stories" [178; 265].

This irony—about outperforming writing through writing—might make a nice point in a deconstructive reading, a generalizable or abstract point that could follow from the personalized ironies about Bruno's unstable difference from Johnny. And if we cared to circle back in order to insist on the virtual collapse of differences between the cautious *Schriftsteller* and the daring *Dichter*, we could develop the point about Johnny's capacity for intellectual speculation being more than equal to Bruno's. Johnny does more than merely quote lines from Dylan Thomas; he glosses them. "O make me a mask," the line that frames the story from Cortázar's epigraph to the coda on Johnny's words [220; 313], is an opportunity for the jazzman to extrapolate on the general arbitrariness of signs. His own life, for example, could not possibly be contained in Bruno's biography; it's not even in the records [212; 304]. And his face, for an even more intimate example, could not possibly be an adequate representation of Johnny himself. Instead it's a mask that makes recognition both possible and impossible; it is someone else, to be caught by surprise as he stares from the glass, menacing to pass for and replace the person looking in.[25] Tirelessly driven, Johnny develops the mystery by wondering about words as such, the way they stick to things and overcome them with the connecting slime that passes for meaning.[26]

> Imagínate que te estás viendo a ti mismo, eso tan sólo basta para quedarse frío durante media hora. Realmente ese tipo no soy yo ... lo agarré de sorpresa, de refilón y supe que no era yo.... No son las palabras, son lo que está en las palabras, esa especie de cola de pegar, esa baba. Y la baba viene y te tapa, y te convence de que el del espejo eres tú. [282]

> [Imagine that you're looking at yourself; that alone is enough to

freeze you up for half an hour. In reality, this guy's not me.... I
took it by surprise, obliquely, and I knew it wasn't me.... No, not
words, but what's in the words, a kind of glue, that slime. And the
slime comes and covers you and convinces you that that's you in
the mirror.] [192]

His speculations range in apparent disorder, disorder itself being one theme
in his obsession with "elastic" time. Even more than an obsession, more than
simply a problem to harass him the way it does Bruno, the variability of time
for Johnny is an invitation to study and to speculate. "I [have] read some
things about all that, Bruno. It's weird, and really awfully complicated ... [*sic*].
I think the music helps, you know. Not to understand, because the truth is I
don't understand anything" [165].[27] His own reflections sound distinctly
Bergsonian, about the variable *durée* of experience. Sometimes, Johnny
muses, a suitcase, like a song, will hold more and sometimes less. Other times
it is packed so full that the contents seem limitless. "The best is when you
realize you can put a whole store full of suits and shoes in there, in that
suitcase, hundreds and hundreds of suits, like I get into the music when I'm
blowing sometimes. Music, and what I'm thinking about when I ride the
metro" [168].[28] With this breathless transition, the speculation about
elasticity continues with the subway as a vehicle for musical compression: the
minute-long ride from one stop to another is so crammed with lovingly
detailed reveries that the trip seems impossibly concise [175–76; 260–61].
"Bruno, if I could only live all the time like in those moments, or like when
I'm playing and the time changes then too ..." [173].[29] Timing was always
Charlie Parker's musical frontier, too. "Charlie Parker's idea of rhythm
involves breaking time up. It might be said that it is based on half beats. No
other soloist attaches so much importance to short notes (eighth notes in
quick tempos, sixteenths in slow)," writes André Hodeir early enough for
Cortázar to have read it. Hodeir's *Hommes et problèmes du jazz* was published
in the same place and year as Bruno's biography (Paris, 1954) and became a
standard work for other jazz historians. At about the same time, jazz pianist
Jay McShann was saying that Parker "played everything offbeat. He had it in
his head long before he could put it together" [qtd. in Reisner; qtd. in Collier
353]. And none of his contemporaries ever caught up to him in pursuit of
polyrhythms, the very pulse of the new music.[30] As the period's giant of jazz
(along with Gillespie), Parker pioneered a variety of styles that would
develop into the opposing "hot" and "cool" trends that lesser musicians
would choose between.[31] They appropriated pieces of Parker, mostly his
experiments with melody and harmony. But no one overtook his talent for

timing, not even his most admiring students, like the pianist Hampton Hawes. "It was Bird's conception that ... made me realize how important meter and time is in jazz.... I began experimenting, taking liberties with time, or letting a couple of beats go by to make the beat stand out, not just play on top of it all the time."[32]

To develop a reading of deconstructed oppositions would be to include a counterpoint to our artist's critical acuity. And Bruno the critic has in fact been showing himself to be an unconventional artist. We have already heard him play with the dissonant "chord tensions" (one of Charlie Parker's performative signatures) of an unstable tense. Now we might add that Bruno is also given to the kind of cramming, overpacking, and overloading so characteristic of bebop and of Johnny's particular speculations about music and time. And just to make sure that we get the connection, Bruno thematizes his own performance as he comments on another hanger-on whose language is also "contaminated" [217; 310] by jazz: "When the marquesa started yakking you wondered if Dizzy's style hadn't glued up her diction, it was such an interminable series of variations in the most unexpected registers ..." [178].[33] Bruno stretches and pads his own story, especially through the long middle section, where linear writing breaks down under the weight of worry. Telling asides erupt through spaces that are visually represented as barely constraining parentheses. In those unpredicted spaces, extradiegetic writing plays with and against Bruno's simpler themes. Crouching inside the breaches and ready to outshout the line of continuity (like Johnny crouches, "lying in ambush" [211; 303]) are pieces of dangerously supplemental information, Bruno's reflexive musings, and his wonder at what he admits to misinterpreting. He squeezes words into his paragraphs like bebop squeezes notes into a melody. It squeezes so hard that the new music verges on exploding the familiar line; melody is not entirely overwhelmed, but it is continually commented on, challenged, critically caressed.[34] And Bruno sees his own project ready to burst from the pressure of overwriting "(I swear I don't know how to write all this)" [210],[35] he confesses in one parenthetical riff.

Readers who notice this visual aid to Cortázar's trespassing from music to manuscript may be surprised—as I was—to know that it may well be borrowed from a jazz critic writing about Parker, perhaps the very critic who inspired Bruno. André Hodeir writes that Parker played "in parentheses. "That is, he suggested as much music as he actually played; "his phrase frequently includes notes that are not played but merely *suggested*.... Thus, anyone who writes down a Parker chorus is obliged to include, *in parentheses* [my emphasis], notes that have hardly been played at all" [*Jazz* 108]. Hodeir's own page then visibly breaks up in parenthetical asides, as if consciously imitating the master. Whether or not Cortázar was imitating, too, whether he took a cue for improvisation from jazz criticism, he certainly played stunning variations. Usually they are doubled solos (between Bruno's nonstop narrative and his preoccupied parentheses), but at least one inspired adaptation sets competitive voices in counterpoint. Regular print and italics alternate and crescendo in a debate about Bruno's book, between an ever-more-anxious biographer and his progressively angrier hero:

—Faltan cosas, Bruno—dice Johnny— ...
—Las que te habrás olvidado de decirme—contesté—bastante picado. Este mono salvaje es capaz de ... (habrá que hablar con Delaunay, sería lamentable que una declaración imprudente malograra un sano esfuerzo crítico que... *Por ejemplo, el vestido rojo de Lan*—está diciendo Johnny—. Y en todo caso aprovechar las novedades de esta noche para incorporarlas a una nueva edición; no estaría mal. *Tenía como un olor a perro*—está diciendo Johnny— *y es lo único que vale en ese disco.* Sí, escuchar atentamente y proceder con rapidez, porque en manos de otras gentes estos posibles desmentidos podrían tener consecuencias lamentables. *Y la urna del medio, la más grande, llena de un polvo casi azul*—está diciendo Johnny—*y tan parecida a una polvera que tenía mi hermana.* Mientras no pase de las alucinaciones, lo peor sería que desmintiera las ideas de fondo, el sistema estético que tantos elogios.... *Y además el cool no es ni por casualidad lo que has escrito*—está diciendo Johnny. Atención.) [300]

["There're things missing, Bruno," Johnny says ...
"The things that you've forgotten to tell me," I answer, reasonably annoyed. This uncivilized monkey is capable of ... (I would have to speak with Delaunay, it would be regrettable if an imprudent statement about a sane, forceful criticism that ... *For example Lan's red dress*, Johnny is saying. And in any case take advantage of the enlightening details from this evening to put into anew edition; that wouldn't be bad. *It stank like an old washrag*, Johnny's saying, *and that's the only value on the record.* Yes, listen closely and proceed rapidly, because in other people's hands any possible contradiction might have terrible consequences. *And the urn in the middle, full of dust that's almost blue*, Johnny is saying, *and very close to the color of a compact my sister had once.* As long as

he wasn't going into hallucinations, the worst that could happen would be that he might contradict the basic ideas, the aesthetic system so many people have praised.... *And furthermore, cool doesn't mean, even by accident ever, what you've written*, Johnny is saying. Attention.)] [208]

One result of all this overwriting is a very long short story. The tale seems compact—a conversation in Johnny's hotel room, a get-together at the marquesa's place, a drink and more talk just before Johnny dies—but the narrative is tellingly stretched beyond the capacity of more conventional stories. Cortázar almost always writes them within twenty pages. More than doubling that length by adding variations, speculations, reveries, and repetitions is the kind of experimental performance that brings Bruno close to bebop.

The analogy between modern music and modern writing is redundantly clear. Even so, Cortázar takes few risks with his readers' interpretive skill. He informs us, outright, that Johnny's jazz is part of a general postwar culture exploding with artistic experiments. "This is not the place to be a jazz critic, and anyone who's interested can read my book on Johnny and the new post-war style, but I can say that forty-eight—let's say until fifty—was like an explosion in music ..." [176].[36] The image of exploding standard forms, the following reference to an ever greater and more avid public, and the timing in the late '40s and early '50s are unmistakable allusions to the Latin American literary "Boom" that Cortázar helped to detonate. So is the geographical displacement that makes American jazz flourish in Paris, the same haven that attracted the most influential new Spanish American novelists: Carlos Fuentes, Mario Vargas Llosa, and Cortázar himself, among others. As a late and supremely self-ironizing wave of modernist experiments, Boom writing distinguished itself from the kind of expository prose that Bruno's biography stands for. The genre of biography in Cortázar's Argentina had in fact been extolled by the great nation-builder Domingo F. Sarmiento. For him and for generations of practical and productive disciples, biography was the most effective guide to personal and political development.[37] And Bruno's book about the bebop artist who "turned the page" [177; 266] on music history might well have fit the mold of celebrating exemplary men in a mimetic effort to become one.

Cortázar is presumably offering a critique of this self-improving genre by replacing biography with a story that tracks the troubled afterthoughts about the very possibility of writing a life. But he may be even more self-promoting than simply preferring his own type of experimental prose to the biographical developmentalism that stays beyond the scene of writing like some guilty pretext for the drama. Cortázar may also be objecting to some of his own interpreters who have tried to tidy up his really unpredictable production into a story of development.[38] Both they and Bruno the biographer tend to lose focus on the mystery pursued, on the nonchronological play that, ironically, can make artistic history. Conceivably, the story is meant to leave Cortázar's critics in the dust raised by his own superior flair for speculative interpretation and by his endless pursuit of forms that describe desire without controlling it.

Without denying the possibility of Cortázar's self-promotion or self-defense, and far from discarding the deconstructive reading that I've been describing, I want to argue a different point here. It sidesteps immediate self-interest and gets beyond the kind of deconstruction that heaps glaring ironies onto inconsistent oppositions in order to level the feeble differences between Bruno's project and Johnny's performance. The story, I would boldly point out, is not merely about the ultimate naiveté of binary oppositions. It is also—and most powerfully—about a refusal to overcome difference. The agonists resist the leveling effect and remain in murderous tension with one another. Johnny refuses to be contained in Bruno's smug prose. And Bruno strains to be free of Johnny, of the self-doubts and the complexity he inflicts. I am saying, in other words, that the "naive" interpretation that a familiar version of deconstruction would override survives the sophisticated assault, in a more responsible deconstructive practice. This survival is most palpable, as I will repeat, in the diegetic passages and at the level of grammar. Whereas a standard deconstructive reading (more de Manian than Derridean) would focus on Bruno's bebop style, on the futility of keeping oppositional categories clear, the "agonistic" emphasis I prefer to give this story keeps an eye on the energy invested in safeguarding the oppositions. The differences between the agonists are evidently not essential, not organic. But their very fragility, their almost arbitrary constructedness, makes the characters whose identity depends on them nervous enough to insist on distinctions.

The fact that Bruno and Johnny overlap as personae and performances is no happy liberation from the tensions of difference; instead it is a threat to the difference that gives each character his specificity, his life. "([M]aybe I'm a little afraid of Johnny, this angel who's like my brother, this brother who's like my angel)" [174; 263]. To override that respectful distance between self and other, a distance that provides the ground for dynamic social relationships, is to risk reducing sociability to solipsism. Closing up distances and coming perilously close to the other threatens to overtake one in a gesture of an ontological appropriation that Levinas calls "totality."[39] Both Bruno and Johnny threaten one another in this way. Each implicates the other in the deadlock of ethical engagement.

Bruno cannot help but perfect his living subject into an inanimate object of discourse. That is the cost of writing a life. Mikhail Bakhtin almost benignly called the process "consummation," in an early philosophical essay titled "Author and Hero in Aesthetic Activity." It is an especially suggestive piece for reading Bruno's relationship to Johnny.[40] Consummation, for Bakhtin, describes the process whereby an author contextualizes and completes his hero from a necessarily exterior vantage point: for example, from Bruno's perspective on Johnny. Critics, Bruno protests after feeling especially stupid, are more necessary than they sometimes think, "because the creators ... are incapable of extrapolating the dialectical consequences of their work, of postulating the fundamentals and the transcendency of what they're writing down or improvising" [208–09].[41] To hear this almost funny, hollow, and impersonal academic jargon, after Johnny has just complained about being left out of Bruno's biography, is to get Johnny's point. Bruno has had to fictionalize his friend, to flatten and substitute him, in order to celebrate him. We are already remarking the culpability of completing a character. And Bakhtin is explicit, at points, about the violence inherent in the process, although the thrust of his sometimes rambling essay is to define a properly ethical engagement between authors who respect their heroes' qualified autonomy, even as the writers help to confer it. The violent surplus of establishing pleasing contours for a hero, whose interior sense of himself cannot appreciate his own outline, is that to confer coherence on a character is, necessarily, to finish him.

> Artistic vision presents us with the whole hero, measured in full and added up in every detail; there must be no secrets for us in the hero with respect to meaning; our faith and hope must be silent. From the very outset, we must experience all of him, deal with the whole of him: in respect to meaning, he must be dead for us, formally dead.
>
> In this sense, we could say that death is the form of the aesthetic consummation of an individual.   [131]

Cortázar's fans may remember his own repeated explorations of the murderous price authors pay for congealing incoherent lives into perfected fictions. In fact much, if not most, of Cortázar's writing is driven ahead of the danger posed by fixing and finishing. He will resist perfection, characteristically, by deforming his grammar, with "shifty" pronouns as well as oxymoronic verbs.[42] Perhaps the most dramatic example of the danger is, predictably, a story that succumbs to it. "We Love Glenda So Much" (1981) is practically a parable about deadly perfectibility. That story ends once Glenda's fans conspire to kill her in order to polish the movie-star image that stabilizes their devotion. The very last lines draw an unmistakable parallel with another necessary sacrifice to cultish heroism: "We loved Glenda so much that we would offer her one last inviolable perfection. On the untouchable heights to which we had raised her in exaltation, we would save her from the fall, her faithful could go on adoring her without any decrease; one does not come down from a cross alive" [16].[43] Sacrifice and deification also menace Bakhtin's essay to describe the dynamic between hero and author. But his efforts run directly into the paradoxical possibility that the hero can be redeemed by the author's finishing work. Love runs the risk of fixing and killing the beloved, but it also promises to raise him or her to another, more perfect plane.

> It is only love (as an active approach to another human being) that unites an inner life (a *subiectum's* own object-directedness in living his life) as experienced from outside with the value of the body as experienced from outside and, in so doing, constitutes a unitary and unique human being as an aesthetic phenomenon.
>
> [82–83]

> [T]he enrichment in this case is formal, transfigurative in character—it transposes the recipient of the gift to a new plane of existence. And what is transposed to a new plane, moreover, is not the material, not an object, but a *subiectum*—the hero. It is only in relation to the hero that aesthetic obligation (the aesthetic 'ought') as well as aesthetic love and the gift bestowed by such love are possible.   [90]

Some pages earlier, Bakhtin had spelled out the fundamentally Christian and paradoxical nature of this consummating and redemptive love. In that passage, Bakhtin might have capitalized the word *author* because he casts himself as one possible creation. The mystery of redeeming a life through death can be read here as one result of Christ's synthetic embrace of traditions, a synthesis that allows for slippages from one plane to another.

> In Christ we find a synthesis of unique depth, the synthesis of
> ethical solipsism (man's infinite severity toward himself ...) with
> ethical-aesthetic kindness toward the other. For the first time,
> there appeared an infinitely deepened I-for-myself... one of
> boundless kindness toward the other.... [Thanks to Christ,] God
> is no longer defined essentially as the voice of my conscience....
> God is now the heavenly father who is over me and can be
> merciful to me and justify me where I, from within myself, cannot
> be merciful to myself and cannot justify myself ... What I must be
> for the other, God is for me. What the other surmounts and
> repudiates within himself as an unworthy given, I accept in him
> and that with loving mercy as the other's cherished flesh. [56]

To become "the other's cherished flesh"—it is a phrase passionate enough to
send chills through readers of "Glenda," where passion achieves its sacrificial
meaning and the heroine's fans (short for fanatics) become living shrines to
her memory. By the time he writes this story, Cortázar is himself a venerated
superstar, or a venerable monument as vulnerable to his carping critics as
Glenda was to her fans. "As always, why don't you live in your country, why
was *Blow-Up* so different from your story, don't you think writers should be
committed? And ... chez Saint Peter there'll be no difference, don't you think
that down below you used to write too hermetically for regular people to
understand?" ["Apocalypse at Solentiname" 119].[44] "Glenda," therefore,
may be a cautionary tale about loving the beloved to death. But such a
reading would diminish the meaning of love, shrink it into simple,
cannibalistic appropriation. Glenda's fanatics could not possibly have loved
her, Cortázar is probably saying, not in the generous and tolerant sense that
Bakhtin gives the word. No one among the "faithful" could have justified
Glenda in her imperfections, forgiven her for that which she could not
forgive herself. Therefore, no one could have consummated the character
with the pleasing coherence achieved only outside one's own intolerant
"ethical (or aesthetic) solipsism."

Bakhtin's idea of redemptive love is obviously inimical to the ritual
cannibalism of Glenda's celebrants. In the least case, their cannibalism
digests away the tension between interiority and exteriority that makes
writing possible. The expression of their love means the end of Glenda, as a
character and as a narrative. Even an autobiographer, Bakhtin observes,
needs to define a tension between author and hero in order to write himself
[151]. And beyond the aesthetic need to keep them apart, there is an ethical
imperative for the author to maintain, or regain, a respectful distance from

his hero: the distance allows the hero's fullness to come into focus [26]. "What's hard is to circle about him and not lose your distance," Bruno reminds himself, "like a good satellite, like a good critic" [197].[45] But despite Bakhtin's own cautions about overtaking or being overtaken by the other, despite repeated warnings against the undifferentiating empathy that offers cheap rushes of feeling and shirks the labor required for consummation [64, 81, 88], his essay seems so steeped in the paradox of redemption through death that even his supremely reflexive and careful kind of loving nudges the argument toward the foot of a cross. An author's loving justification hardly allows for struggle; instead it would seem to stop the hero, to perform for him by substituting his development for an external and more pleasingly coherent perspective.

Maybe there is no help for approaching the cross. Writing, even or especially writing with love, tends to flesh out characters, to finish them off and then to finish narrating. Therefore, to read from the ending, at the point of closure, is almost inevitably to read the violence loosed on life when it is stabilized as a story. But more specific and interesting observations are to be made before the inevitable endings, during the engagement between author and hero, sometimes, that is, between characters cast in those roles. The particular process of consummation, rather than its mere fact, gives a narrative its specificity. And Bakhtin himself would later sharpen his critical focus on the almost open-ended dynamic he called dialogism, so characteristic of modernity, rather than on the consummate promise of salvation as the end of writing. Consider how different are Glenda's fans from Johnny's biographer. Their refusal to engage her is a brutal narrative short-cut, a dime-store deification, while Bruno's vulnerability to Johnny keeps the hero, their conversations, and therefore the narrative alive for many, many pages. The temptation to crucify Johnny is there for Bruno, too, but it is openly and self-critically there. So, besides being an unavoidable trap, temptation is also a goad for more writing: "Basically we're a bunch of egotists," Bruno admits in this rehearsal of Glenda's demise, "under the pretext of watching out for Johnny what we're doing is protecting our idea of him, ... to reflect the brilliance from the statue we've erected among us all and defend it till the last gasp" [182].[46] Later on, Bruno will even imagine the others looking at him looking at Johnny, as if Bruno were "climbing up on the altar to tug Christ down from his cross" [204].[47] The first to reproach him was Johnny himself, and to the extent that they struggle against one another, author and hero survive the violence. The story flows between them, through the fissures of Bruno's fictional but still functional authority. Compared to Glenda's fans and to privileged narrators who stay in business by being willfully stupid (like the one who keeps missing the connections in *Cecilia Valdés* and like Bartleby's boss in Melville's story), Bruno seems almost defenseless.

Yet he menaces Johnny by the very fact of taking his life down, of getting it right. And Johnny reciprocates by dismissing Bruno's capacity to understand him. Why, he practically demands of Bruno, don't you leave biographical logic alone and do as I do, pursue the inarticulable energy behind art, even in the uncooperative medium of writing. "Bruno, maybe someday you'll be able to write ..." [167]. Each makes unsatisfiable demands on the other; yet each resists those demands and remains himself. It is the resistance that safeguards their vexed but dynamic sociability. The agonists depend on one another in their differences, and they know it. Bruno needs the unfettered genius as the featured subject of an academic career and the goad to his own probing performance, while Johnny needs Bruno's sensible attentions in order to survive. He also needs the critic's trained ear to elicit more music and more talk. "You ought to have been happy I put on that act with you," Johnny tells him a few days after the scene in the hotel room. "I don't do that with anybody, believe me. It just shows how much I appreciate you. We have to go someplace soon where we can talk ..." [181].[48]

But Johnny usually prefers not to admit his entrapment; and refusal suggests the bad faith of a man who declines any real engagement with another. "I understand nothing" [165; 254], he protests to the critic who is supposed to understand. Johnny objects that any text would betray him, that any meaning assigned to him would be a falsification. "Right away you translate it into your filthy language ..." [213; 305]. The filth, the slime that makes language work also makes Bruno's book "like a mirror" [207; 300], as falsifying and substitutive as a mirror. Bruno apparently gets it wrong even when he modestly writes that Johnny's real biography is in the records. The point is that the biography cannot be written, or made right, because Johnny's life is driven by inarticulable desire. "And if I myself didn't know how to blow it like it should be, blow what I really am ... you dig, they can't ask you for miracles, Bruno" [212].[49] But Bruno tries to content himself with less than miracles, as he translates Johnny's objection to being left out of his own biography with a literary-critical commonplace: "Basically, the only thing he said was that no one can know anything about anyone, big deal. That's the basic assumption of any biography, then it takes off, what the hell" [213].[50]

Of course his dismissal of the problem doesn't make it go away. Right before Johnny dies, and just as the biography was going into its second edition, Bruno indulges in self-critical plans for rewriting. "To be honest within the limits permitted by the profession, I wondered whether it would not be necessary to show the personality of my subject in another light" [217; 310]. But he controls himself. Another light might promote a "literary infection," Bruno's colleagues worry, and weaken the points about Johnny's music, "at least as all of us understood it" [218; 310]. Whether the infection is *of* literature (Bruno's biography) or *by* literature (Johnny's poetic version of finally ineffable experience) seems purposefully ambiguous. In any case, Bruno closes the prophylactic cover of his book against any possible disease. It is a characteristically self-preserving move.

For all of his repeated admissions of intellectual and spiritual inferiority, Bruno usually braces himself against Johnny. To be in Johnny's company is to lose composure, to become a misfit in time. The parallels with Johnny's experiments (present perfects, future for the past, and the parenthetical riffs) are problems for Bruno the character, as opposed to opportunities for Cortázar the writer. Bruno's problem would perhaps not be so profound if his *ressentiment* were not so obviously driven by jealousy along with self-defensiveness. Less guilty of provocative bad faith than Johnny's conversation, Bruno's private writing seems brutally self-reflective. "I envy Johnny, that Johnny on the other side, even though nobody knows exactly what that is, the other side.... I envy Johnny and at the same time I get sore as hell watching him destroy himself, misusing his gifts ..." [180].[51] And the solution for problem-solving Bruno is to finish Johnny, to make him perfect and stable in a finite past. "[M]aybe basically I want Johnny to wind up all at once like a nova that explodes into a thousand pieces and turns astronomers into idiots for a whole week, and then one can go off to sleep and tomorrow is another day" [180].[52] Thirty pages later the murderous wish for release recurs: "Sure, there are moments when I wish he were already dead" [210]. Then Bruno undercuts the wish by worrying if release is even possible.

> Sí, hay momentos en que quisiera que ya estuviese muerto.... Pero cómo resignarse a que Johnny se muera llevándose lo que no quiere decirme esta noche, que desde la muerte siga cazando, siga salido (yo ya no sé cómo escribir todo esto) aunque me valga la paz, la cátedra, esa autoridad que dan las tesis incontrovertidas y los entierros bien capitaneados. [302]

> [[H]ow can we resign ourselves to the fact that Johnny would die carrying with him what he doesn't want to tell me tonight, that from death he'd continue hunting, would continue flipping out (I swear I don't know how to write all this) though his death would

mean peace to me, prestige, the status incontrovertibly bestowed
upon one by unbeatable theses and efficiently arranged funerals.]

[210]

But relief and repose finally do come. The last sentences, over Johnny's
consummately finite body, rescue Bruno from the mire of deconstructive
contaminations and tangled tenses. Whatever subtle complications may
haunt the biographer after his hero's death, the writing shows symptoms of
release. Bruno has straightened out his verbs; he has disaggregated past from
present, disengaged himself from the present perfection that Johnny
pursued. Finally, Bruno frees himself from Johnny, after "sticking it out to
the end" [167; 256]. He releases his grip on the unmanageable genius who
has dragged him through relentlessly self-reflexive writing. Now tension
abates. The energizing if tortuous present perfect tense slackens and breaks
down into either a haltingly simple past or a comfortingly stable present. And
the supplementary parenthetical riffs evacuate the text, now hellbent on
setting itself straight.

Only now, in the deadly timing of his verbs and in the cause-and-effect
continuity of the necrological notes, does Bruno show some bad faith. He
shows it clearly in the mildly embarrassed reflection that follows his relief at
Johnny's death. More than relieved, Bruno actually seems happy about the
lucky timing of Johnny's funeral, because it produced pictures for the
improved biography. The book "remained, so to speak, intact and finished.
Perhaps it's not right that I say this," Bruno interjects almost contritely, "but
naturally I was speaking from a merely aesthetic point of view" [220; 313].
Merely aesthetic is what Johnny's life becomes for Bruno, once the hero gets
the finishing touches that fix him in a satisfying story. Therefore, the
embarrassed aside is hardly exculpating. Instead, it belies an unhappy
conscience. Although Bruno manages to play a kind of happy note in the last
paragraph, he knows that the note is drowning out much richer music. He
holds that easy note long enough to stop everything else, as if to say that
counterpuntal melodies no longer matter, as if dissonance were now merely
cacophony, a problem to be solved. Again, it is Bruno's grammar that plays so
convincingly. Whatever information we may or may not get about Bruno's
will to survive, that will is *felt* through his newly orthodox verbal conjugations.
Willfully simple, Bruno evokes here the purposefully deaf narrators of *Cecilia
Valdés* and "Bartleby," self-serving narrators who defend their privilege by
defending against understanding. All Bruno wants to know, as he gets on with
his life, is what fits into the disaggregated, perfectly simple past and present
tenses that end Johnny's story. The hero died, and the book is finished.

NOTES

I am indebted to conversations with Adam Zachary Newton, about Bakhtin and about Bruno, as this essay developed.

1. To facilitate reading this essay, I quote Cortázar in the notes and the English version—sometimes adjusted to capture Cortázar's style—in the text. Where two page numbers are cited, the first refers to the translation and the second to the Spanish.

2. Could Bruno be "the brilliant André Hodeir" [qtd. by Marshall W. Stearns in his discussion of Charlie Parker]? It seems plausible, given the respect Hodeir's book commanded, the year of publication (a year before Parker's death), and his characterization of Parker as "the most perfect example" of the jazzman: "L'oeuvre de ce genial improvisateur est l'expression la plus parfaite du jazz moderne" [128]. Stearns concurs: "The giant of giants was saxophonist Charlie Parker" [227].
But a retrospective view questions Parker's stature over Gillespie. "Today Parker is given the lion's share of the credit for inventing the harmonic changes bop brought to jazz, but on the evidence of the records it seems clear enough that Gillespie was making the same discoveries on his own, possibly in advance of Parker" [Collier 350].

3. "El compañero Bruno es fiel como el mal alient" [149].

4. For one of many examples, see Collier: "Parker ... was already (1944) exhibiting the personality problems from which he suffered. He missed jobs; slept through others.... [W]here Charlie Parker wasted his talent on the *pursuit* of the moment, Gillespie managed his career with intelligence and skill "[my emphasis]. Collier begins the chapter "Charlie Parker: An Erratic Bird in Flight" [362–76] by calling him a "sociopath ... who managed in a relatively short time to destroy his career, every relationship important to him, and finally himself" [363], largely through drugs and the arrogance that needed every desire fulfilled immediately.

5. "Pienso en la música que se está perdiendo, en las docenas de grabaciones donde Johnny podría seguir dejando esa presencia, ese adelanto asombroso que tiene sobre cualquier otro músico" [255].

6. For a more developed discussion see, for example, my "Resistant Texts and Incompetent Readers," *Poetics Today*, Spring 1995; and "Taking a Life: Hot Pursuit and Cold Rewards in a Mexican Testimonial Novel," *Signs*, forthcoming. These will be part of a book on literary strategies that refuse intimacy with readers.

7. I thank Heloisa Buarque de Hollanda for pointing this out.

8. See, as a representative piece, "The Reading Process." For a study of the operations readers perform and the "spurs" that texts provide for interaction with the reader, see *The Act of Reading*. In *The Implied Reader* Iser offers readings of representative novels based on their requirement of active readerly participation. Among his many essays, one that is most promising for the readings I attempt here is "Narrative Strategies As Means of Communication." It focuses on the particular shape of readings as imposed by the author's regulation of the process.

9. In the "Discussion "[Macksey and Donato 73–88] that follows Poulet's paper, he responds that, unlike reading, conversation "becomes instead, quite the contrary, a sort of battle, a radical opposition, an insistence of differentiation. The act of reading, as I conceive it, is ... above all an acceding, even an adherence, provisionally at least, and without reserve" [73].

10. That unreflective, universalizing love can produce perverse confusions between pets and partners is provocatively argued in Marc Shell's "The Family Pet."

11. According to Gérard Genette, Roman Jakobson is associated with the lapidary, and by now generally accepted, statements about ambiguity being inherent in poetry and in literature more generally [10]. Specifically, for example, reader-response criticism begins from assuming the negotiable ambiguity of a text. For a transatlantic view, see Lisa Block de Behar, *Una retórica del silencio*.

12. Among other critics concerned with related issues, see Tobin Siebers, *The Ethics of Criticism*. In general, this is an almost shrill rejection of contemporary criticism, from New Criticism to poststructuralism, on the grounds that it assumes that decisions in reading literature are necessarily oppressive, totalitarian, and unethical. From a narrow reading of Kant, and then of Nietzsche, new critics insist on the autonomy of art and then of language, free from considerations of intentionality. Society and art are necessarily opposing terms, for them, the undecidability of art giving the realm of freedom that society tries to limit by law.

13. Public interest in bop didn't last long—the musicians themselves seemed to go out of their way to discourage it—and the threat in bop soon became more psychological than economic. But the young and formerly admiring bop musician did not hesitate to tell the old-timer: "If you don't dig these new sounds, man, you're real square." In fact, he made a point of doing so—in a variety of ways—and many older musicians felt this hostility keenly. The revolt in bop was frequently revolting.... The switch from "hot" to "cool" as the epithet of highest praise goes deeper ... he refused to play the stereotype role of Negro entertainer, which he rightly associated with Uncle Tomism. He then proceeded to play the most revolutionary jazz with an appearance of utter boredom, rejecting his audience entirely. [221]

In his review of the militant journalism that accompanied the "bebop" revolution, Martin Williams points out that the battle was pitched between those who claimed that bop had blasted everything else out of the field and those who claimed it was a passing aberration. See his introductory note to Ross Russell's 1948–49 articles in *The Record Changer* [Williams 1851].

14. "Bruno, si un día lo pudieras escribir.... No por mí, entiendes, a mí qué me importa" [256].

15. "[D]espués de la maravilla nace la irritación, y a mí por lo menos mepasa que siento como si Johnny me hubiera estado tomando el pelo" [262].

16. "Sonrío lo mejor que puedo, comprendiendo vagamente que tiene razón, pero que lo que él sospecha y lo que yo presiento de su sospecha se va a borrar como siempre apenas esté en la calle y me meta en mi vida de todos los días" [262].

17.The ideas of Parker and Gillespie were not so very novel from an academic viewpoint, and would have come into jazz anyway. By the 1940s conservatory-trained musicians were beginning to enter jazz, and they were bringing with them similar ideas worked out by master composers in the previous century. Indeed, it may not be coincidental that Hawkins's "Body and Soul," virtually an exercise in chromatic chord movement, had become, late in 1939, one of the biggest jazz hits of the period. But Parker and Gillespie set about building a whole music around this concept, and, perhaps more important, they had the courage to insist that they were right. [Collier 351]

Parker, like Johnny, was reluctant to admit debts of gratitude and respect, even to mentor musicians [Collier 365]. See also Stearns [218, 224].

18. "como lo que era en el fondo: un pobre diablo de inteligencia apenas mediocre ..." [311].

19. "Knowledge has always been interpreted as assimilation. Even the most surprising discoveries end by being absorbed, comprehended, with all that there is of 'prehending' in 'comprehending.' The most audacious and remote knowledge does not put us in communion with the truly other; it does not take the place of sociality; it is still and always a solitude.... Sociality will be a way of escaping being otherwise than through knowledge" [Levinas, *Ethics and Infinity* 60–61].

20. "'Hace rato que nonos veíamos—te he dicho a Johnny—. Un mes por lo menos.' 'Tú no haces más que contar el tiempo—me ha contestado de mal humor. El primero, el dos, el tres, el veintiuno. A todo le pones un número, tú' [250, my emphasis].

21. "Johnny ... seguía haciendo alusiones al tiempo, un tema que le preocupa desde que lo conozco. He visto pocos hombres tan preocupados por todo lo que se refiere al tiempo" [252].

22. "Esto lo estoy tocando mañana.... Esto ya lo toqué mañana, es horrible, Miles, esto ya lo toqué mañana" [253].

23.

> I'd been getting bored with the stereotyped changes that were being used all the time ... and I kept thinking there's bound to be something else. I could hear it sometimes but I couldn't play it.

> Well, that night, I was working over Cherokee, and as I did, I found that by using the higher intervals of a chord as a melody line and backing them with appropriately related changes, I could play the thing I'd been hearing. I came alive. (qtd. in Shapiro and Hentof 340)

24. "no es victima, no perseguido, sino perseguido" [287].

25. The suggestion of Lacan's essay on the mirror stage is so strong here, it makes one wonder if Cortázar had read the piece or heard it referred to in a later seminar. In that essay, Lacan develops the idea of mirror images as fictional representations likely to cause paranoia in the onlooker who suspects that the coherent image knows more about him than he does himself.

The scene also evokes Bakhtin's "Author and Hero in Aesthetic Activity," although Cortázar almost certainly did not know this piece:

> The mirror can do no more than provide the material for self-objectification, and even that not in its pure form. Indeed, our position before a mirror is always somewhat spurious, for since we lack any approach to ourselves from outside, in this case, as in the other, we project ourselves into a peculiarly indeterminate possible other, with whose help we then try to find an axiological position in relation to ourselves.... I am not alone when I look at myself in the mirror: I am possessed by someone else's soul. More than that. At times, this other soul may gain body to the point where it attains a certain self-sufficiency. Vexation and a certain resentment, with which our dissatisfaction about our own exterior may combine, give body to this other–the possible author of our own exterior. Distrust of him, hatred, a desire to annihilate him become possible. [32–33]

26. That slime or "drool" is the same stuff that obsesses the photographer in "Blow-Up" ("Las babas del diablo").

27. "He leído algunas cosas sobre todo eso, Bruno. Es muy raro, y en realidad tan difícil ... [*sic*]. Yo creo que la música ayuda, sabes. No a entender, porque en realidad no entiendo nada" [254].

28. "Lo mejor es cuando te das cuenta de que puedes meter una tienda entera en la valija, cientos y cientos de trajes, como yo meto la música en el tiempo cuando estoy tocando a veces. La música y lo que pienso cuando viajo en el métro" [257].

29. "Bruno, si yo pudiera solamente vivir como en esos momentos, o como cuando estoy tocando y también el tiempo cambia ..." [262].

30. "Perhaps the most controversial aspect of bebop jazz is its rhythmic organization. Bebop rhythmics, or better polyrhythmics, are so revolutionary that they have been largely misunderstood and, since no jazz can exist without a solid beat, the new style has been suspect among many uninformed listeners" [Russell 189].
Miles Davis has this telling memory of Parker revolutionizing the rhythm section: "Like we'd be playing the blues, and Bird would start on the 11th bar, and as the rhythm sections stayed where they were and Bird played where he was, it sounded as if the rhythm section was on one and three instead of two and four. Every time that would happen, Max used to scream at Duke not to follow Bird but to stay where he was. Then eventually, it came around as Bird had planned and we were together again." Davis adds that Parker's "turning the rhythm section around" so frustrated him that for a while he would quit the group every night [qtd. in *Metronome* (June 1955) 25; qtd. in Stearns 231–32].

31. Hodeir writes that Parker was the real leader of the bebop movement. Like Armstrong around 1930, Parker got jazz out of a rut [*Jazz* 101].
Later the standard attribution was to Parker and Gillespie. Their contributions and the differences of personal style between them are put succinctly by Leonard Feather, whose early *Inside Bebop* became required reading for other jazz historians. In *The Pleasures of Jazz* he writes, "the emergence of bebop, a new and enduring genre, was primarily the creation of Charlie Parker—whose pleasures during his appearances took several forms: odd quotes during an improvised solo, caustic comments to an apathetic or uncomprehending audience—and of Dizzy Gillespie, whose fame as a comedian has often enhanced the undimmed grandeur of his musical contribution" [21].
Keeping Gillespie in view tempers more romantic and self-destructive assumptions about great music, such as the one Robert George Reisner repeats in "I Remember Bird" [*Bird* 11–27]: "Bird was neurotic, but the great strides in the arts are not made by happy, well-adjusted people. Art is a form of sublimation and is created by neurotics and compulsion-ridden people, not by the happy, nine-to-five, family man" [19]. This brings to mind some of Spike Lee's reasons for making Mo' Better Blues, his memorial to musical family men, including his own father.

32. From the liner notes to "Hampton Hawes Trio," Contemporary Records LP C3505, quoted by Lester Koenig (26 August 1955) [Stearns 228]. Hodeir had already made the point: "It is clear that he [Parker] created a school.... But, as we shall see, the new generation has not completely assimilated his acquisitions, particularly in the field of rhythm" [*Jazz* 104].

33. "Cuando la marquesa echa a hablar uno repregunta si el estilo de Dizzy no se le ha pegado al idioma, pues es una serie interminable de variaciones en los registros más inesperados ..." [268].

34. André Hodeir describes Charlie Parker as a musical magician, "making appear and then disappear scraps of a melody that should have been rendered in full, hiding them up his sleeve" ["The Genius of Art Tatum" 175].

35. "([Y]o ya no sé cómo escribir todo esto)" [302].

36. "Este no es el momento de hacer crítica de jazz, y los interesados pueden leer mi libro sobre Johnny y el nuevo estilo de la posguerra, pero bien puedo decir que el cuarenta y ocho—digamos hasta el cincuenta—fue como una explosión de la música ..." [266].

37. "Biography is the most original kind of book that South America can produce in our times, and the best material we can offer history" [Domingo Faustino Sarmiento, *Recuerdos de provincia* (1850), in the appendix on biography].

38. I find Jaime Alazraki unconvincing, for example, when he applauds Cortázar's fiction for maturing from an obsessive focus on plot to being "more concentrated on characters, more vital and less dependent on plot" [94]; but his partiality to character development is consistent with his appreciation for Cortázar's mastery as a writer of faction. Cortázar, of course, kept mastery at enough distance to incite innovation. He always feared writing too easily or too well. Even if Alazraki is not wrong about the initial shift of focus, it is only one shift, and Cortázar is a moving target for his readers.

39. His *Totality and Infinity* is an extended critique of the tradition of Western philosophy, a fundamentally ontological tradition that moves out in appropriative concentric circles from the subject. In its stead, Levinas appeals for an ethics based in the other, the locutor who preexists the subject and constructs him as a necessary listener. Only an appreciation for the radical and inassimilable alterity, and primordialness of the other can ground ethical relations.

40. I thank Adam Zachary Newton for the general turn of this argument to the question of ethical engagement, and specifically for pointing out the relevance of Bakhtin for Cortázar. He develops his own reading in chapter 2 of his masterful *Narrative Ethics: Readers and Fiction in Each Other's Hands*, forthcoming from Harvard University Press. Newton's focus is on the duration of the enabling engagement between author and hero.

41. "Que los críticos son mucho más necesarios de lo que yo mismo estoy dispuesto a reconocer ... porque los creadores, desde el inventor de la música hasta Johnny ..., son incapaces de extraer las consecuencias dialécticas de su obra, postular los fundamentos y la transcendencia de lo que están escribiendo o improvisando" [300–01].

42. See my "A Nowhere for Us." My focus is on his experiments with the very components of literary and common language, that is, on the arbitrarily produced linguistic signs he shows to be constructed, changeable, flexible, and as unstable as the world they allegedly represent.

43. "Queríamos tanto a Glenda que le ofreceríamos una última perfección inviolable. En la altura intangible donde la habíamos exaltado, la perservaríamos de la caída, sus fieles podrían seguir adorándola sin mengua; no se baja vivo de una cruz" [28].

44. "lo de siempre, por qué no vivís en tu patria, qué pasó que *Blow-Up* era tan distinto de tu cuento, te parece que el escritor tiene que estar comprometido? A esta altura de las cosas ya sé que la Última entrevista me la harán en las puertas del infierno y seguro que serán las mismas preguntas, y si por caso es chez San Pedro la cosa no va a cambiar, a usted no le parece que allá abajo escribía demasiado hermético para el pueblo?" [95].

45. "Lo difícil es girar en torno a él sin perder la distancia, como un buen satélite, un buen crítico" [288].

46. "En el fondo somos una banda de egoístas, so pretexto de cuidar a Johnny lo que hacemos es salvar nuestra idea de él ... sacarle brillo a la estatua que hemos erigido entre todos y defenderla cueste lo que cueste" [272].

47. "que se trepara aun altar y tironeara de Cristo para sacarlo de la cruz" [296].

48. "Deberías sentirte contento de que me haya portado así contigo; no lo hago con nadie, créeme. Es una muestra de cómo te aprecio. Tenemos que ir juntos a algún sitio para hablar ..." [271].

49. "Y si yo mismo no he sabido tocar domo debía, tocarlo que soy de veras ... ya ves que no se te pueden pedir milagros, Bruno" [304].

50. "En el fondo lo único que ha dicho es que nadie sabe nada de nadie, y no es una novedad. Toda biografía da eso por supuesto y sigue adelante, qué diablos" [304–05].

51. "envidio a Johnny, a ese Johnny del otro lado, sin que nadie sera qué es exactamente ese otro lado.... Envidio a Johnny y al mismo tiempo me da rabia que se esté destruyendo por el mal empleo de sus dones ..." [269–70].

52. "y quizá en el fondo quisiera que Johnny acabara de una vez, como una estrella que se rompe en mil pedazos y deja idiotas a los astrónomos durante una semana, y después uno se va a dormir y mañana es otro día" [270].

WORKS CITED

Alazraki, Jaime. "From *Bestiary* to *Glenda*: Pushing the Short Story to Its Utmost Limits." *Review of Contemporary Fiction* 3.3 (1983): 94–99.

Andrade, Oswald de. "Cannibalist Manifesto." Trans. Leslie Bary. *Latin American Literary Review* 19.38 (1991): 35–47. Trans. of "Manifesto antropofago." 1928.

Armstrong, Louis. "Bop Will Kill Business unless It Kills Itself First." *Down Beat* 7 Apr. 1948: 2.

Bakhtin, Mikhail. "Author and Hero in Aesthetic Activity." *Art and Answerability: Early Philosophical Essays by M. M. Bakhtin*. Ed. Michael Holquist and Vadim Liapunov. Austin: U of Texas P, 1990.

Barthes, Roland. *The Pleasure of the Text*. New York: Hill and Wang, 1975.

Behar, Lisa Block de. *Una retórica del silencio: Funciones del lector y procedimientos de la lectura literaria*. México: Siglo XXI, 1984.

Chambers, Ross. *Room for Maneuver: Reading (the) Oppositional (in) Narrative*. Chicago: U of Chicago P, 1991.

Collier, James Lincoln. *The Making of Jazz: A Comprehensive History*. Boston: Houghton Mifflin, 1978.

Cortázar, Julio. "Apocalypse at Solentiname." *A Change of Light and Other Stories*. Trans. Gregory Rabassa. New York: Knopf, 1980. 119–27. Trans. of "Apocalipsis en Solentiname." *Alguién que anda por ahí*. Madrid: Alfaguara, 1977.

———. "Graffiti." *We Love Glenda So Much and Other Tales* 33–38.

———. "Blow-Up." *Blow-Up and Other Stories* 100–15. Trans. of "Las babas del diablo." *Las armas secretas*. Buenos Aires: Sudamericana, 1959.

———. *Blow-Up and Other Stories*. Trans. Paul Blackburn. New York: Collier, 1967.

———. "The Pursuer." *Blow–Up and Other Stories* 161–220. Trans. of "El perseguidor." *Las armas secretas*. Buenos Aires: Sudamericana, 1959. 149–313.

———. "Return Trip Tango." *We Love Glenda So Much and Other Tales* 60–77.

———. "We Love Glenda So Much." *We Love Glenda So Much and Other Tales* 8–16.

———. *We Love Glenda So Much and Other Tales*. Trans. Gregory Rabassa. New York: Knopf, 1983. Trans. of *Queremos tanto a Glenda*. México: Nueva Imagen, 1980.

de Man, Paul. "Autobiography As Defacement." *MLN* 94 (1979): 919–30.

Feather, Leonard. *Inside Bebop*. New York: Robbins, 1949.

———. *The Pleasures of Jazz*. New York: Horizon, 1976.

Fish, Stanley Eugene. *Surprised by Sin: The Reader in Paradise Lost*. New York: St. Martin's, 1967.

Genette, Gérard. *Figures of Literary Discourse*. Trans. Alan Sheridan. New York: Columbia UP, 1982.

Hodeir, André. "The Genius of Art Tatum." Williams 173–80.

———. *Jazz: Its Evolution and Essence*. Trans. David Noakes. New York: Grove, 1956. Trans. of *Hommes et problèmes du jazz*. Paris: Portulan, 1954.

Iser, Wolfgang. *The Act of Reading: A Theory of Aesthetic Response*. Baltimore: Johns Hopkins UP, 1978.

———. *The Implied Reader: Patterns of Communication in Prose Fiction from Bunyan to Beckett*. Baltimore: Johns Hopkins UP, 1974.

———. "Narrative Strategies As Means of Communication." *Interpretation of Narrative*. Ed. Mario J. Valdés and Owen J. Miller. Toronto: Intl. Colloquium on Interpretation of Narrative, U of Toronto, 1978. 100–17.

———. "The Reading Process: A Phenomenological Approach." Tompkins 50–69.

Lacan, Jacques. *Écrits*. Trans. Alan Sheridan. New York: Norton, 1977.

Lee, Spike, dir. *Mo' Better Blues*. Universal, 1990.

Levinas, Emmanuel. *Ethics and Infinity: Conversations with Philippe Nemo*. Trans. Richard A. Cohen. Pittsburgh: Duquesne UP, 1985.

———. *Totality and Infinity*. Pittsburgh: Duquesne UP, 1969.

Macksey, Richard A., and Eugenio Donato, eds. *The Structuralist Controversy: The Language of Criticism and the Science of Man*. Baltimore: Johns Hopkins UP, 1972.

Poulet, Georges. "Criticism and the Experience of Interiority." *The Structuralist Controversy: The Language of Criticism and the Science of Man*. Macksey and Donato 56–72. Rpt. in Tompkins 41–49.

Reisner, Robert George. *Bird: The Legend of Charlie Parker*. New York: Da Capo, 1973.

Russell, Ross. "Bebop." Williams 186–214.

Sarmiento, Domingo Faustino. *Recuerdos de provincia*. 1850. Buenos Aires: Emecé, 1944.

Shapiro, Nat, and Nat Hentoff. *Hear Me Talkin' to Ya*. New York: Rinehart, 1955.

Shell, Marc. "The Family Pet, or the Human and the Animal." *Children of the Earth: Literature, Politics, and Nationhood*. New York: Oxford UP, 1993. 148–75.

Siebers, Tobin. *The Ethics of Criticism*. Ithaca: Cornell UP, 1988.

Sommer, Doris. "A Nowhere for Us: The Promising Pronouns of Cortázar's 'Utopian' Stories." *Dispositio* 11 (1986). Rpt. in *Discurso literario* 4.1 (1986–87): 231–63.

Stearns, Marshall W. *The Story of Jazz*. New York: Oxford UP, 1956.

Tompkins, Jane, ed. *Reader-Response Criticism: From Formalism to Post-Structuralism*. Baltimore: Johns Hopkins UP, 1980.

Williams, Martin, ed. *The Art of Jazz: Ragtime to Be-bop*. 1959. New York: Da Capo, 1980.

Zamora, Lois Parkinson. "Movement and Stasis, Film and Photo: "Temporal Structures in the Recent Fiction of Julio Cortázar." *Review of Contemporary Fiction* 3.3 (1983): 51–64.

ISABEL ALVAREZ BORLAND

Cortázar: On Critics and Interpretation

> En algún lugar debe haber un basural donde están amontonadas las explicaciones. Una sola cosa inquieta en este justo panorama: lo que pueda ocurrir el día en que alguien consiga explicar también el basural.
> —Julio Cortázar, *Un tal Lucas* 66.

Cortázar's writing overtly challenges and invites the reader to participate in the act of creation, engaging him/her to consider the creative act from multiple perspectives. He has explicitly dealt with his poetics in "Apuntes para una poética" (1945), and with a theory of the short story in *Ultimo Round* (1969). Starting with *Rayuela* (1963), a great portion of his fiction has been self-consciously dedicated to exploring the aesthetics of the creative act. Given his interest in the subject, a question is raised by the fact that while his essays and fiction on the creative process defend and praise the craft and role of the artist, his portrait of literary critics as characters or as subjects of his essays has displayed an intense suspicion regarding the critic's role vis-à-vis the work of art.

The present study concerns specific stories and essays by Cortázar in which the literary critic functions as the main character. Central to our goal would be to explore how, in these fictions, Cortázar establishes a dialogue with the reader through which he addresses the subject of interpretation. In

From *INTI: Revista de Literatura Hispanica*, nos. 43–44 (Primavera-Otoño 1996). © 1996 by INTI.

order to identify a subtext common to the stories as well as the essays, two questions must be directed to these narratives: 1) What is the role of the protagonist/critic in providing the reader with a particular perspective of the critical act? 2) How does the critical language employed by these protagonists/critics differ from the familiar language of fiction, and what are the implications of these differences? By answering these questions through a careful study of the narratives' fictional processes, we will be concerned with identifying not only the critic as a literary character, but also with exploring Cortázar's awareness of the dynamics of literary interpretation[1].

"El perseguidor" has received considerable attention from scholars as Cortázar's testament on the subject of jazz[2]. Narrated in the first person of a critic named Bruno, the story takes place in the world of music, offering us an account of a talented jazzman's last years, his drug and alcohol dependency, his self-destructive impulses and, finally, the beauty and power of his music. The story is an autobiographical account of Bruno, a critic who is writing a biography on jazzman Johnny Carter. Bruno's view of himself and his profession dominate the story since it is through this critic's perspective that all other events are presented to the reader. As the story opens, the reader is presented with a sordid scene at Johnny's apartment: Johnny lies in bed, sick from his drug habit and desolate because he has lost his saxophone. Bruno, the artist's "friend," is there to promise another saxophone and perhaps additional money. The roles are clearly delineated in this first scene: Johnny will be the exploited genius of jazz while Bruno will be the provider as well as the parasite, the "selfless" critic who follows Johnny around in order to exploit his talents. The story is chronologically told, its language straightforward, its motives and themes rather transparent. However, soon the reader realizes the deceptive character of this narrative, for in this story the narrator and the reader reach different conclusions about the portrait of Johnny Carter as drawn by his critic/pursuer, Bruno. The gap caused by the narratorial unreliability of Bruno's first person, allows the reader to detect inconsistencies in Bruno's portrait of the artist.

There are several aspects in the telling of "El perseguidor" that allow the critical reader to look at this account as the story of the dynamics of exchange between critic and artist, between pursuer and creator. Moreover, "El perseguidor" dramatizes the critical act from multiple perspectives: the critic's view and exercise of his profession; the critic's portrait of the artist; and finally, the artist's view of the critic.

Bruno, our narrator, lacks imagination both in his critical study of Johnny (the pretext for telling his story) and in his account to us as readers. Early in the story Bruno states: "Soy un crítico de jazz to bastante sensible como para comprender mis limitaciones" (92). For Bruno, a critic is no better than a mercenary: "ese hombre que solo puede vivir de prestado de las novedades y las decisiones ajenas" (130). In fact, Bruno feels that his profession denies him any possible transcendence and this realization fills him with bitterness.

It is precisely this negative self-image ("me siento como un hueco a su lado" [120]) that translates into an account of Johnny which is tainted and colored by Bruno's intense feelings of inferiority. The critic wants to convince the reader of Johnny's unworthiness, of his decadent lifestyle, and of the lack of correspondence between his genius and his personal merits. Moreover, Bruno goes to great lengths to let the reader know that the genius of this artist was totally undeserved:

> un pobre diablo de inteligencia apenas mediocre, dotado como tanto músico, tanto ajedrecista y tanto poeta del don de crear cosas estupendas sin tener la menor conciencia (a lo sumo orgullo de boxeador que se sabe fuerte) de las dimensiones de su obra (148).

Bruno feels envy of Johnny Carter's creative genius. He situates himself and his profession as unworthy when compared to the artist's endeavors: "el Johnny está al principio de su saxo mientras yo vivo obligado a conformarme con el final" (92).

Based on the plot's events, we could assert that "El perseguidor" is simply Cortázar's bitter indictment against the figure of the critic, and against criticism as an empty, meaningless, pursuit. However, if we look further, the negative example of Bruno foregrounds key issues related to the exercise of a satisfactory critical practice: the critic's right to become the artist's author; the critic's responsibility to his readers' and the problematics between the critic and his subject of study.

What in fact is Bruno's critical approach to Johnny's art? It is significant that we are never quite sure of what is actually written in Bruno's book. If on one instance, Bruno writes: "me he impuesto mostrar las lineas esenciales poniendo el acento en lo que verdaderamente cuenta, el arte incomparable de Johnny" (124), later on he contradicts himself: "Se muy bien que el libro no dice la verdad sobre Johnny (tampoco miente) sino que se limita a la música de Johnny" (140). The critical reader is forced to examine gaps rather than presences, omissions rather than assertions. The story's subject, Johnny's portrait, is as elusive to the reader as is Bruno's analysis of its merits.

At times Bruno dialogues with the reader and clearly admits that he has no intention of letting him "read" his critical text: "Este no es el momento de hacer crítica de jazz, y los interesados pueden leer mi libro sobre Johnny y el nuevo estilo" (102). Moreover, when Bruno feels that he is letting on too much information regarding his critical text, he restrains himself from such activity: "Pero de todo esto he hablado en mi libro" (111). Bruno's reluctance to let the reader appreciate his critical acumen is significant and could be indicative of Cortázar's own suspicious view of the language of literary interpretation.

The absence or unavailability of the critic's text leads us to explore the presence of a surrogate reader[3] who comments on the critical text unavailable to us. The final judgment on Bruno's book comes from the artist Johnny, and this has a terrifying effect on Bruno for the latter fears public embarrassment. Johnny, as a reader of Bruno's text, clearly sees the critic's desire for facile and opportunistic criticism. As expected, Johnny accuses Bruno of creating a false portrait of him: "Bruno el jazz no es solamente música, yo no soy solamente Johnny Carter" (142). Johnny becomes the first reader of Bruno's critical interpretation and underscores the critic's dishonest approach and lack of scruples (143). In addition, the jazzman's judgment on Bruno's work has additional significance for it introduces in the story the possibility of an alternative approach to the creative work:

> Faltan cosas, Bruno—dice Johnny—. Tu estás mucho más enterado que yo, pero me parece que faltan cosas ... El compañero Bruno anota en su libreta todo lo que uno dice, salvo las cosas importantes. Nunca creí que pudieras equivocarte tanto. (143)

Johnny's reproaches to Bruno suggest a holistic approximation to the work of art, one that considers the artist's human concerns as well as his craft: "Pero Bruno.... de lo que to has olvidado es de mí.... De mí, Bruno, de mí" (141). The events in this story question the critic's right to become the artist's author; but more importantly, these events underline the basic differences between the language of criticism and the language of art.

The questions posed by "El perseguidor" could perhaps be clarified in the context of a second story on the subject of critics and their practice: "Los pasos en las huellas" published in 1974 as part of the collection *Octaedro*[4]. This story presents manipulation and selection of critical evidence as dangerous temptations for the critic in the practice of his profession. Fraga, an unknown critic, decides to write a study on Romero, a well-known poet who had enjoyed an unexplained reputation in his country both before and after his death. It is Fraga's intention to uncover the obscure reasons for the poet's impact and popularity: "padecía de la falta de una crítica sistemática y hasta de una iconografía satisfactoria" (25).

In "Los pasos", Fraga's research is traced chronologically: the initial stage of gathering data, and the "inventive" stage in which Fraga manipulates his facts in order to produce a version that would guarantee success: "ganar simultaneamente el respeto del mundo académico y el entusiasmo del hombre de la calle" (29). Fraga's critical approach to Romero is biographical, a task which makes him a chronicler/detective of Romero's life. After some months of research, Fraga succeeds in his venture: his new interpretation radically changes the canon on the popular author and becomes "el tema del momento."

However, things do not go as Fraga had expected. Once accepted by his peers and by the public at large, Fraga finds himself unable to continue his farce. Overcome by "un desasosiego inexplicable" he is unable to enjoy his newly found success. He recognizes and admits to the reader that his version had not explored the subject sufficiently; that he had stopped researching when he found suitable evidence; and finally, that he had neglected evidence which would have considerably altered his now "commercial" interpretation on Romero: "Oh sí, lo sabía, vaya a saber como pero lo sabía y escribí el libro sabiéndolo y quizá también los lectores lo saben, y todo es una inmensa mentira en la que estamos metidos hasta el último" (40).

A second visit to his original source, Raquel Marquez, confirms what Fraga already knew: he had neglected to include significant evidence that would have changed the reception of his best seller. Plagued by remorse and conscious of the disastrous results such relations would have for his reputation as a critic, Fraga decides to reveal his hoax to the public. There is an ironic twist at the end of the story when Fraga realizes the commercial value of his 'second' interpretation of Romero. Driven by his ambition and desire to preserve his image, our critic is again ready to misuse his latest and more honest interpretation: "... la cancelación del premio, la negativa de la cancillería a confirmar su propuesta, podían convertirse en noticias que lo lanzarían al mundo internacional de las grandes tiradas y las traducciones" (46). The critic's repentance only serves to sink him deeper into the lie he was trying to correct.

The reader's reception of the events in this story is the result of the distorted accounts of three individuals. First, we witness Romero's own manipulation of his poems in order to create an image for himself. Next, we have the selection of the letters given to Fraga by Raquel Marquez revealing her own desire to withhold events which would produce a new version of

Romero. Finally, we have Fraga's knowing acceptance of Raquel Marquez' practical evidence because it suits his own commercial version. Thus Fraga's interpretation of the artist changes with each new telling, and with each reason for telling it.

Against a biography's mirroring capability, its implicit promise of faithful representation, Cortázar clearly senses its potential for distortion and inescapable otherness, its autonomy as object. Thus the subtle interactions of the object's biography and the subject portrayed (in both Johnny Carter's and Romero's lives) contribute and speak for the problematics of identity of the specific critic and of critics in general. In both these stories, the critics seem to be hampered by their own subjectivity, and also by their own desire to make their object of study be like them. In the case of the critic Fraga, this manipulation of evidence is closely associated with an imposition of his own life into the life of the subject he is creating. This is done very effectively as the omniscient narrator draws intentional parallels between the critic and the artist's life: "Las afinidades entre Romero y yo, nuestra común preferencia por ciertos valores estéticos y poéticos, eso que vuelve fatal la elección del tema por parte de biógrafo, no me hará incurrir más de una vez en una autobiografía disimulada?" (28).

Both Fraga and Bruno manipulate evidence in order to produce a sellable, commercial interpretation of their artists. In "El perseguidor," the artist is alive and becomes a critical reader of Bruno's text, while in "Los pasos" Fraga has total and unchecked freedom to forge whatever image of Romero is most suitable to him. The presence of Johnny Carter as a surrogate reader in "El perseguidor", ensures our negative reaction to the critic's unfair behavior. On the other hand, in "Los pasos," Fraga's self-censorship reveals remorse for his dishonest critical practice. In both stories the question of authorship of a critical treatise is a serious one for it involves the risk of dishonesty and deviousness.

While "El perseguidor" and "Los pasos en las huellas" have given us a fictional depiction of failed critics, Cortázar's short essays have sometimes approached the subject ironically once again depicting critics in a negative light. Two fitting examples are his essays: "Noticias de los Funes" (1969) and "Texturologías" (1979).

In "Noticias de los Funes" Cortázar communicates the same derogatory attitude towards the labor of the critic that we had witnessed in his fictions:

> ... un tal Julian Garavito de la revista *Europe* viene y escribe pero entonces usted y el hilo secreto que va uniendo sus cuentos.... La

crítica es como Periquita y hace lo que puede, pero eso de que ahora se dedique a la costura conmigo prueba lo que va de cualquier realidad a cualquier interpretación. (120)

This essay is of interest because our author attempts to answer a critic's interpretation of his own work. In Garavito's[5] particular case, Cortázar is surprised because this critic manages to find unity in what Cortázar viewed as a totally haphazard collection of short stories (120). Curiously, Cortázar is not totally censorious of this critics. The essay concludes by thanking Garavito for having "illuminated" Cortázar's creative work: "sin ironía alguna le doy las gracias a Julian Garavito, tejedor al lado de la luz" (121).

"Texturologías," on the other hand, effectively demeans the labor of the critic by dramatizing the futility of a critical language. The essay reproduces fictitious quotes from six critical interpretations of a poet named Lobizón. Each critic appears as a critic of the previous critic, each successive essay outdoing the next in its pedantry and obscurity, forgetting its main concern which should have been the artist's work. The critic's quotes, which make up the main body of the essay, are followed by Cortázar's own ironic closing sentence: ¿Qué agregar a esta deslumbrante absolutización de lo contingente?". In "Texturologías," we find a telling instance of the misuse of the language of interpretation.

Cortázar's own biography tells us that he himself started as a critic and as a teacher of literature[6]. As a student he labored over the work of Keats and Poe, translated their work, and wrote critical treatises on them. In fact some of Cortázar's writings on these two authors have been identified by critics as essential in the understanding of Cortázar's poetics and his view on what constitutes artistic creativity. "Para llegar a Lezama Lima," Cortázar's essay on Lezama's *Paradiso*, provides an excellent opportunity to examine Cortázar's own approach to the creative work of others.

The essay begins by discussing biographical facts about Lezama such as his lack of familiarity with foreign languages, and his relatively unknown status in Europe. As the essay progresses, it becomes obvious to the reader that Cortázar's method of analysis consists of quoting extensively from the original. Few opinions are formulated by Cortázar on *Paradiso* and when they do appear, they tend to be subjective and emulatory of Lezama's own style (72). Cortázar seems contaminated with Lezama's style and uses nouns and terms which would be recognized as *lezamianos*. Here Cortázar reaches the same union with his text that he had prescribed as essential for creators in "Apuntes para una poética". Cortázar urges the reader to come into direct contact with *Paradiso*, for only by establishing a communion with the artistic text it will be possible for any reader to grasp Lezama's poetic imagery and the power of his prose. Fittingly, Cortázar concludes this essay with a humble assessment of his, critical practice as he labels his own criticism as "un pobre resumen de un libro que no los tolera." As a critic, Cortázar feels awed by the power of Lezama's artistry. The critic, displaced by the artist, is forced to summarize rather than to interpret.

Cortázar's non-fictional writings on the subject of the artist seem to suggest that critics and creators should adhere to the same professional criteria. In his classic essay on creativity, "Apuntes para una poética," Cortázar discusses the qualities needed to create literature: faith, intuition, and a belief by the artist that he will be possessed by the art he is creating. The critic, like the artist, must be able to join in and communicate intuitively with the text: "Yo creo que un gran crítico y un gran creador están absolutamente en el mismo nivel" (Apuntes, 130). Cortázar's insistence on the communion between the artist and his object, is of great relevance to our consideration of the author's stance on critics since it allows us to understand Cortázar's suspicion and lack of trust in the language of criticism.

In a key essay on Cortázar's poetics, Sara Castro Klaren describes the significant influence of phenomenology—specifically Merleau Ponty's writings—on Julio Cortázar's stance of the subject of artistic creation. Castro Klaren specifies two main postulates as defining Cortázar's poetics. The first is the poet's "porous" or open condition to the world's experiences. The second addresses the relationship between the artist and the object of his creation, "the poet thirsting for being, manages to fuse his anxious being to the ontological qualities of the contemplated object" (141).

By juxtaposing the critic's and the artist's use of language in the fictional pieces we have studied, Cortázar explores the limits of critical language to portray the truth. If a good critic should be at the same level as the artist, then it follows that a critic should be able to achieve the same fusion with his subject (the artist) as the artist achieves with his (the work of art). Yet, is this a realistic goal for any critic? For Cortázar, a basic difference between the language of the artist and the language of the critic lies in their respective premises. The artist's truth does not depend on the facts, it has a freedom which is not available to the literary critic. Cortázar's fictional pieces on critics and his own essays on the creative act seem to support this view.

In an interview with Evelyn Picón Garfield, published five years before his death, Cortázar spoke briefly about the language of fiction versus the language of criticism:

> La crítica a veces se llama una especie de creación de segundo
> grado, de segunda etapa, es decir que el cuentista escribe
> partiendo de una especie de nada y el crítico crea partiendo de
> una cosa que ya está hecha.... A mí me gustaría ser una especie de
> síntesis de las dos cosas aunque fuera un día: solo un día de mi
> vida me gustaría ser a la vez un creador y un crítico. (19)

The passage is significant because it underlines once again Cortázar's
dualistic feelings towards the critical act. It also explains what to Cortázar is
the critic's dilemma "a veces hay una especie de corte con la vida, con los
impulsos vitales" (16). In the words of Bruno, a critic's labor consists of
"sancionar comparativamente," that is, to sanction comparatively always
hoping to arrive at a definitive reading of the work of art. Bruno, Fraga,
Garavito, and Lobizon dramatize the problematics of interpretation by
creating critical fictions which have as their futile objective rational and
definitive interpretations.

NOTES

1. Catherine Belsey's *Critical Practice* as well as Stein Haugom Olsen's *The Structure of Literary Understanding* are pertinent and influential to my own reading of Cortázar's views on literary interpretation.

2. Critics have shown considerable interest in "El perseguidor" and I have included in my bibliography articles on this story which have appeared in the last ten years. Pertinent to my own reading are the following pieces which look at the aesthetics of this story: Roberto González-Echevarría , "*Los reyes*: Cortázar's Mythology of Writing"; Lanin Gyurko, "Quest and Betrayal in Cortázar's El perseguidor"; Noe Jitrik, "Crítica satélite y trabajo crítico en El perseguidor"; Amalia Lazarte-Dishman, "Otro enfoque a "El perseguidor"; Maria Lima, "El perseguidor" una segunda lectura"; Antonio Skármeta, "Trampas al perseguidor"; and Saul Sosnowski, "Pursuers." None of the above articles have traced the figure of the fictional critic to Cortázar's other texts on critics.

3. Although Iser's work on reader response is seminal for the kind of reading I'm doing here, more specific studies on embedded readers and writers within fictional texts have influenced my investigation. See specific studies by: S. Daniels, Prince, and, Shor.

4. In contrast to the great number of articles written on "El perseguidor", Cortázar's "Los pasos en las huellas" has received little attention. One exception is Lanin Gyurko's "Artist and Critic as Self and Double" (1982). Gyurko's perspective differs from mine considerably.

5. As it turns out, this critic was not 'invented' by Cortázar. See: Julián Garavito's "Julio Cortázar: *Gites*."

6. See Jaime Alazraki's excellent overview of Cortázar's biography in his introduction to *Final Island*.

WORKS CITED

Alazraki, Jaime and Ivar Ivask eds. *Final Island*. Oklahoma: WLT, 1971. (See essays by Linda Aronne Amestoy; Jaime Alazraki; Sara Castro Klaren).

Belsey, Catherine. *Critical Practice*. London & New York: Methuen, 1980.

Carter, E-D. "La sombra del *Perseguidor*: El doble en *Rayuela*." *Explicación de Textos Literarios* 17 (1988–89): 64–110.

Cortázar, Julio. "El perseguidor." *Las armas secretas*. Madrid: Alfaguara, 1982.

———. "Los pasos en las huellas." *Octaedro*. Madrid: Alianza, 1971.

———. "Del cuento breve y sus alrededores;" "Noticias de los Funes." *Ultimo Round*. México: Siglo Veintiuno, 1969.

———. "Situación de la novela." *Cuadernos Americanos* 4 (1950): 223.

———. "Apuntes para una poética." *Torre* 7 (1945): 121–138.

———. "Para llegar a Lezama Lima." *La vuelta al día en ochenta mundos*. México: Siglo Veintinuno, 1967.

———. "Texturologías." *Un tal Lucas*. Madrid: Alfaguara, 1979.

———. *Ultimo Round*. México, Siglo Veintiuno, 1969.

Daniels, S. "Readers in Texts." *PMLA* 96 (1981): 848–63.

Fiddian, Robin. "Religious Symbolism and the Ideological Critique in *El perseguidor*." *Revista Canadiense de Estudios Hispánicos* 2 (1985): 149–163.

Garavito, Julian. "Julio Cortázar: *Gites*." *Europe* 473 (1968) 17–8.

González-Echevarría, Roberto. "Los Reyes: Cortázar's Mythology of Writing." *Voice of the Masters*. Austin: University of Texas Press, 1985.

Gyurko, Lanin. "Quest and Betrayal in Cortázar's *El perseguidor*." *Hispanófila* 31 (1988): 59–78.

———. "Artist and Critic as Self and Double in Cortázar's *Los pasos en las huellas*." *Hispania* 65 (1982): 352–64.

Hernández, Ana. "Camaleonismo y vampirismo: La poética de Julio Cortázar." *Revista Iberoamericana* 45 (1979): 475–92.

Hudde, Hinrich. "El negro fausto del jazz." In *Lo lúdico y lo fantástico en la obra de Cortázar*. Madrid: Fundamentos, 1986, 37–47.

Jimenez, Antonio. "El sensualismo y la otra realidad." *Mester* 19 (1990): 49–54.

Jitrik, Noe. "Critica satélite y trabajo crítico en "El perseguidor de Julio Cortázar." *Nueva Revista de Filología Hispánica* 2 (1975): 337–368.

Iser, Wolfgang. "Interaction between Text and Reader." In *The Reader in the Text*. Ed. Susan Suleiman and Inge Crossman. Princeton: Princeton University Press, 1980. 106–19.

Kadir, Djelal. "A Mythical Re-enactment: Cortázar's *El perseguidor*." *Latin American Literary Review* 2 (1973): 63–73.

Lazarte-Dishman. Amalia. "Otro enfoque a *El perseguidor*." *Alba de América* 8 (1990): 187–202.

Lima, Maria H. "El perseguidor: una segunda lectura." *Discurso Literario* 6:1 (1988): 23–34.

Olsen, Stein Haugom. *The Structure of Literary Understanding*. Cambridge: Cambridge University Press, 1978.

Prince, Gerald. "Introduction a l'étude du narrataire." *Poetique* 14 (1973): 178–196.

Shor, Naomi. "Fiction as Interpretation/Interpretation as Fiction." In *The Reader in the Text*. Ed. Susan Suleiman and Inge Crossman. Princeton: Princeton University Press, 1980. 165–83.

Picón-Garfield, Evelyn. *Cortázar por Cortázar*. México: Universidad Veracruzana, 1981.

Skarmeta, Antonio. "Trampas al *Perseguidor*." *Mapocho* 20 (1970): 33–44.

Soren-Triff, Eduardo. "Improvisación musical y discurso literario en Julio Cortázar." *Revista Iberoamericana* 57 (1991): 657–63.

Sosnowski, Saul. "Pursuers." *Books Abroad* 3 (1976): 600–608.

Suleiman, Susan. *The Reader in the Text*. Princeton University Press, 1980.

ILAN STAVANS

Justice to Julio Cortázar

The aspects of things that are most important to us are hidden because of their simplicity and familiarity.

—*Ludwig Wittgenstein*

"Anybody who doesn't read Julio Cortázar is doomed," the Chilean poet and diplomat Pablo Neruda once said and, at least on this particular issue, he wasn't off target. The Argentine (1914–1984), a colossus of Latin American letters, is responsible for one of the continent's two twentieth-century masterpieces: *Hopscotch*, published in 1963 (the other one is Gabriel García Márquez's *One Hundred Years of Solitude*). But he is also responsible for catapulting the region into an intellectual coming of age: his artistic talent and his political views amazed and infuriated many, and forced the post–World War II Latin American intelligentsia to become part of the banquet of Western Civilization.

To read Cortázar at the peak of his international reputation was to submerge oneself in the art of improvisational, empirical narrative. He perceived fiction as an indispensable tool in the understanding of history and philosophy. An unconventional man of letters and a philosophical explorer born in Brussels and exiled in Europe since 1951 but a fervent Argentine from head to toe, Cortázar would trot the globe denouncing human rights

From *Southwest Review* vol. 81, no. 2 (Spring 1996). © 1996 by Southern Methodist University.

violations and would spend hours in front of the typewriter professing to own a unique method of writing short stories, essays and novels not unlike those developed by the French surrealist André Breton and the American beatnik Jack Kerouac: a story, he would claim, is born in a sparkle, a thunderous strike of inspiration, and requires very little by way of processing. A decisive impulse, the necessary concentration—and it's ready. He perfected the technique known as "automatic writing," in which the writer, much like Samuel Taylor Coleridge when drafting *Kubla Khan* after an opium-induced dream, must learn to trust his guts: almost no rewritings and virtually no additional editing are needed once the text appears on the page; as if literature were only the product of a supernatural Spirit dictating its craft to scribes everywhere on the globe. He wrote a handful of tales that are among the best this century has delivered.

Novels, on the other hand, were for Cortázar the result of accumulation and a cut-and-paste development. His plots were often restricted to the bizarre and unexplained, even when a political message was intermingled. Although his fantastic tales deal with themes typical of two major influential writers on his work, Edgar Allan Poe and Jorge Luis Borges, such as the double, the labyrinth, transformations of humans into beasts, he injected in them a dreamlike, surrealistic cadence. He described Anton Chekhov's style as directed toward explaining, in minute detail, a man's routine, while his own approach to literature, following the rhythm of chance, was interested in exceptions to a rule—not the investigation of senseless repetitions of an act but the sudden abolition of a habit.

Energetic, outspoken, incredibly prolific, Cortázar probably died of AIDS (although his friends deny it) just as the epidemic was gaining world attention. His unconventional style, his interest in drugs and in altered states of consciousness, his love of jazz and his passion for experimentalism, make him a contemporary of the Beat Generation and Alain Robbe-Grillet, who in 1956 inaugurated a new trend in French novel writing subscribed to by Michel Butor, Claude Simon, and Nathalie Sarraute. And yet, since his death his work has fallen out of fashion—a casualty of our changing ideological mood. It is seldom read beyond limited college courses; his style and voice are seen as the legacy of an era long gone and buried, one that took jazz out of the nightclub and into the concert hall, and was obsessively involved in experimenting with drugs to reach alternative levels of consciousness.

More than a decade after his death, a revaluation is urgently needed. Cortázar is in need of justice because the conservative atmosphere of today has had the effect of dulling his reputation. What new readers ought to get is a full-length biographical investigation in which his creativity serves as the backbone to understand the political and intellectual transformation Latin America has undergone in the twentieth century. After all, he was present at every turning point and involved with the most urgent issues, both in politics and in culture: Peronismo, existentialism, surrealism, the Cuban Revolution, the French *nouveau roman*, the Sandinistas in Nicaragua, exile as a permanent stigma for Latin American writers, detective fiction, guerrilla fighting, the AIDS epidemic, and the literary boom that swept Latin America in the late 1960s. He befriended luminaries like Che Guevara, Eden Pastora, Fidel Castro, Ernesto Cardenal, Georges Perec, Alaide Foppa, as well as Borges, Carlos Fuentes, Italo Calvino, José Donoso, Gabriel García Márquez, and Mario Vargas Llosa. His novel *Hopscotch* created a huge controversy and his response helped shape the aesthetics of the Latin American novel just as the world was awakening to its enchantments. His work left a deep mark on writers worldwide, and in Latin America Cortázar is considered a god-like figure, his birthplace and houses up until his exile turned into shrines and museums.

An exact contemporary of the Mexican poet and essayist Octavio Paz, the 1990 winner of the Nobel Prize of Literature, with whom he would occasionally collaborate and who would write a moving obituary at the time of his death, Julio Florencio Cortázar was born in Brussels on 26 August 1914 into a middle-class milieu, just as the First World War was spreading throughout the Old Continent. His family tree is full of itinerant travelers: a child of Argentine parents, from his paternal side he was a descendant of immigrants from the Basque Province in Spain; and his maternal lineage is traceable to France and Germany. Not surprisingly, Europe, his birthplace, would stimulate more than transient passion in him: it would play an important role throughout his life, becoming Cortázar's permanent address from the moment he turned thirty-seven, when Peronismo pushed him out of the southern hemisphere. As it happened, when he was born his father, also called Julio Cortázar, was temporarily stationed in Europe, as a specialist in economic affairs attached to the Argentine Embassy in Belgium. He would stay in Brussels until 1918, when, after a short visit to Spain, the elder Cortázar returned with his wife Maria Scott and the rest of the family to their native Argentina.

They settled in Bánfield, the lower-middle-class suburb of urban Buenos Aires where "The Poison" and some other future stories of their son would take place. Located in the southern section of the city, not far from a famous slaughterhouse immortalized in a classic tale by Esteban Echeverría written in the early decades of the nineteenth century, Bánfield was known as an industrial and manufacturing district. It was heavily contaminated. No matter where you looked, an abundance of factory chimneys populated the landscape. It had dusty, unpaved streets and in the early twenties, when Cortázar was still a child, horses still prevailed as one, although not the only, means of transportation.

His parents' difficult marriage and ultimate separation marked him deeply. Cortázar's father abandoned the family when his son was six. Cortázar would not know a thing about his father until news of the elder Cortázar's death, in the Cordoba province of Argentina, arrived many years later. Although emotionally devastated, even in his adult life he would never talk about the split, as if its insurmountable pain needed to remain forever private. Paternal figures populate his fiction, for instance in the allegorical novel *The Prizes*, about a group of civilians awarded a boat cruise as a lottery prize, who are suddenly left unattended at sea, without a captain to guide their boat. The novel is obviously a parable on tyranny and anarchy, and the character of the capricious leader recalls Cortázar's own disappearing father.

He and his sister Ofelia, one year his junior and his only sibling, were raised by his mother and by an aunt in a larger-than-usual house with a backyard, one with numerous rooms and obscure, empty corners that became the model of "House Taken Over." Cortázar and his sister developed a complicated fraternal relationship with incestuous undertones, one he also often refused to discuss in interviews. Cortázar acknowledged having had a recurrent dream of sleeping in the same bed with Ofelia. One should remember that non-incestuous fraternal relationships also abound in his oeuvre. Life in Bánfield was intriguing: Cortázar was curious and bookish, always intellectually driven, with an unconventional point of view, which often scared young friends and made him a loner, a sort-of-pariah and pushing him to the fringes of society. The neighborhood was the playground where he tasted the sweet innocence of childhood. In its landscape he discovered insects (ants, spiders, flies, bees), a quintessential presence in his short fiction, and where his first encounters with death and romantic disillusionment took place. When, in 1937 a doctor recommended to Cortázar's mother that the child, an avid reader and frequent dreamer, stay away from books since they could affect his health, he happily ignored the prescription. He loved radio, commercial films, and Greek mythology. He especially enjoyed reading about adventurous heroes traveling to a distant geography. Not surprisingly, his favorite writer was Jules Verne, and he is said to have read *Twenty Thousand Leagues Under the Sea*, a romance about submarines with Captain Nemo as its villain, several times. He wanted to be a sailor and navigate distant seas. "I will always be a child in many ways," he once wrote, "but one of those children who from the beginning carries within an adult, so when the little monster becomes an adult he carries in turn a child inside and, *nel mezzo del cammino*, yields to the seldom peaceful coexistence of at least two outlooks onto the world."

His genealogical tree resulted in a polyglot education. He spoke fluent French during his boyhood and his library, then as in the years to come, would mainly consist of foreign titles, especially francophone and Anglo-Saxon. (Borges, both one of Cortázar's friends and his nemesis, had a similar upbringing: he was a descendant of British immigrants, who used English at home, a language in which he is said to have first read *Don Quixote*; when time came to find the Spanish original, he was sure he had mistaken it for a poor translation). In order to help support the household, at 18 he received a degree as a secondary school teacher and taught for a decade, from 1935 to 1945, in several Buenos Aires provinces, including Bolivar and Chivilcoy. The job proved to be double-faceted: after his classroom hours, he would spend most of his free time completely alone, a depressing fact that made him feel miserable, specially because the intellectual atmosphere in those provincial communities was nonexistent; on the other hand, he had an enormous amount of time to read and pushed himself to embark on ambitious bibliographical projects: for instance, in a few months he devoured Sigmund Freud's complete oeuvre and the work of the Spanish critic and lexicographer Ramón Menéndez y Pelayo. It was during the Bolivar and Chivilcoy period that Cortázar developed neurotic symptoms he would later on use as inspiration in his short fiction. He suffered intense and inappropriate phobias to things and situations, and a compulsive need to pursue certain thoughts or actions in order to reduce anxiety. He evidenced physical symptoms such as tenseness, fatigue, and excessive employment of defense mechanisms. Frequently, these neurotic aspects are pushed to the limit, becoming forms of psychosis, which involve a loss of the sense of reality. In his work, Cortázar is careful enough never to discuss these mental disturbances and ailments in Freudian terms; he shied away from psychoanalysis (so did Borges), trusting that any hallucination, any form of psychological sickness, ought to be understood, perhaps even overcome, through the best treatment: literature. It would be indeed easy to reduce the Argentine's complex work to mere psychosomatic contrivances, but by doing so, its artistic power would be altogether lost.

Add to it Cortázar's overwhelming physical presence, which often frightened his peers. From his late adolescence, he had a distinctive corporal appearance in that he cut a considerable figure: he was very tall, around six feet six inches, an anomaly for a Latin American. José Lezama Lima, the Cuban author of *Paradiso*, used to say the Argentine had received the gift of eternal youth in exchange for never being able to stop growing taller. His summer house in Saigon, France, had to be remodeled in order for him to fit in the kitchen and bathrooms. Years later, in Paris, he met the Colombian journalist and later Nobel Prize awardee Gabriel García Márquez, who admired Cortázar's early work. They met in October, 1956, at the Old Navy Cafe on the Boulevard Saint-Germain. He was "like an apparition," said the author of *Love in the Time of Cholera*. Cortázar "was the tallest man you could possibly imagine, wearing a voluminous black raincoat which was more like the dark cloak of a widow. His face was the face of a perverse child: wide-set eyes like those of a heifer, so oblique and filmy they might have seemed diabolical had they not been submitted to the domination of the heart."

His bizarre looks, nevertheless, seem not to have made him uncomfortable. Never physically handicapped, his characters are always prisoners of their mental machinations, not their bodies. As friends described him, he was punctilious, affable, straightforward, whimsical, lanky and freckled. And Maria Pilar Serrano, wife of José Donoso, the Chilean author of *Curfew*, would describe him as very introspective and reserved. "He hides behind a curtain of friendliness and courtesy," Donoso argued. "People say he doesn't accept or offer intimacy. Friends that loved him and admired him for various and valuable reasons, told me they would never go to him in times of crisis. They would never speak to him about their problems, and neither did Julio." Critic Luis Harss portrays him as follows: "a true Argentine, [he] is a many-sided man, culturally eclectic, elusive in person, mercurial in his ways. There is something adamantly neat and precise about him.... There is a child in his eyes. He looks much too young for his age. In fact, his generally boyish air is almost unsettling. An eternal child prodigy keeps winking at us from his work."

Since its independence, Argentina had been a stage for political instability and military coups—and twentieth-century Argentina is no exception. In 1945 the country belatedly entered World War II on the Allies' side after four years of pro-Allied neutrality. Juan Domingo Perón, an army colonel who, with a group of military colleagues, seized power a year before, won the elections in 1946 and established a popular dictatorship with the support of the army, nationalists, and the Roman Catholic Church. He remained in power until 1955 and developed a following among workers, clergymen, landowners, and industrialists. He instituted a program of revolutionary measures that were supposed to lead to economic self-sufficiency. At the time, Cortázar taught courses in French literature—

mainly Mallarmé and Baudelaire, his two idols at the time—at the University of Cuyo, Mendoza, and was active in a resistance against Perón. He was even arrested and freed shortly. The incident made it clear a dismissal from his academic job was imminent and, thus, Cortázar resigned his position and returned to Buenos Aires. His opposition to Perón's regime, and his overall political participation, was passive at best. He considered himself an esthete—an intellectual involved with ideas and unconcerned with the daily struggle to overthrow a dictatorship, even one in his own country. He advocated art for art's sake, intellectual freedom and, much like the early Rubén Darío, a crucial Nicaraguan figure in the *Modernista* movement that swept Latin America from 1885 to 1915, identified himself for a while with the Romantic idea of the poet living in an ivory tower—isolated, away from the discomfort of mundane affairs.

Intellectually speaking, Borges already commanded a major influence on Argentine cultural life when Cortázar was in his late twenties. He had published *A Universal History of Infamy* in 1935, and in the next few years, after a near-fatal accident, would produce outstanding short stories like "Pierre Menard, Author of the Quixote." His precise, almost mathematical style had a small but fanatical following in the city's intellectual circles and his reviews in Victoria Ocampo's literary magazine, *Sur*, were eagerly awaited every month. Cortázar, to be sure, admired Borges, but also found him dry, pedantic. At the time he discovered another crucial literary figure to be attracted to: Roberto Arlt, a Buenos Aires crime reporter and anarchist whose remarkable sequence of urban nightmares—*The Rabid Toy*, *Seven Madmen*, and *The Flame-throwers*, published in 1926, 1929, and 1931 respectively—was sold for only a few cents in cheap editions at newspaper stands.

Borges and Arlt were artistic opposites: while the former was known as a crafter of overly sophisticated fictions using—perhaps abusing— bibliographical references and philosophical quotes, the latter was a careless stylist in close touch with the metropolitan masses. Arlt's characters are often anarchists with eccentric ideas plotting to incite the status quo; unable to control their instincts, they run amok and end up destroying themselves. At the time Argentine intelligentsia was divided in two major groups, irrevocable rivals in their esthetic approach: the Florida and Boedo groups, named after the location of cafés where members of each group used to meet to chat about literature and politics. Cortázar identified with the author of "Approach to Almotasim" but was infatuated with Arlt's adventurous plots and his use of *lunfardo*, Argentina's urban slang. Eventually, he would oscillate between one pole and the other, becoming a secret disciple of

Borges while also constantly paying tribute to his other major influence, Arlt, by drafting stories where characters look for existential answers in their convoluted, violent urban environment. Later he moved back to Buenos Aires, to his mother, sister, and aunt, and began working as a manager of Camara Argentina del Libro, a government-run printing association. More or less simultaneously, he applied, was accepted, and registered, in the Department of Arts and Letters at the University of Buenos Aires, but would never finish a degree. At the age of 24, under the pseudonym Julio Denís, he embarked on a young writer's dream to self-publish his first booklet of poems, *Presence*, a collection of Mallarméan sonnets about which he would have little to say later on. While Peronismo was at its peak, Cortázar met José Bianco, Victoria Ocampo, and other Argentina intellectuals, and happily began writing reviews and short essays for *Sur*, the most prestigious journal of ideas of the southern cone, to which numerous writers of international fame contributed between 1931 and 1970, including Roger Caillois, Waldo Frank, and Hermann de Keyserling. Many of Cortázar's critical texts in the journal, while collected in his three-volume *Obra Crítica*, are little known and almost forgotten. They are important in that they trace his intellectual journey, as well as his literary influences, perhaps better than anything he would create afterwards. Aside from *Sur*, he also wrote at the time for other magazines, such as *Cabalgata* and *Realidad*. Altogether, these texts on Graham Greene's *The Heart of the Matter*, on Cyril Connolly, André Gide, Eugene O'Neill, Soren Kierkegaard, Aldous Huxley, and on Luis Buñuel's 1950 film, *Los olvidados*, are a compass that signals the direction in which Cortázar as novelist and short story writer would take his talent.

The invitation to write for *Sur* in particular couldn't have come at a better moment. More than anything else, it meant somehow to be related to Borges and his circle of acolytes, to enter the master's circle of close collaborators. But Cortázar's style and concerns immediately distinguished him from the Borgesian galaxy. In 1948, for instance, he contributed to the magazine an obituary for Antonin Artaud, considered today the first text in which he expressed his views on surrealism, a philosophical and artistic movement he was infatuated with, which left a deep mark on him, and whose promoters, André Breton, Tristan Tzara, *et al.*, he admired. He had become acquainted as well with Francisco Ayala, a Spanish émigré who at the time was editing *Realidad*. "The vast Surrealist experiment," he wrote in 1949 in Ayala's magazine, "seems to me the highest enterprise modern man has embarked upon in an attempt to find an integrated humanism. At the same time, the surrealist attitude (inclined to the liquidation of genres and species) colors the verbal and plastic creation, incorporating to the movement an irrational element." Cortázar wrote for Ayala not only on Breton and Artaud but also his first overly ambitious essay on the contemporary novel, and, a bit later, he gave the Spaniard a review of Leopoldo Marechal's *Adam Buenosayres*, a voluminous Argentine novel considered a classic today but at the time attacked as artistic trash because of its author's loyalties to Peronismo. Putting politics aside, Cortázar celebrated Marechal's style and intelligence and applauded his portrait of national urban life. The review created a small scandal in Buenos Aires. He received death threats and was accused of collaborating with the enemy. The Marechal affair offered Cortázar a type of exposure he was anxious to get.

In 1949, Cortázar published, with his friend Daniel Devoto's money, a theatrical piece (or, as he called it, a dramatic poem): the highly polished *The Kings*, based on the myth of the Minotaur. Earlier, throughout the 1940s, he spent a considerable amount of his time reading pulp fiction. It was not an unusual interest; his entire generation inherited from the adventures of British armchair detectives the passion for literature as sleuthing. Indeed, besides Mallarmé, Keats, Baudelaire, and other Romantics, among Cortázar's adolescent passions in the spirit of the time, was police and crime fiction. It was common for a number of publishing houses in Buenos Aires to invest in thrillers, and some even contracted luminaries like Borges and the novelist Ricardo Piglia, author of *Artificial Respiration*, to direct special series like El Séptimo Círculo. More than any other Latin American country, including Mexico, Argentina embraced the tradition of detective, dime, and hard-boiled novels wholeheartedly. Not only was the subgenre highly commercial, it was also embraced by the sophisticated elite. Aside from writing "Death and the Compass," Borges, together with his longtime collaborator Adolfo Bioy Casares, published his collection *Six Problems for Isidro Parodi*, humorous tales of detection mocking urban jargon and social manners. And one year later, the team brought out *The Best Detective Stories*, an anthology that displayed the subgenre in its most coolly intellectual forms. Cortázar read every highbrow and cheap thriller available and, in his words, became "an expert in the detective story." So together with a friend, he prepared a comprehensive bibliography on every thriller available in Spanish, to be published in the *Revista de Bibliotecología*, sponsored by the University of Buenos Aires. They came up with the pseudonym Morton Heinz, supposedly a distinguished British criminologist in charge of the bibliography. Their research was tremendous: they began with Edgar Allan Poe and continued with Willard Huntington Wright (*a.k.a.* S.S. Van Dine), Ellery Queen, and John Dickson Carr.

Cortázar studied translation and earned a diploma, which allowed him to work for various Argentine publishing houses, including Argos and Iman. He translated G. K. Chesterton's *The Man Who Knew Too Much*, André Gide's *The Immoralist*, Daniel Defoe's *Robinson Crusoe*, Jean Giono's *The Birth of the Odyssey*, Louisa May Alcott's *Little Women*, and Marguerite Yourcenar's *Memoirs of Hadrian*, among other titles. He also embarked on an ambitious translation of the complete prose works of Edgar Allan Poe, a writer profoundly influential in his early career. A slow enterprise, the two-volume project on the author of *Eureka* (1848) and "The Purloined Letter" (1845) would not appear until 1956, under the aegis of the University of Puerto Rico and Spanish thinker José Ortega y Gasset's magazine, *Revista de Occidente*. (Cortázar's future wife, Aurora Bernárdez, would help him accomplish the task and decades later would be the major force behind Cortázar's multivolume *Complete Works*.) As a young man in his twenties, he had loved Rainer Maria Rilke's *Notebooks of Malte Laurids Brigge*, but was now enamoured of the British Romantic poet John Keats. Around 1946 he even published a now-forgotten essay on "Ode on a Grecian Urn" and less than ten years later, would embark on a translation of Lord Houghton's *Life and Letters of John Keats* into Spanish.

Cortázar's adult life materialized in France, first in Paris and then in the small southern town of Saignon. 1951, indeed, proved to be crucial. His literary apprenticeship was over. His views on fiction versus reality, on nationalism, on the role of the intellectual in Latin America, were already formed by then (he was thirty-six). Although he had begun writing novels, he understood the short fiction genre as the most valuable tool to explore his own neurosis and that of South America. He knew it was a most difficult genre to master: you have to be brief and put the right word in the right place; your reader will expect to finish the text in one sitting, which means the reader's attention span is short and precious. Cortázar soon realized that his challenge in short fiction was to find the peculiar and bizarre in the routine—to intertwine dreams and reality. To succeed, he would need to find ways to disappear as the author, to be detached, to bring the surreal into daily life. As he put it, "I know I have always been irritated by stories in which the characters have to wait in the wings while the narrator exploits details or developments from one situation to another." He added: "For me the thing that signals a great story is what we might call its autonomy, the fact that it detaches itself from its author like a soap bubble blown from a clay pipe."

Things happened very quickly. In opposition to the Peronist regime, Cortázar rejected a chair at the University of Buenos Aires. Almost simultaneously, he was awarded a scholarship from the French government to study in Paris. Suddenly, exile became an alternative he was happy to embrace. He thus moved to France, where he would live until his death more than thirty years later, dividing his time between a small Paris studio in the Latin Quarter and, later on, an apartment on Place du Général Beluret, and his summer home in the Provençal town of Saignon, Vaucluse. While in Europe, he first worked for four months as a translator from French and English into Spanish for UNESCO but afterwards devoted himself fully to literature and his passions, boxing and the jazz trumpet.

Choosing exile in France seemed the best option for an avid reader, would-be writer and polyglot with a perfect command of Voltaire's language. Away from Argentina, he would be able to explore his country's idiosyncracy through fiction. Distance offers perspective, and perspective brings maturity. He would have time to meditate and read voraciously, an activity he adored. More than anything else, he would live at the center of culture, the apex of civilization, a fact very important since the depressing epoch when he taught secondary school in Bolivar and Chivilcoy. Deep at heart, Cortázar was tired of an existence on the periphery. Besides, there's an old saying among Latin American writers: "To be acclaimed at home, one first needs to be recognized abroad." He had been born in the Old Continent, where he received a cosmopolitan education during his first few years of life; he was now anxious to return to his roots. Ironically, once in France, he began missing Argentina. Exile, he understood, is a universal state, every human an island in an eternal diaspora. One lives constantly divided, neither here nor there. His linguistic dilemma soon acquired difficult implications. To be exposed to another language on a daily basis, *to live* in another idiom, could eventually be detrimental to his work. His grammar and syntax were very much a part of the urban slang on the River Plate. Like Roberto Arlt, he was deeply involved in recovering through literary tools the *arrabal* idiosyncracy where *lunfardo* was spoken. Would he consider renouncing Spanish and writing in Rabelais' tongue? Could a literary career in two languages—two universes—be possible?

Borges served as a useful paradigm. His verbal style was unlike anything ever written in South America: a rigorous attack against arbitrariness, against clumsiness—an attempt to turn a Romance language into a meticulous artifact. If anything, Cortázar could inject the French flavor into his native tongue. After 1951, when the setting of his oeuvre expanded from Buenos Aires to Paris and to the globe at large—Martinque, Cuba, Montevideo, Costa Rica, London, Solentiname, etc.—Argentina was turned into memory. Neither here nor there, he would spend his life investigating the painful destiny of exile.

The month of his departure for Paris, *Bestiary*, his first volume of stories, was published by the respected Buenos Aires house, Editorial Sudamericana. Together with his next two collections, it would be translated into English, although only in part, some seventeen years later, as *Blow-Up and Other Stories*. Although, as with *The Kings*, the reception was rather poor, this most impressive book would slowly become a favorite among young readers and critics, a true original in the Latin American tradition of short fiction. Then, between 1956 and 1958, he published two other collections. Juan José Arreola (b. 1918), the Mexican master storyteller who authored *Confabulario* and was promoting a new literary generation that included José Emilio Pacheco and Salvador Elizondo, invited him to submit *End of Game* to Los Presentes, for a series under his directorship. The volume was published in 1956, and expanded with eighteen more stories in 1964 in a Buenos Aires edition by Sudamericana. And a couple of years later, *Secret Weapons* was published also by Sudamericana. The playful (in his own Spanish wording, *lo lúdico*) provides a constant theme in all of this work, a sense of play offering an elaborate set of rules controlling human behavior. The approach, of course, extends to adulthood and often has serious overtones. What the Argentine was suggesting was that behind our daily routine, behind what we call reality, another universe, richer yet chaotic, seductive yet fabulous, lies hidden, ready to be seized. His objective was to invite the reader to unveil what at first sight looks like the quotidian: a trivial laughing stock, a childish stratagem. in an interview in *Revista de la Universidad de México*, Cortázar said: "In my case, the suspicion of another dimension of things, more secret and less communicable, and the fecund discovery of Alfred Jarry, for whom the true study of reality did not depend on the knowledge of its laws, but in the exception to such laws, have been some of the directing principles in my personal search for a literature at the margin of every naïve realism."

Humor was also his trademark. His literature attempts to be comic, albeit not in a light-hearted way. His esthetic approach is to intertwine parody and sarcasm, to generate a nervous smile on the reader's face and, simultaneously, to reflect on a certain mysterious aspect of daily life. His short fiction investigates the exception to the laws of nature, in Alfred Jarry's approach, as if the reader, not the author, were in full charge. Which brings me to the second element common in his stories published between 1951 and 1959, from *Bestiary* to *Secret Weapons*: the fantastic—*lo fantástico*. "Almost all the short stories that I have written," he once said, "belong to the genre called 'fantastic' for lack of a better name, and they oppose the false realism that consists in believing that all things can be described and explained according to the philosophical and scientific optimism of the eighteenth century; that is, as part of a world ruled more or less harmoniously by a system of laws and principles, of cause and effect relationships or defined psychologies, of well-mapped geographies." The fantastic was in vogue in Buenos Aires in the 1940s. Borges himself is a most distinguished practitioner. From "The Circular Ruins" to "The Book of Sand," he intertwined reality and fiction in essays and tales. Around 1941, in collaboration with his friends Adolfo Bioy Casares and Sylvina Ocampo, he edited a now-legendary *Antología de literatura fantástica*—translated into English as *The Book of Fantasy*, with a prologue by Ursula Le Guin. Curiously, Borges and Bioy Casares decided not to include Cortázar in their volume. He would finally make it in the second, 1965 edition. Several other Argentines had also been selected, including José Bianco, Santiago Dabove, Macedonio Fernández, Leopoldo Lugones, Carlos Peralta, and Manuel Peyrou.

In 1953 Cortázar married Aurora Bernárdez, another Argentine translator, a very bright and educated woman with whom he visited Italy and Greece, where he began developing his characters Cronopios and Famas. In a memoir published in the Mexican magazine *Vuelta*, which was later used as the preface to Cortázar's *Complete Stories*, the Peruvian-born Spanish novelist Mario Vargas Llosa recalls meeting the couple: "I met them ... [in 1958]," he writes, "in the house of a common friend, in Paris, and since then, until the last time I saw them together, in 1967, in Greece—where the three of us were translators in an international conference on cotton—I never stopped being astonished by the spectacle of listening to their dialogue ad tandem. Everybody else looked like an uninvited guest. Everything they said was intelligent, sophisticated, enjoyable, vital. I thought many times: 'They can't be always like this. They must rehearse this type of conversations, at home, in order to impress the listeners with unexpected anecdotes, brilliant quotes and jokes that, at the correct moment, loosen up the atmosphere a little bit.'" And Vargas Llosa adds: "It is hard to determine who had read more and better and which of the two offered more acute comments on books and writers. The fact that Julio wrote and Aurora *only* translated (in her case the word *only* means something altogether different than its normal connotation) was something I supposed to be provisional, Aurora's transitory sacrifice so that in the family there would only be one writer."

After 1958, Cortázar, his reputation still limited to a circle of initiated few, made a fundamental artistic shift: he abandoned the short fiction genre and devoted himself to the novel. *The Winners* was his first one published. He thought he needed to explore new narrative horizons and "The Pursuer" was proof of a desire to expand and be inclusive. After visits to the United States, mainly Washington, D.C., and New York, he devoted himself to a transitional work: *Cronopios and Famas*, playful pseudo-essays now almost totally forgotten, half non-fiction, half fiction. After he finished the section on Cronopios, at first mimeographed as a private edition and distributed to friends, someone suggested he expand certain sections and, thus, the volume was born. When published, the reaction, unlike the applause he got welcoming *End of the Game* and *Secret Weapons*, was negative. While poets loved it, critics attacked it for its lack of serious intentions, as if the novelist had abandoned his style and themes for sheer frivolity. Lacking unity, the volume, written between 1952 and 1959, in Italy, France, and Argentina, is, in Cortázar's own words, "really a game, a fascinating game, very amusing: ... almost like a tennis match. There were no serious intentions." Cortázar's fame became international when *Hopscotch* was published in 1963. Along side García Márquez's *One Hundred Years of Solitude*, many critics consider it one of the premier Latin American literary works of the twentieth century.

Since it appeared, *Hopscotch* transformed an entire generation. Divided into two parts, one taking place in France, the other in Buenos Aires, it's a pastiche in which news items, recipes, philosophical disquisitions, letters, and other forms of writing cohabit. The author suggests at least two ways of reading the volume, although more can be found. It was quickly imitated and critics continue to praise it as a crucial highlight in what has come to be known as "the encyclopedic novel," a type of epistemological novel in which alternative forms of knowledge find a place. It was immediately celebrated and had a deep impact on writers like Salman Rushdie, Georges Perec, Michel Butor, Robert Coover, Fernando del Paso, Carlos Fuentes, John Barth, and Susan Sontag.

Cuba, the third cultural center in Cortázar's odyssey, is essential to understanding him. Indeed, his role under Fidel Castro's regime is helpful in understanding the way in which Castro attracted intellectuals only to manipulate their work and actions. He was initially ecstatic about Havana's socialism, but as time went by, in the eyes of many he became a puppet of the regime in Havana, and as a result of his liaison to Castro, his literary work lost power and respectability. Indeed, in 1966 Cortázar visited Cuba for the first time. Since early 1959, Fidel Castro had become a regional idol and Spanish-speaking intellectuals, after Castro's invitation to "see the island for themselves," considered their role crucial in reeducating the masses along the road to socialism. Cortázar fell under the tyrant's spell and became an active supporter of the revolution. Although he had been involved in

Argentine politics in his adolescence, this no doubt was a reversal of considerable importance. As stated, in his early creative period (1945–1966) he had ignored social causes. When critics suggested ideological readings of his work, he quickly rejected their interpretations. But this attitude changed in the 1960s. According to Eduardo Galeano's trilogy *Memory of Fire*, Cortázar, at least politically speaking, "... went from the end toward the beginning; from discouragement to enthusiasm, from indifference to passion, from solitude to solidarity." In a letter to his friend the Cuban intellectual Roberto Fernández Retamar, editor of the cultural magazine *Casa de las Américas*, dated 10 May 1967, Cortázar wrote:

> At times I wonder what my work would have been like if I had remained in Argentina; I know that I would have continued writing because I'm not good at anything else, but judging by what I had done by the time I left my country, I am inclined to believe that I would have continued along the crowded thoroughfare of intellectual escapism I had traveled until then and which is still the path of a great many Argentine intellectuals of my generation and my taste. If I had to enumerate the causes for which I am glad I left my country (and let it be very clear that I am only speaking for myself as an individual and not as any sort of model), I believe the main one would be the Cuban revolution. For me to become convinced of this it's enough to talk from time to time with Argentine friends who pass through Paris evincing the saddest ignorance of what is really happening in Cuba; all I have to do is glance at the newspapers read by twenty million of my compatriots: that's enough to make me feel protected here from the influence that is wielded by U.S. information in my country and which an infinite number of Argentine writers and artists of my generation do not escape, even though they sincerely think they do; every day they are stirred by the subliminal mill wheels of United Press and "democratic" magazines that march to the tune of *Time* and *Life*.

In essays and lectures he began to support the idea that, while involved in social and political issues, the writer needs to be left alone to write literature. He recognized his intellectual responsibility toward the future of humankind, and yet railed for artistic freedom and against the Communist concept of Socialist Realism, an esthetic approach to art that had reduced to silence many Soviet and Eastern European writers like Isaac Babel, the author of *Odessa Stories* and *Red Chivalry*, during and after the Second World War. In 1969, Cortázar participated in a controversial debate with Vargas Llosa and Oscar Collazos, in which the latter, in the Uruguayan magazine *Marcha*, attacked the Latin American boom writers as derivative, ideologically inconsequential, and sold to the establishment. Cortázar responded ferociously in an essay entitled "Literature in Revolution & Revolution in Literature," in which his views of Socialist Realism and his attitude toward a revolutionary art became even clearer as he denounced those on the left who fail to reach a consciousness that "is much more revolutionary than the revolutionaries tend to have." In a debate preposterous from today's perspective, Cortázar kept on defending the revolutionary nature of his books. And shortly after, when the Heberto Padilla affair exploded in 1971, he joined a number of Latin American writers who signed a letter of protest.

Nevertheless, unlike Octavio Paz and Vargas Llosa, when the affair became acrimonious he refused to turn his back on the Cuban regime. His stand put him in a difficult position: he was in favor of artistic freedom but backed a government that jailed a poet for his writings and later forced the prisoner to denounce himself openly as counterrevolutionary after what was clearly a brain-washing and torture session. Cortázar's deepest political transformation took place in May 1968, when the student uprising hit Paris while civil upheaval shook Mexico's Tlatelolco Square and Prague's Spring erupted. Suddenly, he found himself participating on barricades, handing out fliers denouncing the establishment, and talking about "the imagination of power."

When Cortázar died, Octavio Paz wrote a touching obituary in his literary magazine *Vuelta*. "He was a cornerstone of contemporary Latin American letters," he wrote. "He was my age. Although he lives in Buenos Aires and I in Mexico, I met him early on, in 1945; the two of us contributed to *Sur*, and thanks to José Bianco, we soon began exchanging correspondence and books. Years later we coincided in Paris and for a while we saw each other frequently. Later on, I abandoned Europe, lived in the Far East and returned to Mexico. My relationship with Julio was not interrupted. In 1968 he and Aurora Bernárdez lived with me and [my wife] Marie José in our house in New Delhi. It was around that time that Julio discovered politics and he embraced with fervor and naïveté causes that also ignited me in the past but that, at that point, I already had judged reproachable. I ceased to see him, but not to love him. I think he also kept considering me a friend. Through the barriers of paper and words, we made each other friendly signs."

During the 1970s, Cortázar explored in esthetic terms what I call the art of literary promiscuity. After *All Fires the Fire*, he published two playful, amorphous texts, called "collage books": *Around the Day in Eighty Worlds* and *Last Round*; and in between, *62, A Model Kit*, a sequel to *Hopscotch*, published in 1968 in Buenos Aires by Editorial Sudamericana, about vampires and city landscapes, a theme he began treating in *La otra orilla*. Using traditional genres wasn't enough any more; he needed to surmount barriers, to write prose poems, essayist stories, non-fiction novels—to intertwine separate structures, imposing chaos. This non-conventional drive went even further. In 1975 came another rare experiment: *Fantomas contra los vampiros multinacionales. Una utopía realizable*, an out-of-print "socialist" comic-strip that used a famous dime-novel character placed in an ideological war against aggressive capitalist forces. Just before Cortázar put together his second poetry collection, *Pameos and Meopas*; and published what, according to Ferré, is his most important work: *Observatory Prose*, a volume of illustrated essays. He also wrote another novel, *A Manual for Manuel*, his most politically outspoken to date, and traveled to Argentina with short visits to Peru, Ecuador, and Chile, lectured at the University of Oklahoma, participated in the PEN-sponsored Translation Conference in New York City, and wrote an important introduction to Felisberto Hernández's *Sunk House and Other Stories* and assessment of Horacio Quiroga and Roberto Arlt. Indeed, it was obvious at this point in his career that, aside from Borges, Hernández, Arlt, and Horacio Quiroga had exercised a great influence on Cortázar's short stories. Over the decades, in Hernández, whom the Argentine first read in his thirties, he had found inspiration for stories such as "House Taken Over" and "End of Game," which resemble "Inundated House" and "*Las hortensias*." (Curiously, Hernández and Cortázar lived in Chivilcoy at the same time, in 1939, but apparently they never met). He got from him the capacity to find "the most subtle relationship between things, that eyeless dance of the most ancient elements; untouchable smoke and fire; the high cupola of a cloud and the random message of a simple herb; everything that is marvelous and obscure in the world." Arlt he had read in his twenties. He had admired his "styleless," chaotic street language, "weak" prose, the urgency and anarchy of his plots. He found him to be a great writer who looked for knowledge through the avalanche of darkness and his own artistic power in his infinite weakness. And in Quiroga he had found the raw explorer of the South American jungle, both in the concrete and the imaginary sense, the writer as muscle-man, à la Hemingway—the pathfinder, the pioneer, the trailblazer who would go penetrate inhospitable habitats and return to write a magical story about man's struggle with nature. A decade before his death, Cortázar, through evocative essays and introductions, established genealogical lines between himself and those he recognized as his precursors, making sure his oeuvre would be appreciated in the correct literary tradition.

His political commitment was at its peak in the late 1970s. He had donated the money of the Prix Médicis to the United Chilean Front. His liberalism was in sharp contrast with Borges, who was spending his mature life articulating a right-wing, semi-fascist position in which the artist is glorified *sub specie aeternitatis*. Between 1974 and 1983, Cortázar returned to the short fiction genre to write four more collections. "Politics in a work of literature," wrote Stendhal, "is like a pistol-shot in the middle of a concert, something loud and vulgar, and yet a thing to which it is not possible to refuse one's attention." In the case of Cortázar, the pistol-shot is apparent in a handful of tales, written as he reassessed his whole oeuvre in intellectual terms.

By the early 1980s Cortázar had fashioned a new world of fiction. He accepted President François Mitterand's offer to become a French citizen in 1981. He did it while insisting he was not relinquishing his Argentine citizenship but the event was interpreted as a betrayal by many in Latin America. Since his departure to Europe thirty years before, Cortázar had been attacked by Latin American nationalists as an escapee. In his final collection of prose poems, *Except Dusk*, he included a number of texts written in 1949–1950, concerning his eternal identity dilemma: to live in Paris or return to Buenos Aires—exile or home. Feeling, as he did, an endless searcher for the ultimate Paradise, he could not go back: he wasn't an Argentine anymore—he had given up his native citizenship—but he wasn't a European either because he had immigrated to the Old Continent. Like many of his short fiction characters, he was now a hybrid, a sum of identities. His life had been made of endless farewells and he no longer knew where he belonged. His writing was manifesting this identity conflict in an explicit way.

Mexico and Nicaragua are also crucial to an understanding of Cortázar's odyssey. The first one was a decisive cultural center in the 1960s and 1970s, where innumerable South American exiles sought refuge. The Argentine had a large circle of friends there and many of his books were first published by progressive Mexican houses, including Siglo XXI and Nueva Imagen. As for Nicaragua, his attachment to left-wing causes since the early days of Castro's regime made him sympathize, in the late 1970s and early 1980s, with Darnel Ortega's Sandinistas. Some of his most memorable late-period stories are set in Central America, including "Apocalypse in Solentiname," about reality versus fiction, freedom versus repression in a small Indian town in Nicaragua in which Ernesto Cardenal had built a Marxist community inspired by liberation theology. Also, like Carlos Fuentes, he was honored with the Rubén Darío medal by the Sandinistas.

In 1983 he traveled to Cuba one last time and then to New York to address the United Nations concerning the *desaparecidos* in South America. He felt lonely and isolated, especially now that a strange sickness began taking over his body. He lost appetite, became thinner, and was predisposed to colds. After his divorce from Aurora Bernárdez some fifteen years earlier, he had been involved with a number of women and men, engaging in bisexual affairs. Among his companions was Ugné Karvelis, a blond, tall, Latvian woman who worked for Gallimard and was director of the Spanish section of that publishing house. Karvelis had a son with another man whom Cortázar loved dearly, but he never had children with her or anyone else. When they separated, he became involved with Carol Dunlop. Their relationship was brief but intense—she died in 1983 and as Cortázar told Luis Harss, his solitude was so deep he began to lose trust in his own writing. His most romantic friends still claim he died of "aloneness"—*soledad*.

But it has been rumored for years that he actually died of AIDS. The epidemic was still unknown then, its details elusive to scientists and the masses, so he probably knew little about it. Interestingly, a number of Cortázar tales deal with homosexuality, including "Blow-Up," "The Ferry, or Another trip to Venice," and "At Your Service," the last about Madame Francinet, an old servant woman employed as a babysitter for dogs in a wealthy home. After reading it, Evelyn Picón Garfield asked Cortázar about homosexuality. He answered with a lengthy dissertation on the subject, a history from Greek times to the present social ostracism. "The attitude toward [it]," he added, "has to be a very broad and open one because the day in which homosexuals don't feel like corralled beasts, or like persecuted animals or like beings that everyone makes fun of, they'll assume a much more normal way of life and fulfill themselves erotically and sexually without harming anyone and by being happy as much as possible as homosexual males and females." And he finished by applauding the fashion in which, in some capitalistic societies, they are more accepted. While discussing Cortázar's sickness and death, one should reflect on machismo, homosexuality, and hypocrisy in the Hispanic world, an issue still shockingly absent in cultural debate. In spite of his outspoken political views the Argentine was reluctant to talk openly about his sexuality. And he certainly isn't alone: Manuel Puig, Reinaldo Arenas, and Severo Sarduy, openly

homosexual, also died from AIDS—although only Arenas wanted the world
to know the truth. Which means that, for as much as Latin American writers
are ready to become speakers of the oppressed, only one or two are
committed to assuming their gay identity in the open.

Cortázar died in Paris, on 12 February 1984, and left numerous
imitators and countless literary followers, including Argentines Luisa
Valenzuela and Ana María Shua. I remember the morning I read the headline
in *Excélsior*, Mexico's leading newspaper: "Latin America looses its favorite
child: Julio Cortázar, dead at 69." A continental treasure had been lost and
the sense of sadness was overwhelming. The obituary declared the cause of
his death to be leukemia and heart disease. He died in Saint Lazare hospital
and is buried in Montparnasse cemetery. That same year, four more books
were published: *Nicaraguan Sketches*; *Nothing for Pehujó*, a play in one act;
Except Dusk, a collection of prose poems, and a bit later the prestigious
Spanish publishing house Plaza y Janés brought out a collection of his
political writings. Shortly after *The Exam*, his first novel, written in 1950,
before he left for France and stored in a drawer, finally appeared in print.
The curiosity regarding his background and early literary steps had begun.

Like few others, he seems to embody the refreshing spirit of renewal
and innovation that prevailed in the Woodstock generation: art as liberator,
art as excuse to innovate and unstabilize, to establish a bridge between and
highbrow and pop culture. His name brings back memories of the Vietnam
War and Cuba's Bay of Pigs, an idol of the drugs-for-all fever that
characterized the 1960s. But he was also an incredibly concentrated
storyteller, one with a distinct world view, his oeuvre a masterful cornerstone
in contemporary Latin American literature that led the Hispanic
intelligentsia to new heights. So justice to his talents: The post–World War
II novelistic and short-story genres written in Spanish, and the renewal of the
novel on an international scale, would simply be impossible without Julio
Cortázar.

MARIO VARGAS LLOSA

Translated by Dane Johnson

The Trumpet of Deyá

for Aurora Bernárdez

That Sunday in 1984, I had just set myself up in my study to write an article when the telephone rang. I did something that even then I never did: I picked up the receiver. "Julio Cortázar has died;" the voice of the journalist commanded: "Dictate to me your comment."

I thought of a verse from Vallejo—"Stupid as a Spaniard"—and, babbling, I obeyed him. But that Sunday, instead of writing the article, I kept leafing through and rereading some of Cortázar's stories and pages from his novels that my memory had preserved so vividly. It had been some time since I had heard anything about him. I suspected neither his prolonged illness nor his painful agony. But it made me happy to know that Aurora had been at his side during those last months and that, thanks to her, he had a sober burial, without the foreseeable clowning of the revolutionary ravens who had taken such advantage of him in his last years.

I had met both of them some forty years ago at the house of a mutual friend in Paris. Since then—until the last time I saw them together, in Greece in 1967, where the three of us worked as translators at an international conference on cotton—I had never stopped marveling at the spectacle of seeing and hearing Aurora and Julio converse in tandem. The rest of us seemed to be superfluous. Everything they said was intelligent,

From *The Review of Contemporary Fiction* vol. 17, no. 1 (Spring 1997). © 1997 *The Review of Contemporary Fiction*.

learned, amusing, vital. Many times I thought, "They can't always be like this. They must rehearse those conversations at home in order to dazzle interlocutors with unusual anecdotes, brilliant quotations, and those jokes that, at the opportune moment, burst the intellectual climate."

They tossed subjects from one to the other like two accomplished jugglers. With them, one was never ever bored. I admired and envied that couple's perfect complicity, the secret intelligence that seemed to unite them. I admired, equally, their sympathy, their engagement with literature (which gave the impression of being exclusive and total), and their generosity toward everyone, above all, to apprentices like me.

It was difficult to determine who had read more or better or which of the two said more acute and unexpected things about books and authors. That Julio wrote and Aurora only translated (in her case this *only* means completely the opposite of what it seems) is something that I always supposed was provisional, a passing sacrifice by Aurora so that, in the family, there would be at that moment no more than one writer. Now that I see her again, after so many years, I have bitten my tongue the two or three times I was at the point of asking if she had written much, if she had finally decided to publish. Except for her gray hair, she looks the same: small, petite, with those big blue eyes full of intelligence and the old overwhelming vitality. She climbs up and down the Mallorcan rocks of Deyá with an agility that always leaves me behind with palpitations. She too, in her own way, displays that Cortazarian virtue par excellence: to be a Dorian Gray.

That night at the end of 1958, I sat with a very tall and thin beardless boy who had very short hair and big hands that moved as he spoke. He had already published a small book of tales and was about to re-edit a second compilation for a small series in Mexico directed by Juan José Arreola. I was about to bring out a book of stories too, and we exchanged experiences and projects like two youngsters "who set sail under literary arms." Only upon saying good night did I become aware—stunned—that this was the author of *Bestiario* (Bestiary) and so many texts that I read in Borges and Victoria Ocampo's journal *Sur*, as well as the admirable translator of the complete works of Poe that I had devoured in the two opulent volumes published by the University of Puerto Rico. He seemed to me a contemporary when, in reality, he was twenty-two years older than I.

During the sixties and, especially, the seven years that I lived in Paris, he was one of my best friends and also something like my model and my mentor. I gave him the manuscript of my first novel to read and awaited his verdict with the expectancy of a catechumen. And when I received his letter—generous, with approval and advice—I felt happy. I believe that for a long time I was accustomed to writing presupposing his vigilance, his encouraging or critical eyes over my shoulder. I admired his life, his rituals, his caprices, and his customs as much as the ease and clarity of his prose and that everyday, domestic, and cheerful appearance that he gave the fantastic subjects in his stories and novels. Each time that he and Aurora called to invite me for dinner—first at the small apartment bordering on the Rue de Sèvres, and later at the little house spiraling from the Rue du Général Bouret—it was fiesta and felicity. I was fascinated by his board of unusual news clippings and improbable objects that were picked up or fabricated. I was intrigued by "the room of toys": the mysterious place that existed in their house in which, according to legend, Julio would lock himself up to play the trumpet and enjoy himself like a kid. He knew a secret and magical Paris that did not show up in any guidebook and from which I left loaded with treasures after each encounter with him: films to see, exhibitions to visit, nooks in which to forage, poets to discover, and even a congress of witches at the Mutualité that bored me exceedingly but that he evoked afterward, marvelously, as a jocular apocalypse.

With this Julio Cortázar it was possible to be a friend but impossible to become intimate. The distance that he knew how to impose, thanks to a system of courtesies and rules to which one had to submit to conserve his friendship, was one of his enchantments. It enveloped him with a certain aura of mystery. It gave to his life a secret dimension that seemed to be the source of that restless depth—irrational and violent—that transpires at times in his texts, even the most ragamuffin and cheerful. He was an eminently private man with an interior world constructed and preserved like a work of art to which probably only Aurora had access, and for whom nothing, outside of literature, seemed to matter or, maybe, exist.

This does not mean that he was bookish, erudite, and intellectual in the manner of a Borges, for example, who with all justice wrote: "Many things I have read and few have I lived." In Julio literature seemed to dissolve itself into daily experience and impregnate all of life, animating it and enriching it with a particular brilliance without depriving it of sap, of instinct, of spontaneity. Probably no other writer lent to play the literary dignity that Cortázar did, nor made of play an instrument of artistic creation and exploration so ductile and beneficial. But saying this in such a serious way alters the truth because Julio did not play in order to make literature. For him, to write was to play, to enjoy oneself, to organize life—words, ideas— with the arbitrariness, the liberty, the imagination, and the irresponsibility of children or the insane. But playing in this way, Cortázar's work opened unpublished doors. It arrived to show some unknown depths of the human

condition and to graze the transcendent, something that surely never had
been intended. It is no accident (or, if it is, it is in that sense of the accidental
that he described in *62: A Model Kit*) that the most ambitious of his novels
would take as its title *Hopscotch*, a children's game.

Like the novel, like theater, the game is a form of fiction: an artificial
order imposed on the world, a representation of something illusory that
replaces life. It distracts us from ourselves, serving us in forgetting the true
reality and living—while the substitution lasts—a life apart from strict rules
created by ourselves. Distraction, enjoyment, fabulation—the game is also a
magic resource for exorcising the atavistic fear of humans toward the secret
anarchy of the world, the enigma of our origin, condition, and destiny. Johan
Huizinga, in his celebrated book *Homo Ludens*, maintained that play is the
spine of civilization and that society evolved up to modernity ludically,
constructing its institutions, systems, practices, and creeds starting from
those elemental forms of ceremony and ritual that characterize the games of
children.

In the world of Cortázar the game recovers this lost virtuality of serious
activity that adults use to escape insecurity, to avoid panic before an
incomprehensible and absurd world full of dangers. It is true that his
characters enjoy themselves playing, but many times it has to do with
dangerous diversions that will leave them not only forgotten passengers of
their circumstances but also with some outrageous knowledge or alienation
or death.

In other cases the Cortazarian game is a refuge for sensibility and
imagination, the way in which delicate, ingenuous beings defend themselves
against social steamrollers or, as he wrote in the most mischievous of his
books, *Cronopios and Famas*, "to struggle against pragmatism and the horrible
tendency toward the attainment of useful ends." His games are pleas against
the prefabricated, against ideas frozen by use and abuse, prejudices, and,
above all, against solemnity, the black beast for Cortázar when he criticized
the culture and idiosyncrasies of his country.

But I talk of "the" game and, in truth, I should use the plural. In the
books of Cortázar the author plays, the narrator plays, the characters play,
and the reader plays, obligated to do so by the devilish traps that lie in wait
around the corner of the least expected page. And there is no doubt that it is
enormously liberating and refreshing to find oneself suddenly, without
knowing how, parodying statues, rescuing words from the cemetery of
academic dictionaries to resuscitate them with puffs of humor, or jumping
between the heaven and hell of hopscotch—all due to Cortázar's sleight of
hand.

The effect of *Hopscotch* was seismic in the Spanish-speaking world when it appeared in 1963. It rocked to the foundations the convictions and prejudices that writers and readers had about the means and ends of the art of narration, and it extended the frontiers of the genre to unthinkable limits. Thanks to *Hopscotch*, we learned that to read was a brilliant way of enjoying oneself, that it was possible to explore the secrets of the world and of language while having fun. And we learned that playing, one could probe mysterious layers of life forbidden to rational knowledge, to logical intelligence, abysses of experience over which no one can lean out without grave risks like death or insanity. In *Hopscotch* reason and unreason, sleep and vigil, objectivity and subjectivity, history and fantasy all lose their exclusive condition. Their frontiers are eclipsed. They stop being antonyms in order to become fused. In that way certain privileged beings, like la Maga and Oliveira, and the celebrated "madmen" of his future books, could flow freely. (Like many couples reading *Hopscotch* in the sixties, Patricia and I also began to speak in "gliglish," to invent a private lingo and to translate to its snapping, esoteric terms our tender secrets.)

Together with the notion of play, that of freedom is indispensable when one speaks of *Hopscotch* and all the fictions of Cortázar. Freedom to break the established norms of writing and structuring narrative, to replace the conventional order of the narrative by a buried order that has the semblance of disorder, to revolutionize narrative point of view, narrative time, the psychology of the characters, the spatial organization of the story, and its logical sequence. The tremendous insecurity that, as the novel proceeds, comes to take possession of Horacio Oliveira in confronting the World (and confining him more and more in an imagined shelter), accompanies the reader of *Hopscotch* as he enters this labyrinth and lets himself be led astray by the Machiavellian narrator in the twists and turns and ramifications of anecdote. Nothing there is reconcilable and sure: not the direction not the meanings nor the symbols nor the ground that one treads on. What are they telling me? Why don't I just understand it? Are we dealing with something so mysterious and complex that it is beyond our apprehension? Or is it a monumental pulling of our leg? We are dealing with both. In *Hopscotch* and in many Cortázar stories, the mockery, the joke, and the illusionism of the salon are often present, like the little animal figures that certain virtuosos conjure up with their hands or the coins that disappear between the fingers and reappear in the ears or the nose. But often, too—like in those famous absurd episodes of *Hopscotch* that star the pianist Bertha Trépat, in Paris, and the one with the plank over the emptiness on which Talita balances, in Buenos Aires—these episodes subtly transmute themselves into a descent to the cellars of behavior, to Its remote irrational sources, to an immutable essence—magic, barbarous, ceremonial—of the human experience that underlies rational civilization and, under certain circumstances, rises up to disturb it. (This is the theme of some of Cortázar's best stories, like "The Idol of the Cyclades" and "The Night Face Up," in which we suddenly see a remote and ferocious past of bloody gods that must be satiated with human victims bursting into the womb of modern life and without a continuous solution.)

Hopscotch stimulated formal audacities in the new Hispano-American writers like few books before or after, but it would be unjust to call it an experimental novel. This qualification emits an abstract and pretentious odor. It suggests a world of test tubes, retorts, and blackboards with algebraic calculations, something disembodied, dissociated from immediate life, from desire and pleasure. *Hopscotch* overflows life from all its pores. It is an explosion of freshness and movement, of youthful exaltation and irreverence, a resonant loud laugh in front of those writers who, as Cortázar used to say, put on their collar and necktie in order to write. He always wrote in shirt sleeves, with the informality and happiness with which one sits at the table to enjoy a home-cooked meal or listens to a favorite record in the intimacy of one's room. *Hopscotch* taught us that laughter was not the enemy of seriousness nor of those illusory and ridiculous things that can nestle in experimental zeal when it is taken too seriously. In the same way that the Marquis de Sade exhausted beforehand all of the possible excesses of sexual cruelty, *Hopscotch* constituted a fortunate apotheosis of the formal game to the extent that any "experimental" novel would be born old and repetitive. For this reason, Cortázar, like Borges, has bad uncountable imitators, but not one disciple.

To un-write the novel, to destroy literature, to break the habits of the "lady reader," to un-adorn words, to write badly, etc.—all that on which Morelli of *Hopscotch* insists so much—are metaphors of something very simple: literature asphyxiates itself with an excess of convention and seriousness. It is necessary to purge it of rhetoric and of commonplaces, to endow it again with novelty, grace, insolence, freedom. Cortázar's style has all of this, above all when it distances itself from the pompous miracle-working prosopopeia with which his alter ego Morelli pontificates about literature, that is to say in his stories. Those, generally, are more diaphanous and creative than his novels, although they do not display the showy rocketry that surrounds those last ones like a halo.

Cortázar's stories are no less ambitious or iconoclastic than his longer texts. But what is original and groundbreaking in the latter is usually more metabolized in the stories, rarely exhibiting in them the immodest virtuousity of *Hopscotch*, *62: A Model Kit*, and *A Manual for Manuel*, where the reader has at times the sensation of being subjected to certain tests of intellectual efficiency. Those novels are revolutionary manifestos, but Cortázar's true revolution lies in his stories. It is more discreet but more profound and permanent because it aroused the very nature of fiction, its indissoluble heart that is the form–depth, means–ends, and art–technique that fiction becomes in the hands of the most successful creators. In his stories Cortázar did not experiment: he found, he discovered, he created something permanent.

In the same way, just as the label experimental writer falls short, it would be insufficient to call him a writer of the fantastic, although, without a doubt, if we were to give labels, he would have preferred the latter. Julio loved the literature of the fantastic and knew it like the back of his hand. He wrote some marvelous stories of that sort in which extraordinary events occur, like the impossible change of a man into a little aquatic beast in the small masterpiece "Axolotl"; or the somersault, thanks to intensifying enthusiasm, of a trivial concert into an immoderate massacre in which the feverish public jumps onto the stage to devour the conductor and the musicians in "Las Ménades" (The Maenads). But he also wrote illustrious stories of more orthodox realism: like that marvel "Little Bull," the story of a boxer's decadence, told by himself, that is, in truth, the story of his way of speaking, a linguistic feast of grace, musicality, and humor, and the invention of a style with the flavor of the neighborhood, of the idiosyncrasies and mythology of the people; or like "The Pursuer," which is narrated from a subtle preterit perfect that dissolves into the present of the reader, subliminally evoking in this way the gradual dissolution of Johnny, the brilliant jazzman whose deluded search for the absolute by way of the trumpet arrives to us by means of the "realist" reduction (rational and pragmatic) carried out by a critic and Johnny's biographer, the narrator Bruno.

In reality Cortázar was a writer of realism and the fantastic at the same time. The world that he invented is unmistakable precisely because of that strange symbiosis that Roger Caillois considered necessary for the right to be called the fantastic. In his prologue to the anthology of literature of the fantastic that he prepared, Caillois maintained that the art of the truly fantastic is not born out of the deliberation of its creator but escapes between his intentions through the work of chance or of more mysterious forces. In the same way, he goes on, the fantastic does not come out of a technique, nor is it a literary image, but rather it is the imponderable—a reality that without premeditation suddenly happens in a literary text. From a long and impassioned conversation in a bistro in Montparnasse about Carriers's thesis, I remember Julio's enthusiasm for it and his surprise when I assured him that that theory seemed to me to fit what occurred in his fictions like a glove.

In the Cortazarian world banal reality begins insensibly to crack and to give in to some hidden pressures that push it up to the prodigious without participating fully in it, maintaining it as a sort of intermediary, tense, and disconcerting territory in which the real and the fantastic overlap without integrating. This is the world of "Blow-Up," of "Cartas de mamá" (Letters from Mama), of "Secret Weapons," of "La puerta condenada" (The Blocked-Off Door), and of so many other stories of ambiguous solution that can be equally interpreted as realistic or fantastic since the extraordinary in them is, perhaps, a fantasy of the characters or, perhaps, a miracle.

This is the famous ambiguity that characterizes certain classics of fantastic literature, exemplified in Henry James's *The Turn of the Screw*: a delicate story that the master of the uncertain managed to tell in such a way that there would be no possibility of knowing if the fantastic that occurs in the story—the appearance of ghosts—really occurs or is the hallucination of a character. What differentiates Cortázar from a James, from a Poe, from a Borges, or from a Kafka is not the ambiguity or the intellectualism—which are propensities as frequent in him as in them—but that in Cortázar's fictions the most elaborate and learned stories never die and transfer themselves to the abstract. They continue rooted in the daily reality, the concrete. They have the vitality of a soccer match or a barbecue. The surrealists invented the expression "the daily marvelous" for that poetic reality—mysterious, loosened from contingency and scientific laws—that the poet can perceive underneath appearances by way of dreaming or delirium. This marvelous reality generates books like Aragon's *Paris Peasant* or Breton's *Nadia*. But I believe that no other writer of our time fits this definition as well as Cortázar: a seer who detected the unusual in the usual, the absurd in the logical, the exception in the rule, and the prodigious in the banal. Nobody dignified so literally the foreseeable, the conventional, the pedestrian of human life than he, who, with the juggling of his pen, denoted a hidden tenderness or exhibited an immoderate face, sublime and horrifying—to the extent that, passed by his hands, instructions for winding a watch or ascending a staircase could be, at the same time, anguished prose poems and laughter-inducing pseudometaphysical texts.

Style is the explanation of that alchemy in Cortázar's fictions that fuses the most unreal fantasy with the merry life of the body and of the street, the unconditionally free life of the imagination with the restricted life of the body and of history. His is a style that marvelously feigns orality, the fluent ease of common speech, spontaneous expression, with neither the makeup nor the impudence of the common man. We are dealing with an illusion, because, in reality, the common man expresses himself with complications, repetitions, and confusions that wouldn't work if translated to writing. The language of Cortázar is also an exquisitely fabricated fiction, an artifice so effective that it seems natural, like talk reproduced from life that flows to the reader directly from the mouths and animated tongues of men and women of flesh and blood. It is a language so transparent and even that it blends with that which it names—the situations, the things, the being, the landscapes, the thoughts—to show it better, like a discreet glow that illuminates from within their authenticity and truth. Cortázar's fictions owe their powerful verisimilitude to this style. It is the breath of humanity that beats in all of them, even in the most intricate. The functionality of his style is such that the best texts of Cortázar seem *spoken*.

Nevertheless, this stylistic clarity often deceives us, making us believe that the content of these stories is also diaphanous, a world without shadows. We are dealing with more skilled sleight of hand because, in truth, that world is charged with violence. Suffering, anguish, and fear relentlessly pursue its inhabitants, those who often take refuge (like Horacio Oliveira) in madness or something that appears much like it to escape what is unbearable in their condition. Ever since *Hopscotch*, the mad have occupied a central place in Cortázar's work. But madness begins to appear in it in a deceptive way, without the accustomed reverberations of threat or tragedy. It is more like a cheerful, even tender, impudence, the manifestation of the essential absurdity that nestles in the world behind its masks of rationality and good sense. Cortázar's madmen are most affectionate and almost always benign, obsessive beings with disconcerting linguistic, literary, social, political, or ethical projects to—like Ceferino Pérez—recorder and reclassify existence according to delirious nomenclatures. Between the chinks of their extravagances, they always leave a glimpse of something that redeems and justifies: a dissatisfaction with the given, a confused search for another life, more unforeseeable and poetic (at times nightmarish) than that in which we are confined. Sometimes children, sometimes dreamers, sometimes jokers, sometimes actors, Cortázar's madmen radiate a defenselessness and a fortune of moral integrity that, while awakening an inexplicable solidarity on our part, also makes us feel accused.

Play, madness, poetry, humor—all become allied like alchemic mixtures in those miscellanies (*Around the Day in Eighty Worlds*, *Ultimo Round* [Last Round], and the testimony of that absurd final pilgrimage on a French highway, *Los autonautas de la cosmopista* [Autonauts of the Cosmopike]) where he overturned his inclinations, manias, obsessions, sympathies, and phobias with a happy adolescent brashness. These three books are other poles of a spiritual autobiography, and they seem to mark a continuity in his life and work, in his manner of conceiving and practicing literature as a permanent impudence, a jocular irreverence. But we are also dealing with a mirage because, at the end of the sixties, Cortázar underwent one of those transformations that, as he would say, "occur only in literature." In this, too, Julio was an unpredictable "cronopio."

Cortázar's change (the most extraordinary that I have seen in any being and a mutation that it occurred to me often to compare with that of the narrator of "Axolotl") took place, according to the official version—which he himself consecrated—in France of May 1968. He was seen in those tumultuous days on the barricades of Paris, distributing pamphlets of his own invention, mixing with the students who wanted to elevate "imagination to power." He was fifty-four years old; the sixteen that remained of his life would be as a writer engaged with socialism: the defender of Cuba and Nicaragua, the signer of manifestos, and the habitué of revolutionary congresses right up to his death.

In his case, unlike so many of our colleagues who opted for a similar militancy but due rather to snobbism or opportunism (a modus vivendi and a manner of social climbing in the intellectual establishment that was, and in a certain form continues to be, a monopoly of the left in the Spanish-speaking world), the change was genuine. It was dictated more by ethics than by ideology (to which he continued to be allergic) and by a total coherence. His life was organized around it and it became public, almost promiscuous, and a good part of his work was devoted to circumstance and current events. This work even seemed written by another Person, very distinct from the man who, previously, perceived politics with ironic disdain, as something distant. (I remember the time I wanted him to meet Juan Goytisolo: "I abstain," he joked, "he's too political for me.") In this second stage of his life (as in the first, although in a distinct manner) he gave more than he received. Although I believe he was often mistaken—as when he said that all the crimes of Stalinism were a mere "accident de parcours" of communism—even in those equivocations there was such manifest innocence and ingenuousness that it was difficult to lose respect for him. I never lost it, nor the affection and friendship that, although at a distance, survived all our political differences.

But Julio's change was much more profound and encompassing than that of political action. I am sure that it began a year before the events of '68, when he separated from Aurora. In 1967, as I already said, the three of us were in Greece working together as translators. We passed the mornings and the afternoons seated at the same table in the conference hall of the Hilton and the nights in the restaurants of Plaka, at the foot of the Acropolis, where we went invariably to dine. Together we passed through museums, Orthodox churches, temples, and, one weekend, we visited the tiny island of Hydra. When I returned to London, I told Patricia, "The perfect couple exists. Aurora and Julio have learned how to realize that miracle: a happy marriage." A few days later, I received a letter from Julio announcing his separation. I don't think I have ever felt so misled.

The next time I returned to see him, in London with his new partner, he was another person. He had let his hair grow, and he had a reddish and imposing beard like a biblical prophet. He made me take him to buy erotic magazines, and he spoke of marijuana, women, and revolution as he had spoken of jazz and ghosts before. There was always this warm sympathy in him, that total lack of pretension or of the poses that almost inevitably become unbearable in successful writers when they hit fifty. I should add that he had returned more fresh and youthful, but it was hard to relate him to the man I once knew. Every time that I saw him afterward—in Barcelona, in Cuba, in London, or in Paris, in congresses or roundtables, in social or conspiratorial meetings—I remained each time more perplexed than the time before: Was it him? Was it Julio Cortázar? Of course it was him, but this Julio was like the caterpillar that becomes a butterfly or the fakir of the story who after dreaming with maharajas opened his eyes and was seated on a throne surrounded by courtesans who paid him homage.

This other Julio Cortázar, it seems to me, was less personal and creative as a writer than the earlier one. But I have the suspicion that, to compensate, he had a more intense life and, because of this, was happier than the one before in that, as he wrote, existence transformed itself for him into a book. At least, every time I saw him, he seemed to me young, excitable, game.

If anybody knows, it would be Aurora, of course. I am not so impertinent as to ask her about it. Nor do we speak much of Julio, in those warm days of summer at Deyá. Yet he is always there, behind all the conversations, taking the counterpoint with the dexterity of that time. The cottage, half-hidden among the olive trees, the cypresses, the bougainvilleas, the lemon trees, and the hortensias, exhibits the order and mental cleanliness of Aurora, naturally. It is an immense pleasure to feel, on the small terrace next to the ravine, the decadence of the day, the breeze of nightfall, and to see the sliver of moon appear at the crest of the hill. From time to time, I hear a discordant trumpet. There isn't anybody around. The sound comes, then, from this poster in the rear of the living room where a lanky and beardless boy with a military haircut and a short-sleeve shirt—the Julio Cortázar that I knew—plays his favorite game.

LUCILLE KERR

Betwixt Reading and Repetition
(apropos of Cortázar's 62: A Model Kit)

When asked about his views of *62: A Model Kit* and its relation to other of his texts, Cortázar once stated the following: "When I finished *Hopscotch*, and above all when *Hopscotch* was published, readers reacted as they normally do when they wait for the author to write something like a second part to the text.... [but] that seems to me a completely unacceptable requirement. I have a very good relationship with my readers, but not to the extent of following their instructions" (Cortázar/Sosnowski 1985, 47). Despite his resistance to being instructed, as it were, by his readers, and despite his desire, if not design, to break with the project of the 1963 text and take his next novel in a different direction, Cortázar went on to confess that when he actually wrote *62* he found himself explicitly invoking *Hopscotch* by recalling one of its most important figures' proposals. He explained: "When I felt the desire to write another novel I decided to do something that didn't have anything to do with *Hopscotch*. But, oddly, what is said at the beginning in its title, in *62*, is where I take off from a reflection of Morelli in one of his brief notes in *Hopscotch*, to see if it is possible to write a novel that rejects psychological behavior, the law of causality that determines the different interactions between individuals "based on their feelings" (48).[1]

Cortázar's reference to the well-known explanation of the novel's title in what has generally been read as an authorial preface to *62* might be viewed

From *Julio Cortázar: New Readings*. © 1998 Cambridge University Press.

in a number of ways. If one takes his observations as a possible, even necessary, frame for an overall consideration of *62*, one is led not only around that text but also among questions that pertain to how one might read his work overall. Moreover, Cortázar's comments about the 1968 novel and its relation to *Hopscotch* recall the literary and theoretical questions engaged both by his most famous work and by its successor. Though different stories are told in each of these novels, between the two texts Cortázar addresses pivotal notions about narrative fiction and interrogates conventional critical figures (e.g., author, reader, character) in an idiosyncratic but not insignificant manner.

Cortázar's insistence on authorial prerogative in the face of his readers' actual or potential demands is an odd but apt disclosure. As we recall, *Hopscotch* would have initially involved its readers in a seemingly democratic, if not entirely egalitarian, relation between this same author and his audience.[2] Cortázar's return to the 1963 text's proposals—or rather to the proposals of its resident author-theorist, Morelli—is a telling gesture that both repeats and repositions some of his provocative notions about narrative literature. The author's uncontrollable return to a previous text would, it seems, prescribe the route that any reader of *62* might appear to have to take in order to read the 1968 text properly.

The reading model implicitly proposed by the author, however, would have the reader execute some unsettling maneuvers. The route required for that reading would virtually repeat an authorial operation that is supposedly at the origin of *62*, a text whose originality, and unconventionality, the requisite return to *Hopscotch* also disputes. Furthermore, such a reading would run the risk of belying the redundant, if not tautological, operations that the "required" reading of *62* could entail. However, the readings already produced around this text suggest that it may be difficult, and for some impossible, to resist returning to the previous novel. For many readers it has also been difficult to resist repeating the author's words—more specifically, his critical terminology—that seem to resonate so forcefully around, and also within, *62*. Indeed, Cortázar's novel recalls the uncontrollable repetitions that inform both his authorial activity and the critical corpus generated by this novel.[3]

The author's word around this text (as represented by the quotations above), as well as the authorial words that seem to initiate it (i.e., in the prefatory statement) push one to interrogate the parameters for reading *62* and perhaps even Cortázar's literary project as a whole. One of the questions one might ask after reading, or rereading, *62* is whether it is possible to talk about this text without in some way privileging the author's word about it. By opening with what the reader is urged to take as an authentic authorial statement, and under the guise of guiding the reader to read independently (like *Hopscotch* that precedes it), *62* would underscore the apparent difficulty of reading on one's own. It suggests that one must turn to the author's word not only for instructions about how to read but perhaps also for information about what is being read.[4] From the outset *62* poses a variety of questions about reading, questions that seem to be anticipated if not answered in the prefatory comments where the author appears to speak directly to the reader about the novel. As we recall, the authorial statement raises expectations about the possibility of breaking with conventional concepts and practices ("Not a few readers will notice various transgressions of literary convention here"; 3).[5] These opening words, which have received much attention, predict readers' reactions to some of the text's unsettling narrative strategies (i.e., it is imagined that some readers "might possibly be startled"; 3). The words guarantee "the reader's option" to read and make meaning independently of the arrangements found in the text prepared and presented by the author (3–4). The statement also locates the text's narrative and theoretical origins in chapter 62 of *Hopscotch*, from which the novel openly derives its title. (The text mentions "the intentions sketched out one day in the final paragraphs of Chapter 62 of *Hopscotch*, which explains the title of this book" and speculates that "perhaps those intentions will be fulfilled in the course of it"; 3.)

That *62* is presented as both a literary experiment and a quasi-theoretical proposition is not insignificant. As both experiment and proposition, it asks questions about narrative categories, and about the formal concepts that may well continue to frame (even if only indirectly) the reading and writing of narrative fiction (i.e., concepts such as verisimilitude and character, author, and reader). As experiment and proposition, it also questions the relation between writing (also reading) and theorizing, and draws connections between these operations. The interrogation staged in this text's narrative—in whatever may be called its story—is explained, however, as the result of a formal inquiry that was begun both abstractly and practically in *Hopscotch*, and in particular in its chapter 62.

The untitled paragraphs of the introductory statement send both a warning and a welcome to the reader. There *62* is characterized as unconventional and transgressive, in both its theory and its practice. The virtual solution to the 1968 text's difficulties, the preface proposes, can be sought and found in the writing and reading of the 1963 novel, which *62* thereby identifies as a "key" for reading.[6] As we recall, the theoretical proposal contained in Morelli's note in *Hopscotch*'s chapter 62 is plainly about the matter of character, a critical concept that has more recently caught the attention of literary theorists and critics unaware of Cortázar's literary practice and proposals. (We recall that Morelli, himself an elusive character in *Hopscotch*, posits the foundation for a future book in which psychological causality would cease to govern characters' actions; in such a book, most of the principles of conventional verisimilitude would also be suspended [*Hopscotch*, 361–3]. What may seem most revolutionary is that Morelli's literary theory is supposedly based on the research of a Swiss neurobiologist who proposes that human behavior is caused by chemical changes in the brain rather than by psychological motivation.)[7]

In reading *62* one may therefore be persuaded to consider among others, the "question of character" independently, if not also in relation to the "question of verisimilitude," precisely because one seems to be instructed, directly or indirectly, to do so. However, one's attention may be drawn to such topics not so much because the authorial preface suggests them, but rather because the narrative also engages—indeed, problematizes—those concepts' conventionality within its own literary activity. The difficulties of making sense of *62*'s narrative would prod one to consider what terms such as "story" or "character" have been taken to mean, and how they might be adapted to new narrative projects. Moreover, one's attention may be drawn to such concepts, and the overarching questions to which Cortázar seems to connect them in *62*, precisely because it is difficult to sort them out from within the text. One may be compelled, as many have been, to talk not only about character, for example, but also about why one can't talk about the characters of *62* in conventional ways, even though that is precisely the grid against which one is constrained to measure them. "Character" is, for Cortázar's text, as much a controversial concept as it is a conventional category.[8]

Given *62*'s apparent challenge to such conventional terms and concepts, one might be tempted to rely on another vocabulary, one apparently ready-made for reading Cortázar. Indeed, in trying to describe the novel's narrative—that is, in attempting to summarize its story in the wake of the theoretical announcement made in its prefatory page—one might feel compelled to engage the literary material of *62* with a vocabulary that belongs as much, perhaps more, to Cortázar's own lexicon than to that of literary poetics more generally. Such privileged Cortazarian concepts and vocabulary (especially *figura*) precede and yet, the authorial voice of the preface implicitly claims, follow on the writing of *62*. But the reading difficulties announced in the prefatory passages appear not so much as abstract critical matters to be analyzed but rather as practical narrative obstacles to be surmounted.

Indeed, in reading *62*, one must navigate, as it were, through pages in which various figures appear and reappear in episodes and scenes whose temporal and spatial parameters are not always clearly delineated, but which nonetheless, and contrary to what the initial paragraphs suggest, come to make some kind of sense.[9] For example, generally one can say that the novel concerns a group of individuals situated simultaneously in Paris, London, and Vienna, and that it gives glimpses of the relationships and episodes in which they also become involved individually and together. One can name these figures and describe specific scenes or summarize individual events that comprise the novel's narrative material.

However, in speaking further about the text, a good many readers have assumed that one must inevitably move between Cortázar's texts and his theories, for, the implicit argument goes, one cannot make sense of things without framing the narrative elements with the authorial concepts those elements seem to illustrate or explain.[10] Furthermore, it may appear that one needs to consider not only the relationship between chapter 62 of *Hopscotch* and the whole text of *62: A Model Kit*, but perhaps also the novel's affiliation with other of the author's words around it, whether in personal interviews or in texts that would explain the novel's genesis (e.g., "The Broken Doll" and "Glass with Rose").[11] That is, in going further, readers may feel compelled to return to other texts, to read backward and forward around the novel where "key" references appear to be explained and authoritative explanations provided. Thus one may move to *Hopscotch* and Morelli's statements, where, in a sense, the novel has already been plotted out, where the question of convention, explicitly called up in *62*'s opening paragraphs, is thematized as it is theorized in the voice of an authorial figure who attaches himself to critical as well as literary considerations. And one may move to interviews and essays where the author talks about, even seeks to explain, the aims and origins of the novel and, additionally, the meaning of specific narrative elements.

Indeed, *62*'s prefatory remarks authorize a reading beyond its immediate borders. They suggest that meaning is to be found elsewhere, in a previous theory or critical conceptualization which, one might argue, is merely put into practice in this novel. But such a subordination of narrative text to theoretical or conceptual project, which such reading models presuppose, may also be refuted by *62*, whose sense inevitably seeps beyond the borders of any such project. Although the novel appears to respect the aims of a previously articulated, unconventional theory of narrative or narrative character, it critiques blind adherence to prior projects. And even when it seems to serve its primary aims, the unconventional nature of its accomplishments may well be a matter of dispute. I would argue that *62*'s narrative strategies and anecdotal material also recover conventions and concepts which the previous theory and the present text explicitly challenge.

There are, moreover, a number of ways to situate the novel's prefatory paragraphs. If one takes the preface as an explanation of what the novel will do, one can read the text as the elaboration of a literary project that becomes self-evident in the doing of literature but that nonetheless must also be theorized before the project begins. However, the preface is a retrospective introduction, a statement explaining, after the fact, the aims of the text whose unconventional and potentially controversial effects its readers cannot resist noting and its author, it seems, cannot refrain from explaining. The theory of the novel proposed prior to the narrative is a theory that also follows its own practice; and that practice, in turn, stages what one is supposed to read as its originating theory.

If, as suggested above, one takes the preface at its word, one might be compelled to read *62* as an "application" of theory first proposed in *Hopscotch*.[12] But the 1963 novel can be read as a text that telescopes the distance between theoretical proposal and literary practice, partly because the one form of discourse is mapped onto the other, and partly because the theory *Hopscotch* presents is apparently derived from the discourse assigned to a character in the narrative (i.e., Morelli). Thus, if one finds in *Hopscotch*'s text the supposed origins and aims of *62*, one also finds that the 1963 novel's theoretical authority remains unstable. Just when one might think one may visit the one text so as to return with some theoretical certainty to the other, one finds that one's itinerary has changed. For one is forced to wander between texts, or from a theory that can also be read as a practice to a practice that also functions as a theory, and back again. One may imagine that one is traversing a somewhat foreign (even if vaguely familiar) territory, only to discover that one hasn't really gone all that far from home.

One may read *62* as mapping out a familiar and finally conventional reading territory. One may read Cortázar's novel as reaffirming rather, than revoking conventional reading practices, the conventions of reading against which, the authorial preface suggests, the novel appears to have been fashioned. One may see this text recuperate perhaps more than resist familiar reading patterns; one may read this novel as an effort to reclaim as much as to reject the reader's and author's conventional activities.

Let us recall the novel's structure and its narrative difficulties so as to plot out the territory for that conventional turn. As is true of any text, there are a number of ways to describe this novel and to summarize its narrative. First, one might describe its textual composition. The novel's text comprises a series of narrative segments comparable to chapters in conventional novels, though neither the prefatory segment, which consists of three paragraphs, nor any of the sixty-nine narrative segments, each of different length, bears a title or number to identify or distinguish it from contiguous segments. Then, one might try to summarize its story as it is presented by the text. The narrative material that follows the authorial statement focuses for the first thirty pages or so (the frontier between spaces and scenes is equivocal) on a personage named Juan, who dines on Christmas Eve in the Polidor restaurant in Paris and whose mental associations and analyses on that evening are elaborated in these pages.[13]

The rest of the narrative moves among three cities, as noted above (Paris, London, and Vienna). It registers the interior monologues and dialogues of, as well as the apparently objective reports about, the characters who form the close-knit group of 62.[14] The interrelations among the group's members are such that one can speak not only about various, and often overlapping, couples (Juan and Hélène in Paris, Juan and Tell in Vienna, Marrast and Nicole in London, Celia and Austin in London, Celia and Hélène in Paris, Fran Marta and the English girl in Vienna) but also about the triangles of desire that bind these figures together (Juan–Tell–Hélène, Hélène–Celia–Austin, Marrast–Nicole–Juan).[15]

Although it is possible to name the characters, describe in the barest of terms who they are (e.g., their occupations or professions), and situate them in one or another city or episode, it is not so easy to describe exactly what the narrative comprises.[16] *62: A Model Kit* presents a sequence of interconnected scenes and episodes (one might even argue for describing them as self-contained short narratives) rather than a sustained, coherent linear story.[17] Besides the extended opening scene focusing on Juan in the Polidor, there are other episodes one could describe: for example, that involving members of a group tailed Neurotics Anonymous who are directed by Marrast to examine a painting in the Courtauld Institute in London; or Juan and Tell's voyeuristic pursuit of Frau Marta's seduction of a young English girl in a hotel in Vienna; or Hélène's seduction of Celia in Paris; or Calac and Polanco's comical shipwreck in the shallow waters of a French pond; or the ceremonious unveiling of a statue sculpted by Marrast for the town of Arcueil—and so on. Readings seem inexorably drawn to describing specific scenes and episodes, and to the reiterating characters' ruminations about themselves and others. Readers seem inevitably pushed to summarize and repeat the themes, myths, and motifs that seem to shape the narrative, or to identify the literary and cultural models, the authors and texts, from which 62 may well derive much of its material (e.g., vampirism, "meaningful coincidences," Michel Butor, psychoanalytic discourse).[18]

Despite the acknowledged difficulties presented by the text's rejection of the narrative conventions of realist "psychological" fiction, the "informed" reader may well have the sense that everything does, in the end, make sense in this novel, but perhaps in unexpected ways. The problem the text seems to pose is how to represent any such sense, perhaps how to translate into intelligible terms the peculiar logic, rather than isolated allusions, themes, or scene, that appears to organize the novel's narrative. In confronting the text's apparent impenetrability, critics have seen that task as a one of decipherment, principally as the need to decode the novel's historical, literary, or cultural references. The goal has also been to disclose the associational logic, the unconventional connections, that link these elements and allow them to make sense.

However, in critics' efforts to delineate the connections among characters and episodes so as to make sense of the novel, *62* seems to have occasioned principally elaborate reiterations of the text's details. Cortázar's novel demonstrates, perhaps, how the desire to interpret critically always runs the risk of collapsing, perhaps unintentionally, into an uncontrolled repetition of and absorption into the text from which critical activity would more properly differentiate and distance itself. In the case of *62*, the repetition of the text's thematic motifs (e.g., the vampire myth), and the circular appropriation of its terminology (e.g., the novel as kaleidoscope, the characters as forming a *figura*) seem unavoidable in reading.[19] The matter of repetition, as informing but also as distinct from reading, is perhaps one of the "key" questions raised as one rereads Cortázar's text.

What seem to get repeated in readings of *62* are not only the thematic or anecdotal details of the narrative or the explicit associations among them, but also, if not principally, the authorial theories and terminology proposed within and around the novel. That such repetitions are inevitable if not required for a reading of *62* is an arguable point. Nonetheless, one might wonder, as suggested above, how one can talk about this text without relating it to *Hopscotch*, without framing one's reading with reference to Morelli's theory that is so explicitly recalled in the authorial preface. Or, how one ought to talk about a text that appears to provide metaphors (e.g., kaleidoscope) if not also critical concepts (e.g., *figura*)' apparently so well suited to its own explanation. Or, how, if at all, one can refuse the author's word about the textual relations, theories, terminology, and concepts that seem to figure so weightily in this text and about which Cortázar has so often agreed to elaborate further.

There are, however, different ways to frame such questions. Given the persistence with which the novel's own terms and notions have defined and even subsumed the discourse generated around *62* in critical studies and authorial interviews, one might wonder about the repeated return to such terms, about the dependence on the author's (literary and critical) word. Moreover, one might also wonder whether there might not be something significant in the fact of repetition itself, whether the pattern of tautological reiteration might not unwittingly reveal a significant feature of this novel. On the one hand this feature might demand and, on the other, decry the persistent critical restatement of the text's (or the author's) own words.

Perhaps a return to the much commented upon opening pages of the narrative—those dedicated to Juan at the Polidor restaurant that follow the prefatory paragraphs—will help to suggest another way around Cortázar's writing and around writing about Cortázar. These pages, which have been read as summarizing or already containing all the essential elements of the narrative that follows, are both cryptic and clear. In the broadest terms, they describe the mental rather than physical activity of Juan, who is both subject and object of the narration, which focuses attention on the associative processes that inform his actions and thoughts during his solitary Christmas Eve dinner at the Polidor. Seated facing the dining room's back mirror, he is oddly positioned to see and hear things as they finally need to be seen and heard, for his position allows him access from several positions at once. The process by which he comes to understand how he hears and sees the dinner scene around him seems to acquire significance not only for him, but also, as many readings of the text claim, for the whole novel.[20]

The scene revolves around a sentence, spoken by another diner and heard by Juan in the novel's opening line ("I'd like a bloody castle"; 5). This sentence, which is Juan's automatic, simultaneous translation of "Je voudrais un château [i.e., Chateaubriand] saignant" (5), is the visible—or, rather, audible—result of a process of association of which the reader has no knowledge in the novel's first page but which the text, in the voice both of Juan and of the unidentified narrator, soon explains in subsequent pages of the episode. The pages that follow, and through which additional enigmas and explanations are provided, are notable not only because they present details whose textual resonances are anticipated in these initial pages. (One might emphasize the accumulation for example, of, interrelated references to places [e.g., Transylvania] and personages [the countess Báthory] associated with historical and literary vampire stories. The vampire figure resonates from around the bottle of Sylvaner Juan drinks and the "bloody castle" he "hears" the other diner order, as well as from the mention of "the countess," Frau Marta, the basilisk; see note 18.)

It could be argued that the significance of this episode lies in the reading performed by these pages, and in the reading figures this portion of the text proposes. The novel presents Juan as a character who acts and thinks, and who both subsequently and simultaneously begins to interpret or decipher his own actions and thoughts. As the acting, thinking personage, he is a figure somewhat out of control, because initially he is unable to read properly the text he produces through his actions and associations. He is a figure of unconscious associations, or rather, a figure unconscious of the associations he seems automatically to make among a variety of figures and phrases. As the figure who interprets or translates, and thus reads, the scene in which he is also situated, however, he is a figure of mastery, for he appears finally to understand not only what but also how things mean in this scene. Initially he may be presented (or is presented as presenting himself—the episode is narrated in the first and third persons, with Juan as the object of both internal and external focalization) as unsure of how to read or as doubting in general that something like understanding can be reached (7). But he eventually seems to read things (and be read) correctly, if not also completely.

Juan's doubts about comprehending what he has done and/or seen, and his confrontation with the "useless desire to understand" (7), are incorporated into the process of interpretation and decipherment as well. The question repeated in this episode, and that would finally generate his reading, is "Why did I go into the Polidor restaurant?" (5, 7, 15). (This question is followed by other related interrogatives, for example, "Why did I buy a book I probably wouldn't read?" [5]; "... why did I buy the book and open it at random and read ...?" [7]; "Why did I ask for a bottle of Sylvaner?" [5].) Given the announced authorial project to refuse conventional causal logic, the text appears to remain true to its "theory," as it refuses to provide definitive answers to these questions about Juan's so-called motivation. While it refuses one interrogative ("why?") it nonetheless accepts others ("how?" and "what?" and "where?" and "when?"), as a reading of nonmotivational connections develops within Juan's scene. Indeed, in the voices of Juan and the external narrator, the text replies to virtually all the important questions Juan (or the reader) might have about the relations among the apparently unrelated elements of the scene. This reply—the final interpretation—is constructed in the episode's final pages (20–4, 26–7). The virtual appearance of that "decoding" permits the scene's closure and causes, as it were, Juan to leave the Polidor restaurant, the privileged site of reading, seeing, and hearing in and around 62 (see also note 20).

Juan performs as a reading figure whose curiosity, whose interest in "the old human topic—deciphering" (8), leads him (like any good reader perhaps) to attempt what appears to be an exemplary interrogation of and interpretation for *62*. His questions about the connections among his physical actions and about the meanings of his mental associations, as well as his (or the text's) answers to those questions, figure one of the reading projects that Cortázar's reader might feel compelled to complete. Indeed, around the figure of Juan the text also proposes precisely how to read *62*; furthermore, the text privileges a specific type of reading. Juan's reading, along with the text's reading of Juan, in these crucial initial pages would suggest that there are hidden meanings (if not "keys") that can and must be identified in order to make sense of things.

That reading suggests that only when one has uncovered such meanings (i.e., allusions, references, associations) can one make sense of this episode and also, some readers would argue, the whole novel.

Juan, a translator by profession, appears as a conspicuous figure of interpretation at the beginning of the text. The professional deformation that would compel him to ruminate reflexively about his interpretive activity and to question the reliability of his reading does not, however, obscure the way in which his overall reading is staged in the text or how it offers a reading model that seems so well suited to *62* (see, e.g., 6). The resistance to reading that the scene's initially impenetrable surface presents to Juan (and to the reader) seems finally to be neutralized by a privileged figure of translation whose task it is to uncover hidden linguistic structures and recuperate original meaning. Juan virtually deciphers what at first seems to present itself as incomprehensible. As he does so, he constructs a route into the text, a way to make sense of what otherwise would appear to have little if any meaning. The reading performed both by and around Juan in this episode virtually finds beneath the scene's and the text's surface the references to which one is led to believe that one must have access if one is to read the novel properly.

Through Juan's reading and the reading of Juan presented by these pages, the novel figures a competent, if not ideal, reader for *62*.[21] But the reading figure produced and privileged here calls up a model of reading one can only call authorial. Indeed, the reading performed in this episode succeeds in reading the text only insofar as it seems to repeat, if not reproduce, authorial knowledge and restage authorial activity. For this reading (which, as suggested above, seems to have determined how *62* has often been read) seeks out and apparently succeeds in recovering authorial meaning, the (un)intended meanings presumably required for making sense of *62*. The text's reading of Juan, as well as Juan's seeming success in reading, suggests that much if not all that looks opaque can be rendered transparent in Cortázar's novel—that is, if one is willing to repeat the author's steps in reading. Juan's episode at the Polidor thus has as much heuristic as hermeneutical value; it teaches how to read as much as it tells what might be, or actually is, underneath what is being read.

What are the consequences of becoming a reader like Juan? What are the consequences of following the reading models produced by this "master" episode? And, what, perhaps, does Cortázar's text reveal about itself through this reading proposal? It may well be that the "keys" contained in Juan's reading are more varied than those this figure seems to offer in what is arguably the novel's "key" episode. As suggested above, the figures of reading apparently privileged by Cortázar's text finally appear more conventional than they might at first seem, if not counter to what the authorial preface (and all of Morelli's theories in *Hopscotch*) would propose.

A reading such as Juan's (and of course the narrator's reading of how Juan reads or interprets things) would propose that the recovery of meaning (references, allusions) is not only possible but necessary in this text. Such an attempt to recover meaning following Juan's model is at the same time an attempt to return to authorial aims and ideas rather than to produce an independent reading. The reading proposed at the outset of *62* therefore entails an authorial recuperation along with the recuperation of the traditional notion of original (if not final) meaning. Such recovery would necessarily entail repetition, and such repetition, in turn, would serve as evidence of recovery. To read the way the reader seems to be instructed to read at the beginning of *62* is in a sense to try to return (to) the author's words, words that initially appear to underwrite the reader's recuperative repetition. In order to read properly, the initial episode if not the whole novel seems to propose, one must repeat the, text, one must reiterate and reauthorize the author's word as it emerges from beneath the novel as well as around it. To read like Juan is, in a sense, to read like Cortázar, and that is the only reading, the "master" episode suggests, which can get one through this text.

Is such a reading of *62* inevitable? What are the possibilities for reading *62* without privileging an authorial reading, without in some way repeating the author's terminology and interpretations? One way is to maintain that *62* aims to resist being read otherwise; that its project, put forth as a transgression of canonical critical concepts and literary practices, finally rests on the most conventional of grounds. Indeed, alongside the figure of the unconventional, transgressive author, which is proposed in the novel's prefatory paragraphs and elaborated in authorial interviews, there surfaces a figure of authorial control and containment. While that figure's word is associated with radical ideas about reading and authoring, his writing still conserves conventional practices and principles.

One can read Cortázar's refusal to comply with his readers' desires, cited at the outset of this discussion, also as a statement of authorial resistance. That statement oddly but aptly compels Cortázar's readers to consider how conventional models of reading are not only figured by the novel's initial, exemplary episode but also are implicitly recuperated by the reading apparently required of its own readers. It may well be that in *62* Cortázar has accorded readers what they feel most comfortable with: a text that tells its readers how difficult it is to read but also ("secretly") plots out a reading strategy that would elicit from them the habits of reading they already know how to repeat.[22] Readers who aim to read otherwise, to read against the grain of repetition and recuperation, would have to reject the reading figured by *62* in order to read in the manner theoretically proposed, either there or elsewhere, by Cortázar.

In the end, if there are any reading lessons to be learned from reading *62* and the ways in which it has been read, they may be lessons that inevitably situate us between reading (or rereading) and repetition. As one attempts to maneuver around the words of Cortázar and the contrary models of reading his writing proposes, one is positioned between texts and terms that Cortázar both reconsiders and recycles in *62*. If, while reviewing the readings of *62* and the reading instructions it offers, one considers how this novel works against the "revolutionary" reading practices associated with Cortázar's writing, one might perhaps be able to resist the repetitions inherent in the model of reading it privileges and take one's reading into less conventional territory. However, at the moment one engages the text and moves into its terrain, one is also compelled to respond to, perhaps even by reiterating (but in ways more complex, perhaps, than those who would follow Juan's example), the models of reading that *62* (un)wittingly exposes. It may well be, then, that *62* figures its own reading as a negotiation between alternate practices and principles, which together persist in shaping how one may inevitably wind up reading this text, and possibly others, by Cortázar.

NOTES

Some material in this essay was first offered at the Twentieth-Century Spanish and Spanish American Literatures International Symposium held at the University of Colorado at Boulder, 18–20 November 1993. My thanks for the opportunity to present some of this work go to the Boulder faculty and especially to Luis González-del-Valle, who organized and hosted the conference.

1. With the exception of quotations from Cortázar's texts also published in English, all translations in this essay are mine. See also Cortázar/González Bermejo, 89–90,

Cortázar/Garfield, 36, and Prego, 93–6, for related authorial statements regarding *Hopscotch*'s chapter 62 as the foundation for *62: A Model Kit*.

2. See Kerr, *Reclaiming the Author*, 26–45, 178–82, for my previous discussion of the complex figures of the author that circulate around *Hopscotch* and the contradictory roles proposed for the reader in that text.

3. There is hardly a discussion of *62* that does not mention, if not cite directly, its opening paragraphs as a key to interpreting the novel. Moreover, many readings appropriate Cortázar's critical terms in order to explain the concepts he himself has elaborated in other texts and in personal interviews. Many essays return as well to the text of *Hopscotch*, primarily to cite Morelli's proposals in chapter 62 and often to equate the character's words with those of Cortázar. Such readings presume that the author's word is presented directly to the reader in the prefatory paragraphs of *62*, where Cortázar seems to suggest that if one returns to Morelli's notions one will find a transparent explanation of precisely what is attempted, if not accomplished, in the 1968 text. For a sample of such discussions, see, among others, Alazraki 1978 and 1981, Boldy, 97–160, Curutchet, 107–27, Dellepiane, Francescato, and Sicard.

4. Despite questions raised below regarding the privilege *62* and its readers seem to grant to an authorial reading (i.e., a reading that would aim to recuperate original meanings), there is much helpful material in articles that aim to decipher obscure references or narrative elements in *62*. Among the most suggestive are Boldy, 97–160; Hernández; Incledon; and Nouhaud.

5. These words initiate the statement, and are followed by "a few examples" of the text's transgressive nature, which turn out to consist of transgressions from the laws of verisimilitude; therefore the mention below of this concept, along with that of character, as possible foci for critical inquiry.

6. Many readers have focused on the identification and explanation of certain terms and narrative elements and have made explicit reference to the word *key* in the process; see, e.g., Alazraki 1981, Dellepiane, Gyurko, Hernández, and Incledon. Nouhaud, on the other hand, playfully reminds the reader of the instability of "key" meanings while also suggestively proposing the interpretive possibilities for reading some "keys" (220).

7. One might note in addition that this is an idea to which biomedical and, pharmacological research, as well as psychiatric practice, has more recently given a good deal more credibility than such ideas received in the 1960s, when they were summarily presented in *Hopscotch*. For overviews of developments in modern theories of character and characterization, at least until about 1985, see Martin, 116–22, and also Hochman.

8. Borinsky's reading of how specific figures in the novel may "create the kind of currency needed to undo the psychological integrity of the characters" (90) is the most suggestive contribution on this topic, and Ortega's brief ruminations about the space occupied by the novel's characters develop related points (273–7); Yovanovich has also tried to focus directly on "character" in *62* (132–49). Though other readings do not address the concept of character directly, implicitly all assume the difficulties of reading characters in *62* and offer possible ways of answering questions about them. As I have suggested elsewhere (Kerr, 21), one could argue that Cortázar's text offers yet another opportunity to explore how, in its questioning of fundamental literary concepts (in this case, "character"), Spanish American literature has the potential to teach readers a good deal more than the theoretical materials typically consulted about such concepts.

9. Francescato's early reading of the text argues a related point, going so far as to

declare that, even if readers are unable finally to resolve all the "enigmas," the novel nonetheless can be comprehended quite well (368); Figueroa Amaral's early discussion also emphasizes the text's "clarity" (377).

10. This argument is made implicitly by all the critical and authorial discussions of concepts such as "figura," "constellation," and "coagulation," through which, it is claimed, one may not only understand what *62* is about but also connect the novel to Cortázar's previous works; see, for instance, Dellepiane, Gyurko, Sicard, Yurkievich. The analyses that pay special attention to *62*'s own peculiar idiom (the concepts "the city," "my paredros," "the zone") and that rely on the novel's explicit definitions of these terms or on Cortázar's statements about his lexicon to explain the novel, include Alazraki 1978 and 1981; Boldy, 97–160; Curutchet, 107–27; Garfield, 115–31; Peavler, 107–10; see also Cortázar/González Bermejo, 93–5; Cortázar/Prego 87–9, 94–6. Cf. Ortega's refusal to read the text in terms of such authorial conceptualizations (232–3).

11. These two short texts are companion pieces, published a year after *62*. Whereas "Glass with Rose" clarifies a notion mentioned in "The Broken Doll," the latter constitutes the author's revelations about the varied sources of *62* and his explanations of many "key" references. Critics have both repeated and pursued further these references and have thereby fulfilled, as it were, the reading of *62* already begun by Cortázar. These texts are also mentioned in Boldy, 98, 110, and Incledon, 283, and in Cortázar/González Bermejo, 86–9, 91, 93, and Cortázar/Prego, 89.

12. Alazraki calls *62* the author's "novelistic answer" to Oliveira's search for alternatives or to "Morelli's program" (1978, 14; 1981, 162), and sees it as "the implementation" (15) or "realization" of Morelli's project (1981, 155); Francescato describes it as "the result of the elaboration of the notes by the author Cortázar created in *Hopscotch*" (367); Yurkievich sees the novel as a "sequel" to *Hopscotch* (precisely the notion Cortázar claimed to resist) or as the "putting into practice of Morelli's narrative proposals," but he also qualifies those descriptions when he claims that *62* is "effective as a novel" but "defective with respect to the program that motivated it" (463); Sicard sees *62* as an "attempt" to produce the "novel of figuras" whose "theoretical bases" are presented in chapter 62 (234).

13. Juan, an Argentine in Paris who works as an interpreter, has been identified as a figure of Cortázar and as a central character, if not protagonist (given their shared biographical details, author and character seem "naturally" identified with each other). This transparent identification is not unlike the Morelli–Cortázar or Oliveira–Cortázar (*Hopscotch*) and Persio–Cortázar (*The Winners*) identifications assumed for, and continued from, Cortázar's two previous novels; see, for instance, Dellepiane, 172, Peavler, 108, Sicard, 233–4, 236–7. However, the most suggestive identification with the author's figure may well be of a different sort, as suggested below.

14. Cortázar's predilection for groups or communities of characters whose interrelations rather than individual actions form the basis of the narrative is discussed in Cortázar/Sosnowski, 49. Cortázar's term for the configurations constructed by such interrelations is *figura* (intimately related to, if not imbricated in, the notions of coagulation and constellation), a term proposed in *The Winners*, discussed and implicitly developed in *Hopscotch*, and, apparently, more directly materialized in *62*. Much attention has been paid to this concept's elaboration in *62*, and to repeating what Cortázar has said about it; see, among others, Alazraki 1978 and 1981; Boldy, 97–160; Curutchet, 109–27; Dellepiane; and Sicard; also Cortázar/Garfield, 36; Cortázar/González Bermejo, 91–3; and Cortázar/Prego, 687–9. See also note 10.

15. For more detailed summary descriptions of these dyadic and triadic configurations, see Alazraki, 1981, 159–60; Dellepiane, 165, 173; Garfield, 119–22; Peavler, 108–9. Dellepiane also suggests a four-part division of the narrative related to the locations of the different pairs: The first comprises the Polidor episode with Juan in Paris; the second revolves around both the Marrast/Nicole and the Juan/Tell pairs in London and Vienna; the third focuses mainly on Hélène and Celia in Paris as well as on the previously mentioned pairs in the other cities; and the fourth moves principally to Paris where the characters all converge (171). Paz's comments on the novel's spatial, temporal, and erotic orders, as well as his play on the novel's title in Spanish (*62* as the transformation of a "modelo para amar" into a "modelo para armar"), suggest still other ways to consider these characters' relations (Paz/Rios, 37–9)

16. Most of the characters are engaged in artistic, musical, literary, scientific, or educational activities, and are therefore identified with the world of high culture (as, we recall, are most of the principal characters in Cortázar's other novels): Juan is an interpreter, Hélène a physician, Marrast a sculptor, Tell an illustrator, Calac a writer, Celia a university student, Austin a musician. See Jones's observations on the "economic idyll" enacted by the characters in their arguably "pastoral" gathering (29).

17. Dellepiane, 180, and González Lanuza, 75, argue that *62*'s narrative techniques demonstrate Cortázar's superior abilities as a short-story writer rather than his accomplishments as a novelist.

18. While Hernández reads *62* as a vampire novel, seeing "the central theme of vampirism as a common basis" for the novel's "complex system of cross-references and allusions" (109), Alazraki argues that it would be a mistake to read the novel exclusively in terms of that code (1981, 156). On the myriad associations with literary and legendary vampire stories and figures, see, besides Hernández's detailed discussion, Boldy, 113–19, 129–35; Curutchet, 108–9; Francescato, 368–9; and Garfield, 125–8. On the Jungian notion of "meaningful coincidences" or "synchronicity" which has been suggested as an explanatory model for the novel's logic and the notion of *figura*, see Boldy, 116, Curutchet, 108, and Dellepiane, 163–4. On the pivotal references to Butor's texts, see Alazraki 1981, 157, Boldy, 115, 141–3, Garfield, 124. On the reference to or reliance on the logic of psychoanalysis and the figure of Freud, see Nouhaud's and Borinsky's readings. On other possible literary, mythological, and cultural derivations and affiliations, see Figueroa Amaral, Jones, Incledon, Boldy passim, and also Cortázar/Prego, 92–3, 96–7, Cortázar/Garfield, 87–8, Cortázar/González Bermejo, 89, 95–6, and of course Cortázar's "The Broken Doll."

19. The kaleidoscope image, which is taken directly from the novel's vocabulary (e.g., 48, 49), is privileged as the "key" critical metaphor by Alazraki, who argues that "the novel is put together like a kaleidoscope" (1981, 158); he is not the first nor the only critic to prefer this authorial term; see, e.g., Francescato, 368 and Garfield, 116. See also note 10.

20. For detailed discussion of this scene, see Boldy, 115–17 (he reacts it as a "model of how the text itself produces the figural," 117); Curutchet, 108–10 (he also reads the scene as illustrating the concepts of *figura* and "significant coincidences," 108); Hernández, 109–10 (in her reading, the scene mainly serves the theme of vampirism); Alazraki 1981, 157–8 (he views the scene as "defining an ideogram that the rest of the text deciphers or attempts to decipher," 157). For the present discussion, Nouhaud's is the most suggestive reading (214–18); she engages the figures of the reader and the author through notions both derived and distant from the text (e.g., translation, mutilation, transportation) but

which are used to elaborate horizontally, as it were, on the text's associative possibilities rather than vertically on its definitive meanings,

21. That the reader is a very special, if not specialized, figure tied to high culture, a figure with a specific kind of cultural experience and literary knowledge—an experience and knowledge perhaps equal only to that of the novel's author—has been noted by Curutchet, 109, González Lanuza, 72–3, and Nouhaud, 218, 220.

22. If one were tempted to read the author's figure as a figure of secrets and secret maneuvers, one could look to Borinsky's reading and to the perverse figure of M. Ochs for other suggestive reading possibilities.

REFERENCES

Alazraki, Jaime. "Introduction: Toward the Last Square of the *Hopscotch*." In Jaime Alazraki and Ivar Ivask, eds., *The Final Island: The Fiction of Julio Cortázar*, 3–18. Norman: University of Oklahoma Press, 1978.

———. "*62. Modelo para armar*. Novela calidoscopio." *Revista Iberoamericana* 47 [116–17] (1981): 155–63.

Alazraki, Jaime, and Ivar Ivask, eds. *The Final Island: The Fiction of Julio Cortázar*. Norman: University Oklahoma Press, 1978.

Boldy, Steven. *The Novels of Julio Cortázar*. Cambridge University Press, 1980.

Borinsky, Alicia. "Fear/Silent Toys." *Review of Contemporary Fiction* 3, no. 3 (1983): 89–94.

Cortázar, Julio. "The Broken Doll." In *Around the Day in Eighty Worlds*, trans, Thomas Christensen, 201–10. San Francisco, CA: North Point Press, 1986. Translation of "La muñeca rota," *Ultimo round*. Mexico City: Siglo XXI, 1969. "Primer piso" 104–11.

———. *Conversaciones con Cortázar*. With Ernesto González Bermejo. Barcelona: EDHASA, 1978.

———. *Cortázar por Cortázar*. With Evelyn Picón Garfield. Jalapa, Mexico: Centro de Investigaciones Linguístico-Literarias, Universidad Veracruzana, 1978.

———. *La fascinación de las palabras; conversaciones con Julio Cortázar*. With Omar Prego. Barcelona: Muchnik, 1985.

———. "Glass with Rose." In *Around the Day in Eighty Worlds*, trans. Thomas Christensen, 236–7. San Francisco, CA: North Point Press, 1986. Translation of "Cristal con una rosa dentro," *Ultimo round*. Mexico City: Siglo XXI, 1969. "Planta baja" 98–101.

———. *Hopscotch*. Trans. Gregory Rabassa. New York: Pantheon, 1966.

———. Translation of *Rayuela*. Buenos Aires: Sudamericana, 1963.

———. "Julio Cortázar: Modelos para des armar." Interview with Saúl Sosnowski in *Espejo de escritores: Entrevistas con Borges, Cortázar, Fuentes, Goytisolo, Onetti, Puig, Rama, Rulfo, Sánchez, Vargas Llosa*, ed. Reina Roffé, 41–62. Hanover, NH: Ediciones del Norte, 1985.

———. *62: A Model Kit*. Trans. Gregory Rabassa. New York: Pantheon, 1972. Translation of *62: modelo para armar*. Buenos Aires: Sudamericana, 1968.

Curutchet, Juan Carlos. *Julio Cortázar o la crítica de la razón pragmática*. Madrid: Editora Nacional, 1972.

Dellepiane, Angela, "*62. Modelo para armar*: ¿Agresión, regresión o progresión?" *Nueva Narrativa Hispanoamericana* 1, no. 1 (1971): 49–72. Reprinted in Giacoman, 151–80.

Figueroa Amaral, Esperanza. "Dos libros de Cortázar." *Revista Iberoamericana* 35 [681 (1969) 377–83.

Francescato, Martha Paley. "Julio Cortázar y un modelo para armar ya armado." *Cuadernos Americanos* 3 (1969): 235–41. Reprinted in Giacoman, 365–73.

Garfield, Evelyn Picón. *Julio Cortázar*. New York: Fredrick Ungar, 1975.

Giacoman, Helmy F., comp. *Homenaje a Julio Cortázar*. Madrid/Long Island City, Anaya/Las Americas, 1972.

González Lanuza, Eduardo. "Casualidad y causalidad a propósito de *62. Modelo para armar* de Julio Cortázar." *Sur* 318 (1969): 72–5.

Gyurko, Lanin. "Identity and Fate in Cortázar's *62. Modelo para armar*." *Symposium* 27 (1974): 214–34.

Hernández, Ana Maria. "Vampires and Vampiresses: A Reading of *62*," *Books Abroad* 50, no. 3 (1976): 570–6. Reprinted in Alazraki and Ivask, 109–14.

Hochman, Baruch. *Character in Literature*. Ithaca, NY: Cornell University Press, 1985.

Incledon, John. "Una clave de Cortázar sobre *62. Modelo para armar*." *Revista Iberoamericana* 41 [91] (1975): 263–65.

Jones, Julie. "*62*: Cortázar's *Novela Pastoril*." *Inti* 21 (1985): 27–35.

Kerr, Lucille. *Reclaiming the Author: Figures and Fictions from Spanish America*. Durham, NC: Duke University Press, 1992.

Lastra, Pedro, ed. *Julio Cortázar*. Madrid: Taurus, 1981.

Martin, Wallace. *Recent Theories of Narrative*. Ithaca, NY: Cornell University Press, 1986.

Nouhaud, Dorita. "Hay que armar el modelo 'comilfó.'" *Coloquio Internacional: Lo lúdico y lo fantástico en la obra de Cortázar*, 2: 213–21. Madrid: Fundamentos, 1986.

Ortega, Julio. *Figuración de la persona*. Barcelona: EDHASA, 1971.

Paz, Octavio, and Julián Ríos. "Modelos para a(r)mar." *El Urogallo* 3 [15] (1972): 33–40.

Peavler, Terry J. *Julio Cortázar*. Boston: Twayne Publishers 1990.

Sicard, Alain. "Figura y novela en la obra de Julio Cortázar." *Hommage à Amédée Mas*, 199–213. Paris: Presses Universitaires de France, 1972. Reprinted in Lastra, 225–40.

Yovanovich, Gordana. *Julio Cortázar's Character Mosaic: Reading the Longer Fiction*. Toronto: University of Toronto Press, 1991.

Yurkievich, Saúl. "*62: modela para armar*: Enigmas que desarman." *Cuadernos Hispanoamericanos* 122 [364–6] (1980): 463–73.

ANÍBAL GONZÁLEZ

"Press Clippings" and Cortázar's Ethics of Writing

Call me no longer Naomi, call me Mara, for the Almighty has dealt
bitterly with me.
I went away full, but the Lord has brought me back empty.
—Ruth, 1:20–21

Evil, therefore, if we examine it closely, is not only the dream of the
wicked: it is to some extent the dream of Good.
—Georges Bataille, *La Littérature et le mal*

There was something that made comment impossible in his narrative, or
perhaps in himself....
—Joseph Conrad, "The Secret Sharer"

Since the late nineteenth century, specifically after naturalism and
symbolism in Europe and *modernismo* in Spanish America, it has been
assumed that literature is written, in Nietzsche's phrase, "beyond good and
evil." In fact, this thesis was advanced mostly by literary critics who wished
to distance themselves from the fruitless moralizing of much nineteenth-
century criticism (which, in Hispanic letters, reached its nadir in the work of
Marcelino Menéndez y Pelayo) rather than by the fiction writers themselves,
whose texts continued to display ethical concerns about the act of writing
and the relationship between writer and society.[1] Until recently, such
concerns were usually mediated by ideology: Ideologies, whether from the

From *Julio Cortázar: New Readings*. © 1998 Cambridge University Press.

left or the right, tended to dictate the writers' relation to their society and to their work. We are now witnessing the emergence in Spanish American literature of an "ethics of writing" as a more encompassing phenomenon, one imbued, above all, with a critical, philosophical spirit. Instead of a catalogue of moral injunctions about the writers' responsibility to society (as one finds in nineteenth-century literary criticism as well as in twentieth-century Marxist criticism), the contemporary ethics of writing is an attempt by the writers themselves to figure out the moral implications of their work. Instead of commandments and principles, this ethics of writing formulates questions—questions for which there are no simple, dogmatic answers, such as: What does it mean to be a writer in countries where the vast majority of the population is illiterate? Does fiction writing tend to be complicitous with the sources of social and political oppression or is it, on the contrary, an inherently subversive, antiauthoritarian activity? Can one truly write "beyond good and evil" or does all fiction contain implicit moral judgments?

Like many of his counterparts in the Spanish American narrative "boom," Julio Cortázar attempts to answer some of these questions in his work of the 1970s and early 1980s. Novels such as *A Manual for Manuel* (1973), short stories like "Apocalypse at Solentiname" (1977) and "Press Clippings" (1981), and poems such as "Policrítica a la hora de los chacales" (1971), among others, evidence concerns with the nature of authority and authorship, with the writer's civic duties as an intellectual, and, in general, a questioning of the role of the writer in the power relationships that are at work in literary texts. I have dealt elsewhere at some length with this phenomenon in works by other boom authors such as Carpentier (*The Harp and the Shadow*, 1979), García Márquez (*Chronicle of a Death Foretold*, 1981), and Vargas Llosa (*The War of the End of the World*, 1981), and in younger authors such as Elena Poniatowska (*Massacre in Mexico*, 1971).[2] However, unlike these writers' more distanced and ironic stance, in Cortázar the search for an ethics of writing is frequently presented as a gut-wrenching, intimate experience, similar in scope and intensity to a religious conversion. A conveniently brief but richly suggestive example is his late short story, "Press Clippings," collected in *We Love Glenda So Much and Other Stories* (1981).

Regarded by some of his critics as one of Cortázar's most disturbing stories in a realistic and political vein, "Press Clippings" has also been seen as "the culmination of his overtly political writing, which began with 'Reunión' in *Todos los fuegos el fuego*" (Boldy, 126; see also Peavler, 93).[3] There are, as we shall see, significant parallels (as well as differences) between this story and "Meeting" ("Reunión," 1966). One salient difference is that "Press Clippings" has a female protagonist and first-person narrator who is also an author figure. This is something of a departure in Cortázar's oeuvre and clearly indicates his intention of bringing into this story issues of gender in society and literature.

Briefly, "Press Clippings" is the first-person narrative of Noemí, an Argentine woman and successful author living in Paris, who is asked by a fellow countryman, a sculptor who has done a series of works on the subject of violence, to write a text to accompany a collection of photographs of the works. They meet in his apartment in a seedy neighborhood, and while Noemí studies the sculptures she shows the artist a press clipping that is an open letter written by an Argentine woman living in Mexico, denouncing how the woman's oldest daughter, along with the woman's husband and other close relatives, were kidnapped and murdered by the military junta. Noemí and the sculptor discuss their anguish and feelings of impotence over the facts contained in the clipping. Noemí agrees to write the text about the sculptures, and goes out into the street to take a taxi. On her way to the taxi stand, she comes upon a little girl crying alone in the street. "My papa is doing things to my mama," the girl tells Noemí, and reaching out, practically pulls the writer into a labyrinthine courtyard and toward a shack where Noemí comes upon a dreadful scene: The father has tied the mother to a bedstead and is torturing her by burning her nude body systematically with a lighted cigarette. Following an uncontrollable impulse, Noemí knocks the man unconscious with a stool, unties the woman, and then helps to tie the man to the bedstead. Without exchanging a word with the woman, Noemí, an intellectual who abhors violence, helps her torture the man.

Noemí returns to her apartment in a daze, drinks several glasses of vodka, and passes out. That afternoon, she writes down her experience, which will be the text to accompany the sculptor's works. She then phones the sculptor and, without giving him a chance to interrupt, tells him her story. Several days later, the sculptor sends Noemí a letter with a press clipping from the tabloid *France-Soir* recounting the story of a crime that happened in Marseille, presumably a few days before, in which a man had been tied to a bed and tortured to death. The man's mistress, the clipping says, is a suspect in the crime, and the couple's little girl has been reported missing. The part of the clipping describing the exact details of the man's torture is missing, but the photographs show the shack where Noemí had been. Noemí rushes back to the sculptor's neighborhood, trying in vain to locate the place where, in defiance of space and time, she had had her experience. However, she does find the little girl, and is told by a concièrge that the girl had been found lost in the street and that a social worker would come to get her. Before leaving, Noemí asks the little girl what her last name is, then in a café she writes down the ending to her text on the back of the sculptor's letter, and goes to slip it under his door, "so that the text accompanying his sculptures would be complete" ("Press Clippings," 96).

The complexities in this intense and gloomy story are evident from the beginning, when, after the title, an author's note diffidently advises us: "Although I don't think it's really necessary to say so, the first clipping is real and the second one imaginary" (81). The story is indeed constructed, in a typically Cortazarian fashion, following a series of polar oppositions that are later collapsed: reality/imagination, past/present, literature/journalism, male/female, France/Argentina, Paris/Marseille, and so on. In terms of its structure, binarism and a *mise en abyme* effect also prevail. "Press Clippings" contains two sets of stories, one placed inside the other. The first set comprises the story "Press Clippings," in *We Love Glenda So Much and Other Stories*, written by Julio Cortázar, and the text Noemí writes to accompany the sculptor's works, which is contained in "Press Clippings" and is essentially coextensive with it. The second set includes the two press clippings, each of which presides over one-half of the narrative: the Argentine mother's press clipping in the first half, and the clipping from *France-Soir* in the second half. Cortázar's choice of a female first-person narrator also places the question of narrative authority within a *mise en abyme*: Do we read the story as if it were written by Noemí? or by Cortázar writing as Noemí? or by Cortázar writing as Cortázar writing as Noemí?[4]

As my analysis of the story will show, the principal rhetorical device used by Cortázar to coordinate his use of binary elements and the *mise en abyme* is the chiasmus. This figure, as Richard A. Lanham explains, names "the ABBA pattern of mirror inversion" (Lanham, 33). A well-known instance is a quote from Knute Rockne: "When the going gets tough, the tough get going" (ibid.). Lanham observes that chiasmus "seems to set up a natural dynamics that draws the parts [of the construction] closer together, as if the second element wanted to flip over and back over the first, condensing the assertion back toward the compression of *Oxymoron* and *Pun*" (ibid.). Chiasmus may also be seen as a figure that tends to create indifferentiation, as it "seems to exhaust the possibilities of argument, as when Samuel Johnson destroyed an aspiring author with, 'Your manuscript is both good and original; but the part that is good is not original, and the part that is original is not good'" (ibid.).

Several notable similarities between this story and Cortázar's earlier experiment in politically committed fiction in "Meeting" should be pointed out: Both stories take real-world, historically verifiable events and documents as their point of departure (Che Guevara's *Pasajes de la guerra revolucionaria* [1963] and a 1978 press clipping from the Mexican daily *El País*), and both make use of religious allusions and figural allegory to structure their narrative.[5] Also, like "Meeting," this story can be regarded as the account of an experience so extreme and life-changing as to constitute a "conversion." "Meeting" is the allegorical account of Cortázar's political conversion to Cuban-style Marxism through the first-person retelling of Che Guevara's first guerrilla experiences in Cuba in 1959. Written in the (rather naive) hope of harmonizing revolutionary fervor with the elitist values inherent in literary discourse, "Meeting" succeeds, as I have argued elsewhere, not because it achieves such congruence, but because it artistically distorts and censors the texts by Che Guevara on which it is based ("Revolución y alegoría," 104–5, 109). "Press Clippings," which may be read as a critical rewriting of "Meeting," is the record of an equally radical, though less hopeful, change in Cortázar's outlook. Far more pessimistically and skeptically than in his previous fiction, Cortázar comes face-to-face in this story with the "heart of darkness" that lies at the core of literature.

Journalism is clearly an important element in this context, as it serves to spark the narrative's ethical interrogations. Although the first press clipping does not, properly speaking, belong to any genre of journalism—it is, as I have already indicated, an open letter, written in the style of an affidavit or legal deposition—it is nevertheless disseminated through the newspapers. The clipping's use of legal discourse further heightens its journalistic impact: It is an immediate, direct appeal for justice, and its language therefore carries a powerful performative element. It is not merely a piece of journalistic reporting, but an action carried out by a victim of violence seeking redress. Not unexpectedly, when Noemí and the sculptor read it, the clipping makes them painfully aware of the futility of their own activities to stop the violence:

> "You can see, all this is worth nothing," the sculptor said, sweeping his arm through the air. "Worth nothing, Noemí, I've spent months making this shit, you write books, that woman denounces atrocities, we attend congresses and round tables to protest, we almost come to believe that things are changing, and then all you need is two minutes of reading to understand the truth again, to—" (85)

Noemí responds in a reasonable and worldly-wise fashion to the sculptor's passionate exclamations, reminding him that writing and making art are what they do best, and that their relative weakness and marginality "will never be any reason to be silent" (86). She regards the sculptor's expressions of anguish as a form of "autotorture," and in fact is pleased that the man's works are "at the same time naive and subtle, in any case without any sense of dread or sentimental exaggeration" (82). She is leery of any sort of sensationalism or directness in representing the subject of torture and is sophisticated enough to realize that she herself feels an "obscure pleasure" when evoking images of torture (83).

The second half of the story, which begins when Noemí leaves the sculptor's apartment, is controlled—fittingly, as it turns out—by a hidden journalistic subtext: the crime story in *France-Soir*, which Noemí unknowingly and mysteriously reenacts. This section of the narrative is a descent into darkness, literally and metaphorically: the darkness of the passageways that lead from a street in Paris to a shack in Marseille and the darkness of Noemí's unconscious, which yearns to pay back the torturers in their own coin, in a version of talionic justice like the Old Testament's "an eye for an eye, a tooth for a tooth." (There are other, more direct links with the Bible in the story, as will be seen shortly.) For now, suffice it to note that this section's discourse combines, in a volatile mix, sensationalist journalism with psychoanalysis.

But, why journalism? Why not deal more directly with the question of art and violence, or art and crime, as in De Quincey's *On Murder Considered as One of the Fine Arts* (1827) or, to mention a more recent example, Patrick Süsskind's *Perfume* (1985)? Journalistic discourse, as I have pointed out in a recent study, appears in many works of contemporary Latin American narrative as a marker for ethical inquiry, specifically for what I have called an ethics of writing (González, *Journalism*, 109–11). In literary works up to the nineteenth century, religious discourse was predominant whenever ethical issues were raised; in twentieth-century Latin American narrative, however, it is frequently the figure of the journalist who confronts moral questions and agonizes over them, and in a language that is predominantly secular and philosophical rather than religious. The reasons for this journalism–ethics linkage in Latin American literature are complex,[6] but in general they have to do with that literature's constant return to its own discursive roots and to the historical importance of journalism as one of the founding discourses of Latin American writing. In "Press Clippings," furthermore, the artist characters are confronted by journalism with a transcription of reality unhampered by the norms of artistic and literary taste and decorum as Noemí and the sculptor understand them. The first clipping's performative use of language, and the second's sensationalistic rhetoric, are both able to name what the sculptures and Noemí's own text (as she foresees it at the story's beginning) repress or elide in the name of "good taste" or intellectual sophistication. By dealing openly with violence and crime, the press clippings expose literature's hypocritical denial of its links with evil.

Although this story's ethical inquiries are secular in nature, religious discourse still fulfills an auxiliary function in the text. Cortázar has seen fit to insert it obliquely by the allusion, in his choice of the protagonist's name, to the biblical story of Ruth. The allusion to the Book of Ruth in Noemí's name reinforces the theme of male–female relations in the story, but it also brings into play a figural allegorical framework derived from biblical exegesis similar to the one Cortázar uses in "Meeting."

"Noemí" is the Spanish version of Naomi, who was Ruth's mother-in-law. Though not an unusual name in Spanish-speaking countries, where it is used by Christians as well as Jews, it nevertheless also suggests a figural link between the protagonist and the Argentine mother of the first clipping, who is Jewish.[7] The biblical Naomi, it should be recalled, was an Israelite woman who had gone with her husband and two sons to live abroad in the country of Moab. Her husband and sons die, and she is left alone with her Moabite daughters-in-law, Orpah and Ruth. When she decides to return to her native land, she tells her daughters-in-law to go back to their families, reminding them that they no longer have any obligation toward her, but Ruth is determined to remain: "Where you lodge, I will lodge; your people shall be my people, and your God my God" (Ruth 1:16). The latter verse is a reminder that the story of Ruth, as Bible commentators have remarked, entails profound personal transformations:

> In what amounts to a change of identity, from Moabite to Israelite (for there was as yet no formal procedure or even the theoretical possibility for religious conversion), Ruth adopts the people and God of Naomi. Religion was bound up with ethnicity in biblical times; each people had its land and its gods (cf. Mic. 4:5), so that to change religion meant to change nationality. (*Harper's Bible Commentary*, 263)

The mutual loyalty between Ruth and Naomi throughout the story is seen in the rabbinical tradition as an example of *chesed*, "loyalty or faithfulness born of a sense of caring and commitment" (*Harper's Bible Commentary*, 262). The story of Ruth also develops the theme of family continuity. The males in Naomi's family, who might be expected to perpetuate their family, disappear at the beginning of the story, and it falls to the women, an elderly widow and a non-Israelite, to achieve the continuity of the family through Ruth's marriage to Boaz (ibid.).

Noemí and the Argentine mother stand in a figural allegorical relationship to the biblical Naomi. Like her, both Noemí and the Argentine mother have no husband (in Noemí's case, because she is unmarried), and both seem to be women in their middle age or past it.[8] Like Naomi at the beginning of the Book of Ruth (1:20–1), Noemí clearly harbors a great bitterness (in her case, about her country's situation), and one may surmise that the Argentine mother harbors similar feelings, as her experience of losing her husband and daughters parallels that of the biblical Naomi. Furthermore, like Naomi, both women display *chesed*—loyalty and solidarity—although Noemí does so in an unexpectedly evil fashion, when she helps the tortured woman to turn the tables on her torturer. In contrast, the Argentine mother is closer to the instance of Naomi, because she petitions international organizations like the United Nations, the OAS, and Amnesty International for help in her plight; that is, she acts within a legal framework, as Naomi does to help her daughter-in-law Ruth at a time when Israel is under the rule of the judges (Ruth 1:1).

The figural allegory of Naomi, the Argentine mother, and Noemí clearly breaks down during the scene of violence in which Noemí is an active participant. This is the point when a chiasmatic reversal occurs in the narrative, a mirrorlike inversion of both the story of Naomi and that of the Argentine mother. This section may be read as Noemí's dream or fantasy of wish fulfillment in which, by assuming the male's aggressive role, she ends up displaying the same dark impulses as the male power-figures.[9] The question of gender comes shockingly to the fore in this section. Unlike the powerless women in the Book of Ruth and in the first press clipping, who must appeal to a higher—and masculine—authority for aid, Noemí takes violent action to defend the tortured woman and, in a gesture that connotes not only solidarity with the victim but a distrust of the male-dominated system of justice, helps her to get even in the same brutal way as a male might do.

Despite its rather graphic realism, the atmosphere in this section of the story is oneiric, suggesting a symbolic rather than a literal reading. Earlier, the narrator had indicated a latent desire for wish fulfillment, when she recalled a religious anecdote about the conversion of King Clovis:

> I remembered something I'd read when I was a girl, in Augustin Thierry, perhaps, a story about how a saint, God knows what his name was, had converted Clovis and his nation to Christianity and was describing the scourging and crucifixion of Jesus, and the king rose up on his throne, shaking his spear and shouting: "Oh, if only I could have been there with my Franks!"—the miracle of

an impossible wish, the same impotent rage of the sculptor, lost
in his reading. (87)

As well as prefiguring the story's narrative strategy (the use of wish
fulfillment), the anecdote foregrounds the ambiguous use of the
representation of violence in religious and, by extension, narrative discourse.
King Clovis's naive reaction to the story of Christ's crucifixion uncovers the
violent subtext on which the narrative depends even as it symbolically
suppresses it: Hearing the story, Clovis did not see the cross as a. Christian
symbol of redemption but as an instrument of torture on which Jesus was
being unjustly punished.

Like Clovis, Noemí literalizes in the account of her experience
elements from a symbolic system—in her case, the Freudian "primal scene."
The little girl's complaint ("My papa is doing things to my mama") rings with
a psychosexual double entendre, suggesting a link with Noemí's unconscious,
but also with her literary work: Earlier, Noemí has told the sculptor, "I've
been writing a story where I talk, no less, about the psycho-log-i-cal
problems of a girl at the moment of puberty" (87). It should be stressed that,
in the end, this process of literalization and wish fulfillment does not uncover
Noemí's unconscious so much as it does the hidden impulses behind the
production of a literary text, in this case, the text to accompany the sculptures
about violence. Cortázar's focus in this story, I would argue, is resolutely
fixed on the gray no-man's-land (so to speak) between literature and
psychoanalysis. Thus, the "primal scene" Noemí witnesses is not quite that
of the sexual act between the father and the mother, but yet another
symbolization. Although sexual implications are still present in this scene (in
the symbolic equation of sex with violence and death common to many
cultures), in this instance, like Jesus' crucifixion, the torture of the woman by
the man clearly stands also for something else: writing. The connection with
writing is brought out through a series of conventional symbolic
equivalencies between the sexual act and the act of writing: The lighted
cigarette is the penis/pen, the woman's body "burned from the stomach to
the neck" ("Press Clippings," 91–2) is the page, the "purple or red splotches
that went up to the thigh and the sex to the breasts" (92) are a form of
somatic writings.[10]

As a whole, the tableau that Noemí interrupts suggests an equation
between sexuality, violence, and writing in a context of transgression—a view
that has much in common with that of the French writer Georges Bataille in
Literature and Evil (1957). In his work, Bataille, who sees literature as the
product of an unconscious human desire to exceed all boundaries (whether

legal, religious, or cultural), offers a Nietzschean "hypermorality" as a position *au dessus de la melée*, as it were, from which to judge literature ethically (Bataille, 8). Provocatively, to be sure, Bataille writes as if the question of evil in literature were already settled: "Literature is not innocent. It is guilty and should admit itself so" (82). Cortázar, on the other hand, seeks to go beyond Bataille's rather detached "hypermorality" toward a more personal and critical view of literature's links with evil. Cortázar wishes to show instead that there is no fixed, exterior place from which one can safely pass judgment: Just as the distinctions between male and female, inside and outside, reader and writer, torturer and victim, are blurred in the story, so the possibility of rendering an objective moral judgment about events becomes more difficult, if not impossible—even as the need to do so becomes more urgent.

In "Press Clippings," Cortázar creates a referential *mise en abyme* in which "literature" and "reality" (as both are symbolized in multiple ways in the story) continually reflect and interpenetrate each other at various levels, in a back-and-forth movement that ends in indifferentiation: We have already remarked how Noemí's story stands in a figural allegorical and chiasmatic relation to both Naomi's (in the Book of Ruth) and to that of the Argentine mother; and how, by "gendering" (to use a fashionable verb) the narrator, by making his narrator female, Cortázar encourages an abysmatic reading of his authorial pronouncements in the story (how do we separate Noemí's utterances from those of Cortázar, or from Cortázar writing as Noemí, etc.?). Even when Noemí supposedly comes face-to-face with the grimmest reality in the second half of the story, literature creeps in. Noemí's actions, as said before, are obvious wish fulfillments; but their improbable, conventionally fictional nature is further underscored by the narrator's reference to books and films. After she has struck the man with a stool, she finds a knife and cuts the woman's bonds: "What came afterward I could have seen in a movie or read in a book, I was there as if not being there, but I was there with an agility and an intent that in a very brief time—if it happened in time—led me to find a knife on the table, cut the bonds that held the woman" (92).

In another wish-fulfilling reversal, Noemí and the woman then tie up the still-unconscious man to the bed and proceed to torture him as he had tortured the woman. The narrator refuses to offer the exact details of the man's torture, save by an indirect—and terrifying—reference to a story by Jack London ("Lost Face," 1910), suggesting that the man's fate is different from what he inflicted upon the woman (93).[11] But is this really so? The allusions to the Jack London story suggest a scene not of maenadic frenzy, but of carefully deliberate dismemberment:

> now that I have to remember it and have to write it, my cursed state and my harsh memory bring me something else indescribably lived but not seen, a passage from a story by Jack London where a trapper in the north struggles to win a clean death while beside him, turned into a bloody thing that still holds a glimmer of consciousness, his comrade in adventures howls and twists, tortured by women of the tribe who horribly prolong his life in spasms and shrieks, killing him without killing him, exquisitely refined in each new variant, never described but there, like us there, never described and doing what we must, what we had to do. (93)

The passage suggests that the man is subjected to a process of indifferentiation—he is turned, like London's character, "into a bloody thing"—which appears to be the opposite of what the woman suffered: I have already remarked that the cigarette burns on her body evoke a form of somatic writing, and as such they are connected to differentiation. But it can be argued that what we have here is another chiasmus, "an ABBA pattern of mirror inversion," and that in fact the fates of both the man and the woman are equivalent.

The way in which Jack London's story is alluded to becomes in itself a clearer indication of what happened to the man. Unwilling to repeat in writing the horror in which she participated, Noemí takes recourse to literature in order to avoid describing, while strongly suggesting, what took place. Not surprisingly, given the story's pervasive use of the *mise en abyme*, the passage from London alluded to here also performs the same act of elision by allusion. In "Lost Face," the narrator refers to the torture thus:

> So that thing before him was Big Ivan—Big Ivan the giant, the man without nerves, the man of iron, the Cossack turned freebooter of the seas; who was as phlegmatic as an ox, with a nervous system so low that what was pain to ordinary men was scarcely a tickle to him. Well, well, trust these Nulato Indians to find Big Ivan's nerves and trace them to the roots of his quivering soul. They were certainly doing it. It was inconceivable that a man could suffer so much and yet live. Big Ivan was paying for his low order of nerves. Already he had lasted twice as long as any of the others. (5)

As Noemí says, in London's tale the torture "by the women of the tribe" is "never described but there" ("Press Clippings," 93). Comparing this reference to Jack London with one in "Meeting," one sees that in the latter story London is mentioned indirectly through an edited quote from Che Guevara's *Pasajes de la guerra revolucionaria* that serves as the story's epigraph: "I remembered an old story by Jack London, where the protagonist, resting against the trunk of a tree, prepares to end his life with dignity" (*Todos los fuegos el fuego*, 67). As I show in my essay on this story, Cortázar reads this quote as a convergence between life and fiction, as well as an allegory of death and resurrection, although in fact there is no precise correspondence between Che's circumstances (a guerrilla skirmish in a Cuban forest) and those of Jack London's fictional hero: As Che himself indicates in a phrase that Cortázar chose to cut, "the protagonist ... prepares to end his life with dignity, *knowing that he is doomed to die of the cold in the frozen zones of Alaska*" (quoted in González, "Revolución y alegoría," 104–5; my italics).[12] In "Press Clippings," on the other hand, the allusion to London opens up a vertiginous *mise en abyme* of elisions, cuts, or "clippings": A paraphrase, it is itself already a "clipping," a piece cut from London's text; furthermore, in its content, the passage avoids describing directly the way the trapper dies (another elision), although it strongly suggests that this occurs through some variant of the proverbial "death of a thousand cuts," which is yet another grim metaphor for writing.

Commenting astutely on *Hopscotch* (*Rayuela*, 1963) in his essay "Del yin al yang (Sobre Sade, Bataille, Marmori, Cortázar y Elizondo)," the late Severo Sarduy focuses on chapter 14 of the novel, the episode in which Wong, a Chinese who is a marginal character in the novel, shows the members of the Serpent's Club a portfolio of photographs of the Leng T'che, the "death of a thousand cuts," which he is using for a book on Chinese art, because "In China," as Wong explains, "one has a different concept of art" (*Rayuela*, 70). Sarduy remarks that Wong symbolizes in the novel an alternative to the Western metaphysics of presence and to the yearning for totality that predominates in Cortázar's ideology in *Hopscotch*. Wong and his photographs emblematize the discontinuous, fragmentary nature of literary language, and its links with death and emptiness. However, Sarduy points out, Cortázar's text does not fully develop these implications, perhaps because they are too unsettling to the search for wholeness thematized in the novel (*Escrito sobre un cuerpo*, 24–7). Both the man and the woman in "Press Clippings," therefore, attempt to destroy each other through a mutilation that is emblematic of writing. There is no symbolic death and resurrection here, no possibility of allegorically "healing" the break between the text and its meaning: A panorama of "cuts" or "clippings" extends as far as the eye can see.

"Press Clippings" proposes a view of writing as a cutting or mutilation very similar to Jacques Derrida's notion of "textual grafting":

> One ought to explore systematically not only what appears to be a simple etymological coincidence uniting the graft and the graph (both from *graphion*: writing implement, stylus), but also the analogy between the forms of textual grafting and so-called vegetal grafting, or even, and more commonly today, animal grafting. It would not be enough to compose an encyclopedic catalogue of grafts ...; one must elaborate a systematic treatise on the textual graft. Among other things, this would help us understand the functioning of footnotes, for example, or epigraphs, and in what way, to the one who knows how to read, these are sometimes more important than the so-called principal or capital text. (*Dissemination*, 202–3)

Could it be by chance that the scene of torture in the second press clipping, in which Noemí uncannily (vicariously?) participates, tapes place in a shack next to "a vegetable patch with low wire fences that marked off planted sections, there was enough light to see the skimpy mastic trees, the poles that supported climbing plants, rags to scare off the birds" (90) and with "a vague entrance full of old furniture and garden tools" (91)? Cortázar's use of chiasmus not only negates the possibility of any allegorical interpretation that would give his story a sense of wholeness and transcendent meaning, but it also makes visible the story's dependence on cuts or elisions at every level: from that of writing (as a systematic spacing of signs as well as an operation involving textual grafts), to the structural (the story's binary divisions), to the thematic (the sculptor's works and the instances of torture and mutilation described in the text). Noemí's disjointed thoughts, while self-reflexively harking back to the story's overall theme of cutting or dividing, show that she has witnessed a terrifying truth about herself, not only as a human being, but as a writer: "How could I know how long it lasted, how could I understand that I too, I too even though I thought I was on the right side, I too, how could I accept that I too there on the other side from the cut-off hands and the common graves, I too on the other side from the girls tortured and shot that same Christmas night ..." (93).

The psychoanalytic element in the story helps explain the delayed appearance of the second press clipping, the one from *France-Soir*, as an instance of *Nachträglichkeit*, or deferred action. As Jonathan Culler summarizes it, this is "a paradoxical situation that Freud frequently encounters in his case studies, in which the determining event in a neurosis never occurs as such, is never present as an event, but is constructed afterward by what can only be described as a textual mechanism of the unconscious" (*On Deconstruction*, 163). Arguably, the event that precipitates the deferred action is the encounter with the little girl, which causes Noemí to construct a fantasy in which she acts out her neuroses; what is uncanny about the fantasy is that it is built out of elements from another clipping, one that Noemí had not previously mentioned (although she never denies having seen it before). The story leaves open the possibility, however, that Noemí might have learned about the events in Marseille from the little girl herself, who was the (presumably runaway) daughter of the couple in *France-Soir*, and that what we have read is Noemí's conflation of the little girl's account with her own wish-fulfilling fantasy.

In the end, it matters little. Clearly, there are two opposite ways to read this story: a "fantastic" one, which discounts the story's political and documentary elements (the first clipping) by subsuming everything into fiction; and a "realist" or "symbolic" one, in which the whole second half of the story (after Noemí leaves the sculptor's home) would be Noemí's fictional response to the first clipping, a narrative-within-the-narrative, and thus subject to a "symbolic" rather than a literal interpretation. This reading, however, is based on assumptions that are not fully and unequivocally supported by the text (that the story as a whole, or a large part of it, is a fiction penned by Noemí and therefore attests only to her "state of mind") and essentially acts to suppress the "fantastic" reading. Both readings conflict with each other and do violence to the text. I have been pursuing the latter, more "symbolic" reading, mainly because it has allowed me to focus on the story's many self-reflexive aspects, including the question of the narrator's gender, but it clearly breaks down when I try to explain, in a non-"fantastic" way, the chain of events of the story's second half. The preliminary authorial statement that one of the clippings is real and the other imaginary (81), further muddies the waters by first strictly delimiting two domains—"reality" and "imagination"—and then suggesting that, save for the first clipping, which has been "grafted" into it, the story as a whole belongs to the "imaginary" domain. Nevertheless, even this apparently authoritative statement is subject to fictionalization, and more ruthless readers who want to opt for the "fantastic" view might choose to do this, if they were willing to consider the powerfully performative first clipping to be purely fictional as well—an option that goes to the heart of the ethical issues raised by the story, as will be seen shortly.

The ethical questions in "Press Clippings," however, focus first not on the reader but on the figure of the author. In a curiously perverse (chiasmatic?) version of his old theory of the "lector cómplice" (*Rayuela*, 453–4), Cortázar posits in this story a theory of an "autor cómplice," an "author-accomplice," not of the reader, but of the torturers, the criminals, and any other entity that uses violence as a means to control others. The writer's craft is a sublimated version of the mechanisms of aggression used by those in power and those who wish to have power. To write is to cut, to wound, to hack away at something that is (or seems to be) alive: language, words, texts. Even if texts are viewed as already "dead bodies" or "epitaphs," writing is still a macabre affair, a form of necromancy or necrophilia.

Considering that all of Cortázar's novels after *Hopscotch* have fragmented, collage-like structures in which "expendable chapters" (that are often quotes taken from newspapers and magazines, as in *Hopscotch*) or outright press clippings (as in *A Manual for Manuel*) play a significant role, then "Press Clippings" clearly implies a broad and anguished reappraisal by Cortázar of a large portion of his own oeuvre. And Cortázar, unlike Bataille, seems to find no reassurance in a view of literature as a form of desire and transgression. "Press Clippings" marks a point of crisis in Cortázar's work, a crisis that had been haunting that work at least since chapter 14 in *Hopscotch*, where Wong displays the photographs of the Leng T'che. The source of those photographs, as Severo Sarduy points out, is Bataille's *Les Larmes d'Eros* (1961; *Escrito sobre un cuerpo*, 16, 24–5); "Press Clippings" would thus be merely the latest episode in a long-standing and tense "dialogue" between Cortázar and Bataille's texts. Sarduy also remarks on the narrative distance with which Cortázar approaches this subject, and on the *"perturbation"* (Sarduy's italics) Wong's presence brings into *Hopscotch* (*Escrito sobre un cuerpo*, 25, 27). Cortázar continued to tiptoe around the subject of literature and evil in texts such as "Suspect Relations" (in *Around the Day in Eighty Worlds*, 1967), which can be considered a tepid gloss on De Quincey's *On Murder Considered as One of the Fine Arts*, and in such novels and stories as *Manual for Manuel* and "Apocalypse at Solentiname," which, in their search for ideological solutions, are still merely rough drafts of "Press Clippings." Of course, Cortázar's stories have often featured characters who confront evil and perversity, or who are themselves monstrous;[13] but in "Press Clippings" the terms of the equation (literature, politics, violence) are fully present and clearly laid out, the ethical questioning is deeper, and the sense of crisis is unequivocal.

The discomfort this story generates in both author and readers is directly traceable to the grafting of the first press clipping, that of the Argentine mother. This powerful text unsettles the story and critical readings of it, making them seem superfluous, if not downright immoral. Bringing legal discourse into play, and evoking notions of justice and morality at their most fundamental level, the first press clipping uses ethical discourse as a shield and as a weapon to further its cause.

The clipping's ultimate effect is to make the critical reader feel like an accomplice to the crimes it denounces. It achieves this first through its testimonial nature, which asserts the text's absolute truthfulness and almost literally rubricates it in blood. In general, testimonial narratives are profoundly ethical, in that their stories are built around moral imperatives; one of these is *Thou shalt not lie*. (From the reader's standpoint, this particular imperative translates as Thou *shalt not doubt*.) Despite their frequent claims to objectivity, moralism is pervasive in testimonial narratives, since, like melodrama (to which many of these texts recur), they always deal with fundamental polar oppositions: truth *versus* falsehood, justice *versus* injustice, society versus the individual (Brooks, 4). With the best intentions, these texts often manipulate their readers' emotions, forcing them to judge or be judged, to accept the narrative at face value or risk moral opprobrium. Testimonial narratives impose upon the reader the burden of making a moral choice, partly because they make ethically unacceptable the option of reading them as fiction.

The clipping's second strategy is the use of the performative, which shifts the clipping's textual dimension to the level of an act. A text such as the first clipping addresses itself to the readers, asking, almost demanding, that they do something. But what? Certainly, art or literature is not what first springs to mind. For the artists—Noemí, the sculptor, or Cortázar himself—the clipping poses an almost existentialist dilemma of how to react without betraying their personal identity, of which literature (in Noemí's and Cortázar's case) forms an inseparable part. Cortázar's life and work, in particular, despite his ludic inclinations, were always characterized by his desire to be true to his vocation as a writer, as his sometimes strained but always close relationship with the Cuban Revolution attests: To the demands by the Marxist and *fidelista* hard-liners that he deal with subjects such as revolution and oppression in Latin America and elsewhere, Cortázar replied that he would do so, but "in my own way" ("Policrítica," 128). In interviews, Cortázar insisted on "the horror I feel toward anyone who is an 'engaged writer' and nothing else. In general, I've never known a good writer who was engaged to the point that everything he wrote was subsumed in his engagement, without freedom to write other things. [...] I could never accept engagement as obedience to an exclusive duty to deal with ideological matters" (Prego, 131–2; my translation).

Speaking about *A Manual for Manuel*, Cortázar states that in that novel he tried to "achieve a convergence of contemporary history ... with pure literature.... That extremely difficult balance between an ideological and a literary content ... is for me one of the most passionately interesting problems in contemporary literature" (Prego, 133; my translation). The Argentine mother's clipping, however, does not allow for any such "balance." It is an imperative text, which demands that the reader give an ethically unambiguous reply to its appeal. But is a literary reply ethical? In "Press Clippings," Cortázar addresses the question of how to react ethically *as a writer* to acts of violence and evil, only to discover that literature itself is violent. Like the torturers and their dictatorial masters, literature is impassive and heartless, not given (in Noemí's phrase) to "sentimental exaggeration." In the end, Cortázar appears to agree with Bataille's dictum that "Literature is not innocent." But he does so grudgingly and with profound anguish, as this notion runs counter to Cortázar's publicly stated view of literature as ludic, childlike, and therefore innocent.[14] At the story's end, in a last twist of figuralism and chiasmus, the orphaned little girl becomes a figure for the Argentine mother and for Noemí herself. A witness to the horrors of the second clipping, the little girl, her innocence lost, is to be picked up by a "social worker" ("Press Clippings," 96), swallowed up by society. The best literature can do, it seems, is to "graft" the Argentine mother's clipping onto its own textual body and pass it on to the reader, along with the ethical dilemma it poses.

NOTES

1. My layman's understanding of ethics is heavily indebted to a group of current books that attempt to link ethics with literature, some of which seek to expand on Jacques Derrida's rather cryptic statement in *Signéponge/Signsponge*: "the ethical instance is at work in the body of literature" ("l'instance éthique travaille la littérature au corps"; 52–3). Among those which I have found most useful—although they often differ widely among themselves in approach—are: Geoffrey Galt Harpham's *Getting It Right: Language, Literature, and Ethics* (1992); J. Hillis Miller's *The Ethics of Reading: Kant, De Man, Eliot, Trollope, James, and Benjamin* (1987) and *Versions of Pygmalion* (1990); and Adam Zachary Newton's *Narrative Ethics* (1995). Harpham, whose synthesis of the current problematics of ethics and literature I find persuasive, cautions that "ethics is not properly understood as an ultimately coherent set of concepts, rules, or principles—that it ought not even be considered a truly distinct discourse—but rather that it is best conceived as a factor of 'imperativity' immanent in, but not confined to, the practices of language, analysis, narrative, and creation" (5). Harpham nevertheless identifies certain recurrent traits in discourses dealing with ethics (such as works by contemporary thinkers as diverse as Cavell, Derrida, Foucault, and Levinas) or where it plays a visible role (as in the narratives of Joseph Conrad): A fundamental one is the concern with the Other, particularly with "an otherness that remains other, that resists

assimilation" (6). In his view, "the appearance of the other marks an 'ethical moment' even in discourses not obviously concerned with ethics" (7). Glossing a passage from Paul De Man's *Allegories of Reading* (1979), J. Hillis Miller observes that the ethics of language requires that language be referential (i.e., that it speak of something other than itself), even if that same referential impulse leads it (inevitably, according to De Man) into confusion, error, or falsehood (Miller, 46). In its discursive form, ethics does not escape the same contradiction: It has to be referential, which in its case implies passing judgment, formulating commandments, and making promises about good and evil; but at the same time it happens that such judgments, commandments, or promises cannot be evaluated as to their truthfulness outside the domain of language. Commandments like "Thou shalt not kill," "Thou shalt not lie," or "Thou shalt not commit adultery," for example, are neither true nor false: They simply *are*. Ethical discourse is tautological; it is impossible to verify with reference to any rule or example outside itself (Miller, 49–50). In this, it resembles fiction, since it can be argued that the "falsehood" of any work of fiction can always be recovered as a "truth" on another level. At a strictly referential level, for instance, Góngora's *Fábula de Polifemo y Galatea* (1613) is false, but this is not necessarily the case at a symbolic or an allegorical level. Commandments are also like fictions in that, although they refer to real-world situations in which specific individuals may be involved, they greatly over simplify and generalize these situations.

2. In Chapter 6 of my book *Journalism and the Development of Spanish American Narrative*, I comment extensively on works by García Márquez, Poniatowska, and Vargas Llosa. On Carpentier, see my essay "Etica y teatralidad: *El Retablo de las Maravillas de Cervantes y El area y la sombra* de Alejo Carpentier."

3. Other recent essays that comment on "Press Clippings" are Susana Reisz de Rivarola's "Política y ficción fantástica" and Maurice Hemingway and Frank McQuade's "The Writer and Politics in Four Stories by Julio Cortázar." Unlike Boldy and Peavler, these critics view "Press Clippings" as a story that attempts to reconcile the fantastic with the political.

4. The quandary is similar to that in Borges's short story "Averroes' Search," when, in the final paragraph, the narrator notes: "I felt that Averroes, wanting to imagine what drama is without ever knowing what a theatre is, was no less absurd than I, wanting to imagine Averroes with nothing but a few drams of Renan, Lane, and Ásín Palacios. In the last page, I felt that my narrative was a symbol of the man I was while I was writing it, and that in order to write that narrative I had to be that man, and that to be that man I had to have written that narrative, and so until infinity" (*El Aleph*, 101). All translations are mine, save where otherwise indicated.

5. See my essay "Revolución y alegoría en 'Reunión' de Julio Cortázar," 96–109. The most complete treatment of figural allegory is still Erich Auerbach's classic essay, "Figura." In it, he defines figural allegory as "the interpretation of one worldly event through another; the first signifies the second, the second fulfills the first. Both remain historical events; yet both, looked at in this way, have something provisional and incomplete about them; they point to one another and both point to something in the future, something still to come, which will be the actual, real, and definitive event" (58).

6. For a more detailed explanation, see González, *Journalism*, 109–11.

7. Her maiden name, Laura Beatriz Bonaparte, suggests that (like the biblical Ruth) she is not of Jewish origin, but she is married to Santiago Bruchstein, who is insulted by the military as "a Jew bastard" ("Press Clippings," 86).

8. Noemí's acquaintance with the sculptor dates back twenty years; "Press Clippings," 81.

9. Inquiring about the origin of the wishes that incite dream-wishes, Freud remarks (in a passage that is highly suggestive in terms of "Press Clippings"): "I readily admit that a wishful impulse originating in the conscious *will contribute* to the instigation of a dream, but it will probably not do more than that. The dream would not materialize if the preconscious wish did not succeed in finding reinforcement from elsewhere.... From the unconscious, in fact. *My supposition is that a conscious wish can only become a dream-instigator if it succeeds in awakening an unconscious wish with the same tenor and in obtaining reinforcement from it....* These wishes in our unconscious, ever on the alert and, so to say, immortal, remind one of the legendary Titans, weighed down since primaeval ages by the massive bulk of the mountains which were once hurled upon them by the victorious gods and which are still shaken from time to time by the convulsion of their limbs. But these wishes, held under repression, are themselves of infantile origin, as we are taught by the psychological research into the neuroses. I would propose, therefore, to set aside the assertion ... that the place of origin of dream-wishes is a matter of indifference and replace it by another one to the following effect: *a wish which is represented in a dream must be an infantile one*" (*The Interpretation of Dreams*, 591–2; Freud's emphasis).

10. See Susan Gubar's overview of sexual/textual metaphors and women's writing in "'The Blank Page' and the Issues of Women's Creativity," 244–7.

11. In London's "Lost Face," an exiled Polish patriot, Subienkow, who had joined with Russian fur trappers in Alaska in the early 1800s, faces certain death by torture at the hands of an Indian tribe. As he hears and watches his comrade, Big Ivan, being tortured by the women of the tribe (in the passage alluded to in Cortázar's story), he devises a way to achieve a quick, clean death at the hand of his enemies. Subienkow, who regards himself as "a dreamer, a poet, and an artist" ("Lost Face," 4), uses his wits to trick the chief into beheading him, thus depriving the tribe of the pleasure of torturing him. The narrator makes it clear that Subienkow is no pure, unsullied hero. Despite his cultivated background and his noble dream of an independent Poland, he too had killed innocent people: the traveler in Siberia whose papers he stole (7, 8), and, of course, numerous Indians (7). "It had been nothing but savagery" (7) is a phrase that recurs like a leitmotiv throughout "Lost Face." Interestingly, this is a story that also caught Jorge Luis Borges's attention. Borges translated it into Spanish and included it in an anthology he edited of short stories by London, *Las muertes concéntricas* (1979). It is likely, however, that Cortázar read the story in the original English long before Borges's translation appeared.

12. The story Che had in mind is probably London's "To Build a Fire."

13 As Roberto González Echevarría remarks about the myth of the Minotaur in Cortázar's early play, *Los reyes* (1949): "The confrontation of the monster and the hero constitutes the primal scene in Cortázar's mythology of writing: a hegemonic struggle for the center, which resolves itself in a mutual cancellation and in the superimposition of beginnings and ends.... This primal scene appears with remarkable consistency in Cortázar's writing. I do not mean simply that there are monsters, labyrinths, and heroes, but rather that the scene in which a monster and a hero kill each other, cancel each other's claim to the center of the labyrinth, occurs with great frequency, particularly in texts where the nature of writing seems to be more obviously in question" (*The Voice of the Masters*, 102, 103).

14. "Ever since I began writing ...," Cortázar has said, "the notion of the ludic was

profoundly meshed, confused, with the notion of literature. For me, a literature without ludic elements is boring, the kind of literature I don't read, a dull literature, like socialist realism, for example" (Prego, 136–7). See also, González Bermejo, 103–12, and Picón Garfield's comments on games and the "man-child" in Cortázar's works in *¿Es Julio Cortázar un surrealista?* 189–99.

REFERENCES

Auerbach, Erich. "Figura." In *Scenes from the Drama of European Literature*, 11–78. Minneapolis: University of Minnesota Press, 1984.

Bataille, Georges. *La Literature et le mal*. Paris: Gallimard, 1957.

Boldy, Steven. "Julio Cortázar (26 August 1914–12 February 1984)." In *Dictionary of Literary Biography: Volume 113, Modern Latin American Fiction Writers, First Series*, 119–33. Detroit: Bruccoli Clark. Layman, 1992.

Borges, Jorge Luis. *El Aleph*. Buenos Aires: Emecé, 1972.

Brooks, Peter. *The Melodramatic Imagination: Balzac, Henry James, Melodrama, and the Mode of Excess*. New York: Columbia University Press, 1984.

Conrad, Joseph. "The Secret Sharer." In *The Portable Conrad*, ed. Morton Dauwen Zabel. New York: Viking Press, 1968.

Cortázar, Julio. "Policrítica a la hora de los chacales." In Carlos Fuentes, "Documentos. El caso Padilla." *Libre* 1 (September–November 1971): 126–30.

———. "Press Clippings." In *We Love Glenda So Much and Other Tales*, trans. Gregory Rabassa, 81–96. New York: Knopf, 1983.

———. *Rayuela*. Buenos Aires: Sudamericana, 1972.

———. *Todos los fuegos el fuego*. Buenos Aires: Sudamericana, 1972.

Culler, Jonathan. *On Deconstruction: Theory and Criticism after Structuralism*. Ithaca, NY Cornell University Press, 1982.

De Man, Paul. *Allegories of Reading*. New Haven, CT: Yale University Press, 1979.

Derrida, Jacques. *Dissemination*. Trans. Barbara Johnson. Chicago: University of Chicago Press, 1981.

———. *Signéponge/Signsponge*. Trans. Richard Rand. New York: Columbia University Press, 1984.

Freud, Sigmund. *The Interpretation of Dreams*. New York: Avon Books, 1965.

González, Aníbal. "Etica y teatralidad: *El Retablo de las Maravillas* de Cervantes y *El arpa y la sombra* de Alejo Carpentier." *La Torre (Nueva Epoca). Revista de la Universidad de Puerto Rico* 27–8 (1993): 485–502.

———. *Journalism and the Development of Spanish American Narrative*. Cambridge University Press, 1993.

———. "Revolución y alegoría en 'Reunión' de Julio Cortázar." In *Los ochenta mundos de Cortázar: Ensayos*, ed. Fernando Burgos, 93–109. Madrid: Edi-6, 1987.

González Bermejo, Ernesto. *Revelaciones de un cronopio. Conversaciones con Cortázar*. Montevideo: Ediciones de la Banda Oriental, 1986.

González Echevarría, Roberto. *The Voice of the Masters: Writing azul Authority in Modern Latin American Literature*. Austin: University of Texas Press, 1985.

Gubar, Susan. "'The Blank Page' and the Issues of Women's Creativity." *Critical Inquiry: Writing and Sexual Difference* 8 (Winter 1981): 24.3–63.

Harper's Bible Commentary. San Francisco: Harper & Row, 1988.

Harpham, Geoffrey Galt. *Getting It Right: Language, Literature, and Ethics*. Chicago: University of Chicago Press, 1992.

Hemingway, Maurice, and Frank McQuade. "The Writer and Politics in Four Stories by Julio Cortázar." *Revista Canadiense de Estudios Hisspánicos* 13 (Fall 1988): 49–65.

Lanham, Richard A. *A Handlist of Rhetorical Terms*. 2d ed. Berkeley: University of California Press, 1991.

London, Jack. *Las muertes concéntricas*. Ed. and trans. Jorge Luis Borges and Nora Dottori. Buenos Aires: Ediciones Librería de la Ciudad/Franco María Ricci Editore, 1979.

———. "Lost Face." In *Lost Face*. New York: Macmillan Co., 191 o.

Miller, J. Hillis. *The Ethics of Reading: Kant, De Man, Eliot, Trollope, James, and Benjamin*. New York: Columbia University Press, 1987.

———. *Versions of Pygmalion*. Cambridge, MA: Harvard University Press, 1990.

The New Oxford Annotated Bible. New York: Oxford University Press, 1991.

Newton, Adam Zachary. *Narrative Ethics*. Cambridge, MA: Harvard University Press, 1995

Peavler, Terry J. *Julio Cortázar*. Twayne World Authors Series 816. Boston: Twayne Publishers, 1990.

Picón Garfield, Evelyn. *¿Es Julio Cortázar un surrealista?* Madrid: Gredos, 1975.

Prego, Omar. *La fascinación de las palabras: Conversaciones con Julio Cortázar*. Barcelona: Muchnik Editores, 1985.

Reisz de Rivarola, Susana. "Política y ficción fantástica." *Inti: Revista de Literatura Hispánica* 22–3 (1985–6): 217–30.

Sarduy, Severo. *Escrito sobre un cuerpo*. Buenos Aires: Sudamericana, 1969.

Chronology

1914   Julio Florencio Cortázar, son of Julio Cortázar and María Herminia Scott, is born in Brussels.

1918   The Cortázar family returns to Argentina and the father abandons his wife and two children. Julio is raised by the women of the family: his mother, an aunt, his grandmother and his sister Ofelia.

1928   He attends the Mariano Acosta Normal School for teachers.

1932   He obtains his Normal Teacher Diploma, which allows him to teach first primary and then secondary school.

1935   He studies at the Faculty of Philosophy and Literature, but due to financial difficulty at home he abandons his studies to start teaching.

1937   Appointed teacher at the National School of Bolivar, a small town in the province of Buenos Aires, Cortázar writes short stories that he leaves unpublished.

1938   Using Julio Denis as a pseudonym, he publishes his first poems under the title of *Presencia* (Presence)

1939   Assigned to the Normal School of Chivilcoy.

1944   Cortázar moves to Cuyo, Mendoza where he teaches French Literature at the University. He publishes his first short story, "Bruja" ("The Witch"), and takes parts in anti-Perón meetings.

1945	When Juan Domingo Perón wins the presidential elections Cortázar quits his teaching post and returns to Buenos Aires. His first volume of short stories, entitled *La otra orilla* (*The Other Shore*), appears.
1946	He publishes the short story "Casa tomada" ("The House Taken") in the review *Los Anales de Buenos Aires*, whose director is Jorge Luis Borges.
1947	His short story "Bestiario" ("Bestiary") appears in the review *Los Anales de Buenos Aires*.
1948	Cortázar obtains his certification as Public Translator for English and French.
1949	He publishes the dramatic poem *Los reyes*, the first work to be released under his own name. The work is generally ignored by the critics.
1951	Sudamericana publishes Cortázar's first volume of short stories *Bestiario* (*Bestiary*). He obtains a scholarship from the French Government and he travels to Paris, where Cortázar works as a translator for UNESCO.
1952	The short story "Axolotl" appears in Buenos Aires in *Literaria*.
1953	He marries Aurora Bernárdez, an Argentinean translator.
1954	Cortázar continues to work for UNESCO as an independent translator. He completes *Historias de cronopios y de famas* (*Cronopios and Famas*), which he had begun in 1951.
1956	The collection of short stories *Final del juego* (*End of the Game and Other Stories*) is published in Mexico. Cortázar also publishes a translation of Poe's prose work.
1959	*Las armas secretas* (Secret Weapons), a collection of stories including the short story called "El perseguidor" ("The Pursuer"), appears.
1960	He travels to the United States and publishes the novel *Los Premios* (*The Winners*).
1963	Sudamericana Publishers publishes *Rayuela* (*Hopscotch*); 5000 copies are sold in the first year. That same year, Cortázar visits Castro's Cuba for the first time.
1965	The English translation of *Los Premios* (*The Winners*) is published.
1966	Cortázar releases a collection of stories *Todos los fuegos el*

fuego (All Fires the Fire). His essay "Para llegar a Lezama Lima," on the Cuban writer Lezama Lima, is published in Havana. English and French translations of *Rayuela* (*Hopscotch*) appear in print.

1967   Cortázar publishes his first collage-book, *La vuelta al día en ochenta mundos* (*Around the day in 80 worlds*), which a collection of short stories, chronicles, essays and poems.

1968   Cortázar publishes the novel *62, Modelo para armar* (*62: A Model Kit*) in Buenos Aires.

1968   In *Último Round* (*Last Round*), another collage-book, Cortázar compiles essays, short stories, poems, chronicles and humorous texts. The book also includes a letter written in 1967 to Roberto Fernández Retamar regarding the situation of the Latin American intellectuals. The English translation of *Historias de cronopios y de famas* (*Cronopios and Famas*) appears.

1970   He travels to Chile with his second wife, Ugne Karvelis, to witness the inauguration of President Salvador Allende.

1973   *Libro de Manuel* (A Manual for Manuel) is published in Buenos Aires by Sudamericana. Cortázar receives the "Medici Award" in Paris for this book.

1975   He visits the United States and goes to Mexico City, where he gives a series of lectures about Latin American literature and his own work; two of these appear in *The Final Island: The Fiction of Julio Cortázar* (1978).

1978   English version of *Libro de Manuel* (A Manual for Manuel) appears.

1979   He publishes *Un tal Lucas* (*A Certain Lucas*) in Alfaguara, Madrid. He divorces Ugné Karvelis, and travels with Carol Dunlop, his third wife, to Panama.

1980   Cortázar publishes the short story collection *Queremos tanto a Glenda* (*We Love Glenda So Much and Other Tales*).

1981   Thanks to François Mitterand, Cortázar receives French citizenship. That same year, he is diagnosed with leukemia.

1982   His wife Carol Dunlop passes away in November.

1983   He travels to Havana, Cuba, and later to Buenos Aires to visit his mother after the fall of the dictatorship.

1984   Cortázar dies on February 14 of leukemia and is buried at the Cemetery of Montparnasse in the same tomb were Carol Dunlop rests.

1986   Alfaguara Publishers begin the edition of his complete works.

Contributors

HAROLD BLOOM is Sterling Professor of the Humanities at Yale University. He is the author of over 20 books, including *Shelley's Mythmaking* (1959), *The Visionary Company* (1961), *Blake's Apocalypse* (1963), *Yeats* (1970), *A Map of Misreading* (1975), *Kabbalah and Criticism* (1975), *Agon: Toward a Theory of Revisionism* (1982), *The American Religion* (1992), *The Western Canon* (1994), and *Omens of Millennium: The Gnosis of Angels, Dreams, and Resurrection* (1996). *The Anxiety of Influence* (1973) sets forth Professor Bloom's provocative theory of the literary relationships between the great writers and their predecessors. His most recent books include *Shakespeare: The Invention of the Human* (1998), a 1998 National Book Award finalist, *How to Read and Why* (2000), *Genius: A Mosaic of One Hundred Exemplary Creative Minds* (2002), and *Hamlet: Poem Unlimited* (2003). In 1999, Professor Bloom received the prestigious American Academy of Arts and Letters Gold Medal for Criticism, and in 2002 he received the Catalonia International Prize.

JAIME ALAZRAKI, Professor of Spanish at Columbia University, is the editor of many fundamental scholarly works on Borges and Cortázar, as well as the recent collection entitled *Teorías de lo fantástico* (2001). Professor Alazraki is also the author of *Borges and the Kabbalah: and other essays on his fiction and poetry* (1988) and *Hacia Cortázar: Aproximaciones a su obra* (1994).

ROBERTO GONZÁLEZ ECHEVARRÍA is Sterling Professor of Hispanic and Comparative Literatures. He is the author of numerous scholarly works including *The Voice of the Masters: Writing and Authority in Modern Latin*

American Literature (1985) and *Celestina's Brood: Continuities of the Baroque in Spanish and Latin American Literatures* (1993), editor of *The Oxford Book of Latin American Short Stories* (1997), and co-editor of *The Cambridge History of Latin American Literature* (1996). His most recent publication is *The Pride of Havana: A History of Cuban Baseball* (1999).

STEVEN BOLDY is the author of *Novels of Julio Cortázar* (1980), the work cited in this collection, and *Before the Boom: four essays on Latin-American literature before 1940* (1981). His latest critical study, *Memoria mexicana* (1998), examines Carlos Fuentes' novel *La region mas transparente*.

ANA HERNÁNDEZ DEL CASTILLO is the author of *Keats, Poe, and the Shaping of Cortázar's Mythopoesis* (1981). In addition to critical essays on Cortázar, Professor Hernández has published studies on Horacio Quiroga as well as on Cuban poets including Magali Alabau, Lourdes Gil and Maya Islas.

GORDANA YOVANOVICH is a professor with the School of Languages and Literatures at the University of Guelph. She is the author of *Julio Cortázar's Character Mosaic: Reading the Longer Fiction* (1991) and *Play and the Picaresque: Lazarillo de Tormes, Libro de Manuel, and Match Ball* (1999). Professor Yovanovich has published several critical essays on Cortázar, as well as Nicolás Guillén. She is also the editor of *New World Order: Corporate Agenda and Parallel Reality* (2003), a study of social and political aspects of globalization.

DORIS SOMMER, professor of Romance Languages at Harvard University, has written extensively on Latin American literature and its rhetoric. Professor Sommer is the author of *Foundational Fictions: the National Romances of Latin America* (1991). In addition, she is the editor of *The Places of History: Regionalism Revisited in Latin America* (1999), a study of the relationships of history and regionalism.

ISABEL ALVAREZ BORLAND is Professor of Spanish at Holy Cross College. In addition to many critical essays on Latin American writers such as Gabriel García Márquez and Severo Sarduy, Professor Alvarez-Borland is the author of *Discontinuidad y ruptura en Guillermo Cabrera Infante* (1992) and *Cuban-American Literature of Exile: From Person to Persona* (1998).

ILAN STAVANS, Professor of Spanish at Amherst College, is the editor of several scholarly collections including *Oxford Book of Latin American Essays* (1997) and *Poetry of Pablo Neruda* (2003). Professor Stavans has published extensively on translation, language, and Latin American culture. He is the author of *Julio Cortázar: a Study of the Short Fiction* (1996).

MARIO VARGAS LLOSA, author of countless fundamental works of Latin American literature such as *La casa verde* (*Green House*) (1965), *La ciudad y los perros* (*Time of the Hero*)(1967), and *Conversación en la cathedral* (*Conversation in the Cathedral*)(1969), also has participated in the political scene in his native Peru. Vargas Llosa's political experience informs his recent novel, *Fiesta del Chivo* (*Feast of the Goat*) (2000), based on the brutal regime of Trujillo in the Dominican Republic.

LUCILLE KERR, professor of Spanish at the University of Southern California, has published numerous critical essays on Latin American authors such as Jose Donoso, Carlos Fuentes, and Manuel Puig, as well as Julio Cortázar. Professor Kerr is the author of *Suspended Fictions: Reading Novels by Manuel Puig* (1987) and *Reclaiming the Author: Figures and Fictions from Spanish America* (1992).

ANÍBAL GONZÁLEZ is the Edwin Earle Sparks Professor of Spanish and Portuguese at Pennsylvania State University. In addition to numerous critical essays, Professor González is the author of *La crónica modernista hispanoamericana* (1983) and *La novela modernista hispanoamericana* (1987). His latest publication is *Killer Books: Writing, Violence, and Ethics in Modern Spanish American Narrative* (2001).

Bibliography

Alazraki, Jaime. "The Fantastic as Surrealist Metaphors in Cortázar's Short Fiction". *Dada/Surrealism* 5 (1975): 28–33.

————."Introduction: Toward the Last Square of the Hopscotch" in *The Final Island: The Fiction of Julio Cortázar*. Jaime Alazraki and Ivar Ivarsk, eds. Norman: University of Oklahoma Press, 1978. pp. 3–18.

Alazraki, Jaime, ed. *Critical Essays on Julio Cortázar*. New York: G.K. Hall, 1999.

Alazraki, Jaime, and Ivar Ivarsk, eds. *The Final Island: The Fiction of Julio Cortázar*. Norman: University of Oklahoma Press, 1978.

Alonso, Carlos J., ed. *Julio Cortázar: New Readings*. Cambridge: Cambridge University Press, 1998.

Alvarez Borland, Isabel. "Cortázar: On Critics and Interpretation". *INTI: Revista de literatura hispánica* 43–44 (1996): 157–166.

Amar Sánchez, Ana María. "Between Utopia and Inferno (Julio Cortázar's Version)" in Julio Cortázar: *New Readings*. Carlos J. Alonso, ed. Cambridge: Cambridge University Press, 1998. pp. 19–35.

Axelrod, M.R. *The politics of style in the fiction of Balzac, Beckett, and Cortázar*. London: Macmillan, 1992.

Bennet, Maurice J. "A Dialogue of Gazes: Metamorphosis and Epiphany in Julio Cortázar's 'Axolotl.'" *Studies in Short Fiction* 23(1986): 57–62.

Bloom, Harold, Ed. *Julio Cortázar*. Philadelphia: Chelsea House, 2003.

Boldy, Steven. *The novels of Julio Cortázar*. Cambridge: Cambridge University Press, 1980.

Books Abroad 50 (1976)—Julio Cortázar issue.

Chatman, Seymour. "The Rhetoric of Difficult Fiction: Cortázar's 'Blow-Up.'" *Poetics Today* 1(1980): 23–66.

Cortázar, Julio. *A Change of Light and Other Stories*. Gregory Rabassa, trans. New York: Knopf, 1980.

———. *End of the Game and Other Stories*. Paul Blackburn, trans. New York: Pantheon, 1963. Reprinted by Vintage in 1967 as *Blow-Up and Other Stories*.

———. *Hopscotch*. Gregory Rabassa, trans. New York: Pantheon, 1966.

———. *The Winners*. Elaine Kerrigan, trans. New York: Pantheon, 1965.

———. *Cronopios and Famas*. Paul Blackburn, trans. New York: Pantheon, 1969.

———. *62: A Model Kit*. Gregory Rabassa, trans. New York: Pantheon, 1972.

———. *All Fires the Fire and Other Stories*. Suzanne Jill Levine, trans. New York: Pantheon, 1973.

———. *A Manual for Manuel*. Gregory Rabassa, trans. New York: Pantheon, 1978.

———. *We love Glenda So Much and Other Tales*. Gregory Rabassa, trans. New York: Knopf, 1983.

———. *A Certain Lucas*. Gregory Rabassa, trans. New York: Knopf, 1984.

Ditsky, John. "End of the Game: The Early Fictions of Julio Cortázar". *The Review of Contemporary Fiction* 3 (1983): 38–44.

Garfield, Evelyn Picón. *Julio Cortázar*. New York, Frederick Ungar Publishing, 1975.

González, Aníbal. "'Press Clippings' and Cortazar's Ethics of Writing" in *Julio Cortázar: New Readings*. Carlos J.Alonso, ed. Cambridge: Cambridge University Press, 1998. pp. 237–257.

González Echevarría, Roberto. "*Los reyes*: Cortázar's Mythology of Writing" in *The Final Island: The Fiction of Julio Cortázar*. Jaime Alazraki and Ivar Ivarsk, eds. Norman: University of Oklahoma Press, 1978. pp. 63–72.

Harss, Luis, and Barbara Dohmann. *Into the Mainstream*. New York: Harper and Row, 1966.

Hernández del Castillo, Ana. *Keats, Poe, and the Shaping of Cortázar's Mythopoesis*. Amsterdam: John Benjamins, 1981.

Kerr, Lucille. "Betwixt Reading and Repetition (apropos of Cortázar's *62: A*

Model Kit)" in *Julio Cortázar: New Readings*. Carlos J.Alonso, ed. Cambridge: Cambridge University Press, 1998. pp. 91–109.

King, Sarah E. *The Magical and the Monstrous: Two Faces of the Child Figure in the Fiction of Julio Cortázar and José Donoso*. New York: Garland Publishing, 1992.

Levinson, Brett. "The Other Origin: Cortázar and Identity Politics". *Latin American Literary Review* 22(1994): 5–19.

McNab, Pamela J. "Julio Cortázar's Axolotl: Literary Archaeology of the Unreal". *International Fiction Review* 24(1997): 12–22.

———. "Shifting Symbols in Cortázar's 'Bestiario.'" *Revista Hispánica Moderna*. 50, No. 2 (1997) 335–346.

Moran, Dominic. *Questions of the Liminal in the Fiction of Julio Cortázar*. Oxford: Legenda, 2000.

Mundo Lo, Sarah de. *Julio Cortázar, His Works and His Critics: A Bibliography*. Urbana: Albatross, 1985.

Paley, Francescato, Martha. "Selected Bibliography (1938–1976)". *Books Abroad* 50 (1976): 513–516.

Peavler, Terry J. *Julio Cortázar*. New York: Twayne Publishers, 1990.

Peavler, Terry J. and Peter Standish. *Structures of Power*. Albany: State University of New York Press, 1996.

Point of Contact (1994)—Julio Cortázar issue.

Rabassa, Gregory. "Lying to Athena: Cortázar and the Art of Fiction" in *The Final Island: The Fiction of Julio Cortázar*. Jaime Alazraki and Ivar Ivarsk, eds. Norman: University of Oklahoma Press, 1978. pp. 57–62.

Review 72 (1972)—Julio Cortázar issue.

Rodríguez-Luis, Julio. *The Contemporary Praxis of the Fantastic: Borges and Cortázar*. New York: Garland Publishing, 1991.

Rosser, Harry L. "The Voice of the Salamander: Cortázar's 'Axolotl' and the Transformation of the Self". *Kentucky Romance Quarterly* 30(1983): 419–427.

Sommer, Doris. "Grammar Trouble: Cortázar's Critique of Competence". *Diacritics* 25 (1995): 21–45.

Standish, Peter. *Understanding Julio Cortázar*. Columbia: University of South Carolina Press, 2001.

Stavans, Ilan. "Kafka, Cortázar, Gass". *Review of Contemporary Fiction* 11 (1991): 131–36.

———. "Justice to Julio Cortázar". *Southwest Review* 81 (1996): 288–310.

————. *Julio Cortázar: A Study of the Short Fiction*. New York: Twayne, 1996.

Tyler, Joseph. "From the Fabulous to the Fantastic: The Tiger and its Fearful Symmetry in the Twentieth-Century Spanish American Short Story". *Romance Languages Annal* 9(1998): 710–716.

Vargas Llosa, Mario. "The Trumpet of Deyá". Trans. Dane Johnson. *Review of Contemporary Fiction* 17 (1997): 25–34.

Wight, Doris T. "Fantastic Labyrinths in Fictions by Borges, Cortázar, and Robbe-Grillet". *The Comparatist* 13 (1989): 29–36.

Wood, Don E. "Surrealistic Transformation of Reality in Cortázar's 'Bestiario'" *Romance Notes*. 13, No.2 (1971) 239–242.

Wykes, David. "Cortázar's 'The Night Face Up' and the War of the Flower". *Studies in Short Fiction* 25(1988): 147–150.

Yovanovich, Gordana. *Julio Cortázar's Character Mosaic*. Toronto: University of Toronto Press, 1990.

Acknowledgments

"Toward the Last Square of the Hopscotch" by Jaime Alazraki. From *The Final Island: The Fiction of Julio Cortázar*. © 1978 University of Oklahoma Press. Reprinted by permission.

"*Los reyes*: Cortázar's Mythology of Writing" by Roberto González Echevarría. From *The Final Island: The Fiction of Julio Cortázar*. © 1978 University of Oklahoma Press. Reprinted by permission.

"Libro de Manuel" by Steven Boldy. From *The Novels of Julio Cortázar*. © 1980 Cambridge University Press. Reprinted with the permission of Cambridge University Press.

"Woman as Circe the Magician" by Ana Hernández del Castillo. From *Keats, Poe, and the Shaping of Cortázar's Mythopeoesis*. © 1981 John Benjamins B.V. With kind permission by John Benjamins Publishing Company, Amsterdam/Philadelphia. www.benjamins.com.

"An Interpretation of *Rayuela* Based on the Character Web" by Gordana Yovanovich. From *Julio Cortázar's Character Mosaic*. © 2003 Gordana Yovanovich.

"Grammar Trouble: Cortázar's Critique of Competence" by Doris Sommer. From *Diacritics* 25, no. 1 (Spring 1995), 21–45. © 1995 The Johns Hopkins University Press. Reprinted by permission of The Johns Hopkins University Press.

"Cortázar: On Critics and Interpretation" by Isabel Alvarez Borland. From *INTI: Revista de Literatura Hispanica*, nos. 43–44 (Primavera–Otoño 1996). © 1996 INTI. Reprinted by permission.

"Justice to Julio Cortázar" by Ilan Stavans. From *Southwest Review* vol. 81, no. 2 (Spring 1996). © 1996 by Southern Methodist University. Reprinted by permission.

"The Trumpet of Deyá" by Mario Vargas Llosa. *The Review of Contemporary Fiction* vol. 17, no 1 (Spring 1997): 25–34. © 1997 *The Review of Contemporary Fiction*. Reprinted by permission.

"Betwixt Reading and Repetition (apropos of Cortázar's *62: A Model Kit*)" by Lucille Kerr. From *Julio Cortázar: New Readings*, edited by Carlos J. Alonso. © 1998 Cambridge University Press. Reprinted with the permission of Cambridge University Press.

"'Press Clippings' and Cortázar's Ethics of Writing" by Aníbal González. From *Julio Cortázar: New Readings*, edited by Carlos J. Alonso. © 1998 Cambridge University Press. Reprinted with the permission of Cambridge University Press.

Index

DATE DUE

GAYLORD   PRINTED IN U.S.A.